STAY WILD

Cabins, Rural Getaways, and Sublime Solitude

Escape from the city and get away from it all! Spend some time immersed in nature, and at the end of the day, retire to a cosy retreat under the stars.

Whether you're planning a family holiday or a micro-adventure just for two, disconnect from the day-to-day and reconnect with the great outdoors through meaningful experiences, far from the hustle and bustle. *Stay Wild* is about slow travel and celebrating unique moments in nature. From lakeside yurts deep in the woods to treehouses and even a converted school bus, this book is a journey through *Canopy & Stars*' one-of-a-kind, low-impact getaways, each more secluded than the last.

gestalten
ISBN 978-3-89955-861-6

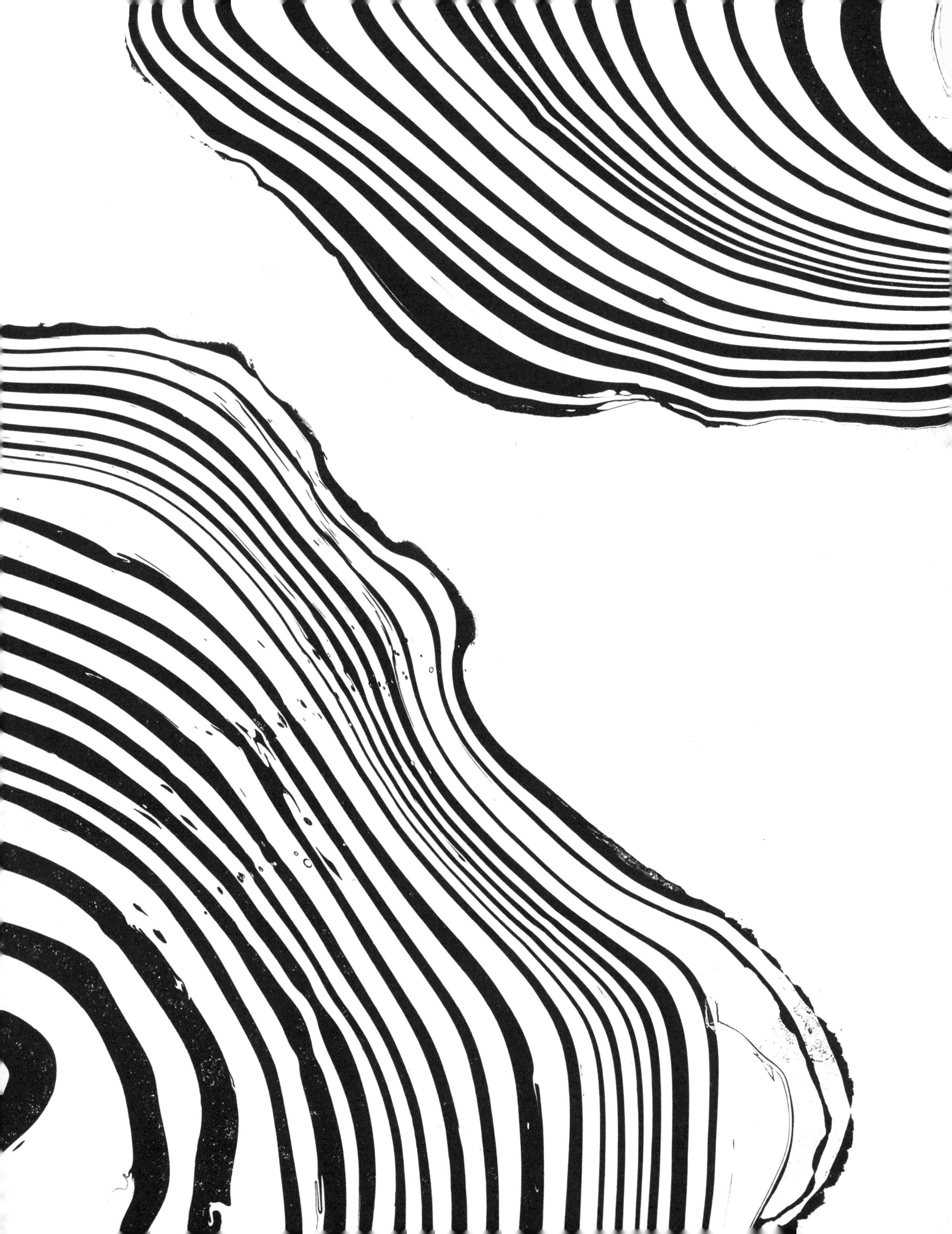

STAY WILD

Cabins, Rural Getaways,
and Sublime Solitude

CANOPY & STARS

gestalten

Table of Contents

4–5	Foreword: The Outdoor Life	64–67	The Chapel Shropshire, England
6–9	The Ferry Waiting Room Loch Lomond and The Trossachs National Park, Scotland	68–73	Lilla Stugan Worcestershire, England
10–15	Orchard Treehouse Worcestershire, England	74–75	Woodland Cabin Cornwall, England
16–19	Hinterlandes The Lake District, England	76–81	Poacher's Cabin Périgord-Limousin, France
20–23	Gwennol Black Mountains, Wales	82–87	The Science of Stepping Outside
24–31	Big Sky Lookout Devon, England	88–91	Kushti East Sussex, England
32–35	Midsummer Meadow Bed Dartmoor, England	92–93	The Beermoth The Cairngorms, Scotland
36–41	Kinton Cloud-House Yurt Shropshire, England	94–95	Humble Bee Devon, England
42–45	The Ultimate Life More Wild	96–99	Log Jam Cabin Cornwall, England
46–49	Layénie Under the Stars Lot-et-Garonne, France	100–105	Rufus's Roost Yorkshire, England
50–53	Star Suite Yorkshire, England	106–109	Our Wild Future
54–55	Stargazer's Wagon Herefordshire, England	110–115	The Island Cabin Agder, Norway
56–59	The Roundhouse Cornwall, England	116–119	7th Room Norrbotten, Sweden
60–63	Dragon Cruck Powys, Wales	120–121	Aurora Dome Lapland, Finland

122–123	**The Bird's Nest** Norrbotten, Sweden	184–187	Weekend Wanderings
124–129	**Mirrorcube** Norrbotten, Sweden	188–195	**The Woodsman's Treehouse** Dorset, England
130–135	**Esko's Cabin** Lapland, Finland	196–199	**Caban Copa** Powys, Wales
136–139	Our Outdoor Pantry	200–205	**Bowcombe Boathouse** Devon, England
140–143	**Dabinett Treehouse** Somerset, England	206–213	**The Danish Cabin** Cornwall, England
144–147	**Sky Den** Northumberland, England	214–219	**Château dans les Chênes** Hérault, France
148–151	**The Lake** Cornwall, England	220–225	**The Vintage Vardos** Devon, England
152–157	Slowing the Pace	226–233	**Macieira Lodge** Beira, Portugal
158–161	The Meaning of (Cabin) Life	234–239	The Joy of Doing Nothing
162–165	**Digital Detox Cabin** Essex, England	240–245	**The Beach House** Kent, England
166–171	**Dragonfly** Norrbotten, Sweden	246–251	**Moinho da Fadagosa** Alto Alentejo, Portugal
172–175	**Blue Cone** Norrbotten, Sweden	252–253	Contributors
176–179	**The Cabin** Norrbotten, Sweden	254–255	Index
180–183	**Le Cèdre Blanc Two** Corrèze, France		

The Outdoor Life

— by Emily Eavis, co-organiser of Glastonbury Festival

Over the years, I've come to understand that Glastonbury Festival — which my dad and I organise here on Worthy Farm — is an event which means so many different things to so many different people: the Pyramid Stage, the performers, the late-night areas, the mud, the magic. But, at its very heart, our festival has always been a celebration of nature and the outdoor life. Each June, we welcome more than 200,000 people to these idyllic Somerset fields and, for those five days, they have no option but to live a simpler, more pastoral life.

They sleep under canvas, get around by foot, and find themselves very closely attuned to the weather. If they need shelter or shade, they'll search out a tree. If they need to relax or slow down for a bit, they'll sit on the grass and have a chat or read the paper (they can't keep looking at their phones, because they need to preserve battery). And the toilet facilities? Well, let's just call them functional.

Yet so many people I meet tell me that Glastonbury is their favourite place in the world, those five days their most cherished. And I'm sure that the back-to-basics rural lifestyle is a huge part of that. It allows people to reset, slow down, and live in the moment. And when they do, they realise what a special thing being outdoors in the countryside is.

Certainly, I feel hugely lucky to have grown up on Worthy Farm, where my family has lived for six generations. I've lived in London, too, where I often found myself yearning for the valley, the trees, and the birdsong. But what I think I missed most was the seasons. When you're in a big city, you might notice whether it's raining or hot, but the seasons — the very indicators of ongoing life and the beauty of the natural world — can pass you by. Now I'm back in Somerset, I take so much comfort in nature: seeing the first snowdrops of spring or the autumn leaves beginning to bronze. That seasonal ebb and flow gives you perspective.

Living here, the wonder and power of nature is all around us, and I think that maybe explains why my dad and I have always seen protecting the planet as such a big part of the festival's mission. For decades now, we've tried to raise awareness of climate change and campaign for ways of living that can help preserve and heal the world. Here on the farm, we have Europe's largest privately owned solar farm (on the roof of the cowshed), we convert the Worthy herd's dung into electricity with our anaerobic digester, and we were very proud to save millions of single-use plastic bottles from going to landfill after we banned the sale of them at the festival.

We're very fortunate to be in a position to make those big, newsworthy gestures — and having that platform is something we take very seriously — but the small things really count too. All of us can make changes and choices that truly will make a difference. And one of those is simply to take the time to enjoy and appreciate the natural world. The countryside is there for all of us. With the help of this lovely book make sure you get out there. Use it, value it, cherish it.

Lost and Found in the Scottish Highlands

Two reclaimed buildings make unlikely partners for a hideout in the wilds of Scotland

THE FERRY WAITING ROOM
LOCH LOMOND AND THE TROSSACHS NATIONAL PARK, SCOTLAND

Standing side by side with uninterrupted views of Balquhidder Glen, a basic bothy and a redundant waiting room make for an incongruous pair. Each was once unceremoniously consigned to the scrapheap, before landing here as one half of this innovative Highland hideout, for which the interiors have undergone renovations to suit the personality of the exteriors. All whitewashed walls, sophisticated textiles, and modern furnishings, the waiting room is a serene bedroom for four. The bothy, meanwhile, with its mishmash of plywood and tongue-and-groove walls, has an altogether more eclectic, rustic fit-out, serving as a small kitchen and sitting room. It goes without saying that both buildings have the most amazing views of their surroundings.

Set in the heart of the Loch Lomond and The Trossachs National Park, the hideout is a wildlife haven, with red squirrels, sparrow-hawks, and red deer right on the doorstep. When out and about, guests can climb Ben More or fish in nearby Lochs Voil or Doine.

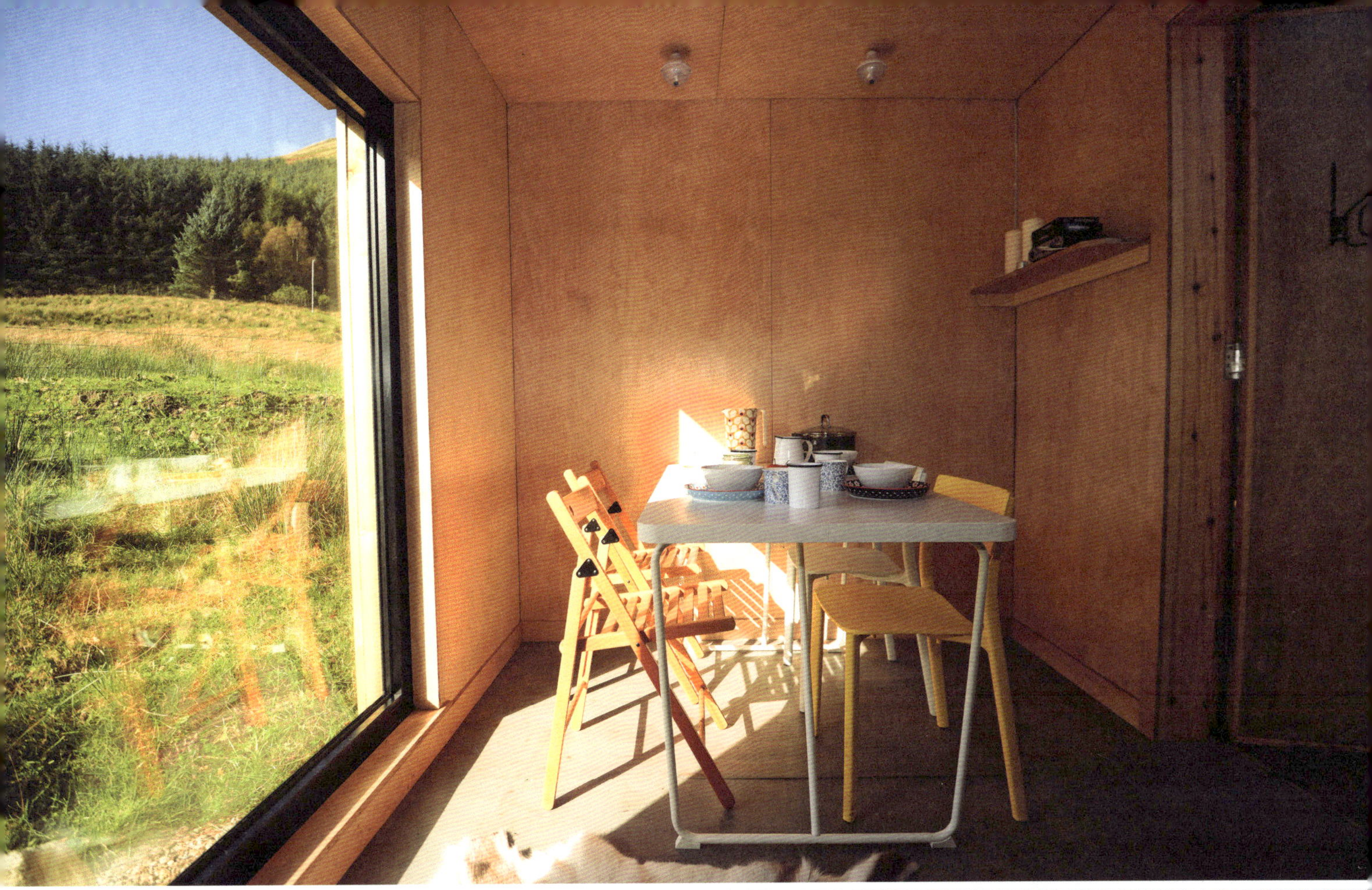

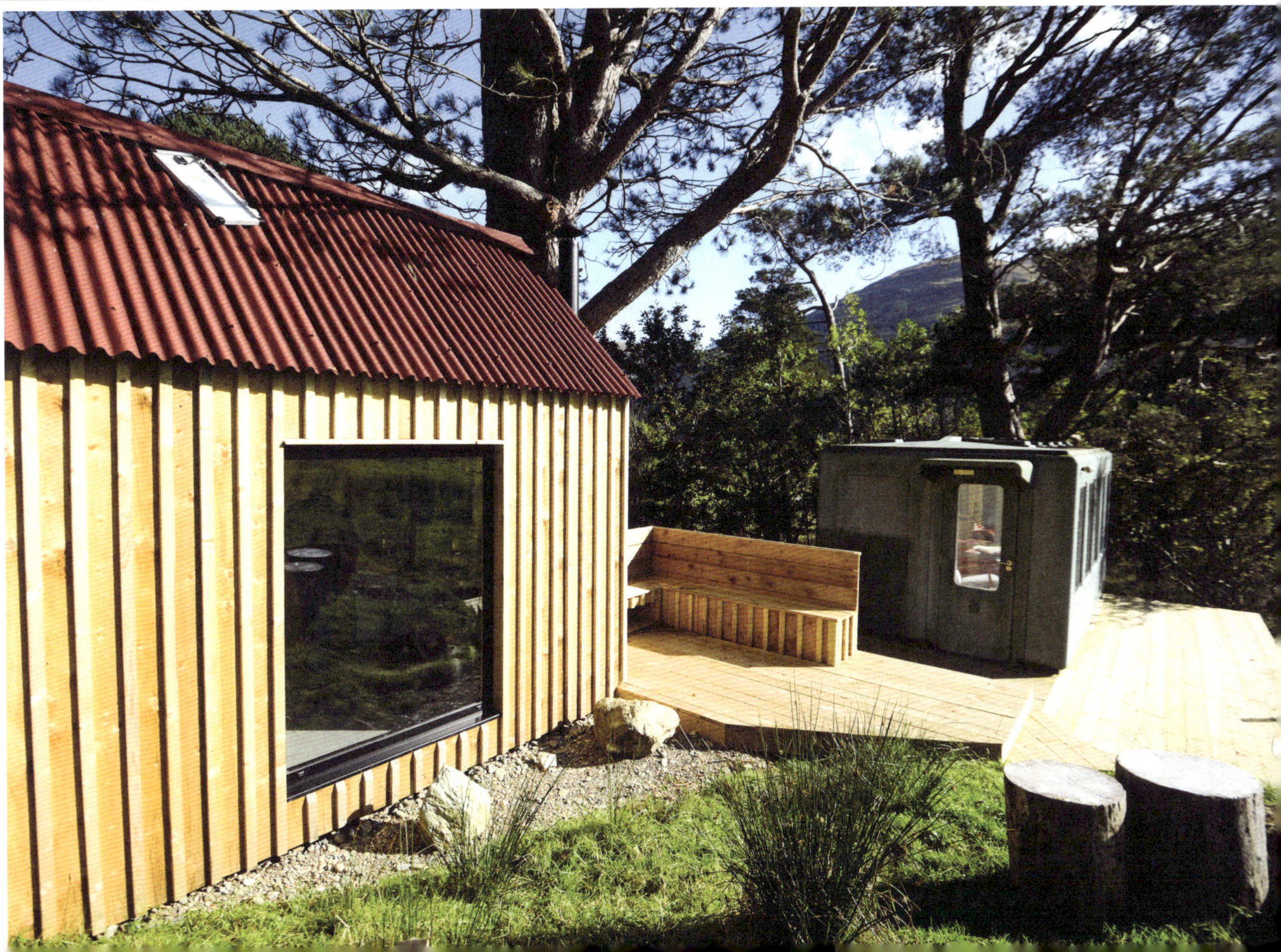

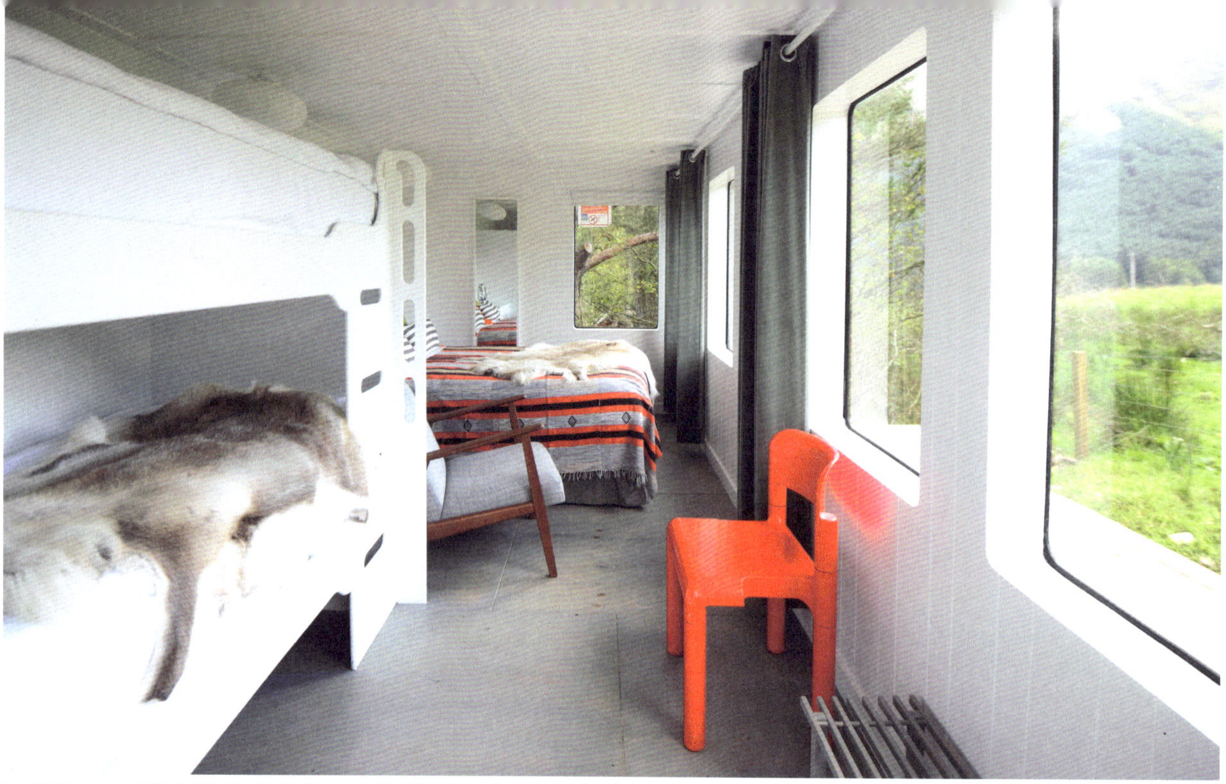

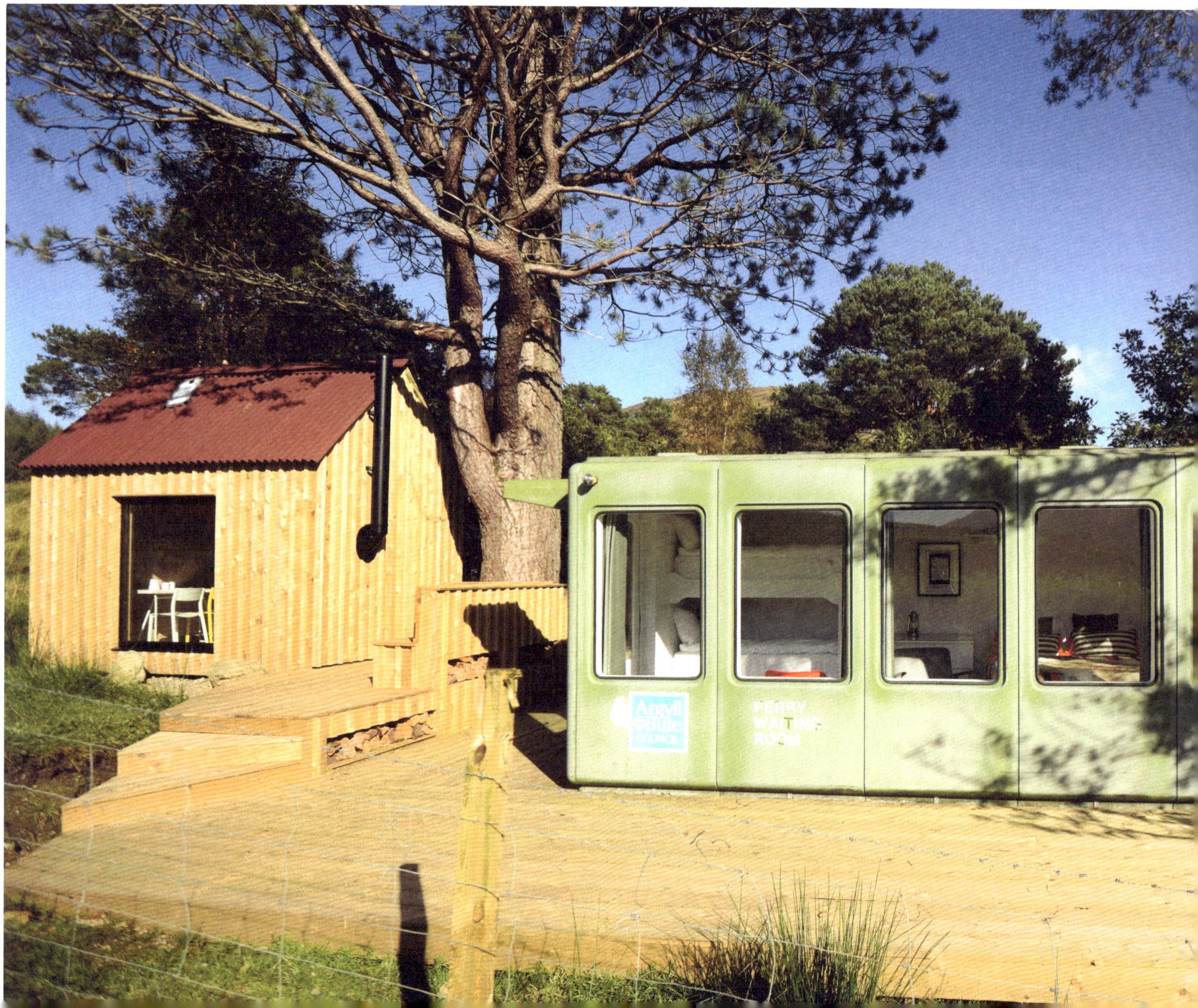
Argyll & Bute
COUNCIL
FERRY
WAITING
ROOM

THE FERRY WAITING ROOM

Run for the Hills

A luxury treehouse sandwiched between two rolling regions of outstanding natural beauty

ORCHARD TREEHOUSE
WORCESTERSHIRE, ENGLAND

On the grounds of a medieval manor house stands a magnificent Cypriot pine tree and, wrapped around it, a most impressive treehouse. With stunning views of the rolling hills of the north Cotswolds in one direction and of the Malverns in the other, Orchard Treehouse is tastefully furnished in neutral tones, with a king-size bed right in the middle. On the mezzanine level, accessed via a spiral staircase, a handsome bathtub squats beside a little window through which guests can watch the sun setting as they bathe. The bathroom has a shower and flushing loo, and there's even a hot tub on the deck, perfect for soaking in the open, high up among the branches. Dotted with fruit trees and crossed by a babbling stream, the surroundings are gorgeously green and terrifically tranquil; guests will delight in spotting wild deer, buzzards, woodpeckers, and barn owls.

ORCHARD
TREEHOUSE

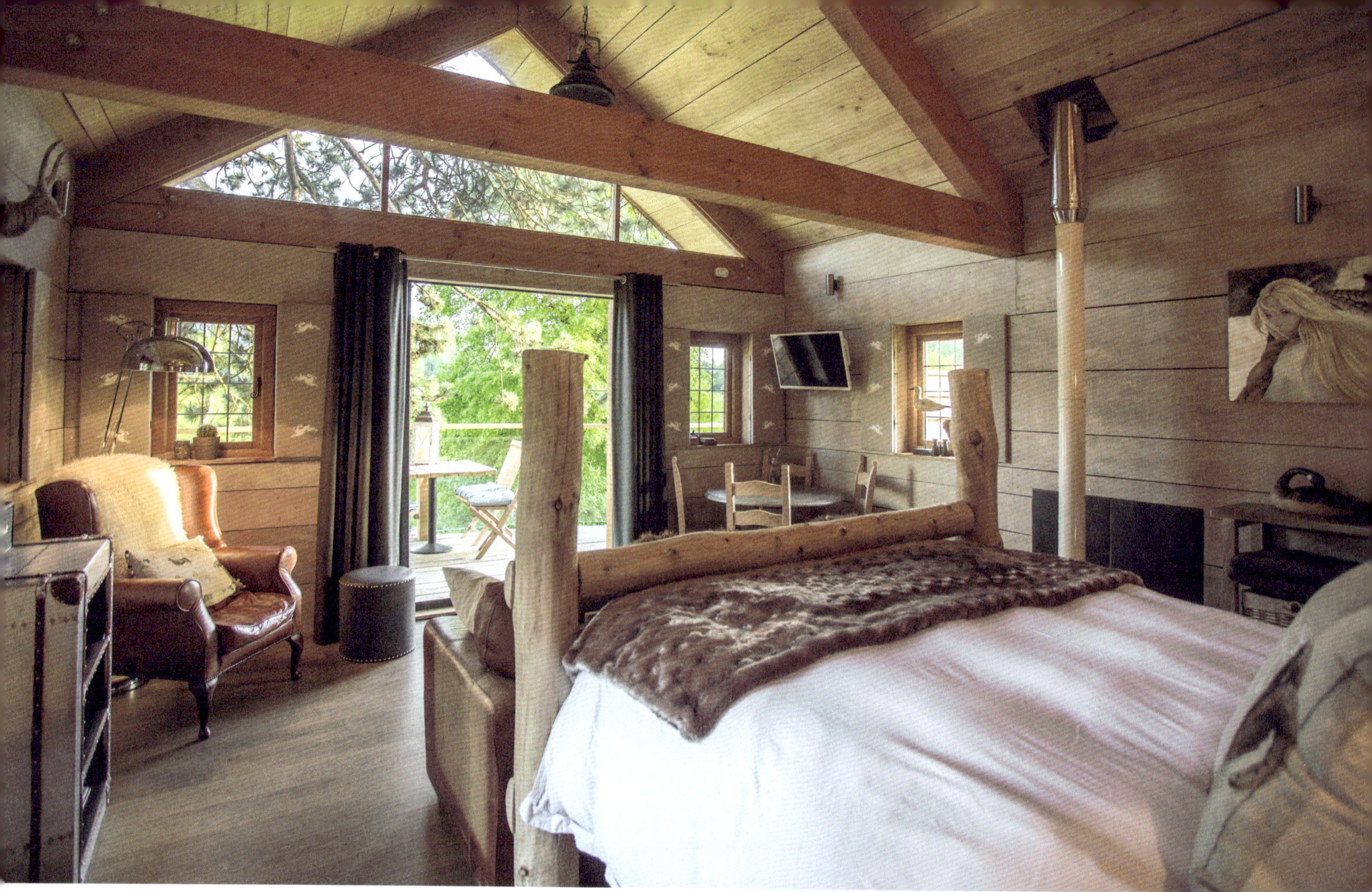

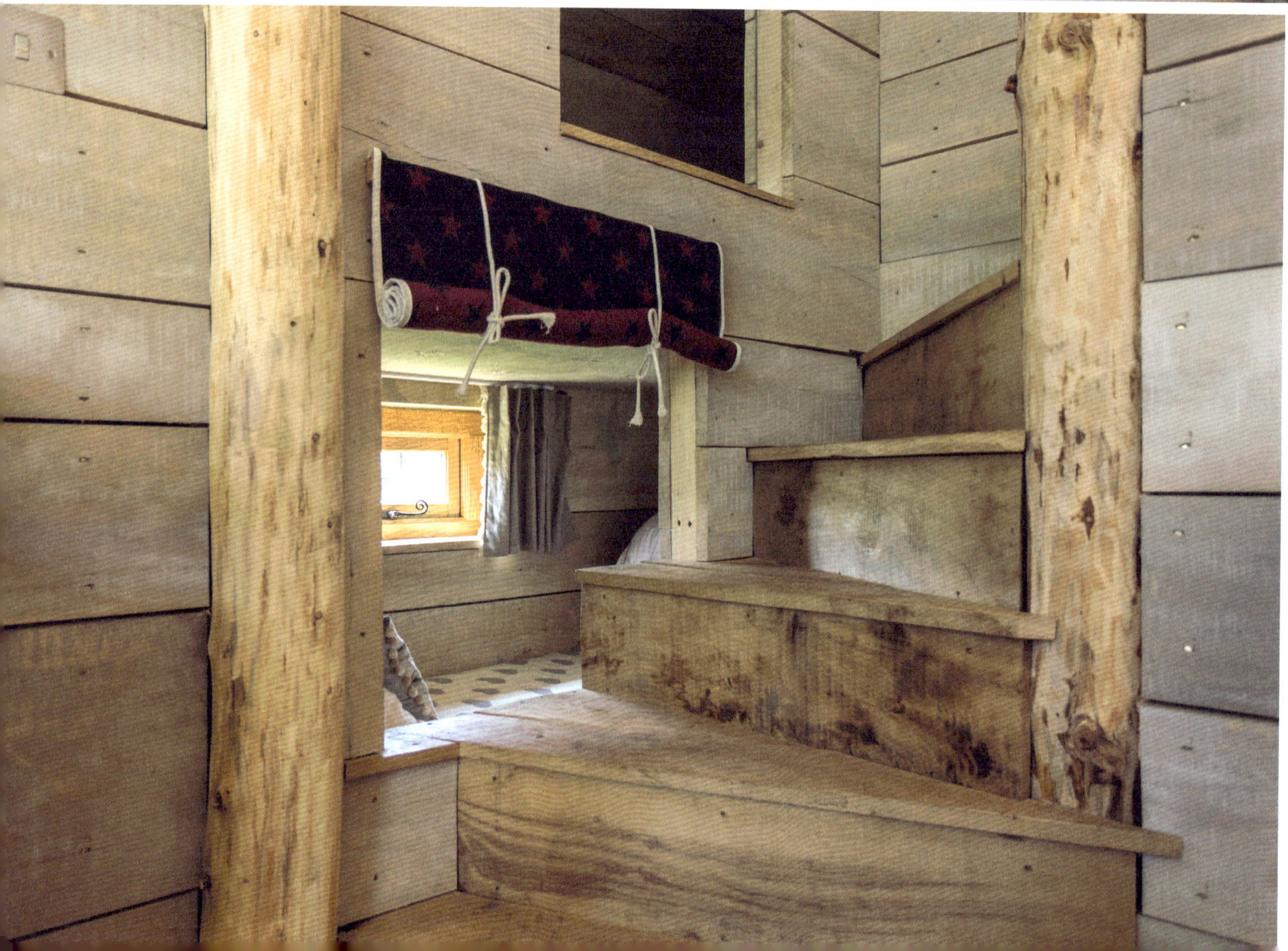

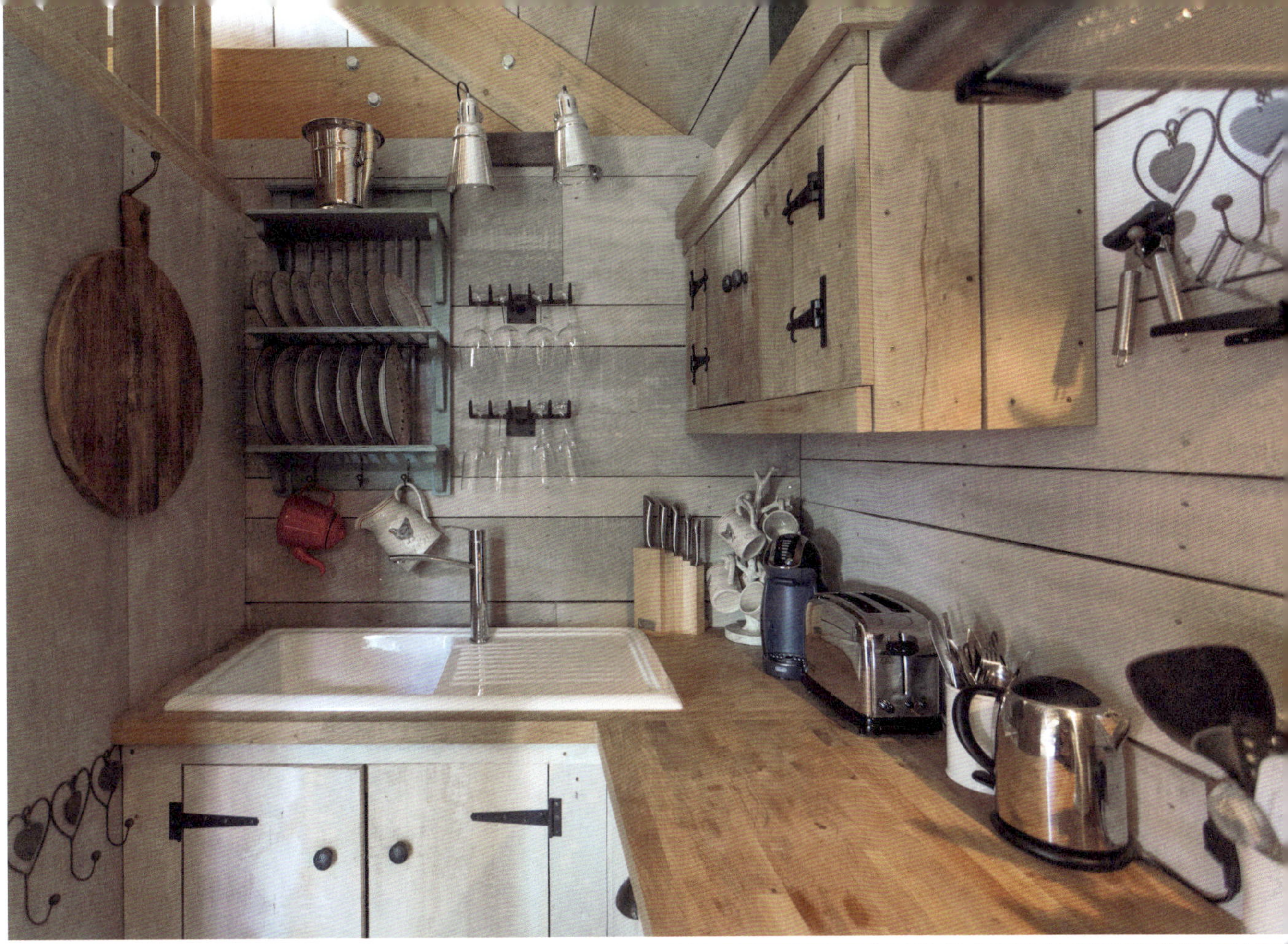

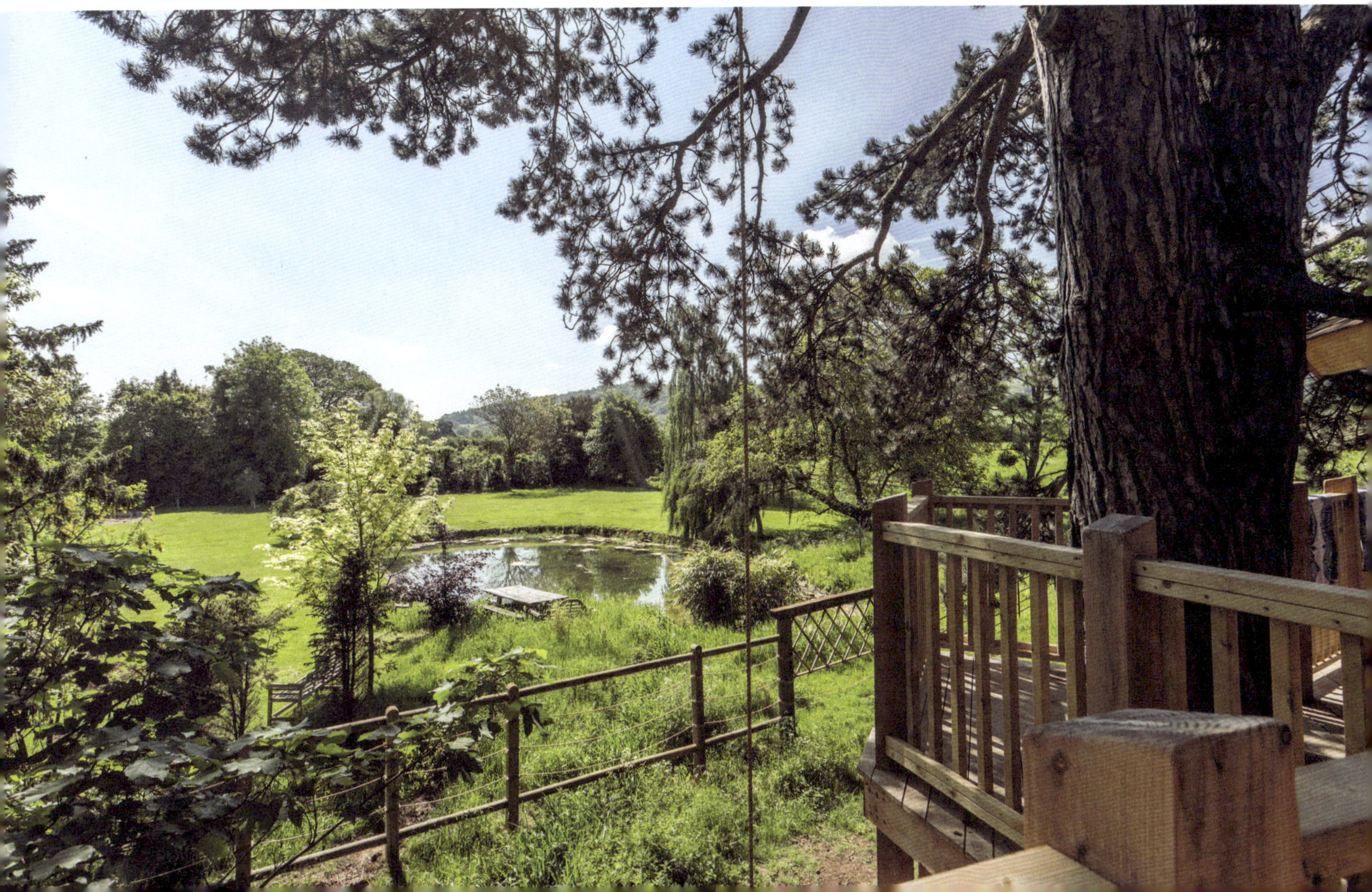

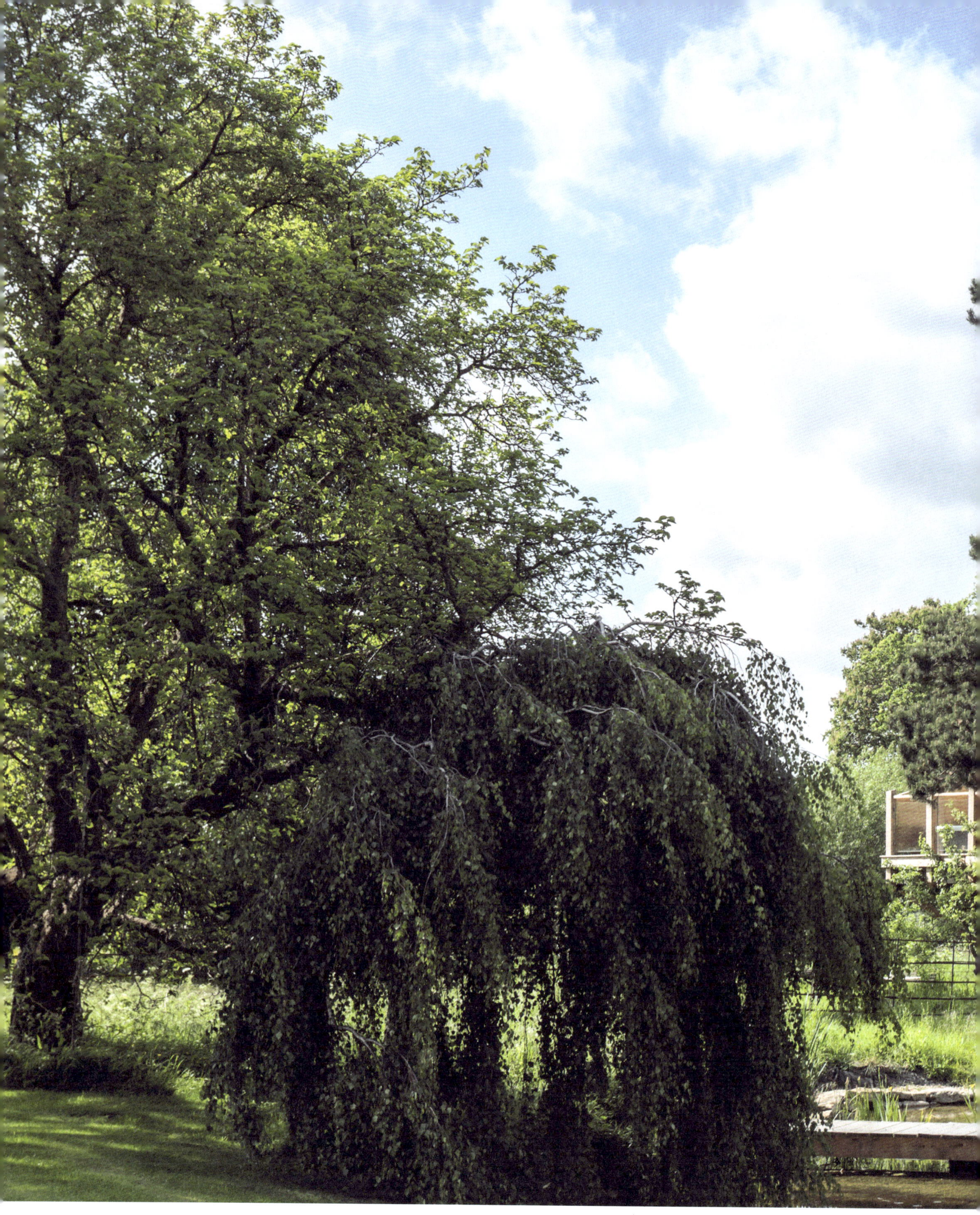

ORCHARD TREEHOUSE

LIFE IS
BETTER
IN THE
MOUNTAINS

One of a Kind Hybrid

This cross between a typical U. S. school bus and a VW camper provides a getaway like no other

HINTERLANDES
THE LAKE DISTRICT,
ENGLAND

This intriguing combination of two vehicles — one stacked on top of the other — can be found in Cumbria's Lake District, England's largest national park and a spectacular destination for spotting wild deer, otters, and birds of prey on the many possible trail walks. The lower bus level of the accommodation comes complete with an AGA cooker, hot shower, and compost loo, while, up a ladder, the camper level provides a bedroom with wraparound windows from which to enjoy the view. And the view is *always* stunning — always, because Hinterlandes moves between several locations throughout the year to help minimise its impact on the environment while making the most of its wild and remote home ground. On one visit, guests might wake up surrounded by curious sheep; on another, their days might be accompanied by the rippling waters of a nearby brook. Wherever Hinterlandes ends up, visitors can be sure to find outdoor seating around a firebowl and a wood-fired hot tub for outdoor soaking.

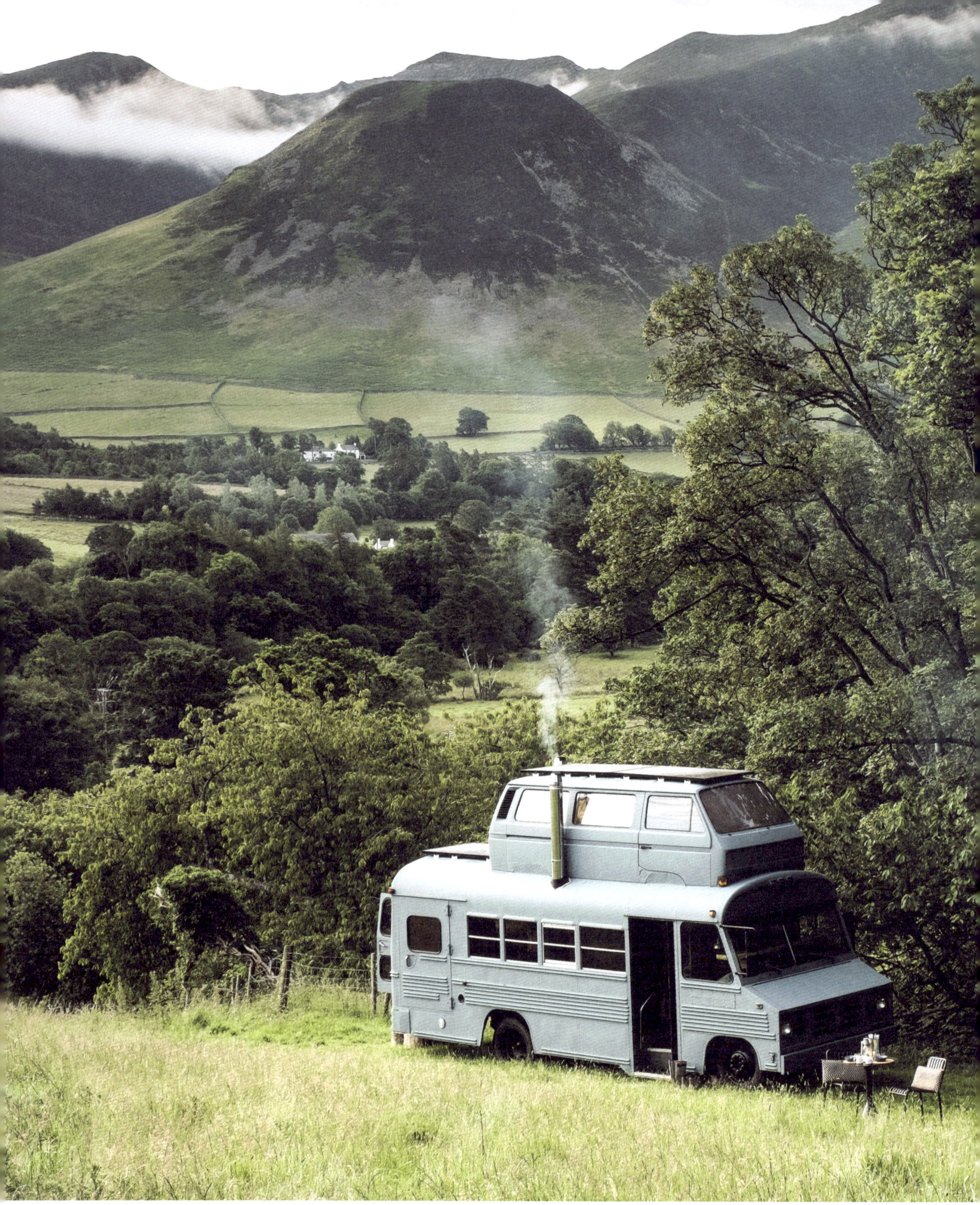

HINTERLANDES

A Humble Hut for Quiet Contemplation

Living in harmony with nature in a wild and isolated dell in the Black Mountains

GWENNOL
BLACK MOUNTAINS,
WALES

This beautifully hand-crafted shepherd's wagon, created by woodsman James Noble, provides owner Molly Gilbert with the perfect eco-friendly refuge away from the day-to-day of city living. Gwennol sits beside a river, in a clearing that's accessible only on foot or horseback, or by bike, and life here is simple. A clay tagine for slow-cooking hangs over the fire pit, and there's an air of tranquillity that urges guests simply to relax and go with the flow. Nearby are numerous hiking trails and a host of other outdoor activities, including pony trekking and canoeing.

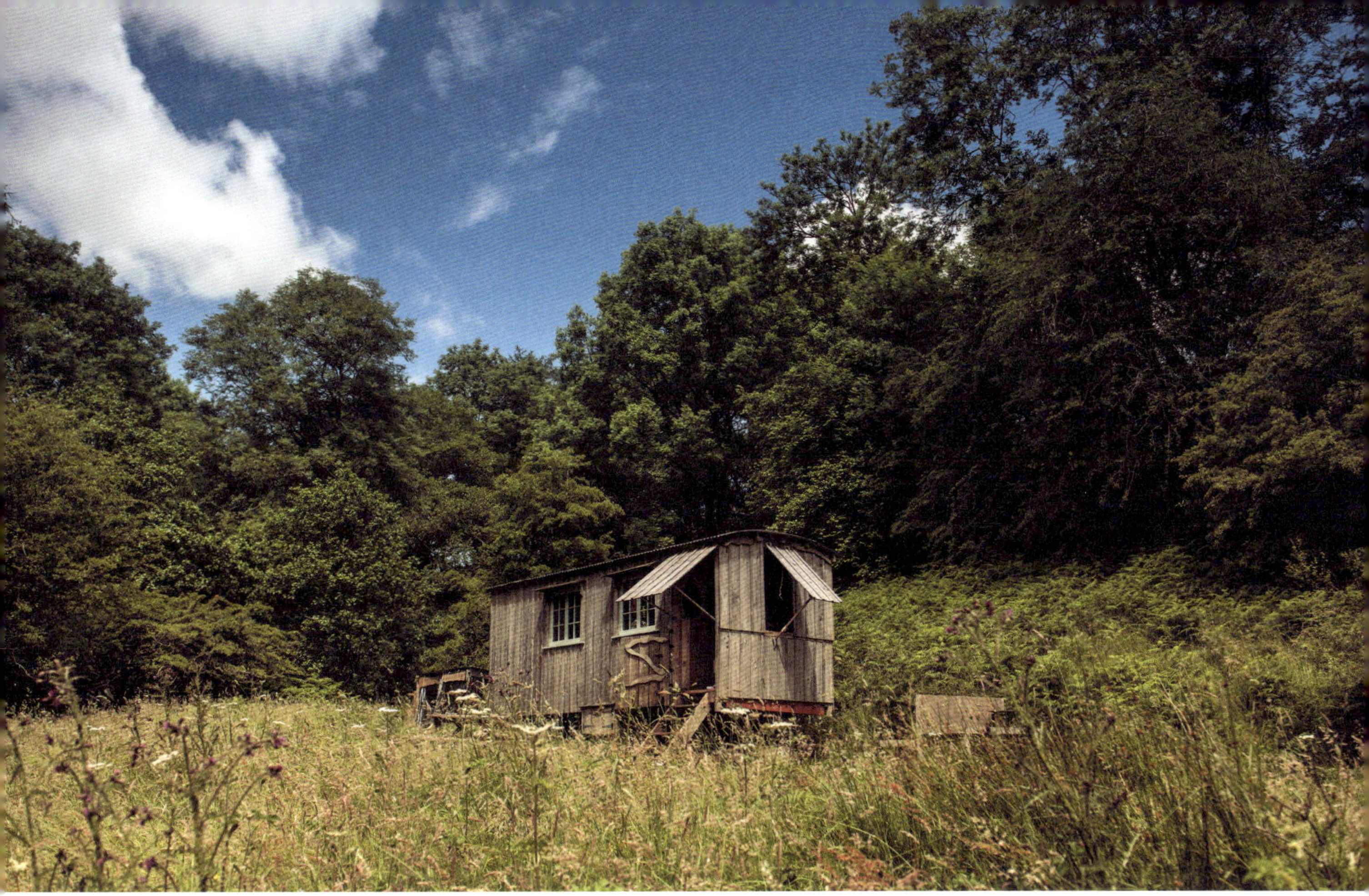

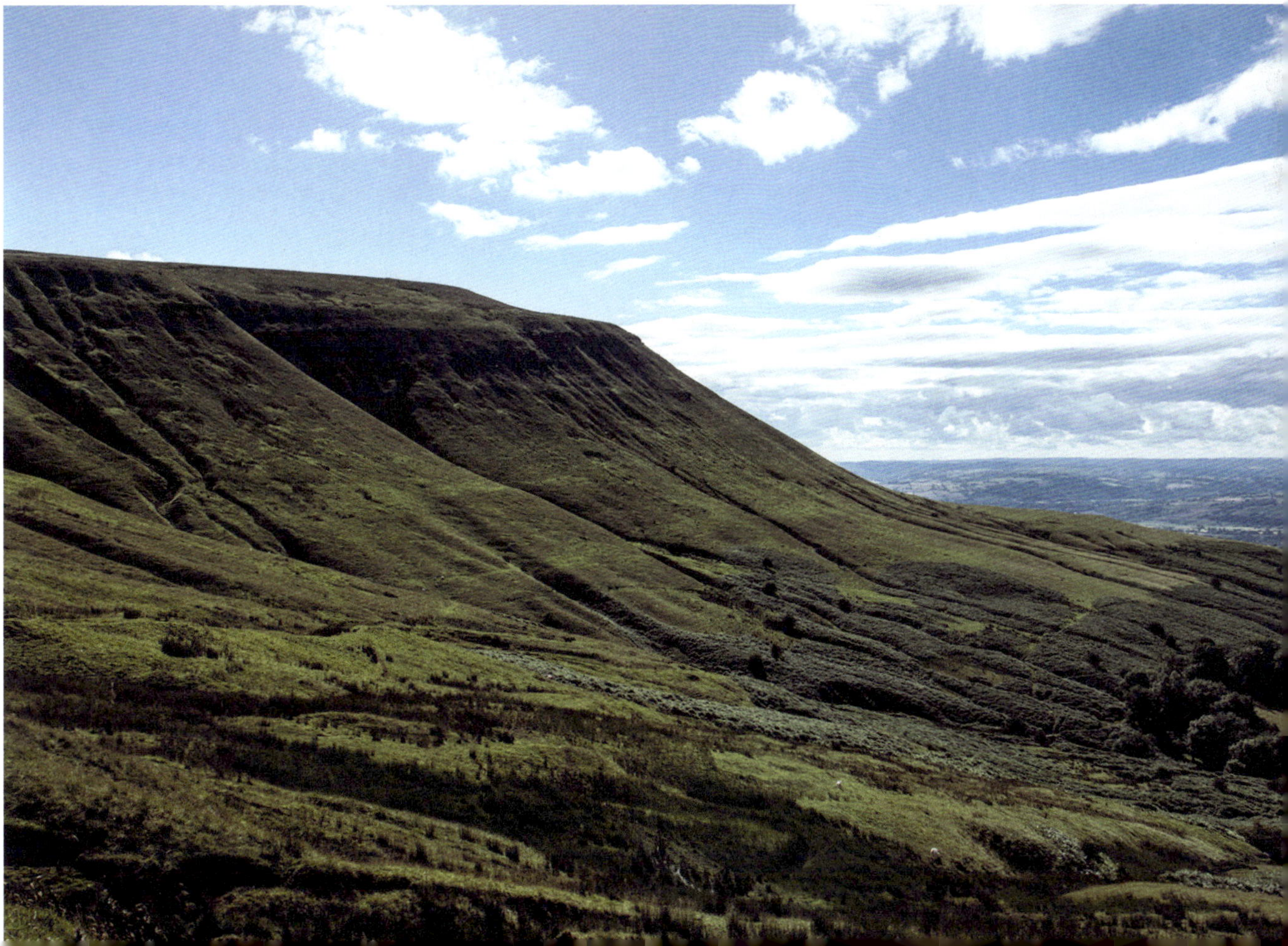

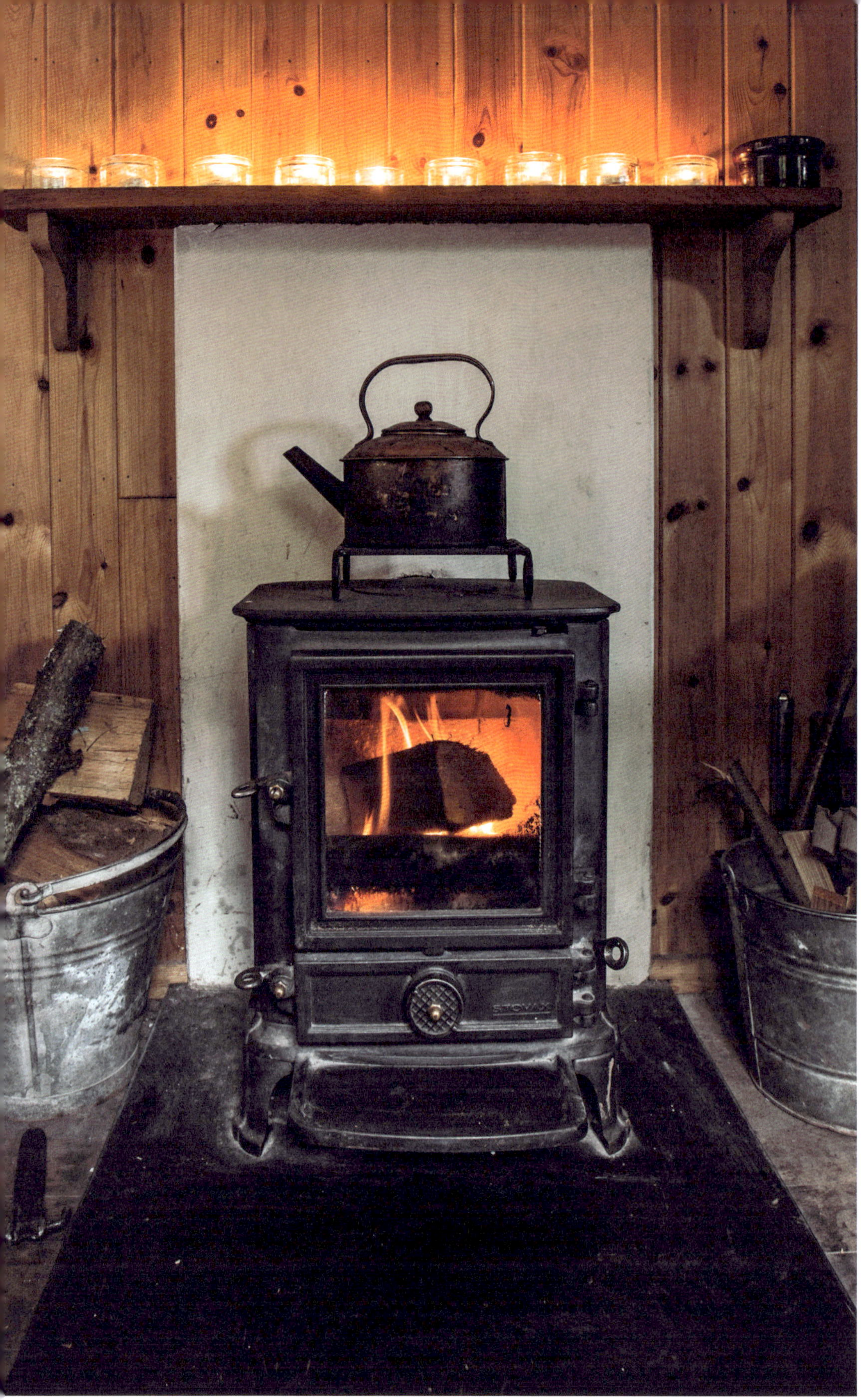

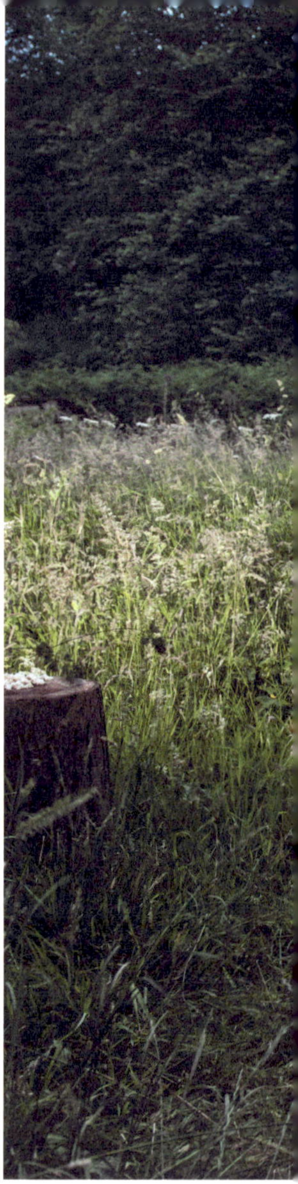

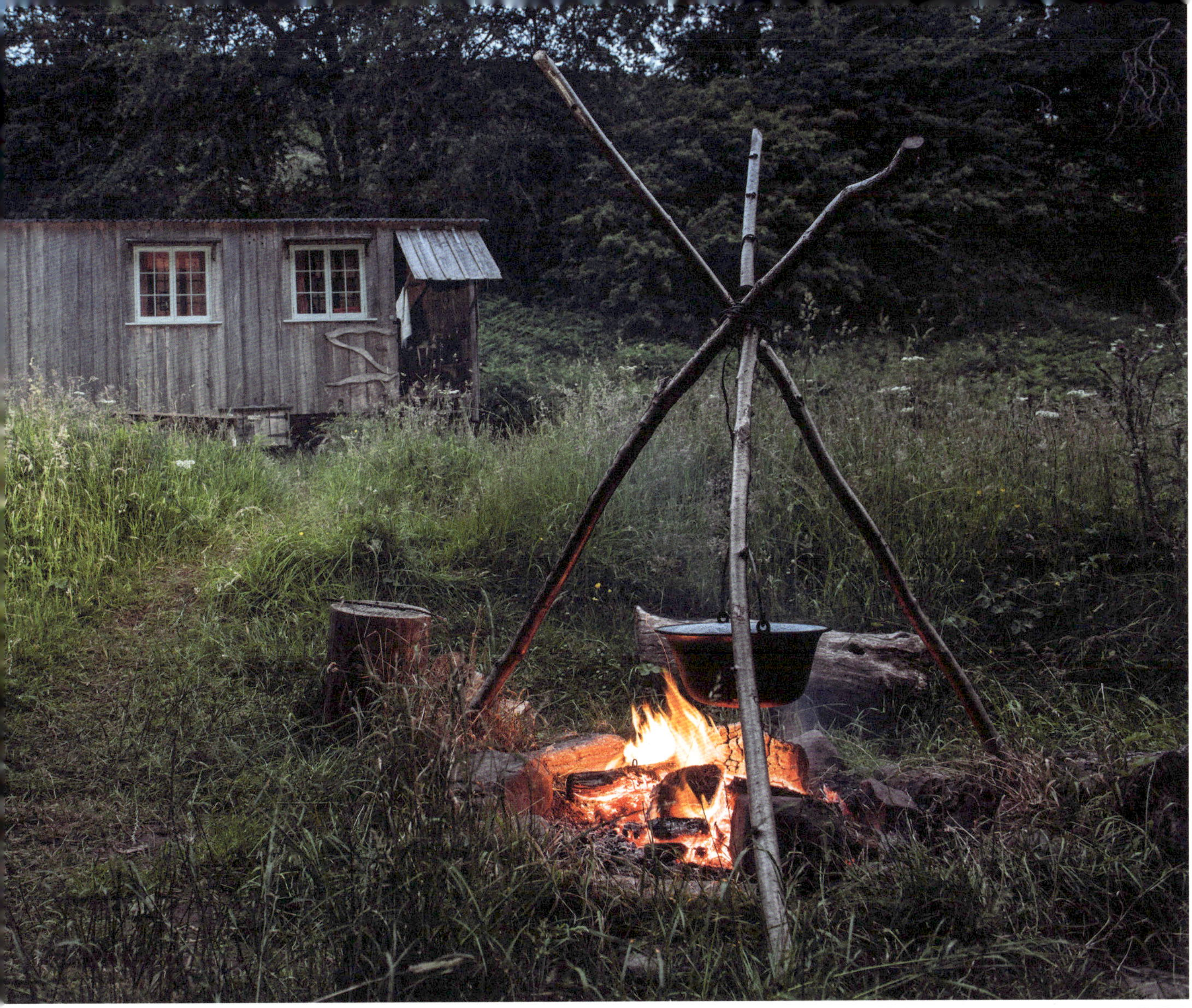

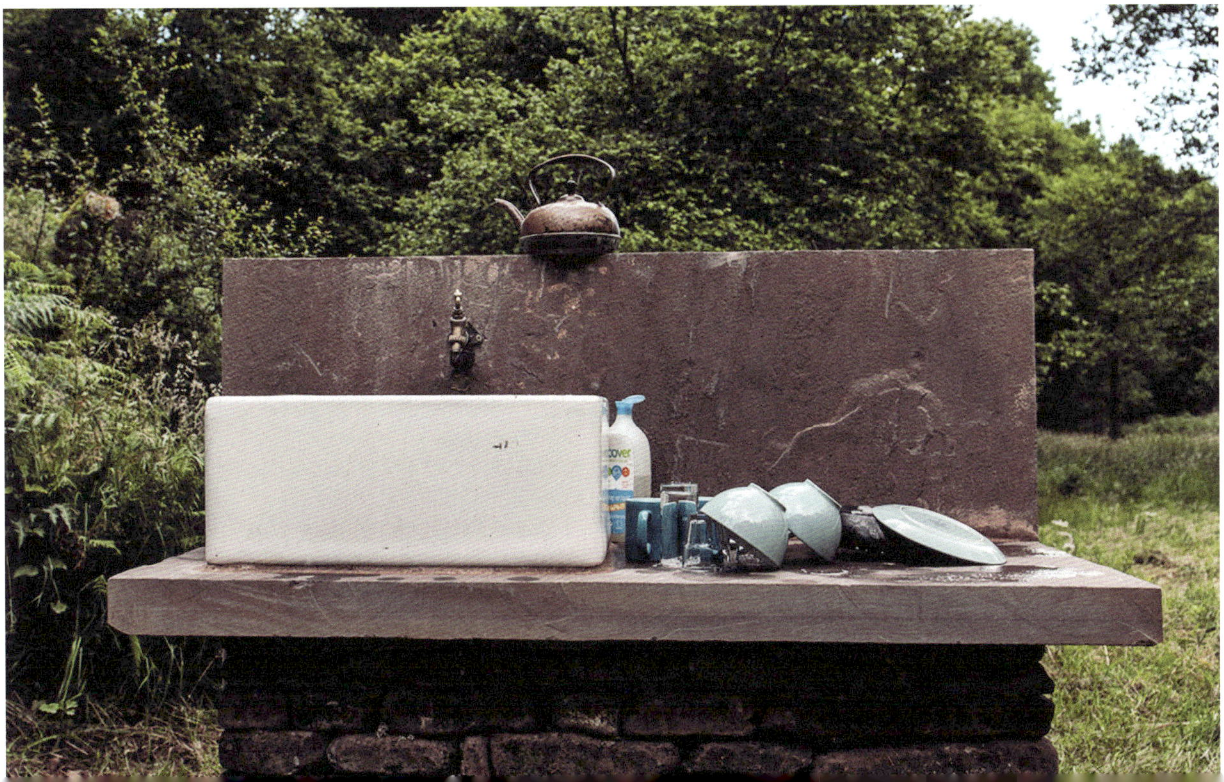

The Whole World at Your Feet

Miles and miles of rolling countryside in one of England's best-loved counties

BIG SKY LOOKOUT
DEVON,
ENGLAND

There is a rural ease and tranquillity that pervades every corner of this woodsy cabin, particularly in summer, when guests can slide open the doors to let the countryside in. Charming in its simplicity, Big Sky Lookout is built from wooden boards: the exterior is a deep, dark blue, and the interior is composed of natural wood, with royal blue frames around the windows. Outside, two swings hang from the nearest tree for daydreamy contemplation of the world at your feet, and, just beyond the deck, there's a tripod fire pit for cooking after a day spent out and about.

With two coastlines and vast expanses of open moorland, Devon has no shortage of outdoor activities for adventurers, from hiking and climbing to kayaking and surfing. But for those looking to simply relax, the retreat offers stunning wildflower meadows in summer and plentiful berry crops come autumn. It's a haven for wildlife where nature lovers will have no trouble spotting butterflies, birds, badgers, foxes, deer, and owls.

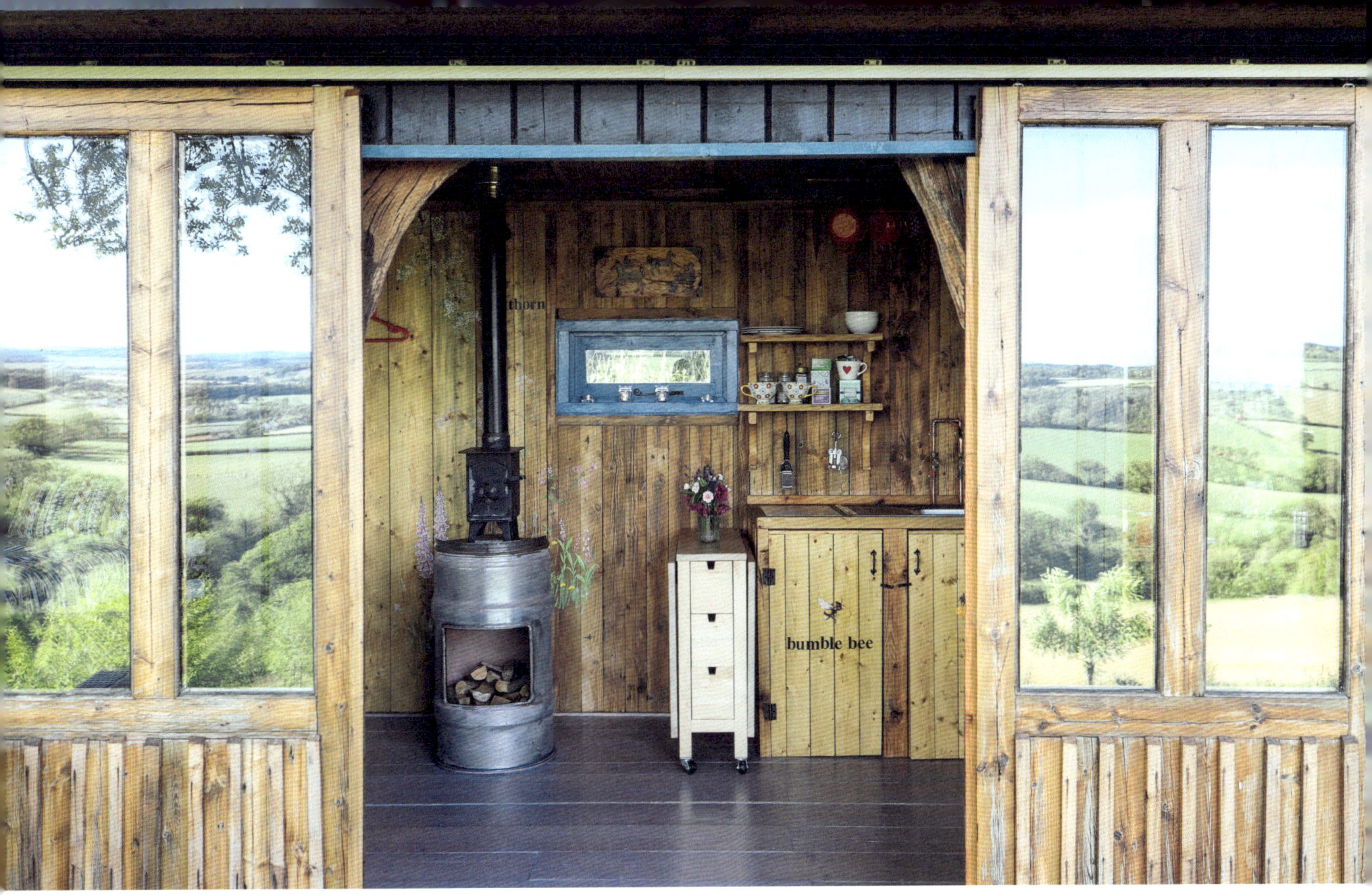
thorn
bumble bee

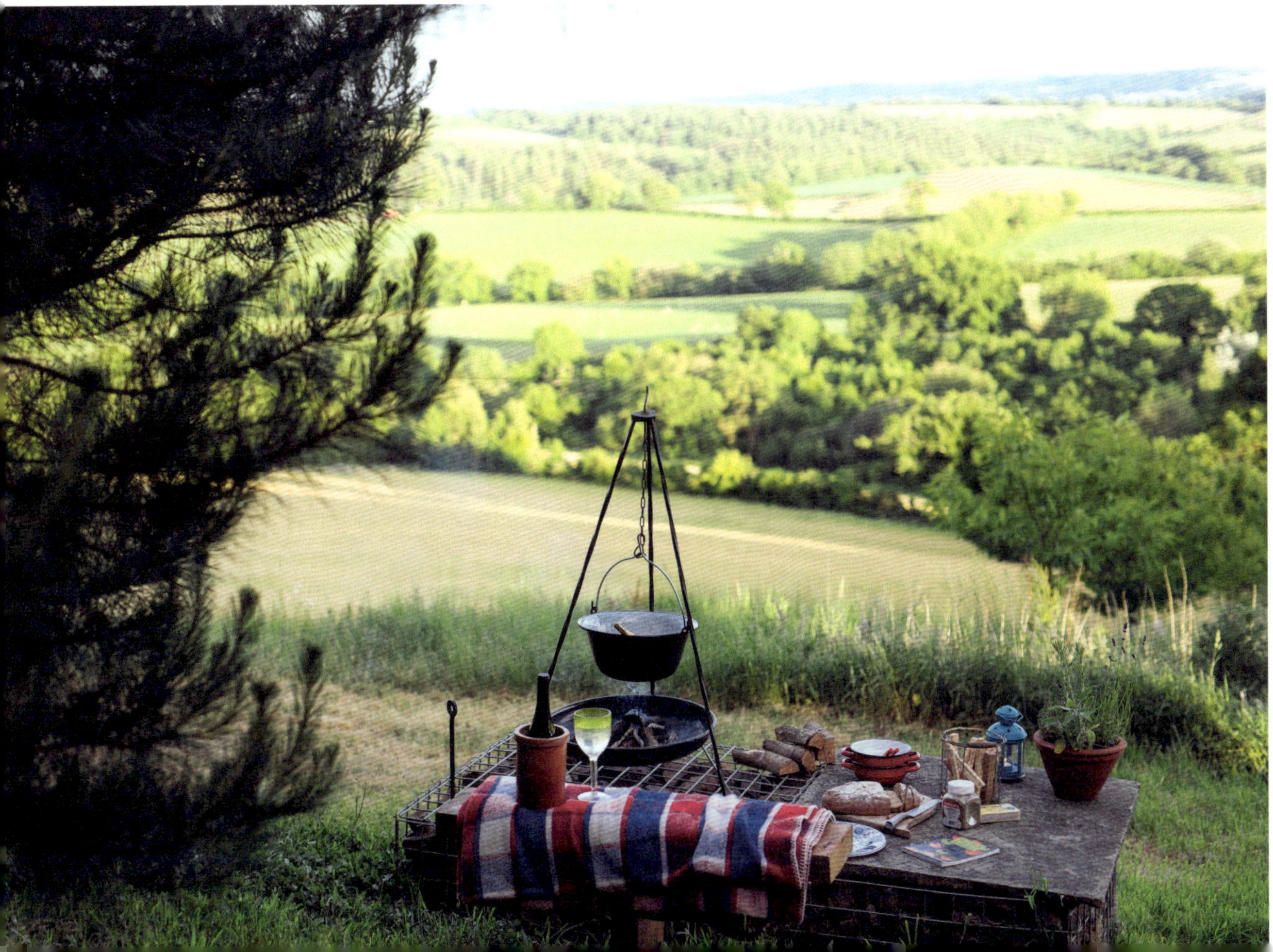

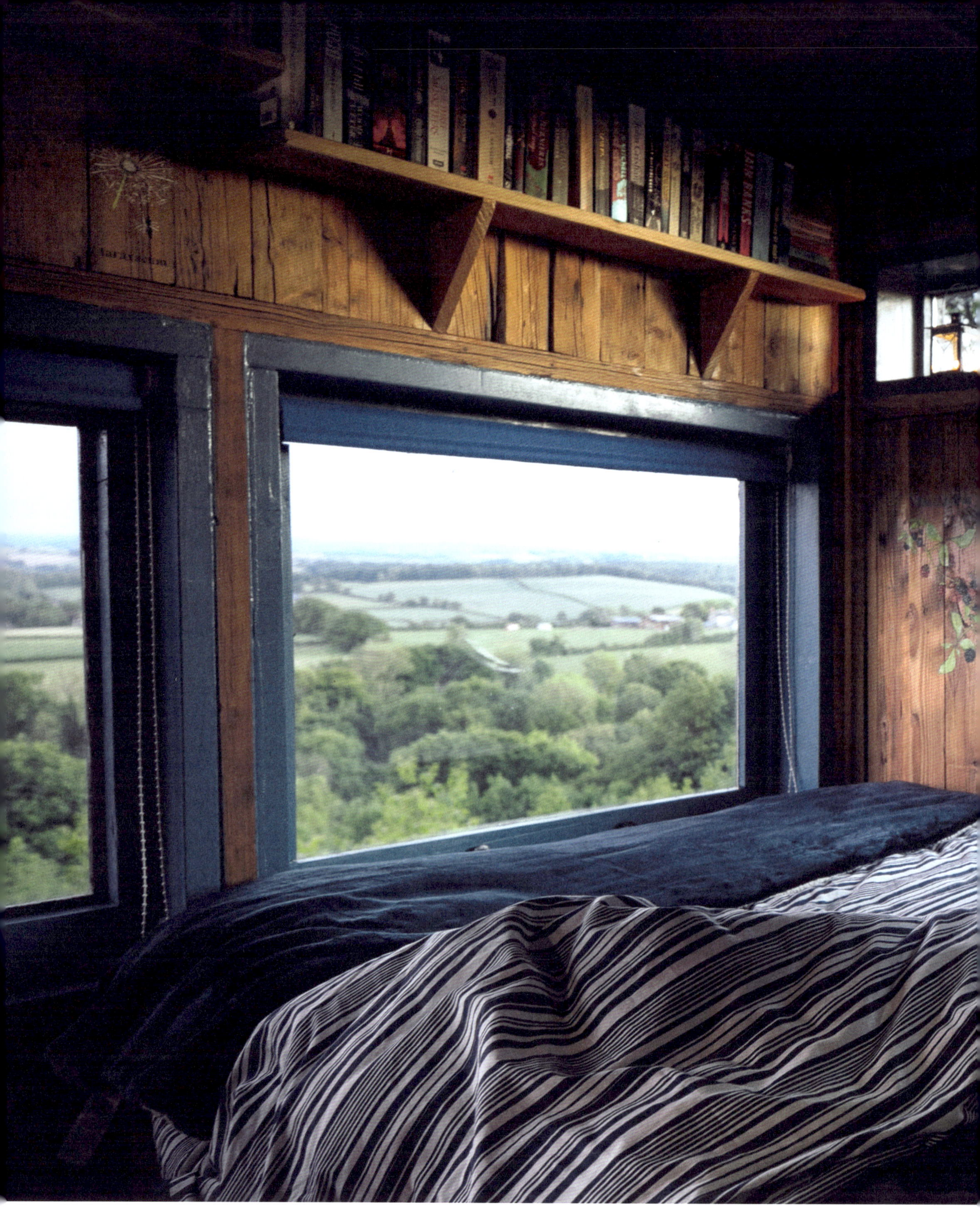

BIG SKY LOOKOUT

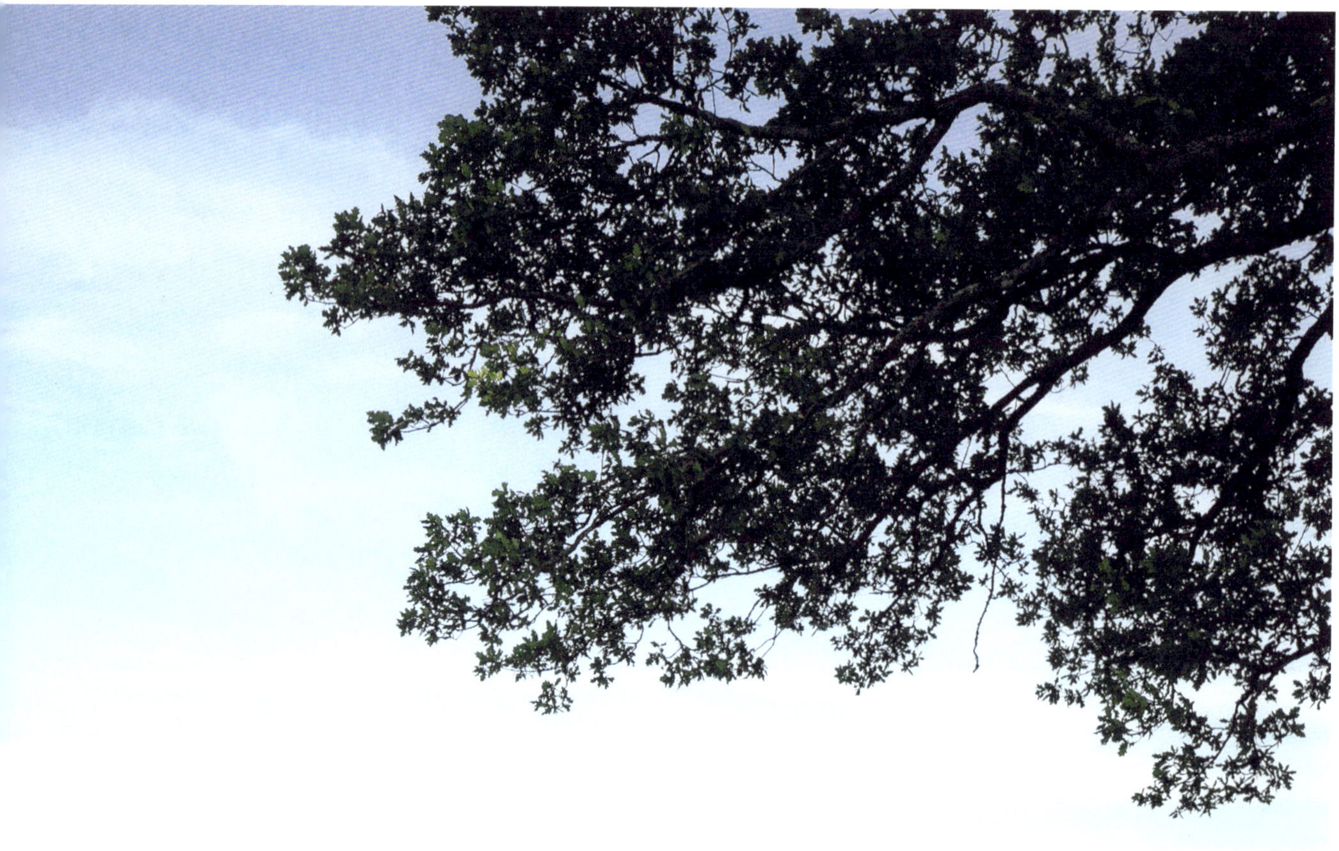

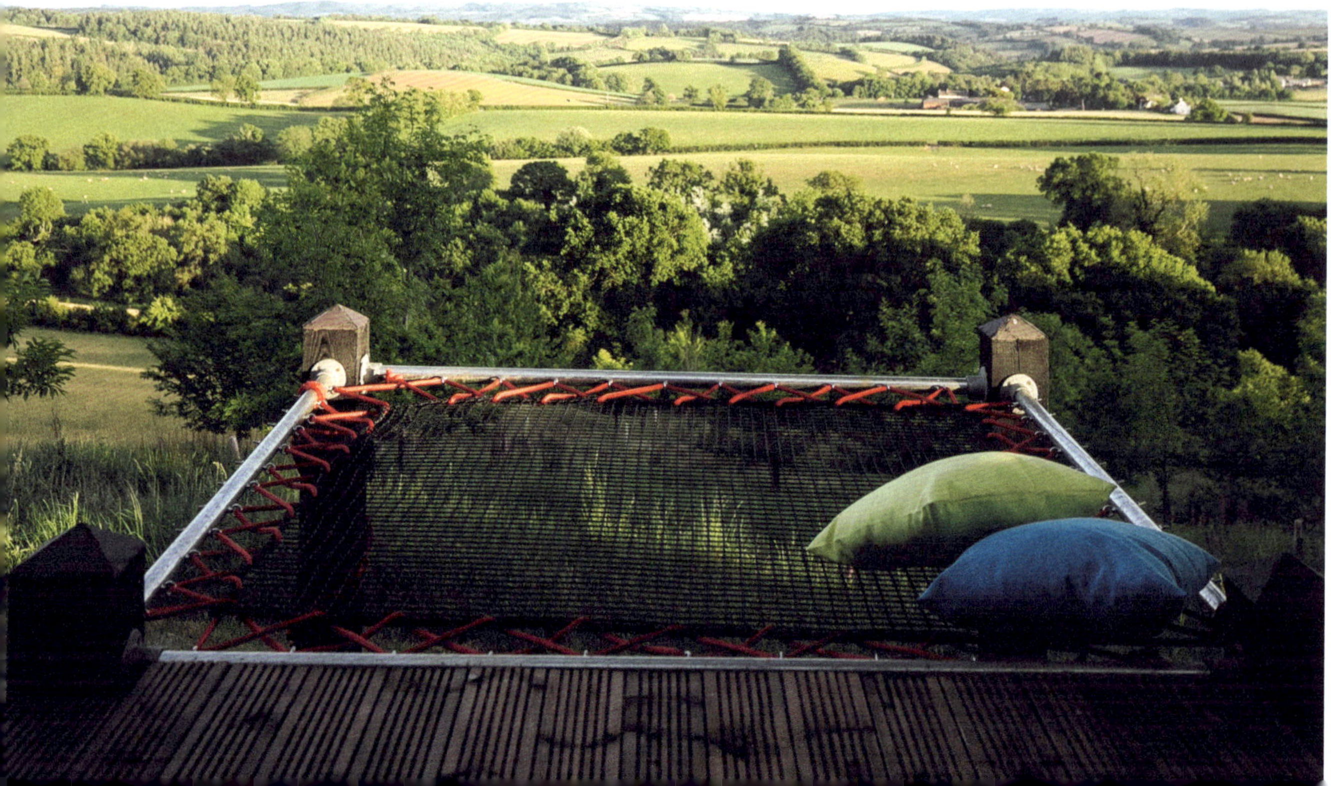

BIG SKY LOOKOUT

BIG SKY LOOKOUT

honeysuckle (*lonicera*)

The Stuff of Fairy Tales

Sleeping in total comfort beneath the stars in an ancient woodland setting

MIDSUMMER MEADOW BED
DARTMOOR, ENGLAND

Picture a sun-blessed glade in an ancient woodland surrounded by wildflowers, their heads bobbing in the gentle summer breeze. There's a bell tent pitched on the grass and, beneath the trees, the most magical four-poster bed carved from the branches of a fallen eucalyptus tree. This idyllic scene is not a fantasy but a glamping-retreat reality crafted by co-founder of Canopy & Stars, Tom Dixon, and his partner Vashti Cassinelli on a Devonshire Dark Sky Reserve in south-west England. Available during the summer months, the Midsummer Meadow Bed offers guests a rare opportunity to sleep in the wild in cushioned and canopied comfort, with only the sounds of the woodland around them. Peeling back the canopy at night reveals a skyful of stars, and the morning hush is accompanied by a breakfast hamper packed with treats. Just a stone's throw away, there's a barn with a private bathroom and tea-making facilities. And the bell tent? It's the perfect place to chill after trail walking or wild swimming in the fairy-tale setting.

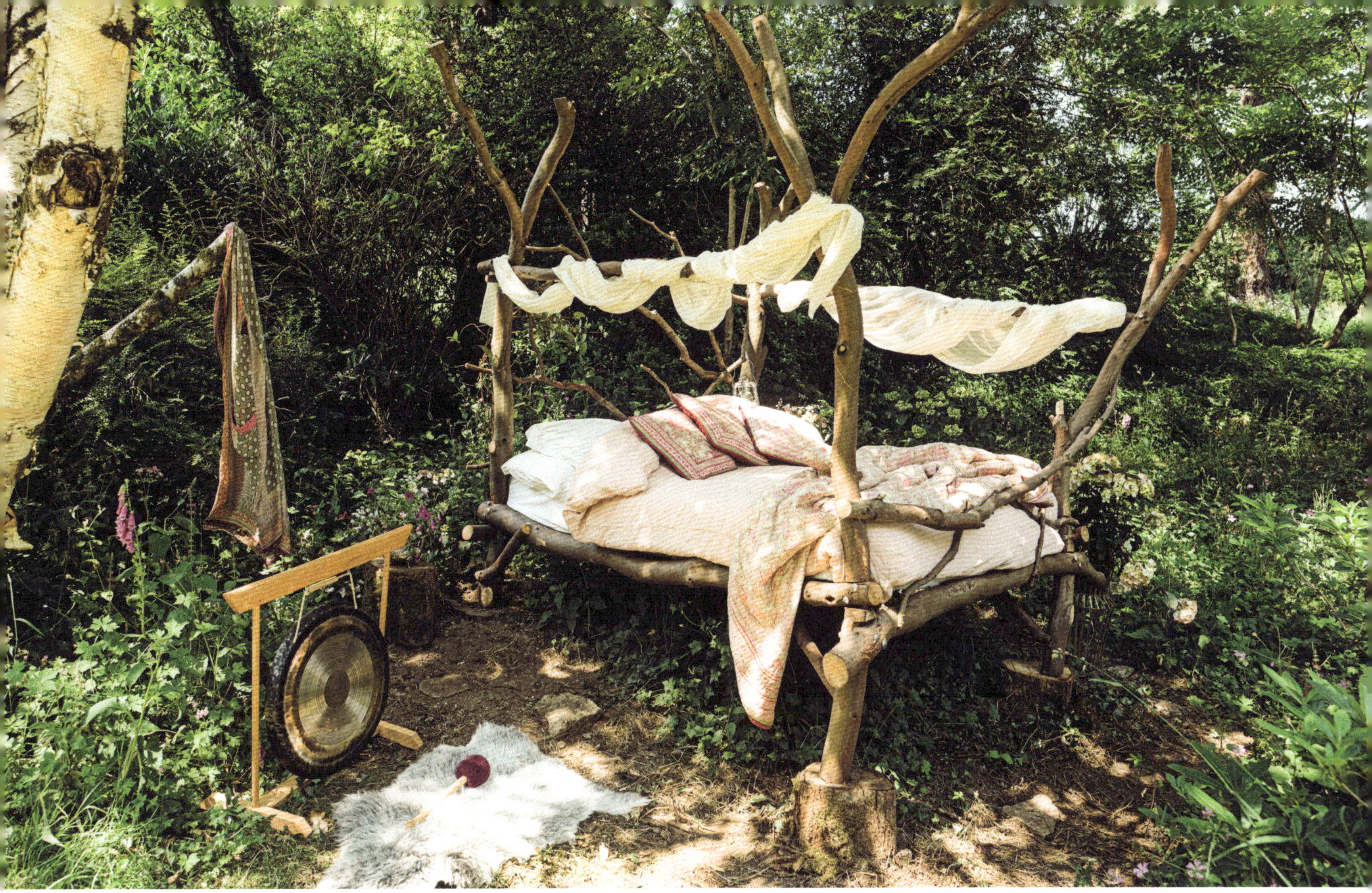
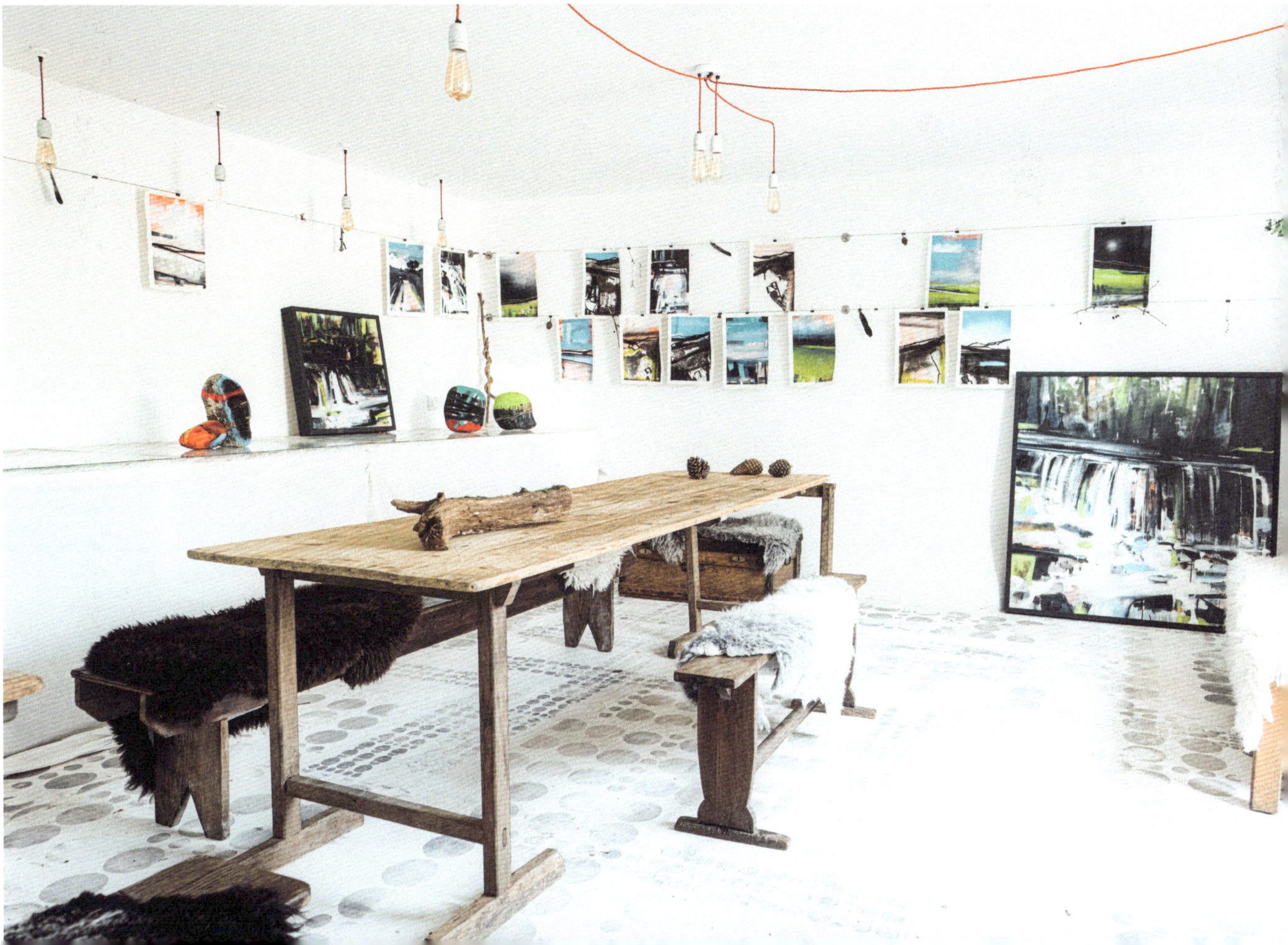

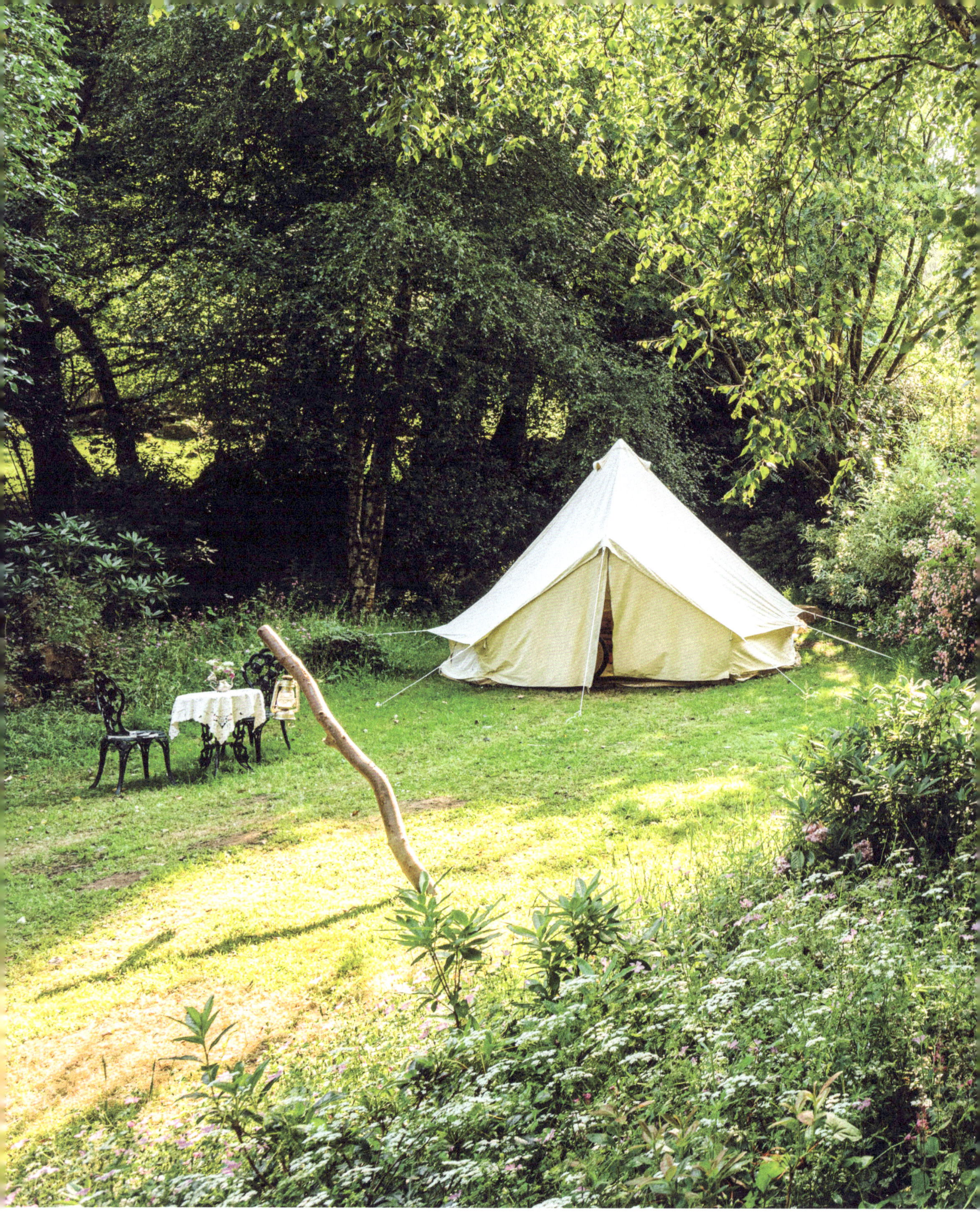

MIDSUMMER MEADOW BED

Chilling Out in a Mongolian-Style Yurt

Enter this kaleidoscopic tent for bohemian-style glamping on the Welsh Borders

KINTON CLOUD-HOUSE YURT
SHROPSHIRE, ENGLAND

Stepping into Kinton Cloud-House — a translation of the original Mongolian term for 'yurt' — guests are greeted with the most fantastic rainbow of colours in the fabrics that span the space's interior. Candles and solar-powered fairy lights conjure a magical atmosphere in which to chill in true bohemian style, and there are plentiful soft fleeces and sheepskins for augmenting the warmth of the wood burner. The yurt occupies a large wooden deck on a private estate with access to a number of designated hiking trails, and in this wildlife haven, red kites are an especially frequent sight.

BLACK BIRD
TURMERIC
DOMAINE DU REMPART
Pomerol
CANTEMERLE

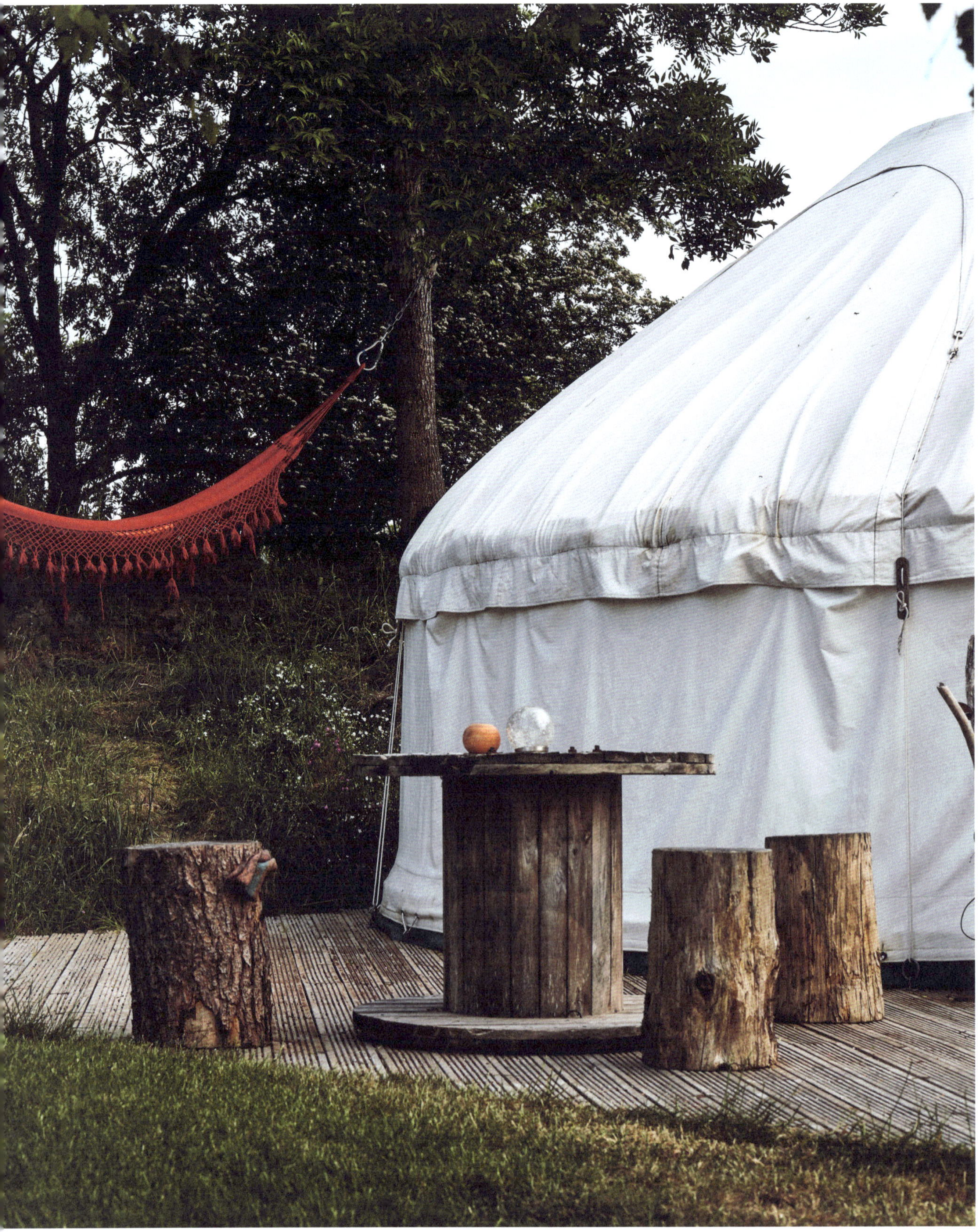

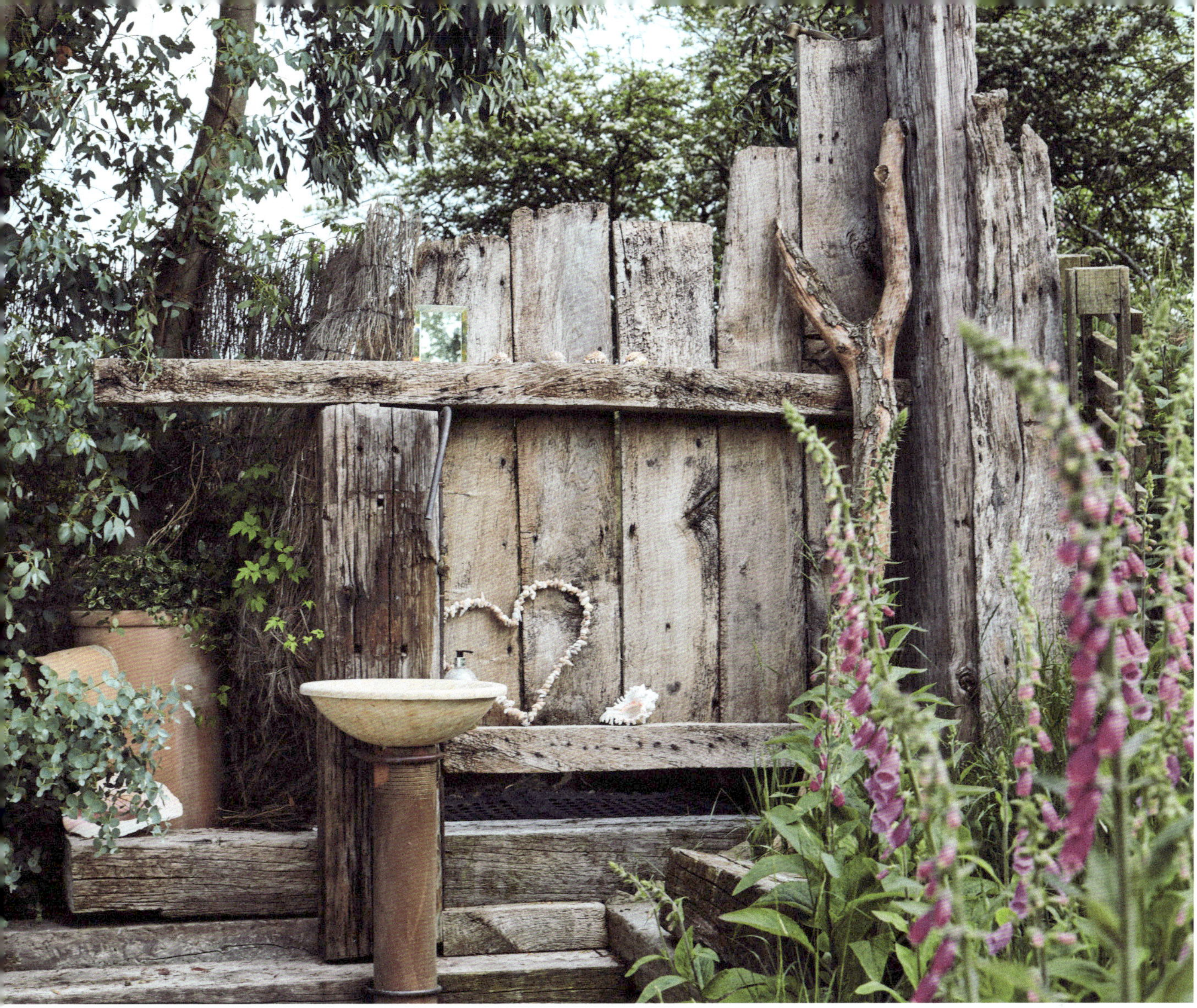

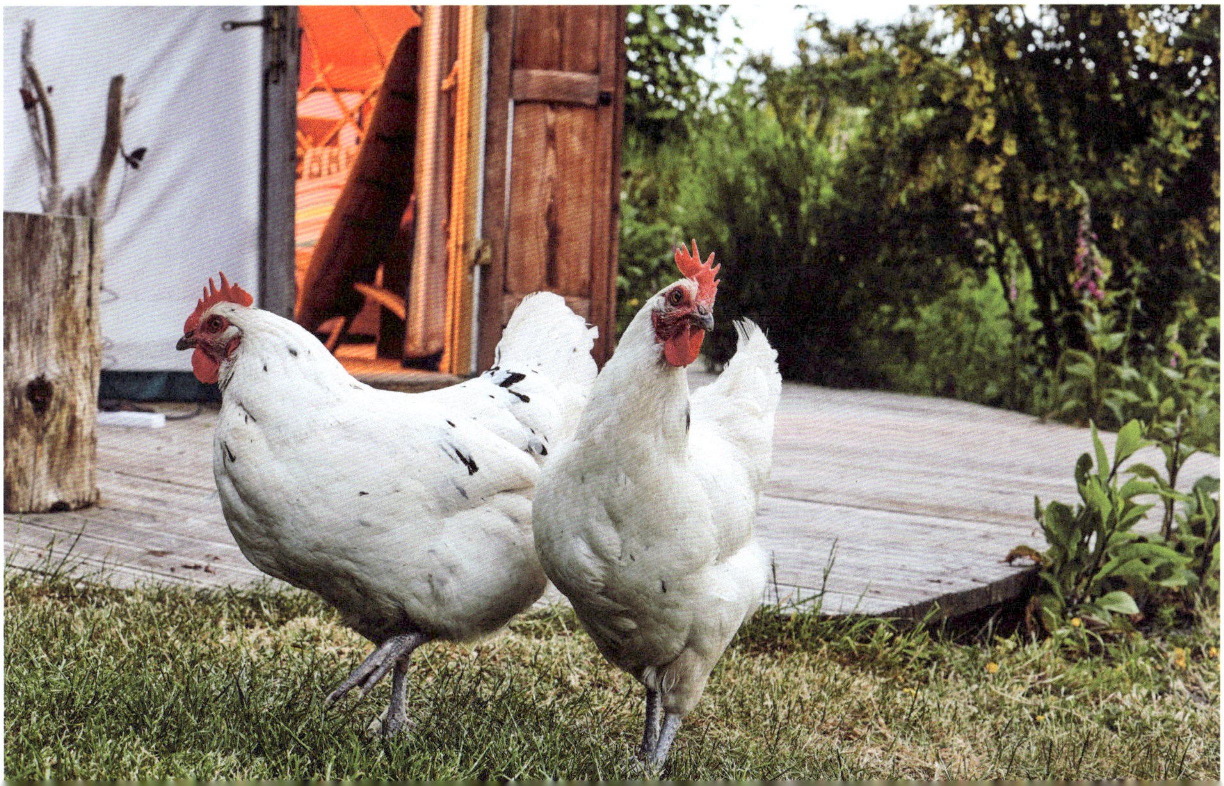

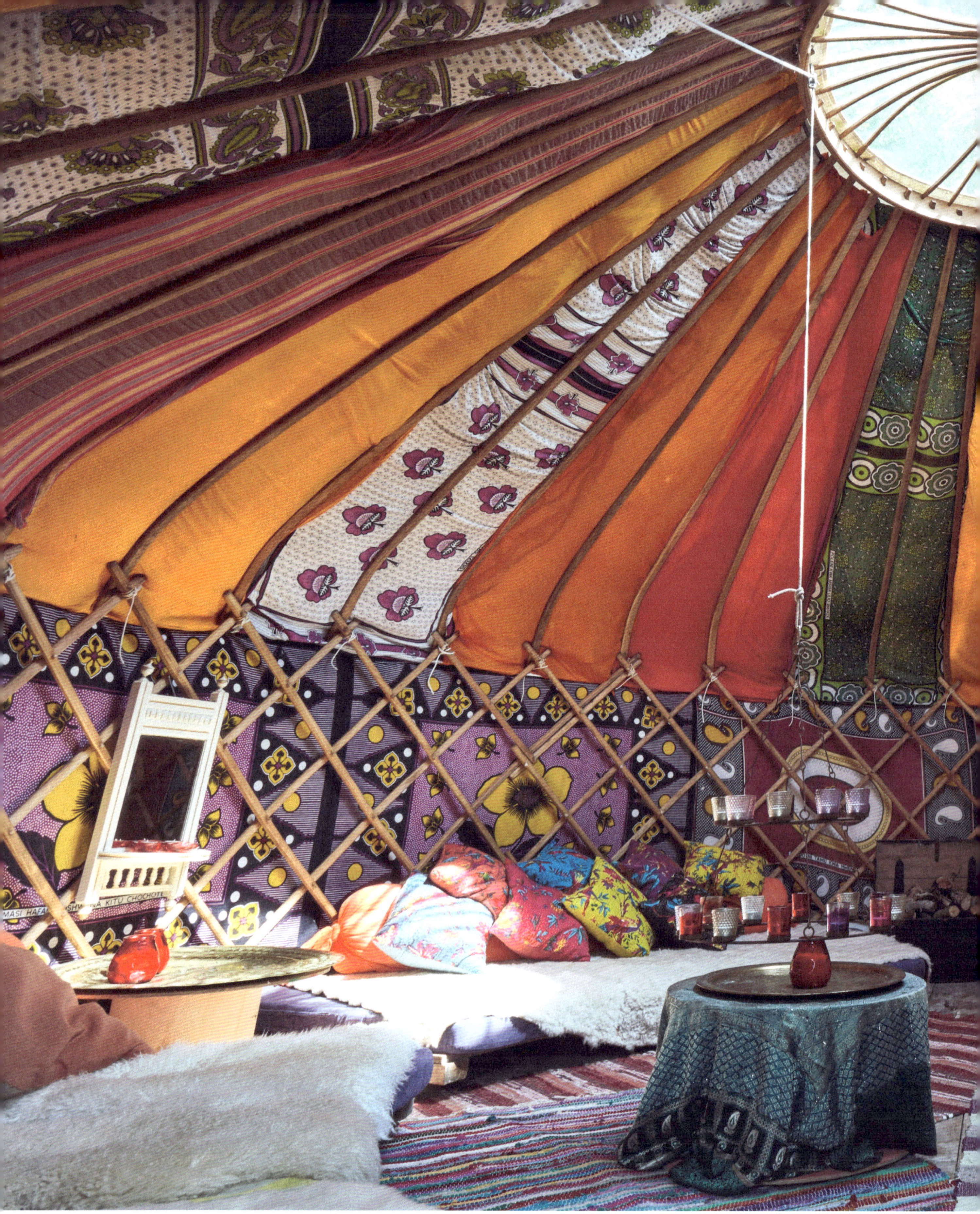

KINTON CLOUD-HOUSE YURT

The Ultimate Life
More Wild

Adventurers who went in search of a different way to live and found a deep connection to nature — three inspiring stories

— by Canopy & Star's Chris Elmes

We've all daydreamed about stepping out of our lives and moving to the country. In our heads we quit our jobs, wave goodbye to the city, and live in harmony with nature. Very few of us ever actually do it, because even working out where to start can be a daunting prospect. Here are three inspiring stories about making the leap and coming to live the ultimate life in the wild — a carpentry apprenticeship that turned into a forest workshop, a wild estate saved by endless invention, and a house on wheels that became the ultimate symbol of freedom.

'Cities are designed to hide the passage of time. Sometimes your lights go on earlier or later, but nothing actually stops. Working outdoors, you stop when it gets dark and you start again when it's light.' This is one of the things that Penny Tasker and her partner, Will Kirby, owners of the treehouses and workshops at Brook House Woods, have rapidly adjusted to since their move to the countryside. They met whilst acting alongside each other in a Chekhov play in London,

> 'The moment you step out of your door in the city, there are a hundred things vying for your attention. Whenever we were in wild spaces, we felt the beautiful absence of all that background noise.'

but Tasker always felt that wasn't where they were destined to be. 'Our flat was a jungle, and we spent every spare moment we could seeking out the city's green spaces,' she says. 'It was clear there was something in us that longed to be closer to nature.' A chance meeting with a green woodworker led to Kirby taking up an apprenticeship and helping out with carpentry courses at Brook House Woods. When the opportunity arose to move, they jumped at it. 'The moment you step out of your door in the city, there are a hundred things vying for your attention,' they say. 'Everything is trying to get you to go somewhere or buy something, or engage with a product. Whenever we were in wild spaces, we felt the beautiful absence of all that background noise. We wanted that to be our whole lives, not something we only experienced at the weekends.' In a dramatic leap, they moved from a London flat to a caravan in the countryside in under six months. In the few years since, they have built six incredible spaces for guests, welcomed scores of aspiring carpenters to their forest classroom, and completely settled into the rhythm of the countryside. 'Life is cyclical, not only in terms of light and dark, but with people. In summer the place is full of guests on woodworking courses, and we eat big communal meals almost every day. In winter it's just the two of us and the wood burner, and we love the quiet. But spring comes around and we're ready for a bit more of the bustle again. It's nice having our lives gently dictated to us by the seasons.'

For Walter Micklethwait, owner of the Inshriach Estate near Aviemore in the wild Scottish Highlands, the dictation isn't so gentle, but he loves the freedom of the land and the space it gives him to be creative. Micklethwait's family came into possession of the estate in the 1970s, when it was 'a not very sporting estate but a nice place to retire to.' In 2008, he gave up his job as an antique dealer and turned his seemingly endless resourcefulness to the task of restoring it. The challenge of innovating and drawing in guests whilst nurturing the area's natural health is one that he relishes. 'For a while,' he says, 'we had nothing but sheep and white horses here. It looked like Narnia sometimes. But the farm is actually much nicer when it's not grazed. Now we have a moth man who comes every year and tells

'I always thought we'd got it all wrong as humans. Everything is complicated and it should be simple.'

me that we have rare species thriving like nowhere else. We've had to make do, reuse and recycle, but that's the part I love — working with materials that have a pattern, a history. I've got an old railway station that I moved down from the hills. Between that and the bits of a Victorian villa I took apart last year, I think we could do something really great.' Whatever comes of those latest acquisitions will sit alongside a small-scale gin distillery, a handmade shepherd's hut, and an old army fire truck driven over 500 miles (800 kilometres) to the location from a museum in the south and converted into a wild living space and artist's bothy. Somewhere in the woods there's a horsebox sauna too. Micklethwait's endless ingenuity means there's no shortage of plans for the future, but he's cautious of overloading the estate and ruining the edge of complete wildness that keeps guests coming back: 'We're lucky to be custodians of this place. It has its own atmosphere and beauty. I'm running out of spaces to put things, because I don't want to pack it full of people.' Looking out on a thick blanket of snow that stretches miles into the distance, he laughs as he declares, 'People ruin stuff, you see. You've got to invite them in sparingly.'

Micklethwait might have been jesting, but for Elizabeth Pearson, who built her own house on wheels in Spain, it was her doubts about modern living that made her seek out a life more wild. 'I always thought we'd got it all wrong as humans,' she says. 'Everything is complicated and it should be simple. I was working a job I didn't enjoy to pay for a flat I didn't really like living in. It didn't make sense.' So she moved to the south coast of Spain hoping that a change of scenery would make the difference, but found herself simply recreating the same life as before. She then realised that she had to completely change her mindset from one of earning enough to live, to one of living simply enough to shift the focus off money. An old metal chassis with a single wheel attached turned out to be the literal foundation of her new life, and she set out to build a home that had everything she really needed in a space small enough to tow. The learning curve was steep.

'I've always been creative,' she says, 'but I'd never done anything like it before. I'd built a rabbit hutch once, but that was about it.' Somehow, from a small cardboard model, hours of YouTube videos, and the odd bit of local help, the house began to rise. Walls were made from wood dumped outside her flat, the kitchen unit was found by the side of the road, and every inch of space was carefully thought through and utilised. Over the course of a year, Pearson found any time she could, working three or four days a week on the build, and she finished with an intense home straight of long days and nights over several months. The result, a three-roomed house taking up the space of most people's lounges, is perfect for the outdoor living of warm Spanish summers, with an incredibly low impact on the environment, and it's easy to heat during the chilly mountain winters. Pearson describes moving it from where it was built to its new home as 'the most incredible yet scary journey of my life', but she knows she has achieved what she'd set out to do. She lived in the Little Wooden House for three carefree years, until the opportunity to put her newfound construction skills to work on a rundown finca proved too tempting. Being able to welcome others to the tiny home, however, has been almost as rewarding as building it. 'Guests come and stay, and they leave inspired,' she says. 'One couple spent their whole time here sketching out the small space they were going to build when they got home. It's lovely to think that the little house is giving people some big ideas.'

Merci de penser
à déposer vos déchets dans le
container mis à votre disposition.
Il y a un container pour le verre
au village.
Welcome

Awash with Bohemian Flair

Laid-back lakeside living in a tumbledown shack in the south of France

LAYÉNIE UNDER THE STARS
LOT-ET-GARONNE, FRANCE

Atop a rickety staircase in a private garden, Layénie Under the Stars spills out onto open decking with stunning views across rural France. The main space of the hand-built wooden shack, equipped with a kitchen, living room, and a bedroom with a canopy bed, bursts with colour and creativity, while a ground-level bathroom provides a hot shower and compost loo. Not far from the historic town of Agen, it's the perfect spot to enjoy the peace and quiet of the countryside. Guests will have no trouble embracing the bohemian vibe, taking local walks by day and listening for the hoots of owls at night.

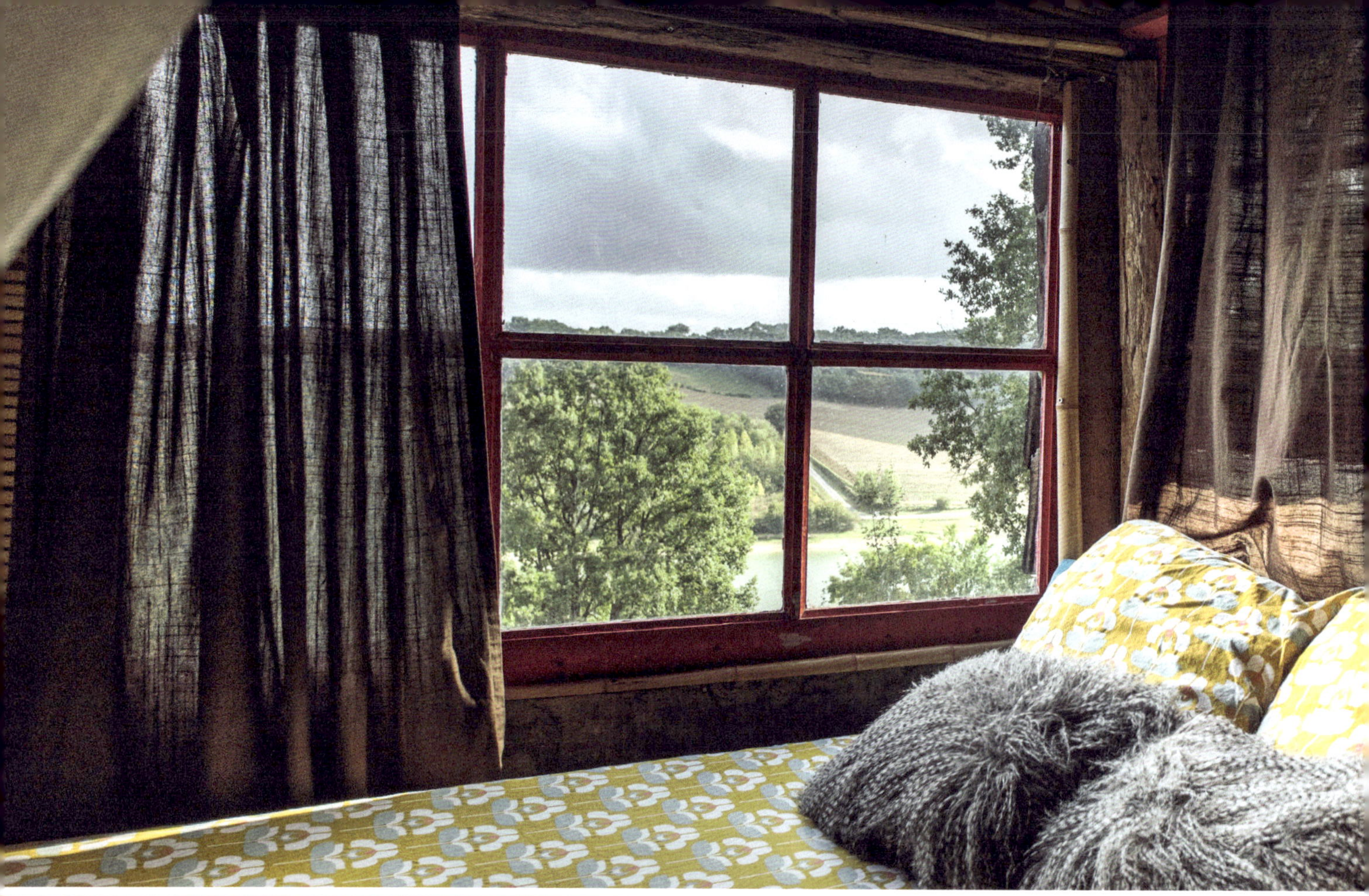

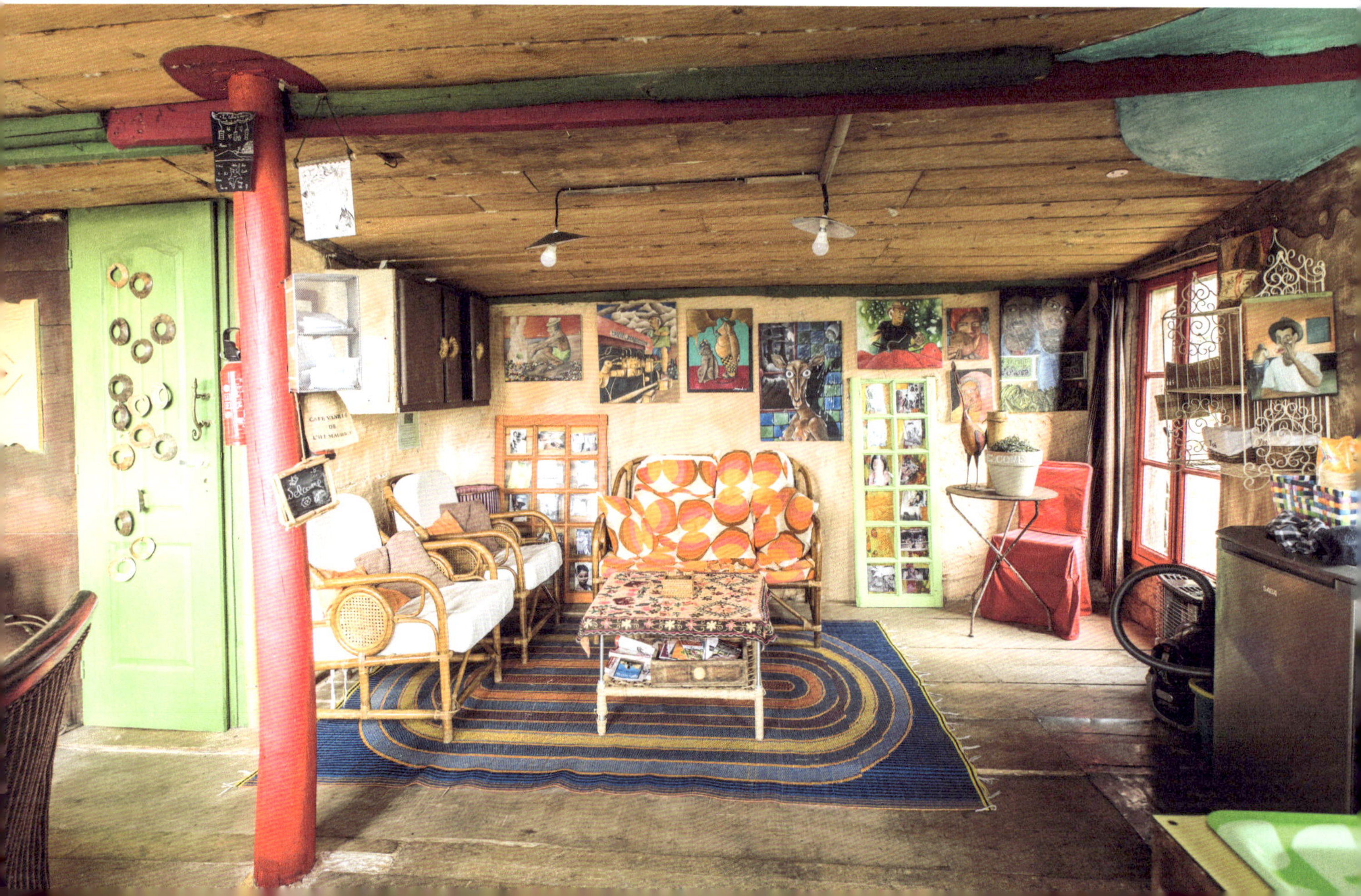

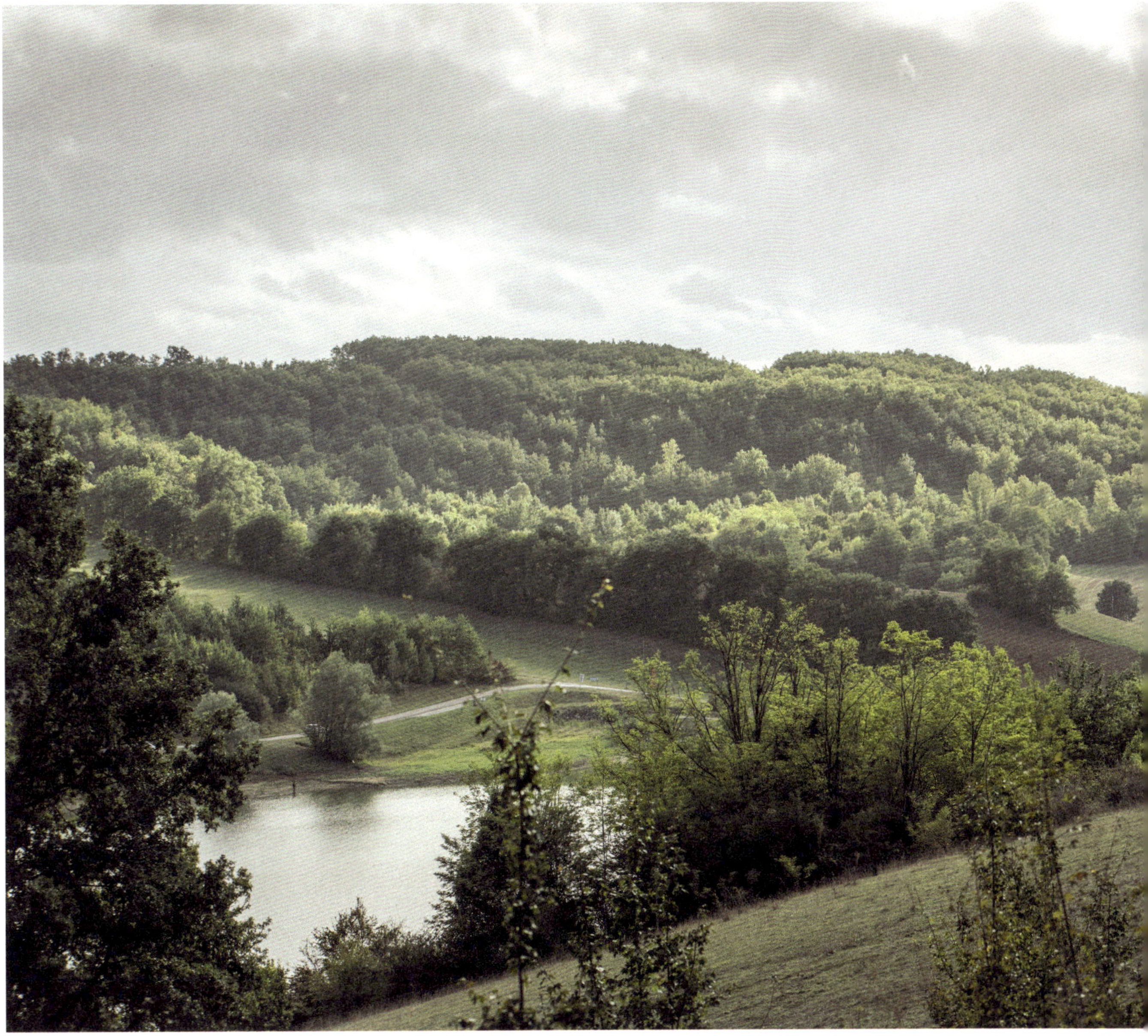

Star Treatment in the Yorkshire Wolds

A rustic suite with campfire camaraderie over toasted marshmallows, and a luxury twist

STAR SUITE
YORKSHIRE,
ENGLAND

In this private suite, the most luxurious of eight such dwellings at the North Star Club, guests get to experience what its owners, multi-award-winning designers Christian and Carolyn Van Outersterp, describe as the 'quintessential woodland retreat'. With its four-poster bed, shiny copper bathtub, canopied BBQ deck, and private sauna, the Star Suite certainly ticks all the boxes for glampsite luxury. And that is just for starters. Set within 200 hectares (500 acres) of English woodland in the peaceful Yorkshire Wolds — and taking inspiration from the rustic wilderness retreats that pampered wealthy American industrialists at the turn of the twentieth century — this beautifully crafted lodge has solid wood floors, a black-marble bathroom, and luxury textiles throughout. There's even a communal chill-out barn where 'club' members can indulge in tea and homemade cake, or share stories with the neighbours while toasting marshmallows around a cosy canopied campfire.

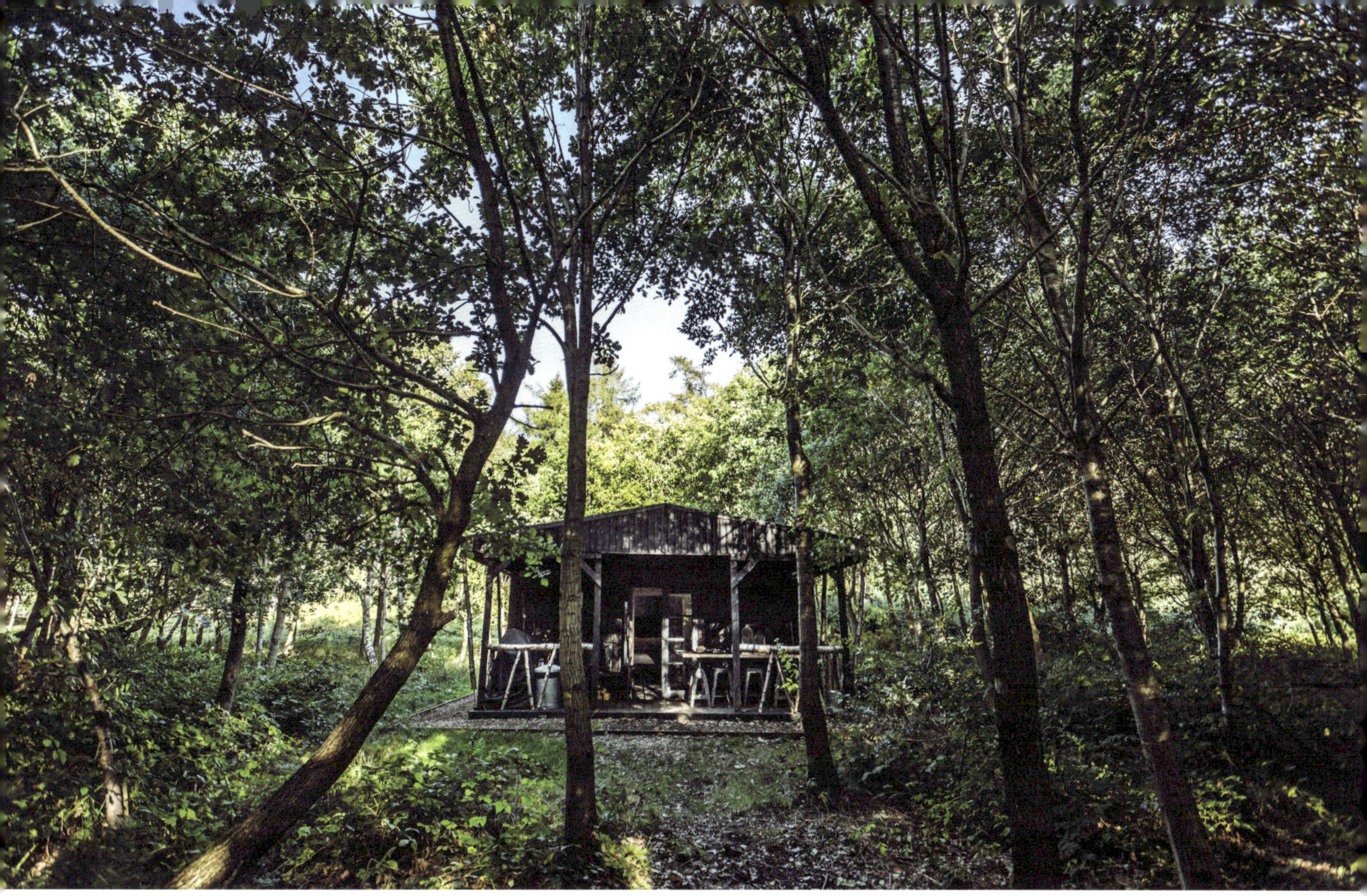

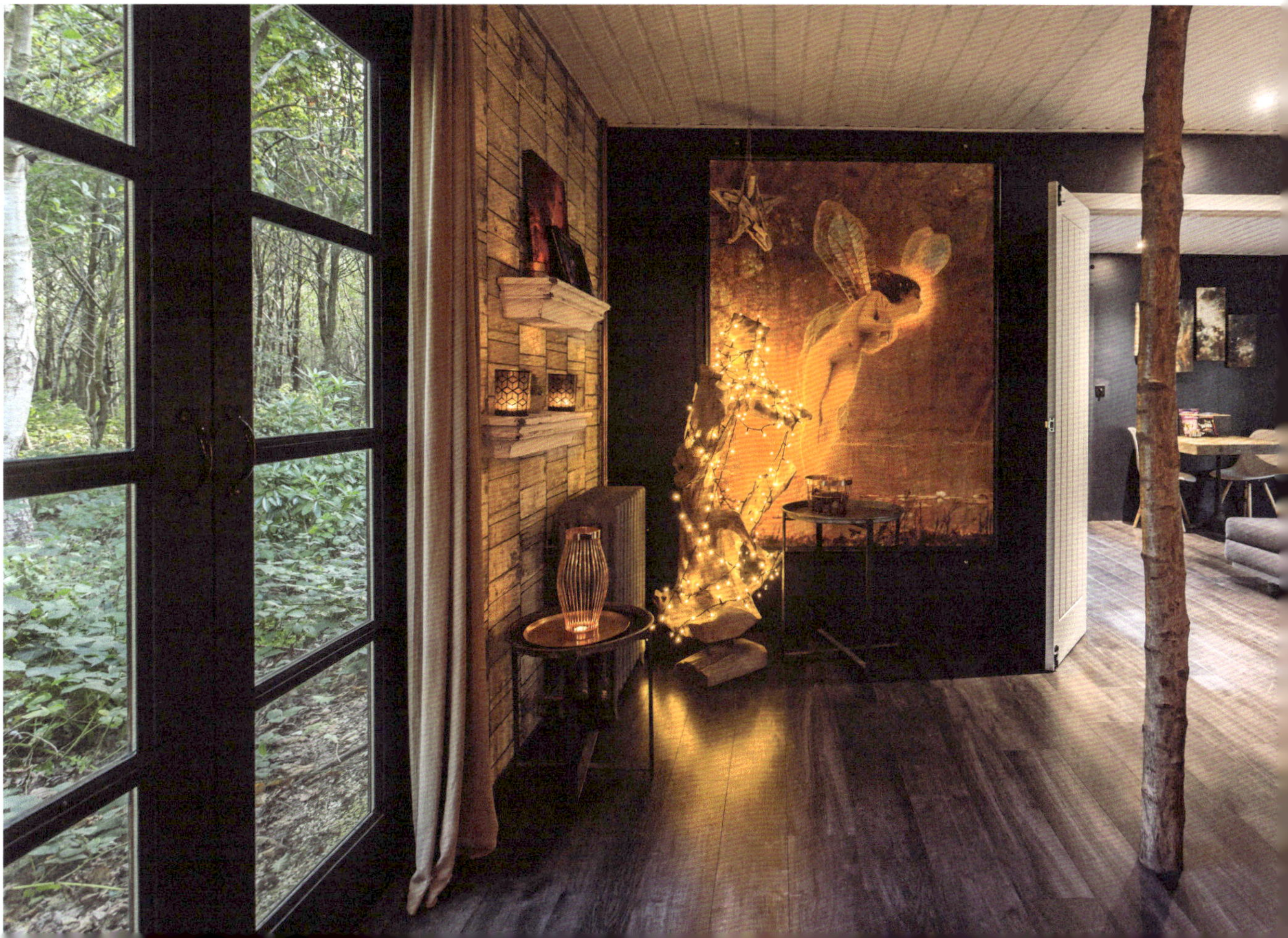

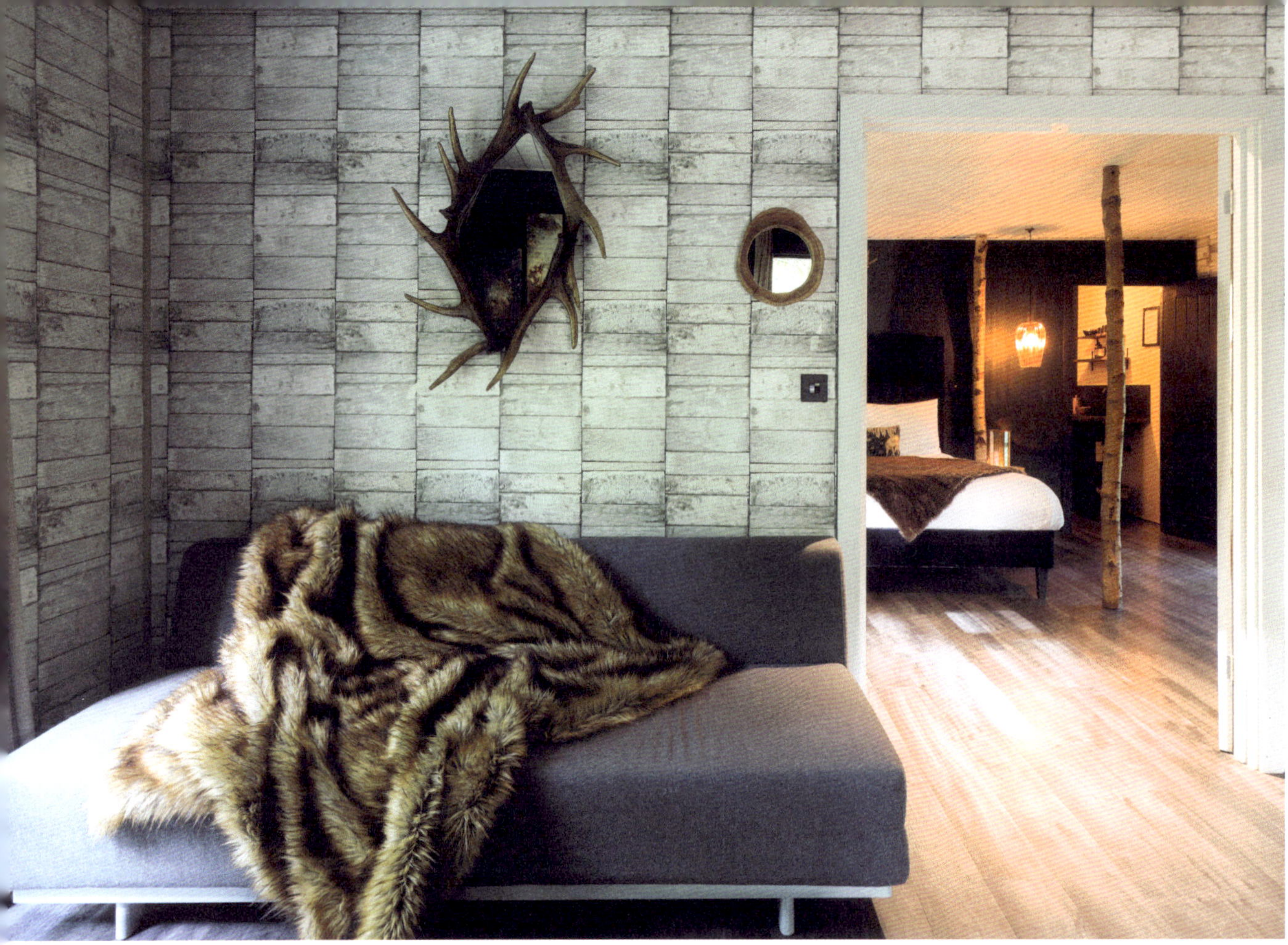

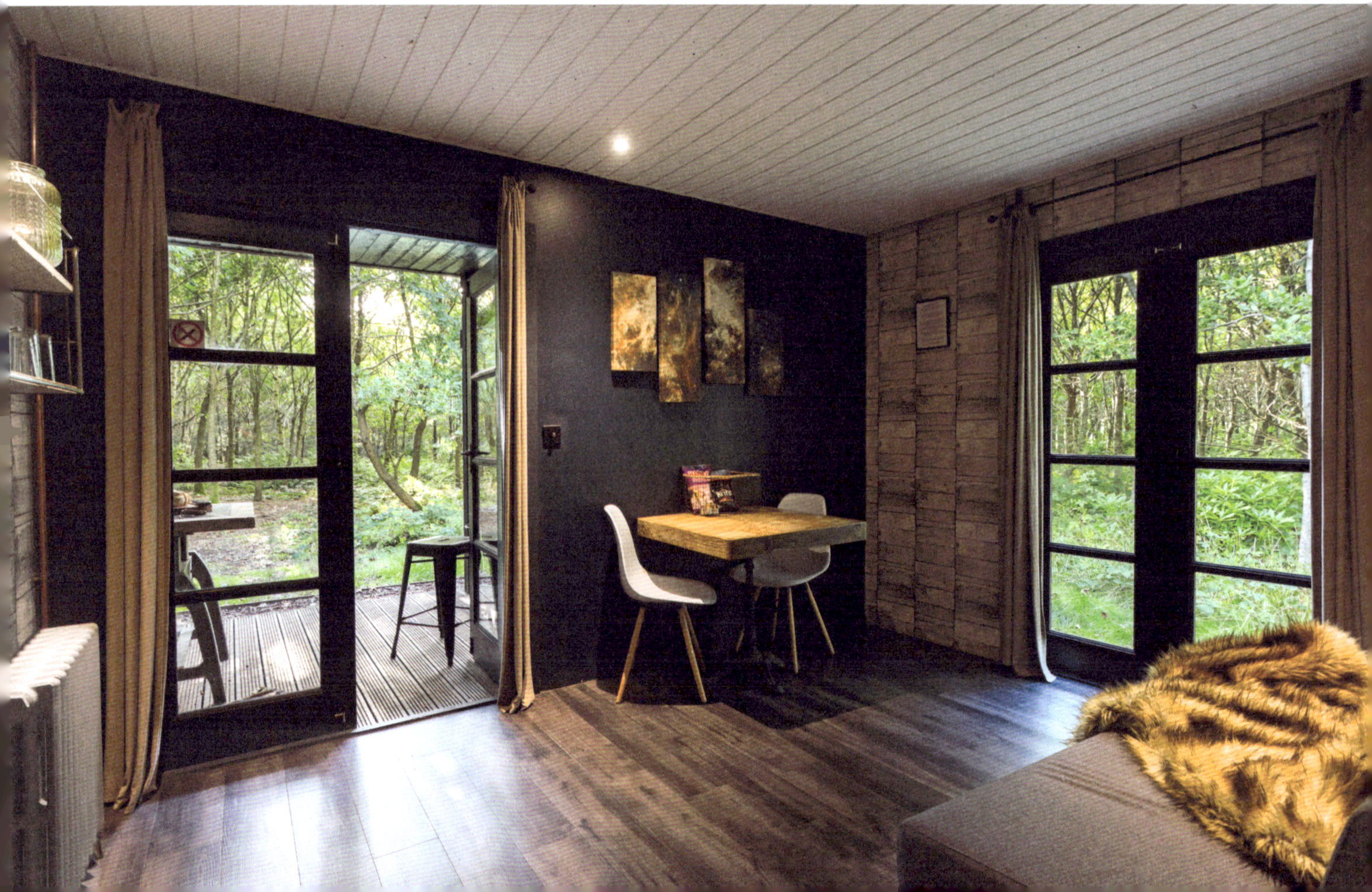

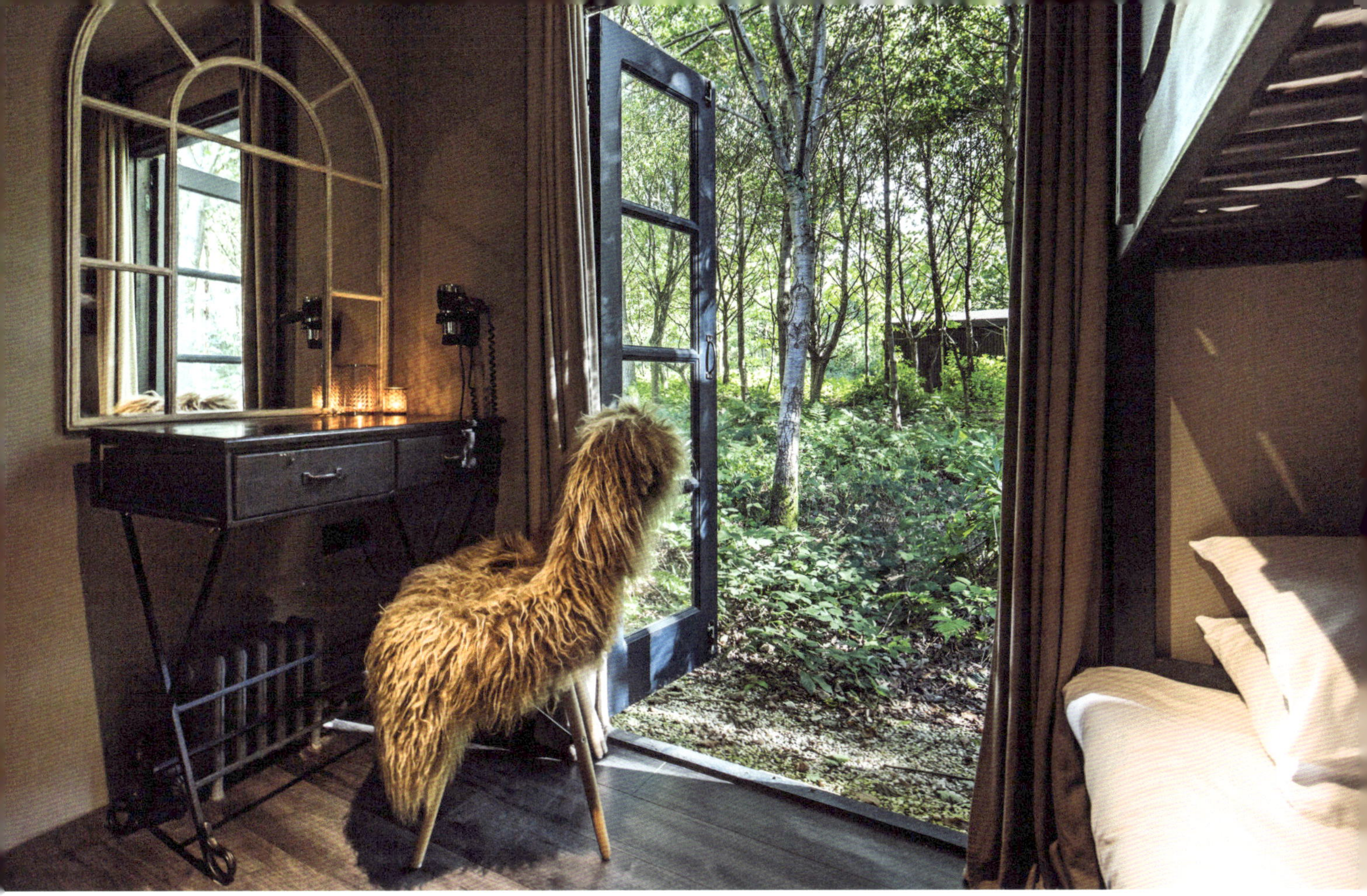

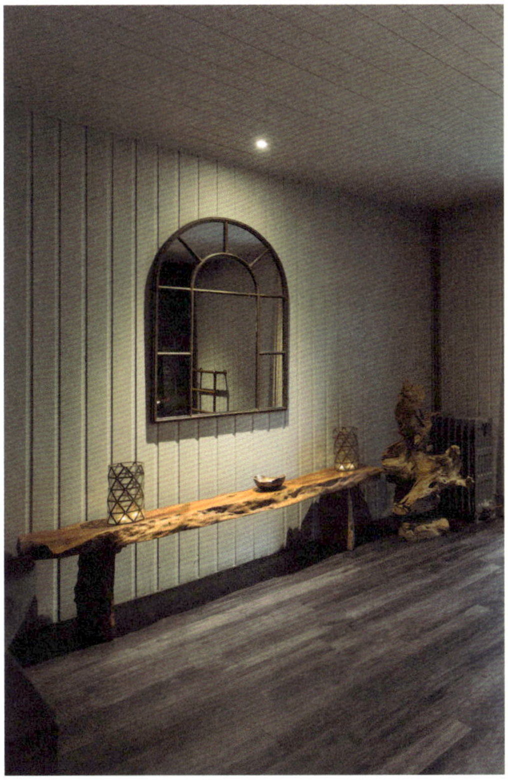

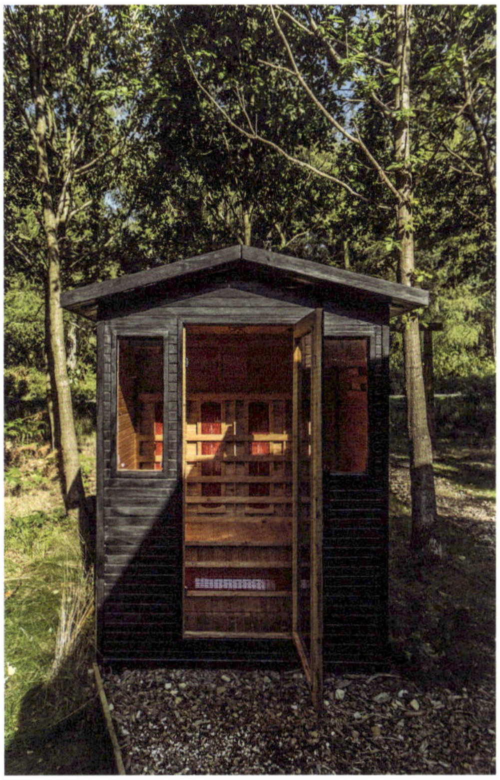

From Circus Wagon to Luxury Living Space

A rural idyll in the heart of Herefordshire, one of England's least-explored counties

STARGAZER'S WAGON
HEREFORDSHIRE, ENGLAND

Perched on a ridge at one end of a two-hectare (five-acre) wildflower meadow, Stargazer's Wagon is off-grid and remote enough for guests to feel totally at one with nature for days on end. Raised on a wooden platform, the handsome wagon faces south, with panoramic views across no fewer than five counties. This is rural England at its best — quiet, gently rolling, and verdantly green in summer. By day, there's plenty to explore in a countryside dotted with old forts and ruins, and by night, guests can light up the fire bowl and loll in a deck-side hot tub, watching dusk descend across the landscape, accompanied by the distant hoot of an owl. Inside, the spacious wagon is kitted out with a double bed at one end, a leather sofa with a cosy wood burner at the other, and fine fabrics in neutral colours throughout. Once settled, visitors can draw on a well-stocked kitchen, but on their first night, they get to tuck into a home-cooked welcome supper, courtesy of hospitable owners Victoria and Chris Draper.

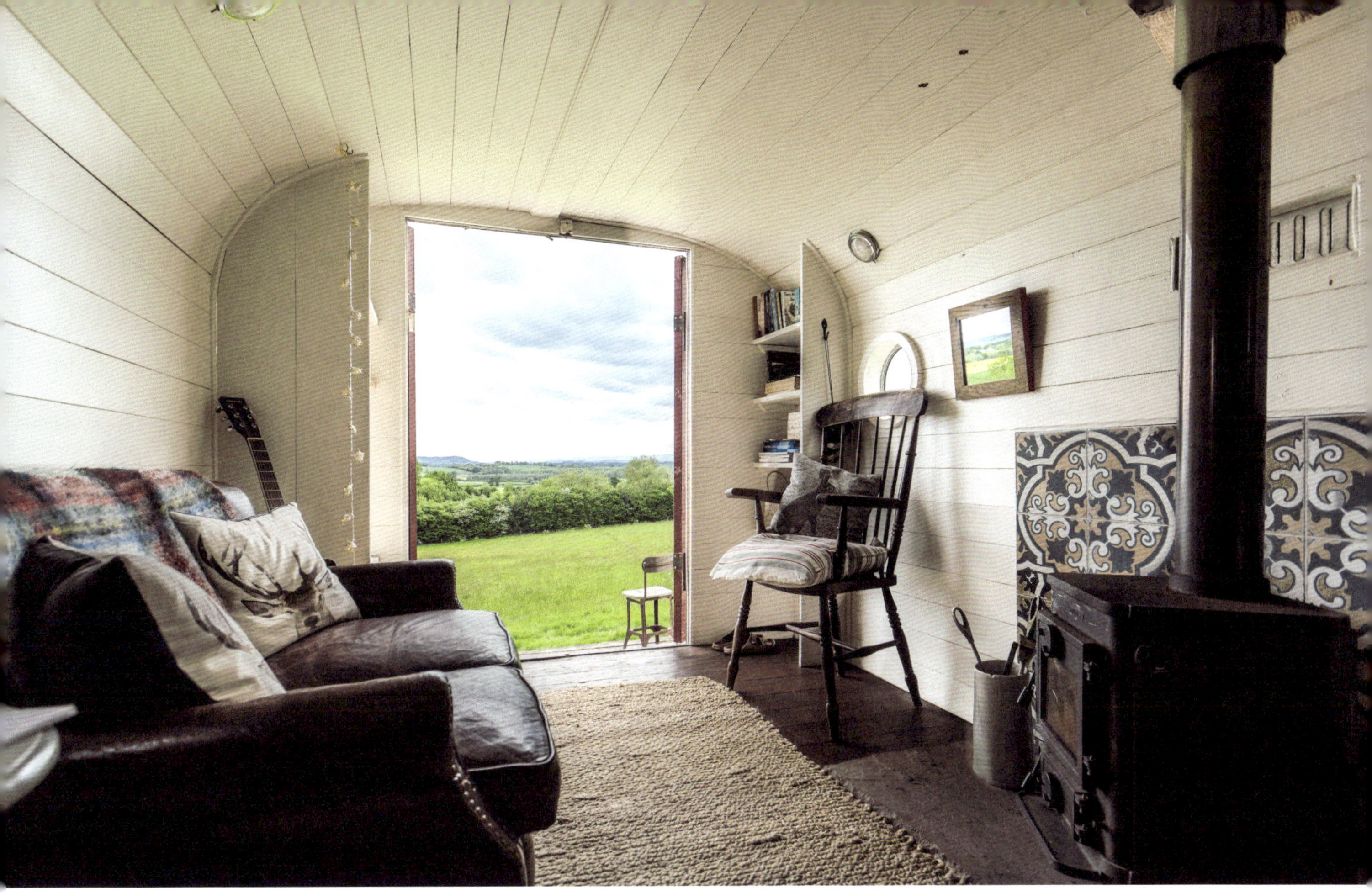

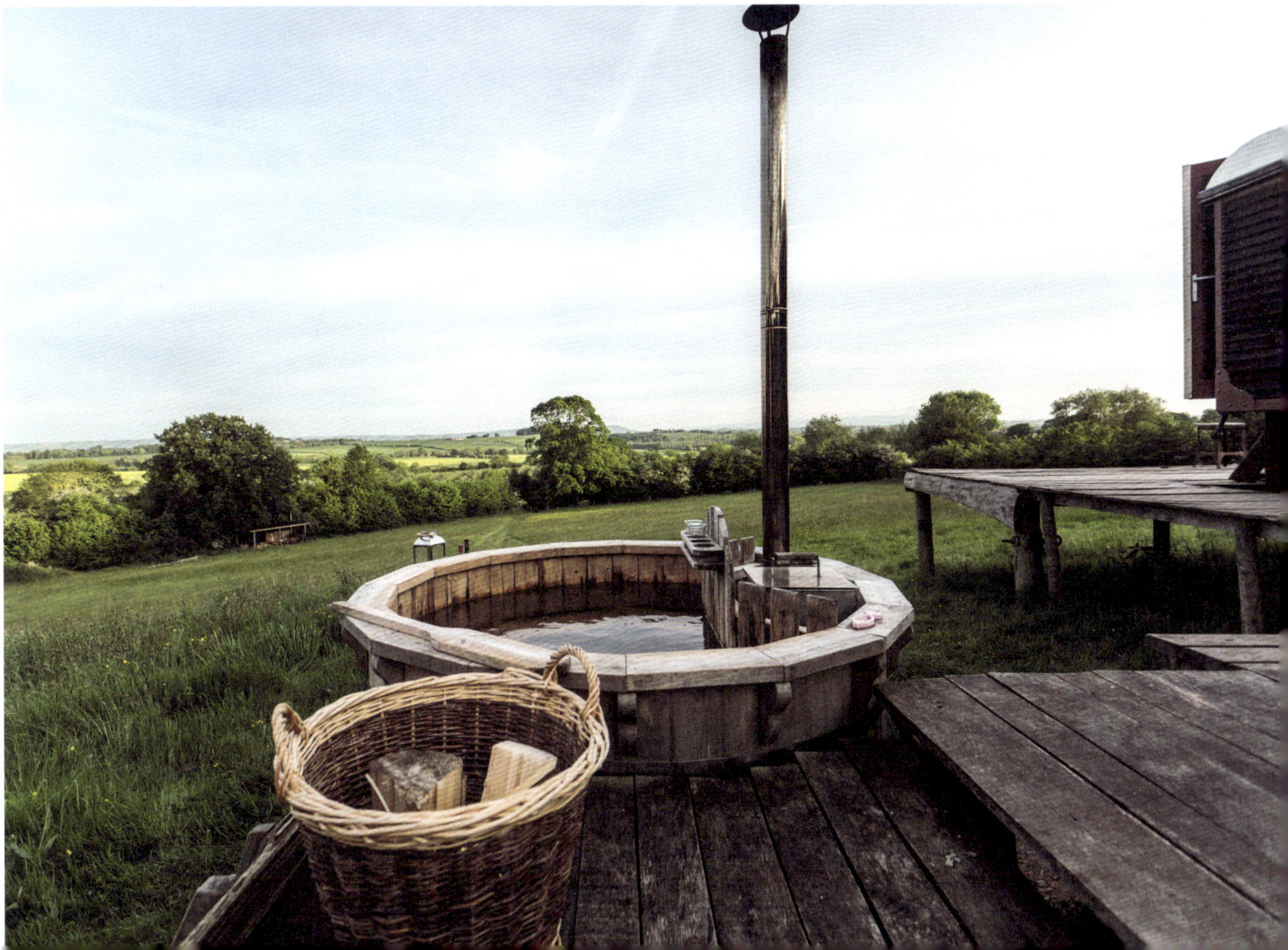

A Slice of Prehistory in Cornwall

Sleeping in ancient grandeur just 400 metres (1,300 feet) from one of Europe's best-preserved Iron Age villages

THE ROUNDHOUSE
CORNWALL,
ENGLAND

The Roundhouse, on the Land's End peninsula of Cornwall, presents a rare opportunity to experience the English countryside in Iron Age style. Occupying a quiet corner of the organic 40-hectare (100-acre) Bodrifty Farm, this particular roundhouse was built by farm owner Fred Mustill at the turn of the twenty-first century — a celebration of the new millennium located less than a mile away from one of Europe's most well-preserved Iron Age settlements. Totally authentic in its stone and thatch execution, Mustill's roundhouse captures the spirit of this distant time. Inside, guests can slumber in a handmade four-poster bed with flowers woven into the willow headboard, to be gently woken by the sound of birdsong come dawn. On the same site, the Treehouse — literally a structure built around a living tree — is equipped with a kitchen, living room, and bathroom.

THE ROUNDHOUSE

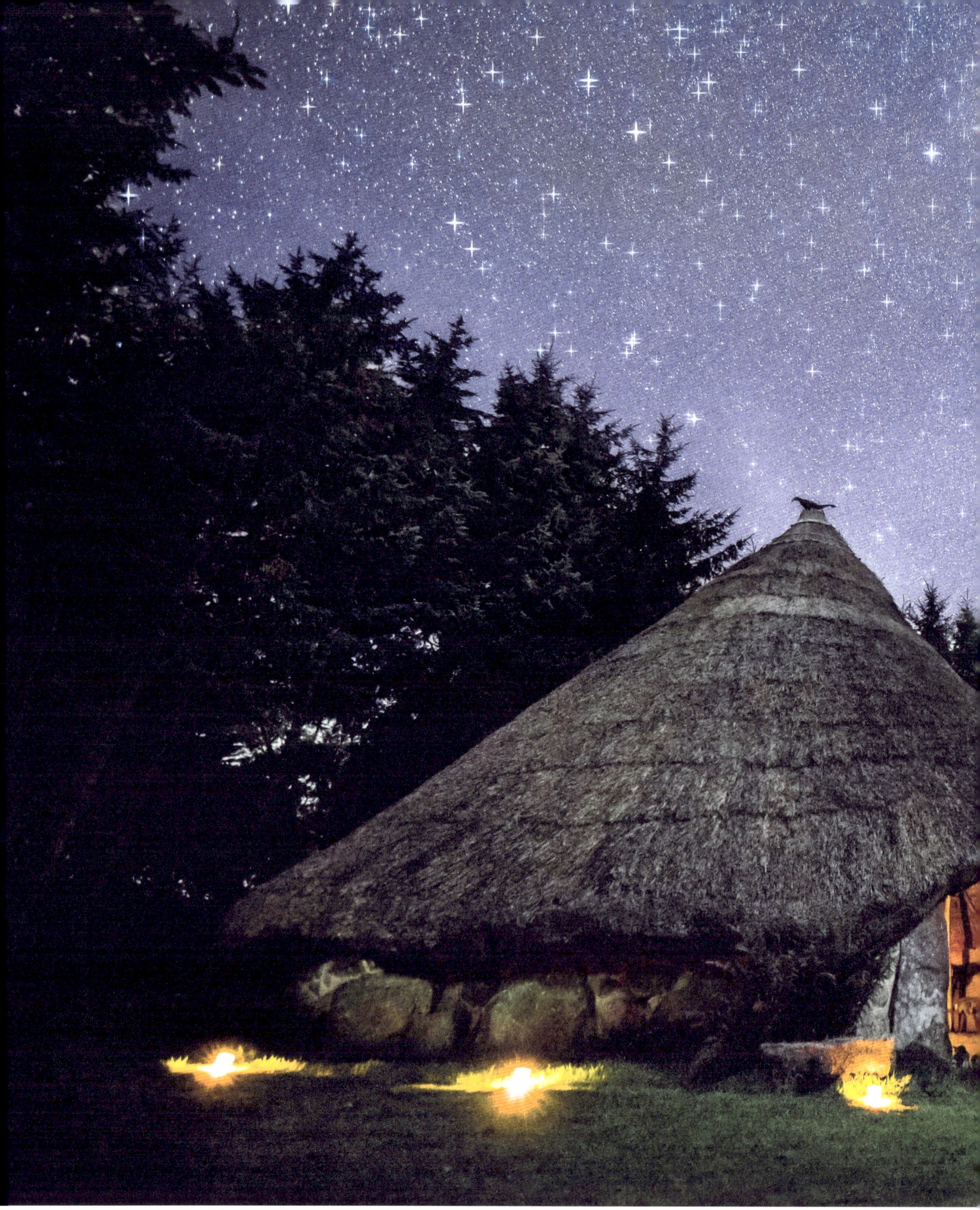

THE ROUNDHOUSE

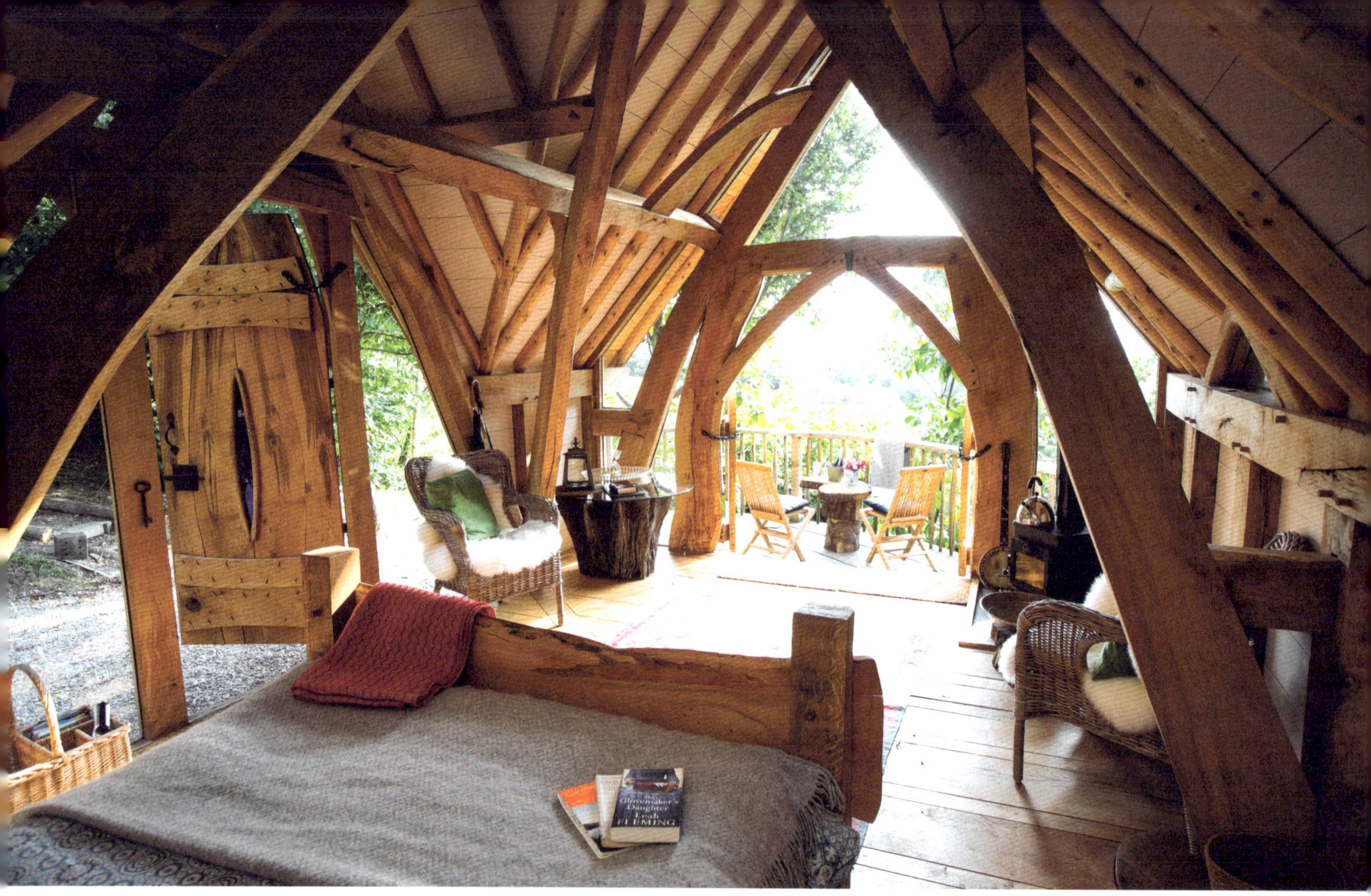
The Glovemaker's Daughter
Leah FLEMING

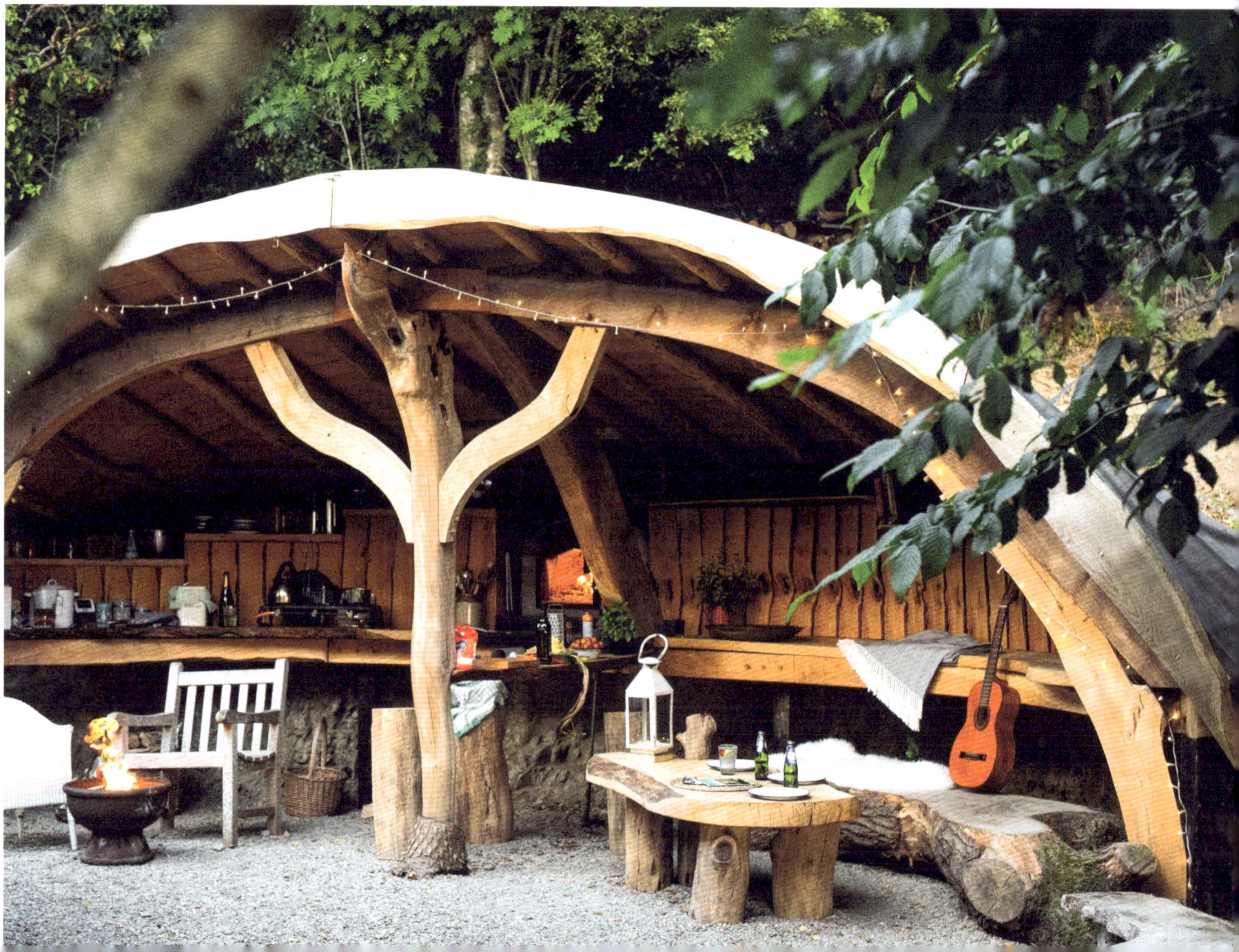

Carved and Crafted by Hand

A sculptural cruck-style structure that takes its name from the dragon joint used in its construction

DRAGON CRUCK
POWYS,
WALES

This one-of-a-kind holiday home for two occupies a prime woodland spot overlooking the Vyrnwy valley in Wales. Hand-crafted by owner Mike Kemp — a tree surgeon — and his team, everything from the shingles on the roof to the curvaceous crucks were made from locally sourced wood. Coupled with an outdoor kitchen, the place has a wonderfully open feel to it, immersing guests fully within their natural surroundings. It's a peaceful spot from which to observe the local wildlife — foxes, badgers, rabbits, and birds, including ravens, jays, and woodpeckers — or to indulge in wild swimming, hiking, and picnicking nearby.

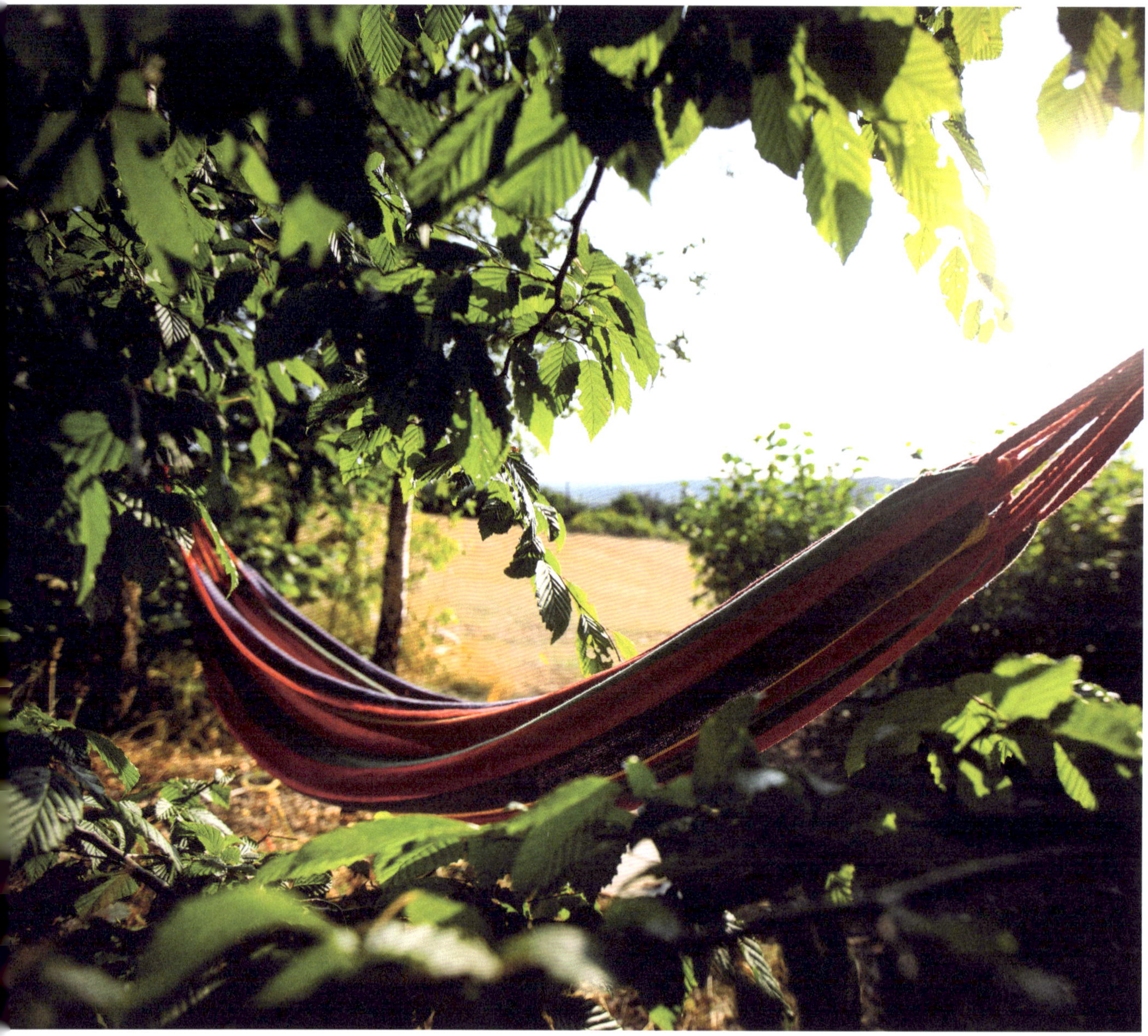

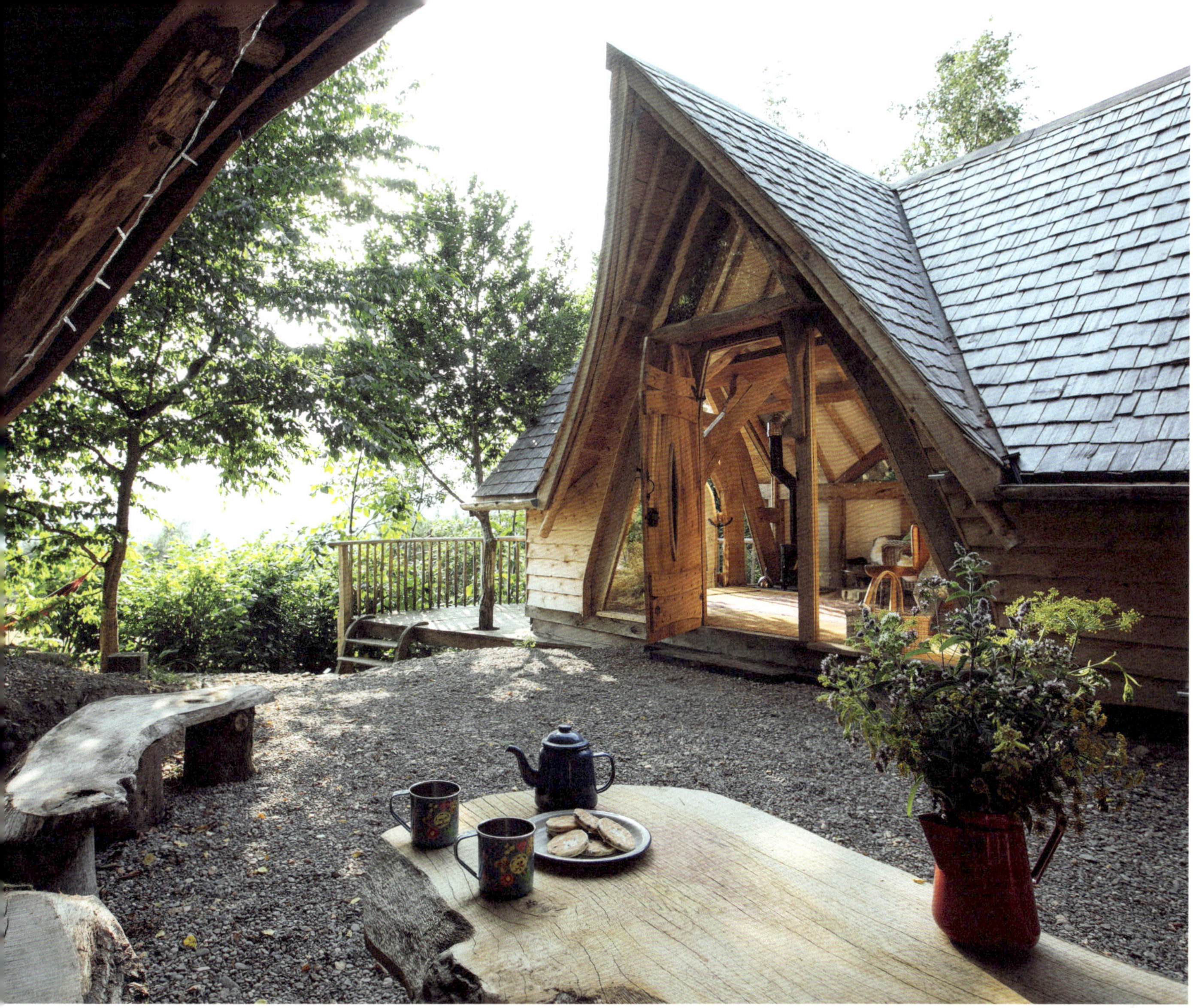

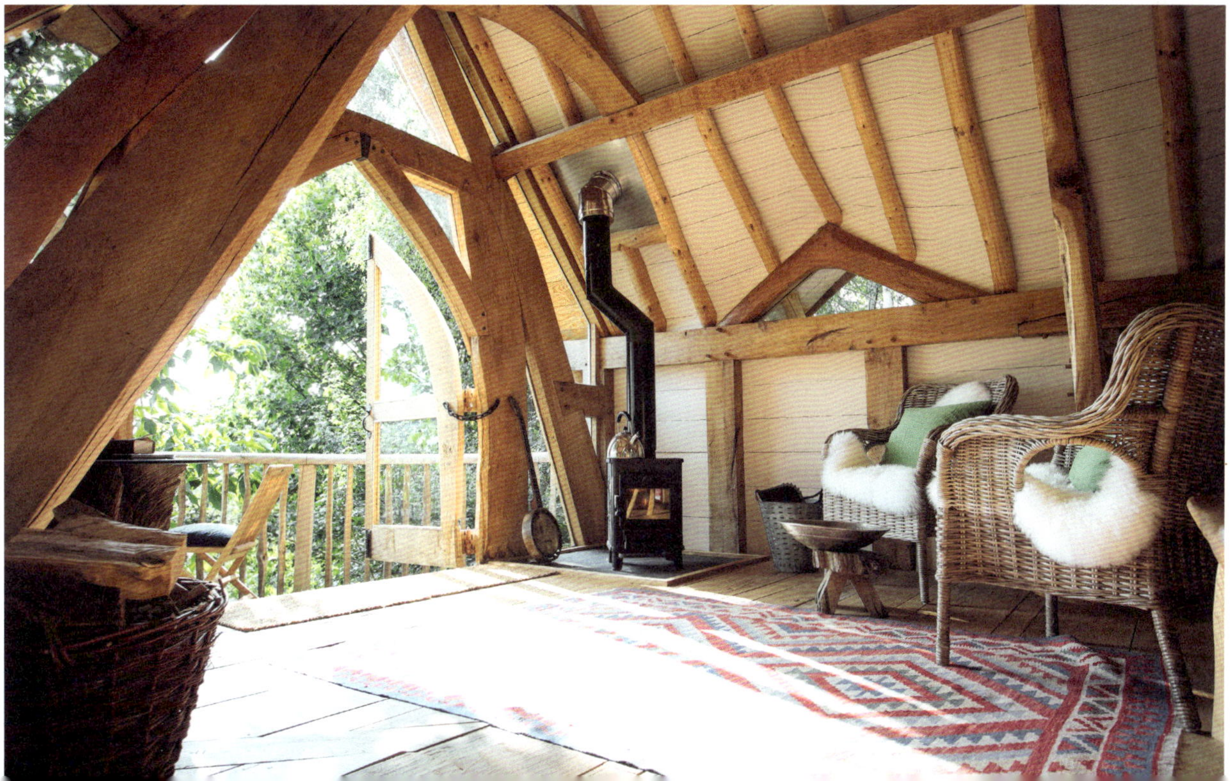

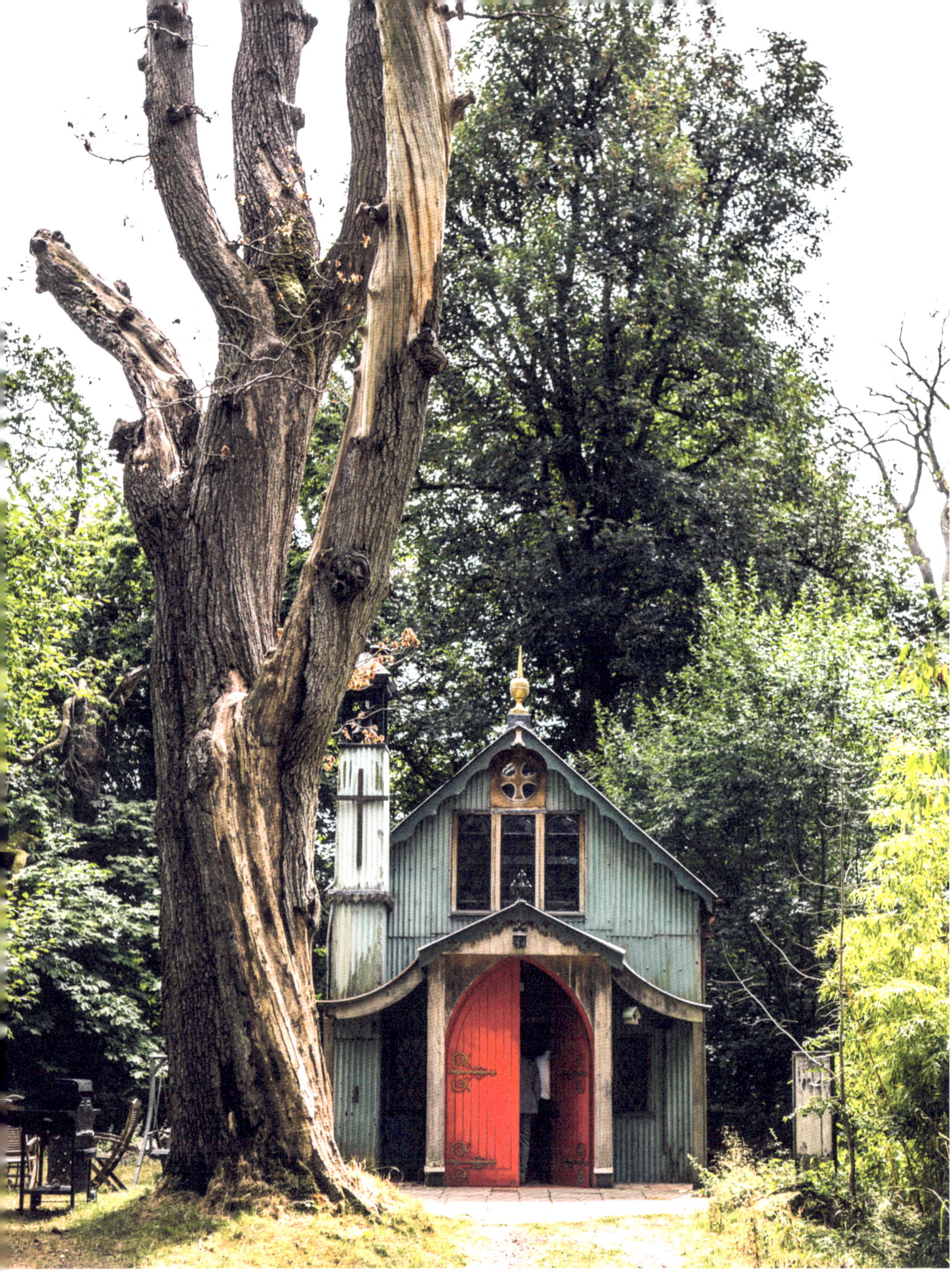

Beneath the Trees Where Nobody Sees

A lovingly restored chapel set deep within the grounds of Shropshire's Walcot Hall

THE CHAPEL
SHROPSHIRE,
ENGLAND

This hideaway offers the unique, almost fairy-tale experience of a life surrounded by dense woodland and wildlife. With an exterior of corrugated tin and a timber-lined interior, the space itself makes for a surreal break from city life. Among the many comforts are a Rayburn range and a deep marble bath, and there are even stained-glass windows and a functional organ. Guests have the run of the land, where a little exploration will lead them to a lush peacock-inhabited arboretum and a woodland lake. Further afield, the Shropshire Hills offer no end of exhilarating country walks.

St John's Mission Church Muxton Parish of Lilleshall

THE CHAPEL

A Little Slice of Sweden in the Malvern Hills

A Scandinavian BBQ hut transformed into an enchanting Swedish-style cottage

LILLA STUGAN
WORCESTERSHIRE, ENGLAND

Standing in a 100-year-old apple orchard, on the edge of the Knapp and Papermill Nature Reserve, this cute house is the work of two generations of a family with Scandinavian heritage. A Swedish vibe pervades every corner, from the structure of the 'little cottage' to the pine-lined interior and the red and blue colour scheme. In amongst the trees is a huge fire pit on which guests can slow cook the odd stew. It's a beautiful spot, with the orchard carpeted with meadow grasses in summer and its boughs heavy with fruit in autumn. There's even a gate leading straight onto the nature reserve.

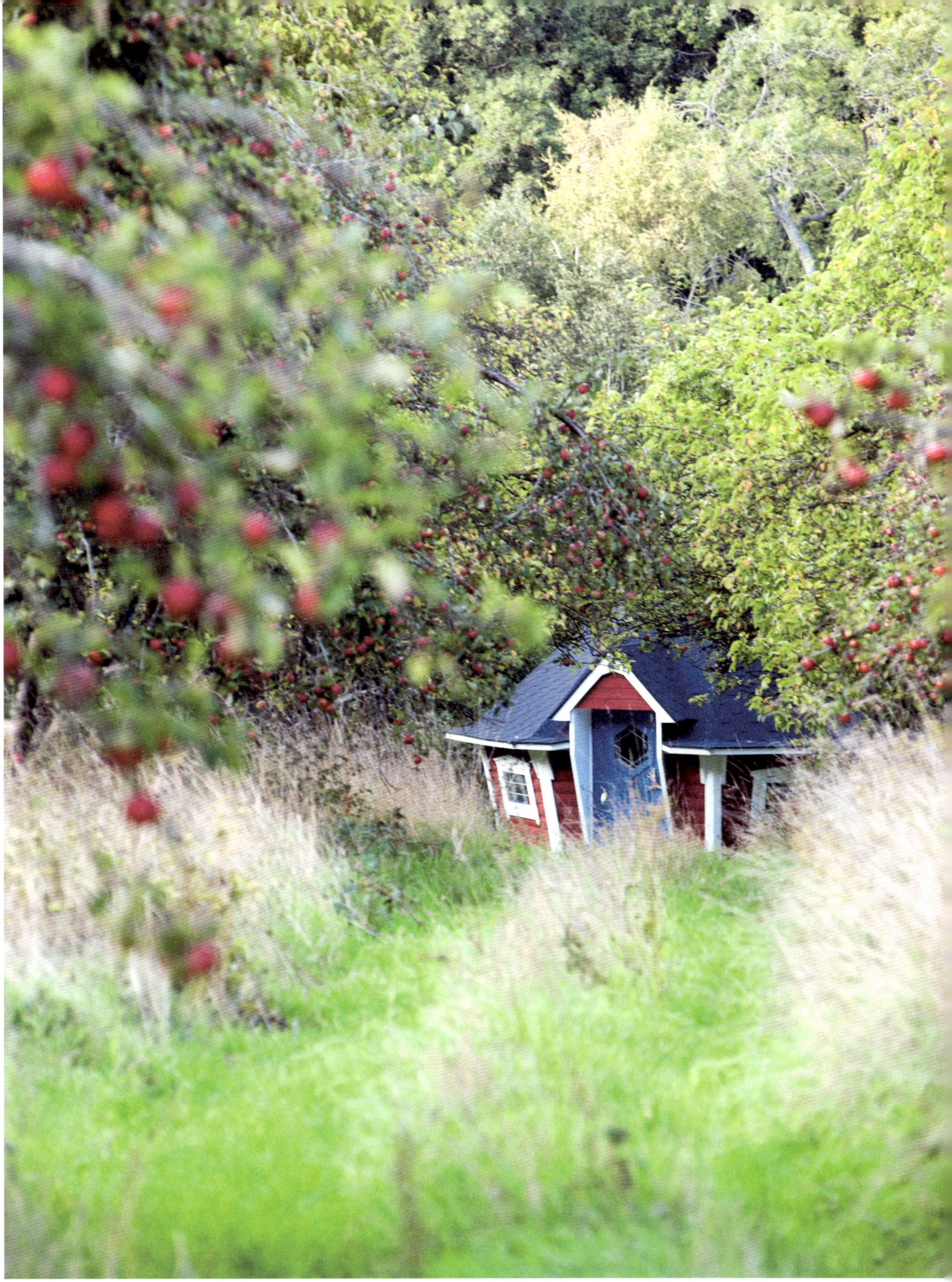

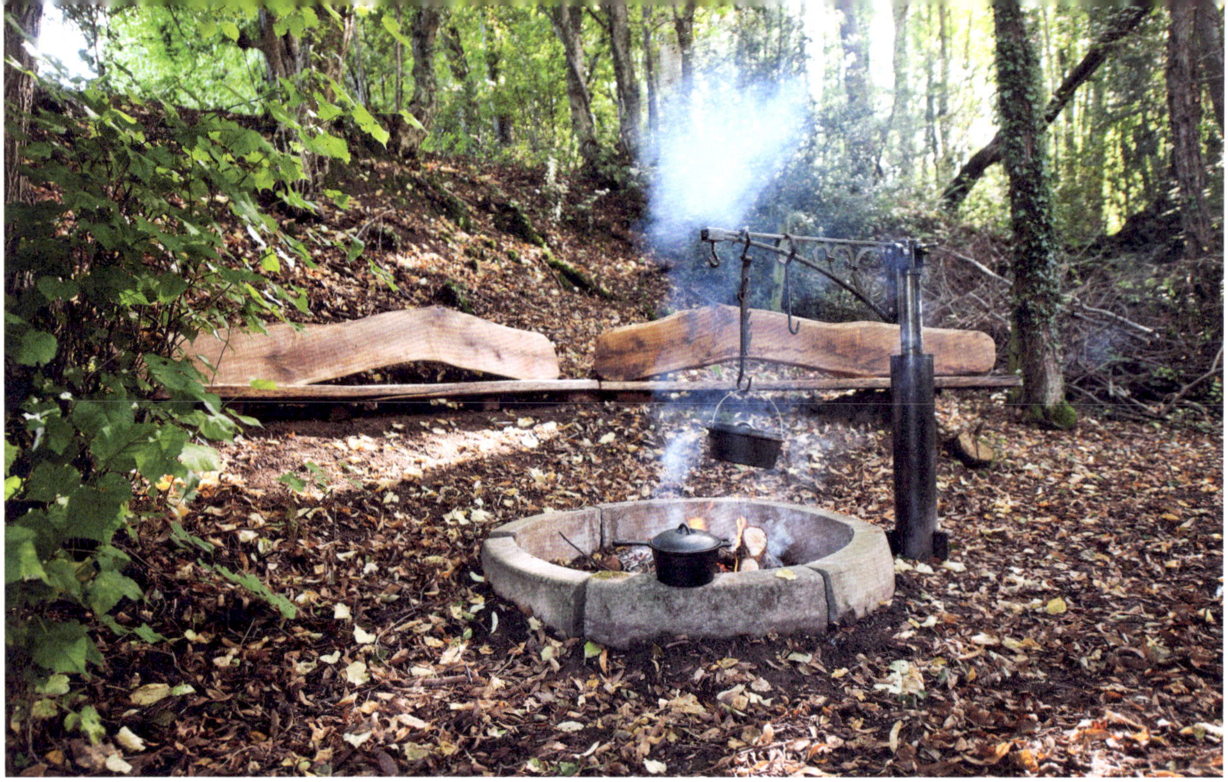

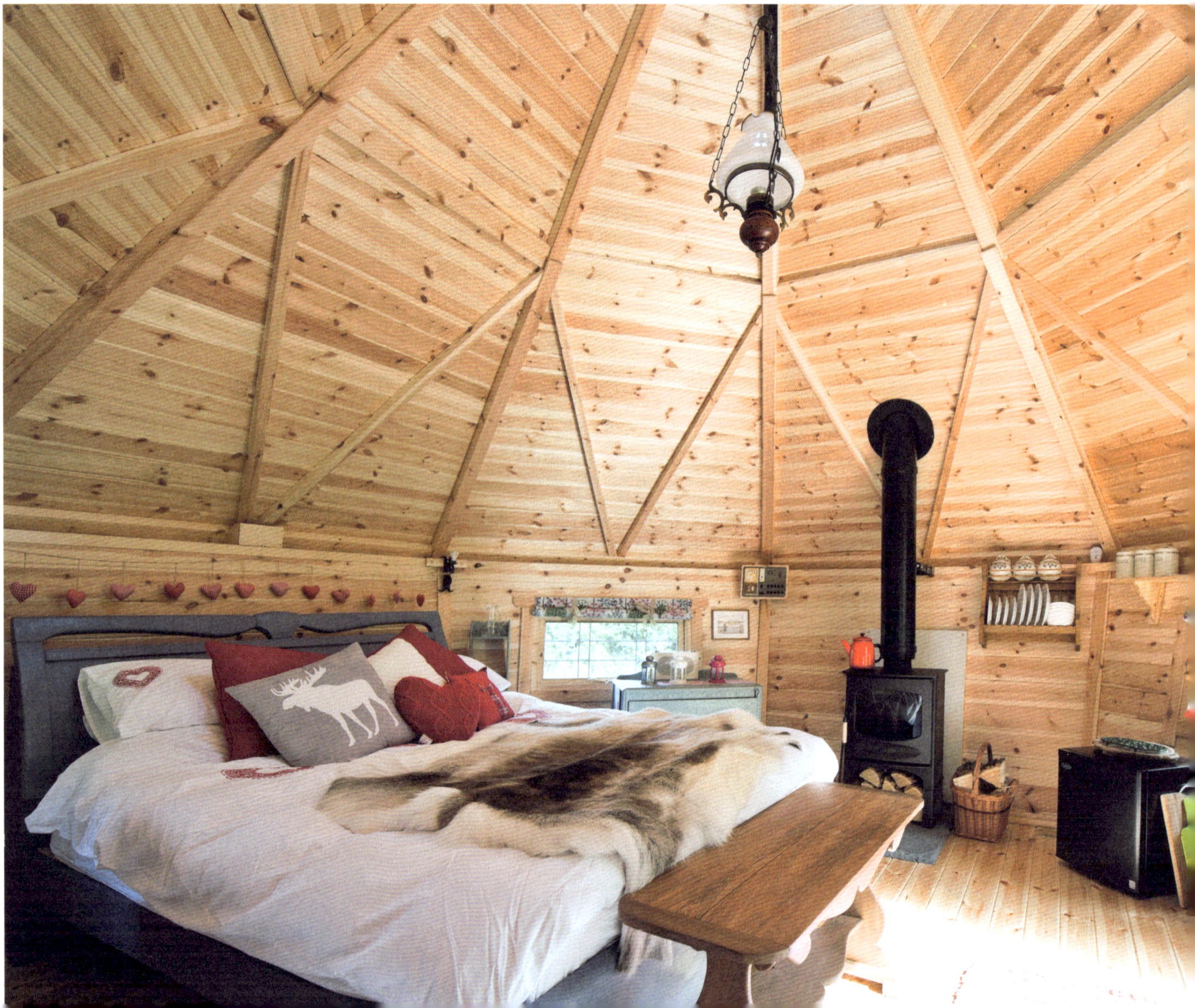

LILLA STUGAN

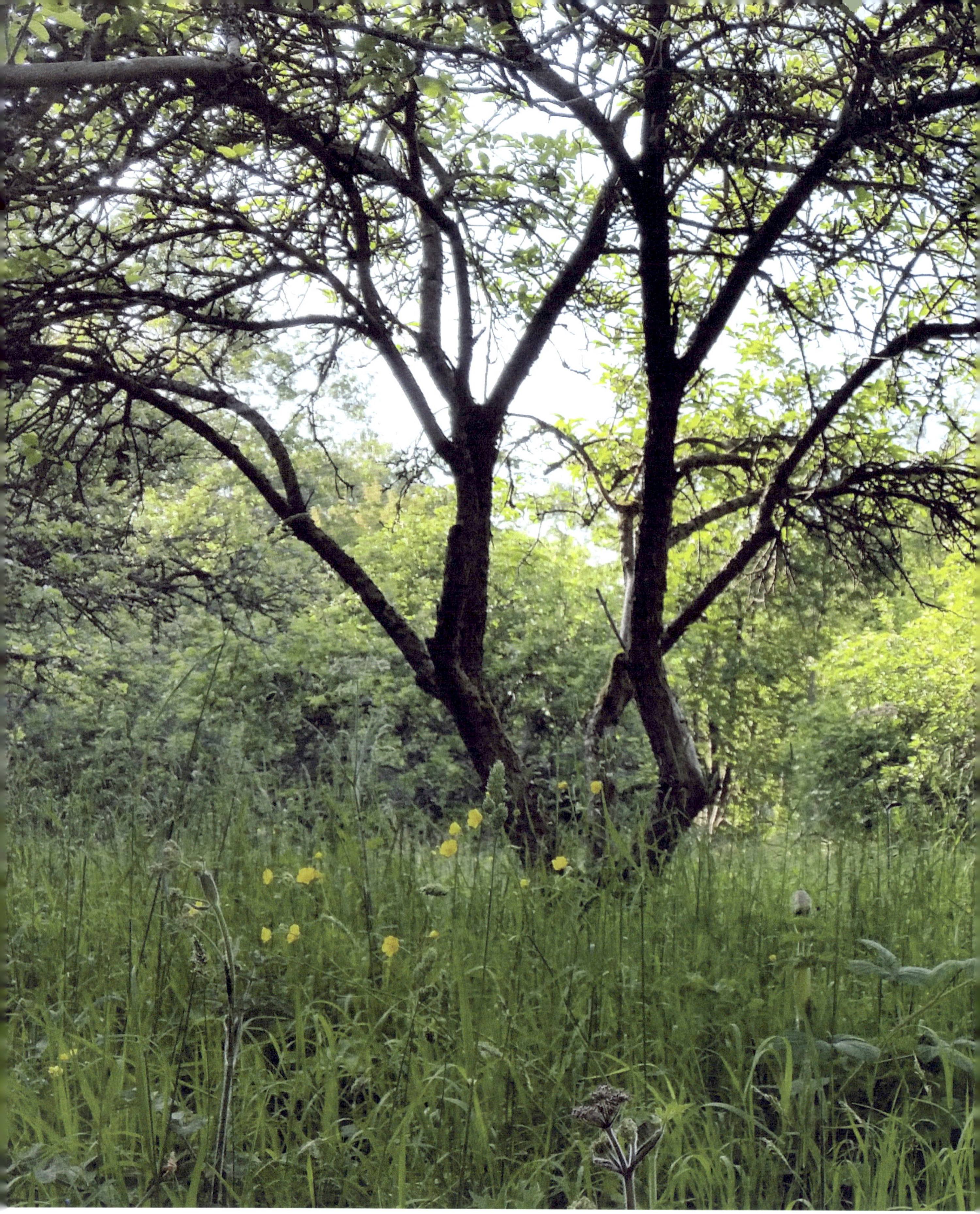

LILLA STUGAN

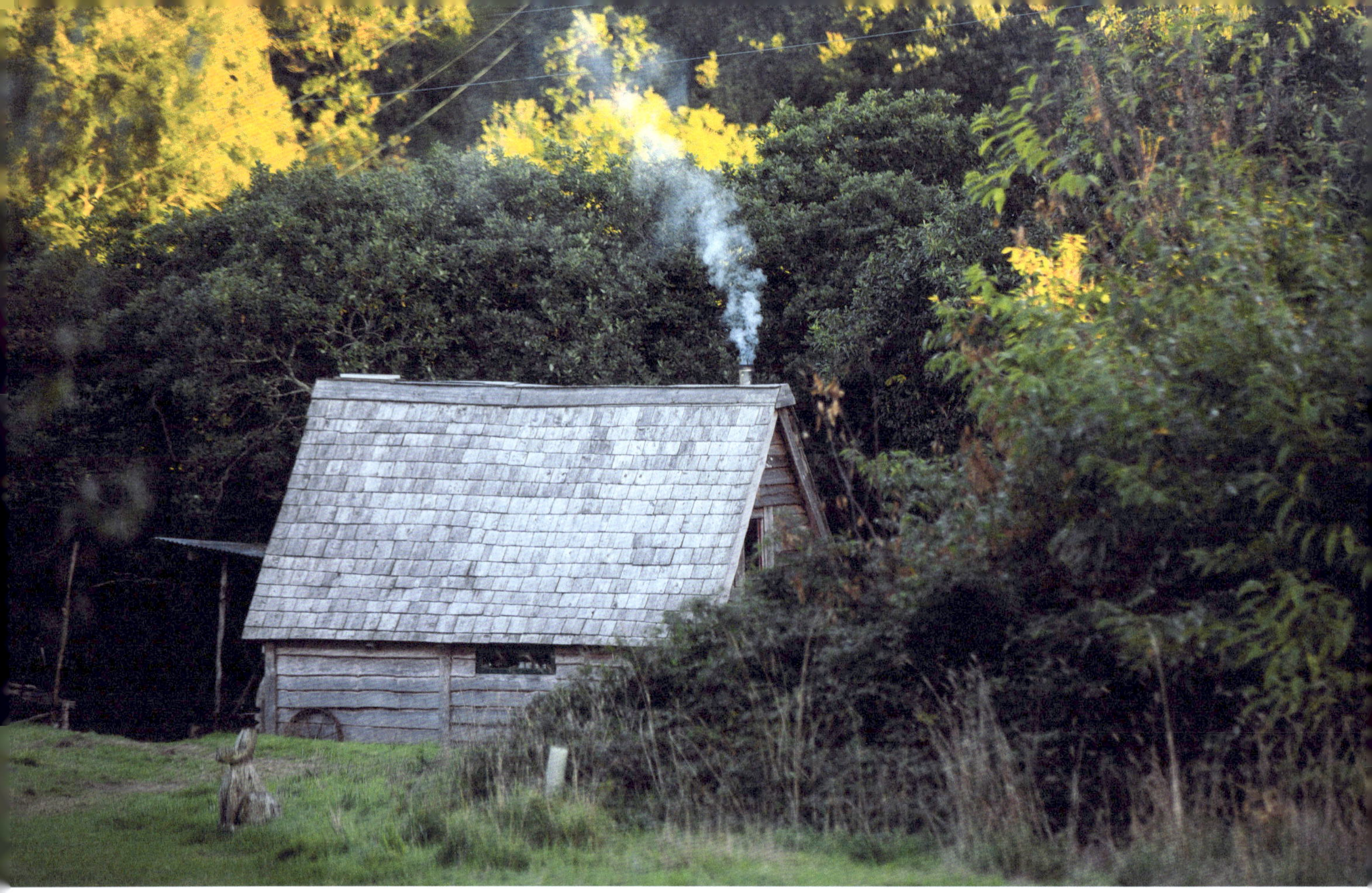

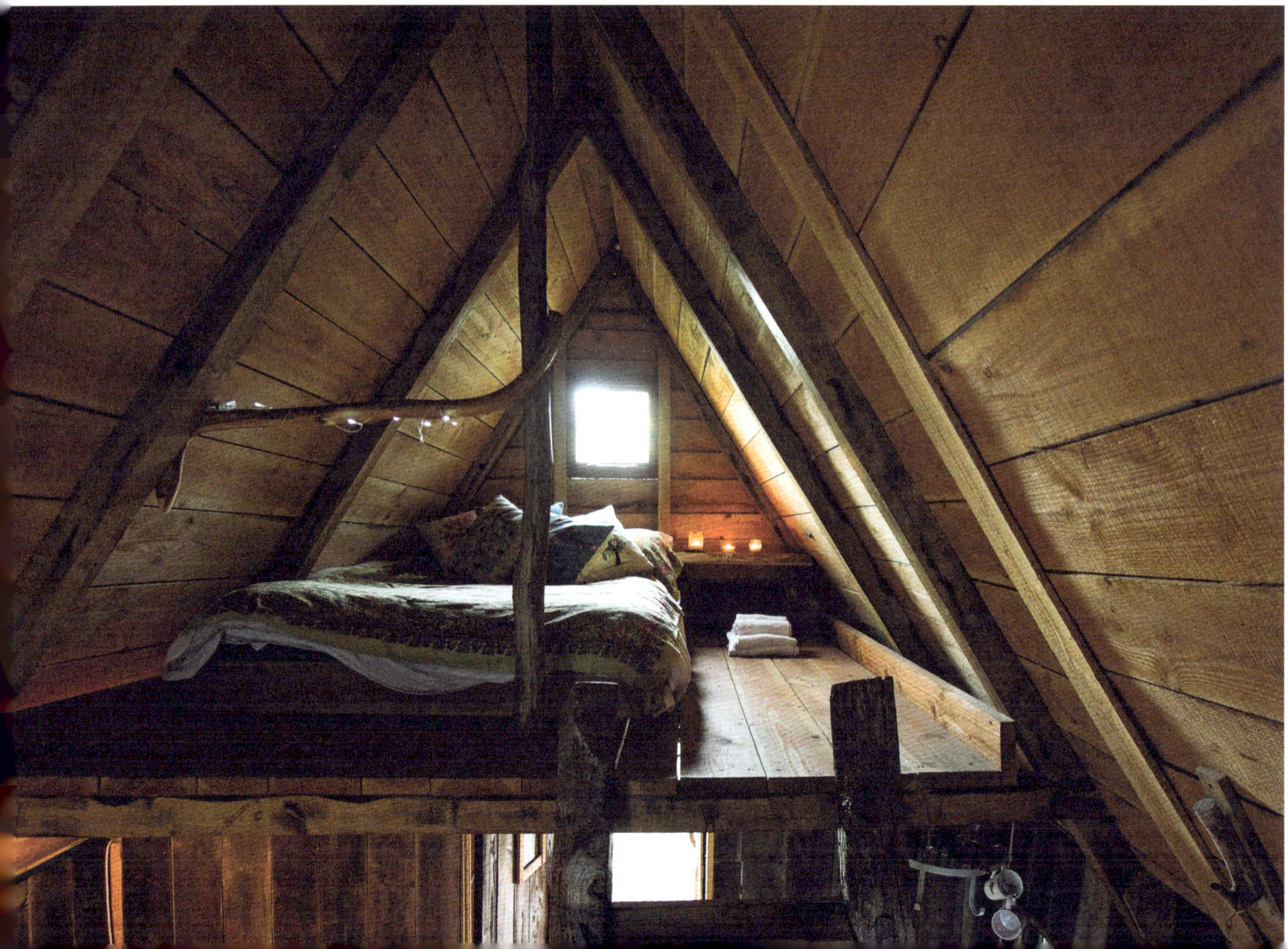

Old-Fashioned Camping in Cornwall

A charmed life in a wooden cabin where guests can truly get back to nature

WOODLAND CABIN
CORNWALL,
ENGLAND

This enchanting woodland cabin was hand-crafted from local and upcycled wood — sometimes, simple is best. Apart from a few solar lights for nighttime comfort, all of the amenities are wood-fired, and the water comes from owners Lisa and Neil Mudie's private borehole. The whole place is imbued with the couple's commitment to sustainable living and a heartfelt desire to return to the romance of old-fashioned camping. Besides roaming freely, foraging for food, and collecting wood for the campfire, daytime wanderings reveal magical woodland walks, winding coastal paths, and a host of inviting village pubs.

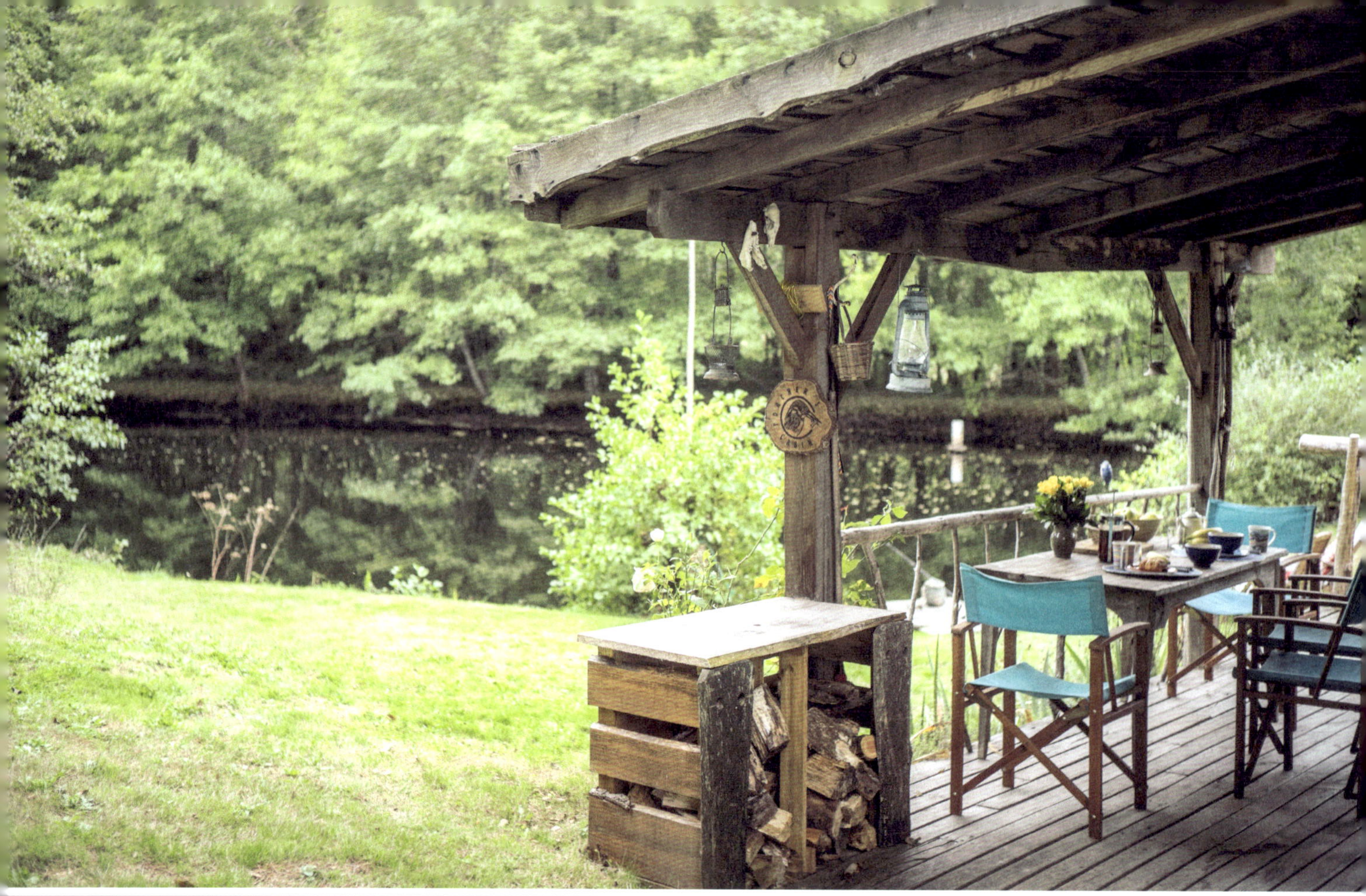

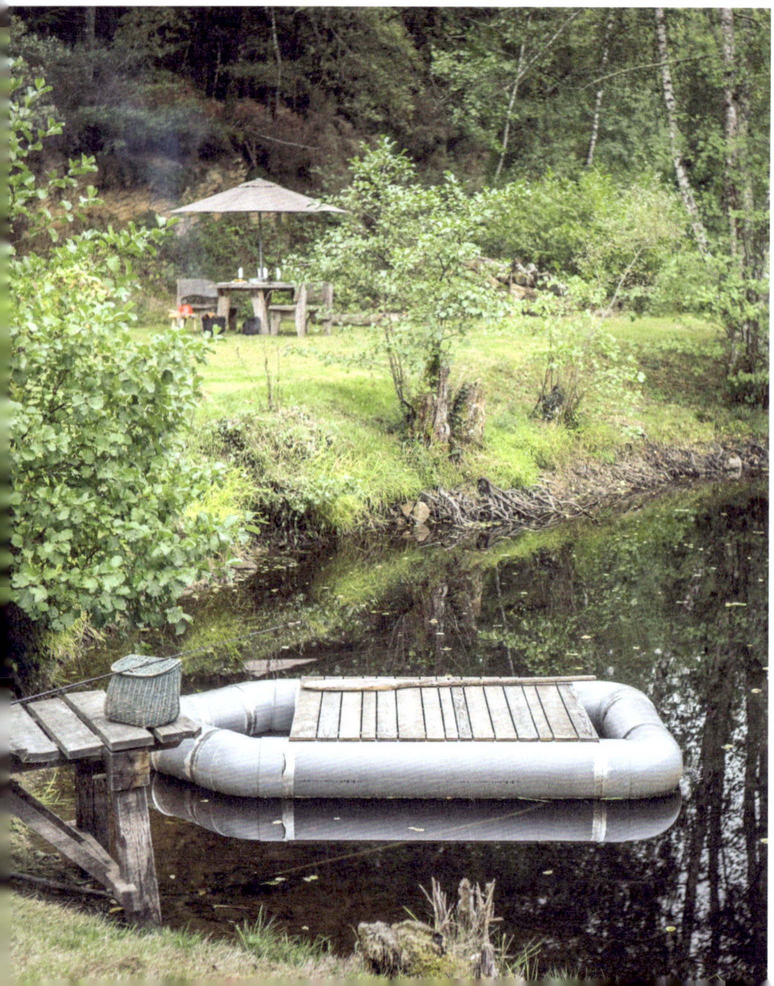

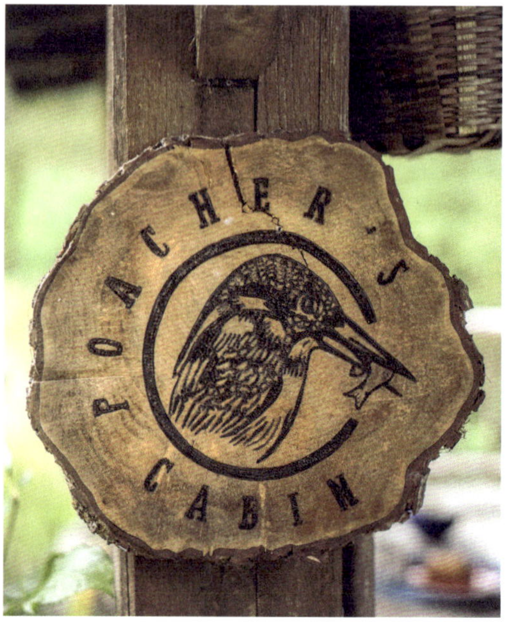
POACHER'S
CABIN

Rustic Solitude in the Woodlands of France

A stylish lakeside cabin for two in the wilds of Périgord-Limousin National Park

POACHER'S CABIN
PÉRIGORD-LIMOUSIN,
FRANCE

This cabin has undergone a sensitive restoration in its transformation from fishing shack to solitary woodland hideaway. Simple in its arrangement — essentially a bedroom above an open-plan living space — the refuge has a rustic feel, with gnarled door frames, planed kitchen work surfaces, and a veranda tiled in chestnut shingles. Off-grid comforts include a gas boiler for the shower, solar-powered lights, and a compost loo. Owned by wildlife TV presenter Kate Humble and her husband, Ludo Graham, it should come as no surprise that there are plenty of off-road cycle paths and trails right on the doorstep.

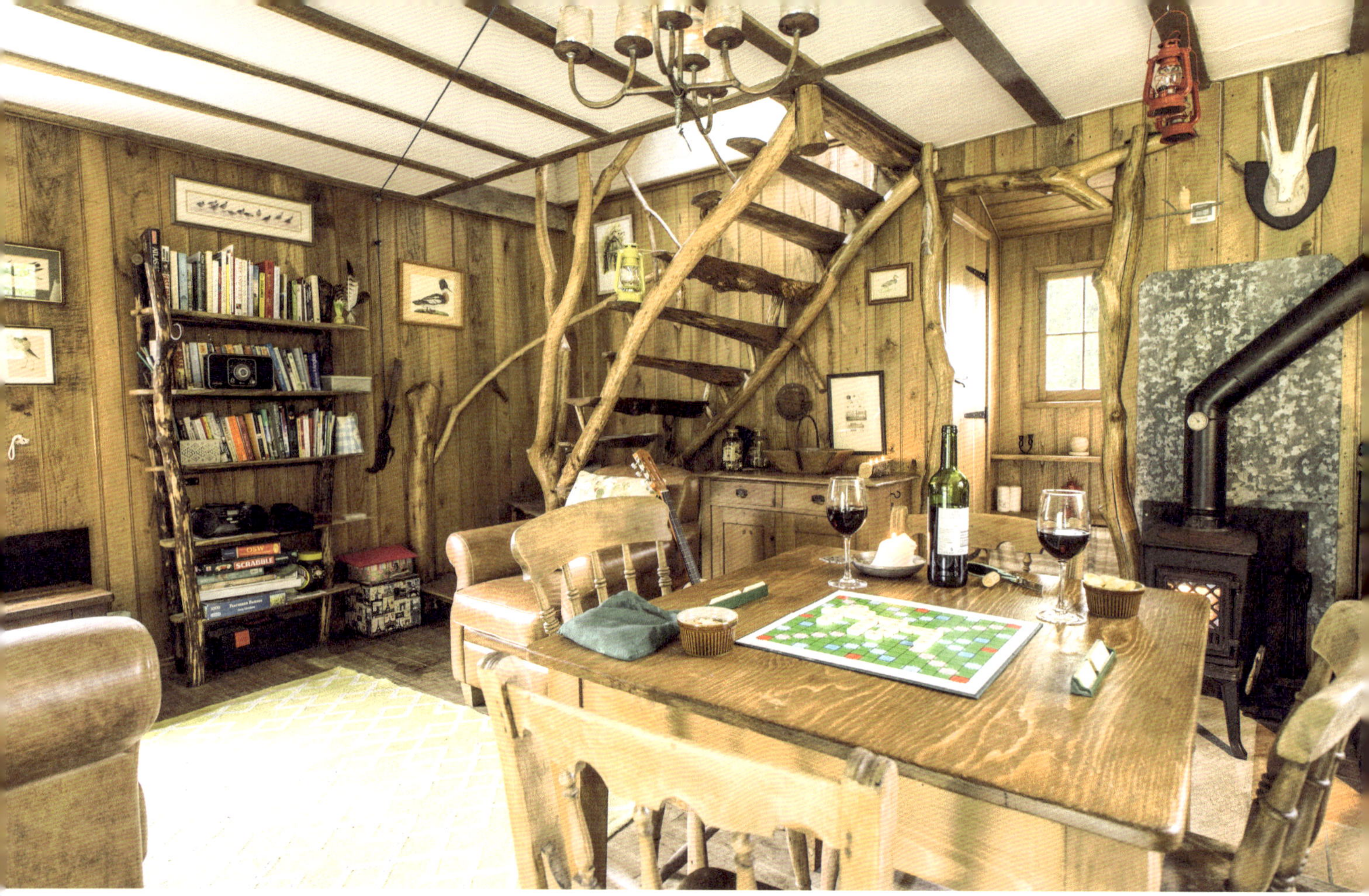
SCRABBLE

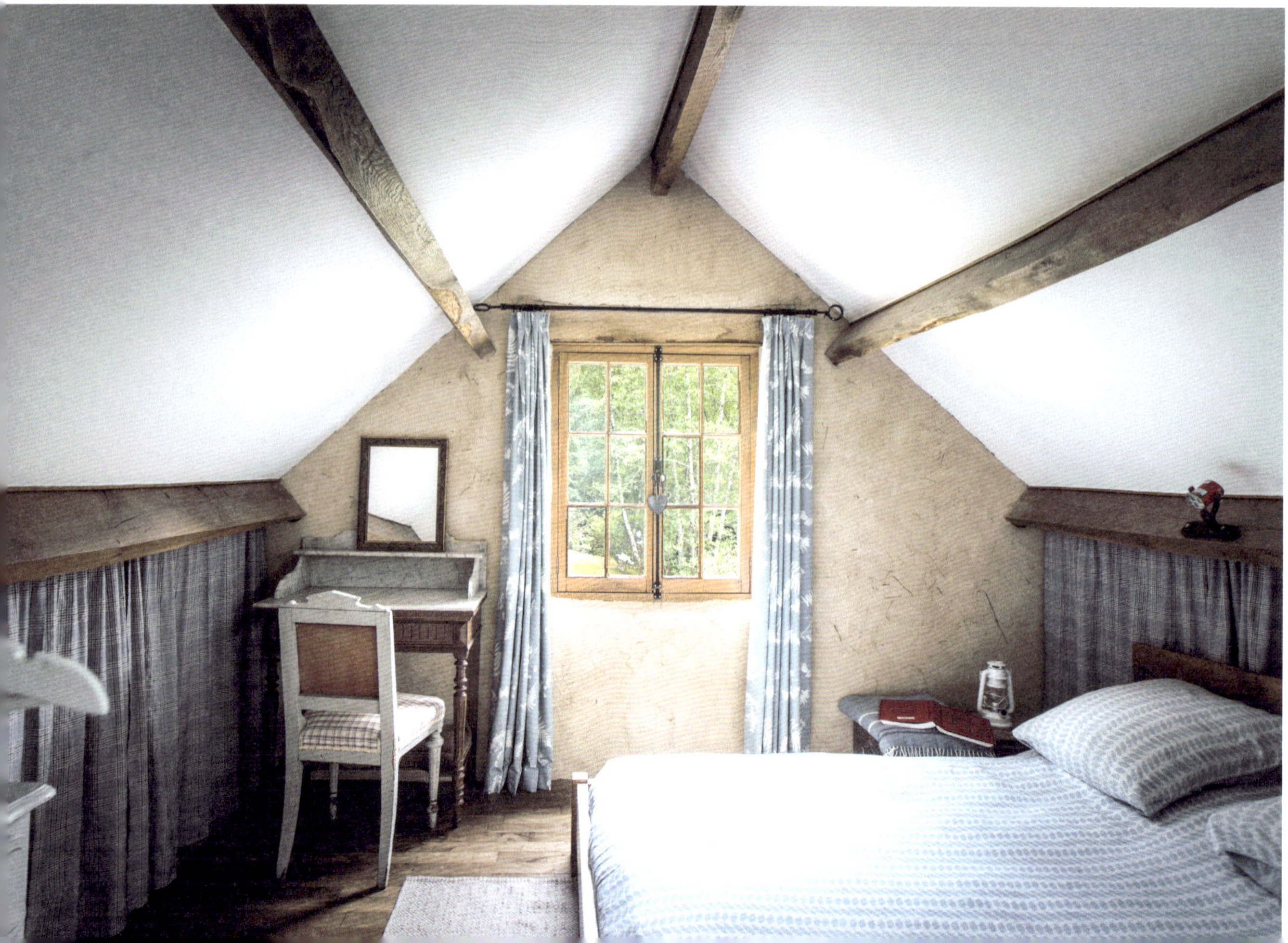

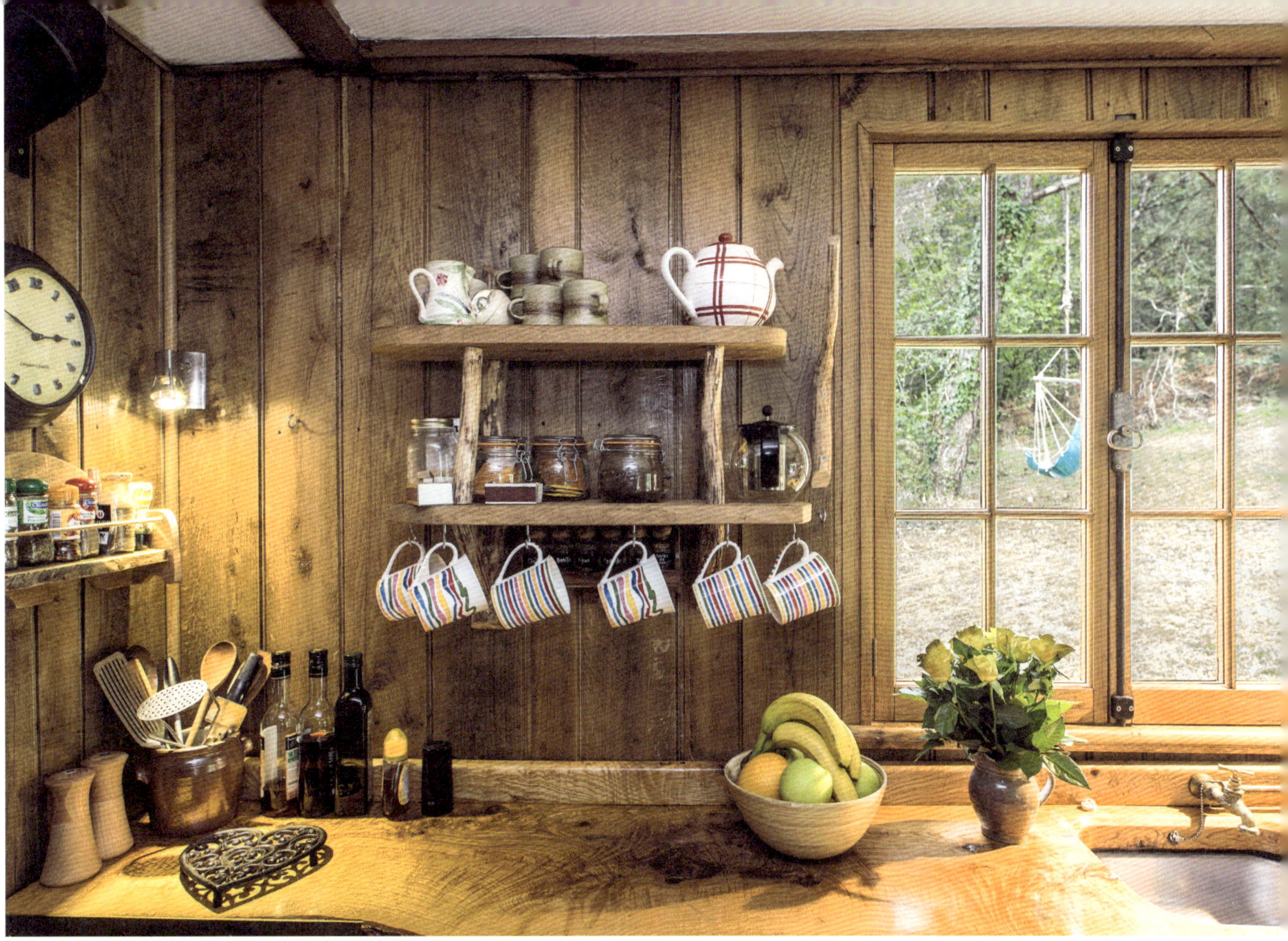

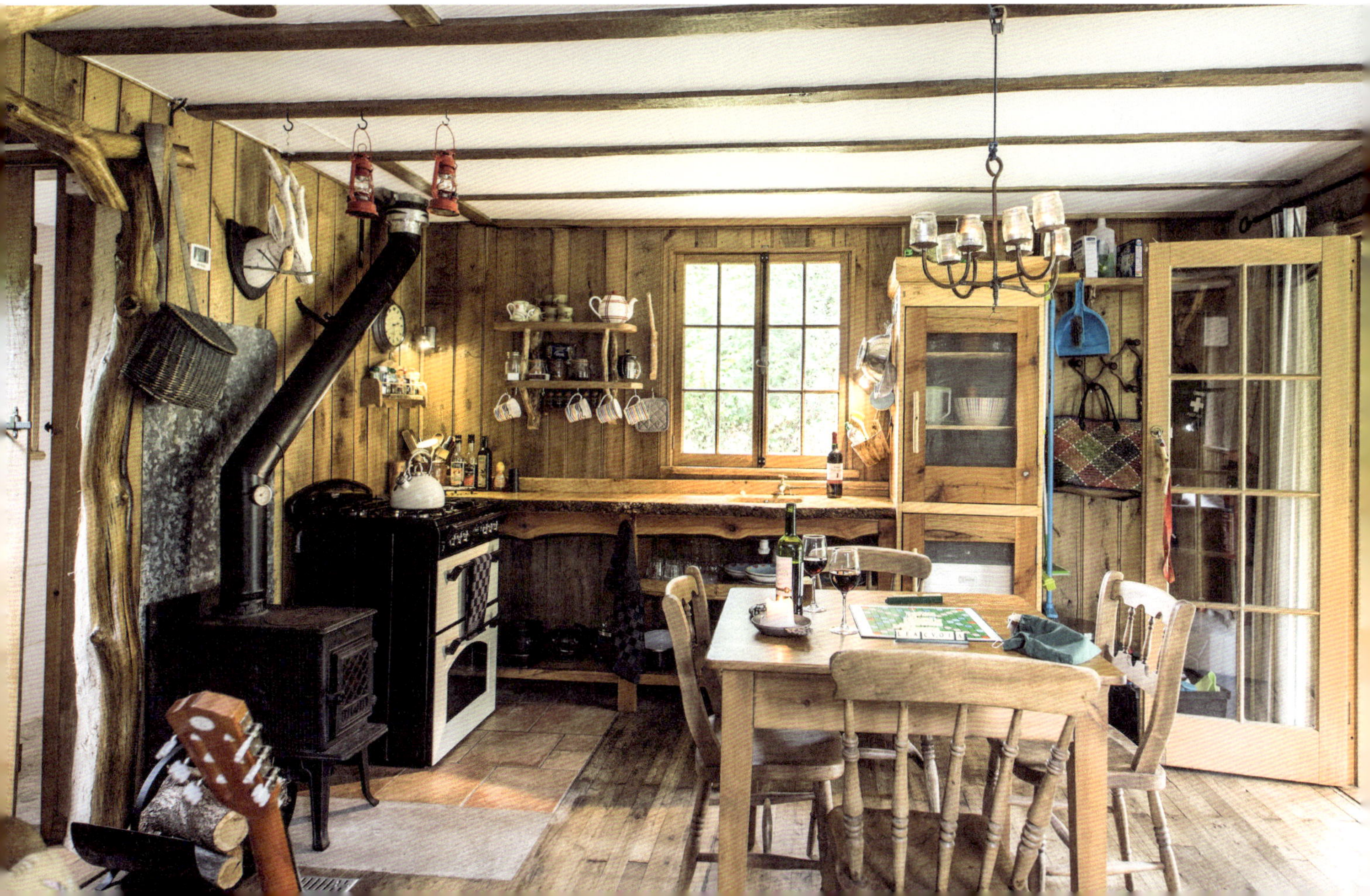

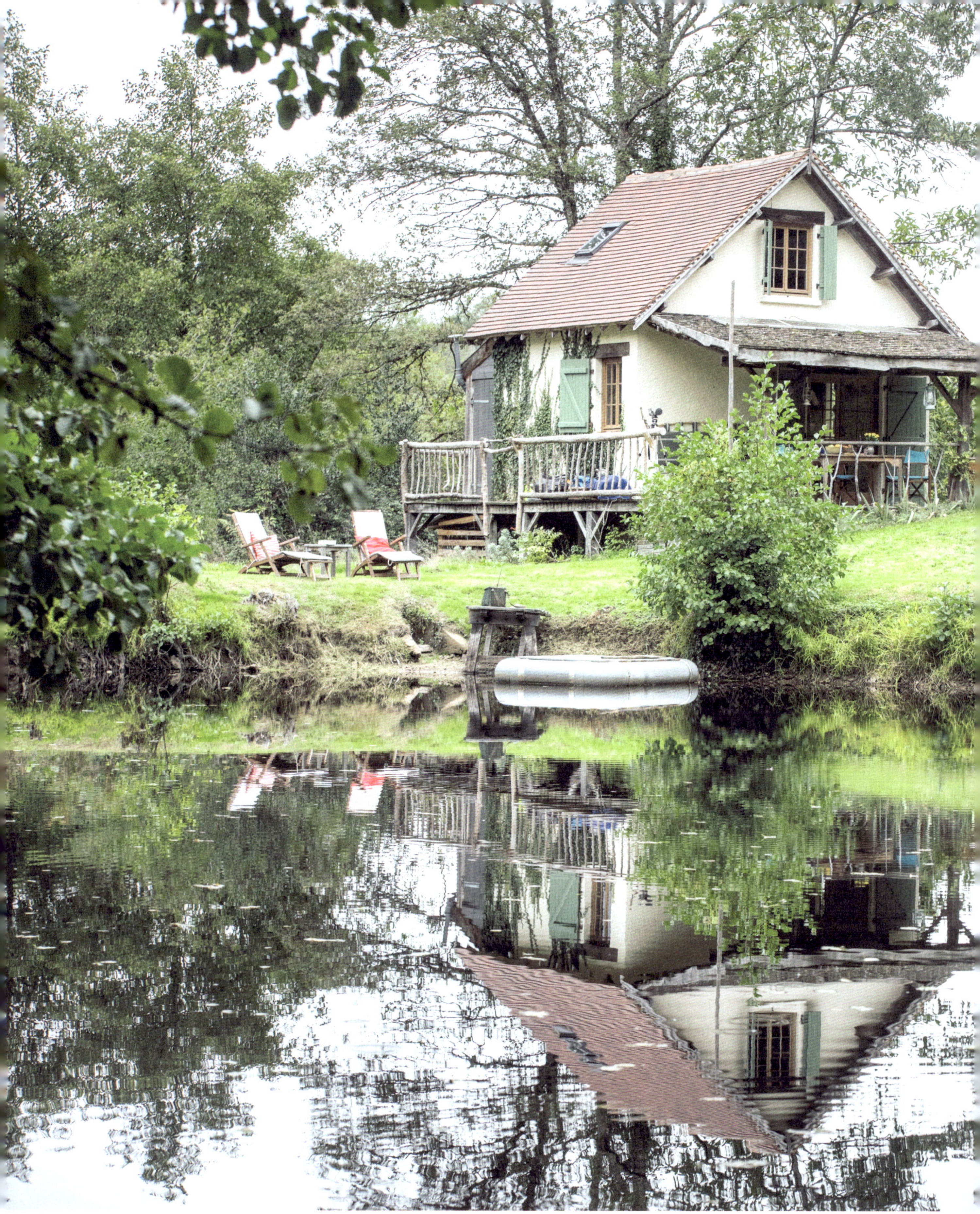

POACHER'S CABIN

The Science of
Stepping Outside

Discover the powerful physical and mental effects that spending time outdoors has on us

— by psychotherapist and writer Ruth Allen

When we go to stay somewhere wild, it is not just the enchanting, curious, and quirky dwellings that we go for. We go because these are beautiful spaces nested within beautiful places, man-made lodgings in nature-made havens. We go because when we stay wild, we get up close and personal with both the absolute best of thoughtful human design, which helps us disconnect, unwind, and relax, and with nature's intrinsic restorative and healing benefits.

Luckily for us, or, perhaps more accurately, as a function of our innate evolutionary connection to the rest of nature, the benefit of time spent in and around the outdoors can be felt with little effort or exertion on our part. You might choose to sit outside quietly,

As a function of our innate evolutionary connection to the rest of nature, the benefit of time spent in and around the outdoors can be felt with little effort or exertion on our part.

go for an aimless wander, or close your eyes and listen to the sounds of wildlife and weather. Some of my most memorable and uplifting times outside have been when I have done nothing more than observe the beauty around me, felt my own glorious smallness, and enjoyed simply *being*. Whilst there will be additional gains taken from a concerted effort to be outside doing immersive activities, the research is clear that we can experience the physical and mental health benefits of natural places even by viewing them through a well-placed window. Imagine, then, the possibility of stepping outside and being surrounded by a world that, whilst not designed for your well-being, is nevertheless deeply supportive of it.

Although many of us intuitively know the power of time spent outside, the empirical study of nature's healing potential is still relatively new, but one well-documented area of analysis is the impact of forest bathing on our holistic health. Research shows that escaping the city to immerse yourself amongst the trees can reduce your blood pressure and stress levels, improve your metabolic health, lower your blood sugar levels, and improve your pain response. We have also discovered that trees produce natural oils called phytoncides, which they

Some of my most memorable and uplifting times outside have been when I have done nothing more than observe the beauty around me, felt my own glorious smallness, and enjoyed simply *being*.

use to communicate with each other. These infuse the already oxygen-rich forest air that we breathe, and have been shown to boost the immune system and even increase the production of anti-cancer proteins. On a psychological level, the oils can also lower the symptoms of depression and anxiety, improve mood, increase concentration and memory, and increase energy levels.

Breathing in the chemicals released by trees, being exposed to the microbial properties of soil, and absorbing the Vitamin D we get from natural daylight have all been shown to stimulate an anti-depressant effect in our brains, and in the case of bacteria, *Mycobacterium vaccae* may also reduce anxiety. When we go outside, not only do our own microbiomes *generally* benefit from wider exposure to a more diverse ecology of bacteria, but our bodies get busy producing neurotransmitters such as dopamine, pain-relieving endorphins, and the hormones serotonin and oxytocin in response to the things we see and do that make us feel good. But it is not just the happy chemicals that nature helps us regulate; taking time outside can also lower the production of the stress hormone cortisol (which many of us are bathing in as a function of our busy, modern lives), reducing our overall stress levels and restoring calm and 'order' to our autonomic nervous system.

And it is not just forests. There is now abundant data revealing similar health benefits of time spent in or near water. Whether it is a walk on a coastal path, swimming in the sea, watching a river flow, or sitting by a peaceful lake, time spent in 'blue spaces' shares many of the same outcomes as 'green spaces', with some notable additions of its own, such as the increased intake of fresh (preferably salty) air, which has been shown — amongst other things — to improve overall lung function. No special effort is required to feel the benefits of time spent in blue or green spaces, other than the intention to make room for it. A couple of hours a week is often enough for long-term improvements, but even 15 minutes will set you on your way.

Evidently, it is not *only* the soulful emotional connection that we make with the landscape, flora, and fauna that keeps us returning outside time and again; the physiological 'match' also keeps us coming back. All the benefits outlined above are experienced because we have an organic, fleshy body that, if we give it the opportunity, attunes well to what the natural world has to offer.

It is through our human senses of sight, touch, smell, taste, and sound that we encounter the rest of the natural world, via messages sent to our brain about what we enjoy, what relaxes us, what invigorates us, and what stimulates a sense of wonder. These moments matter, not just for aesthetics' sake but because beautiful things improve our mood, and when we stimulate feelings of awe, internal inflammation has been shown to reduce, which may in turn decrease the symptoms of chronic inflammatory diseases, and even of depression.

In fact, it is because the natural world appears to be so brilliant at up- and down-regulating our nervous system that we find our time outside to be both restorative *and* energising. Whether you arrive outdoors in need of peace and quiet or mobilisation and stimulation, going outside has something for everybody. Relaxing activities such as sitting quietly and listening to the ambient sounds of birdsong or building a fire and softly gazing at the flames with friends are excellent ways of activating your body's parasympathetic nervous system — sending the message that it is time to de-stress and allow feelings of safety and connection to wash over you. Alternatively, activities that feel exciting, new, and exploratory, or that involve putting your body under a healthy level of exertion, not only benefit the cardio-vascular system, but also energise the sympathetic nervous system out of lethargy and into readiness, sending the message: 'Let's go!' which itself can lift mood, motivation, and overall feelings of well-being.

We have known for a long time that immersing ourselves in the softer light and soundscape of natural places has the potential to restore our attention and concentration when we have become mentally fatigued and overwhelmed in our hyper-saturated, noisy working lives, but now we also know that repeating shapes and patterns in nature provide a visual fluency that is soothing to our brains. We know about the pain-killing properties of a green view and that bilateral movements such as walking or running help us to process our emotions, problem solve, and break our own ruminations. A diverse and fascinating database of scientific evidence that substantiates the human health benefits of nature is growing all the time and revealing the astounding depth and complexity of

No special effort is required to feel the benefits of time spent in blue or green spaces, other than the intention to make room for it. A couple of hours a week is often enough for long-term improvements, but even 15 minutes will set you on your way.

our embodied relationship with the natural world. When I work outside with people in therapy, I see the endless ways that being in a natural environment supports the work we do together, whether it's observing the bodily relaxation that happens as soon as we start walking through the woods together, seeing how we enjoy the sights and sounds moment by moment, or noticing the long-term psychological benefits in a person over time as they learn to connect meaningfully with the world around them. This is my encouragement for you too. Go outside and meet the world with all of your senses in a way that works for you, because the rationale for a closer relationship is clear: to be without nature is to be deprived of its life-giving and life-affirming properties.

At the end of the day, though, it might just be about the simplest of things, about what happens when you step out of your daily life for a while to relax, to play, to breathe in fresh air, to immerse yourself in a new place and do new things — when you have switched off, lit the candles, cooked the food, and settled down to *get away from it all for just a little while*. Scientific research can tell us a hundred different facts about the power of nature on our health and well-being, but sometimes the story is revealed through the simplest of everyday occurrences, in that particular deep and dreamlike sleep you have as you drift off smelling of woodsmoke in the enveloping company of wild things.

```
Go outside and meet the world with all
of your senses in a way that works
for you, because the rationale for a
closer relationship is clear: to be
without nature is to be deprived of its
life-giving and life-affirming properties.
```

That Easy, Comfortable 'Cushty' Vibe

A Sussex woodland retreat offers open-air classes in traditional pastimes and nature crafts

KUSHTI
EAST SUSSEX,
ENGLAND

Visitors to Forest Garden might never leave — there's just so much to do! Owners Charles and Lisa don't just want guests to enjoy their homely accommodation; they want them to make full use of this beautiful woodland retreat and to take part in the wide range of courses in traditional crafts and activities on offer. Amongst the yurts and cabins on the site, the wonderfully traditional Kushti sets the perfect tone for such a stay, featuring painted poles, colourful textiles, and solar-powered fairy lights. At night, guests can look up at the stars through the big crown wheel set in the roof, and in the morning, they can step out into an ancient woodland carpeted with wild garlic, bluebells, or orchids, depending on the time of year. They can also expect to see bunnies and deer, and maybe even a resident heron. Daytime activities might involve taking a course in mushroom foraging or spoon carving.

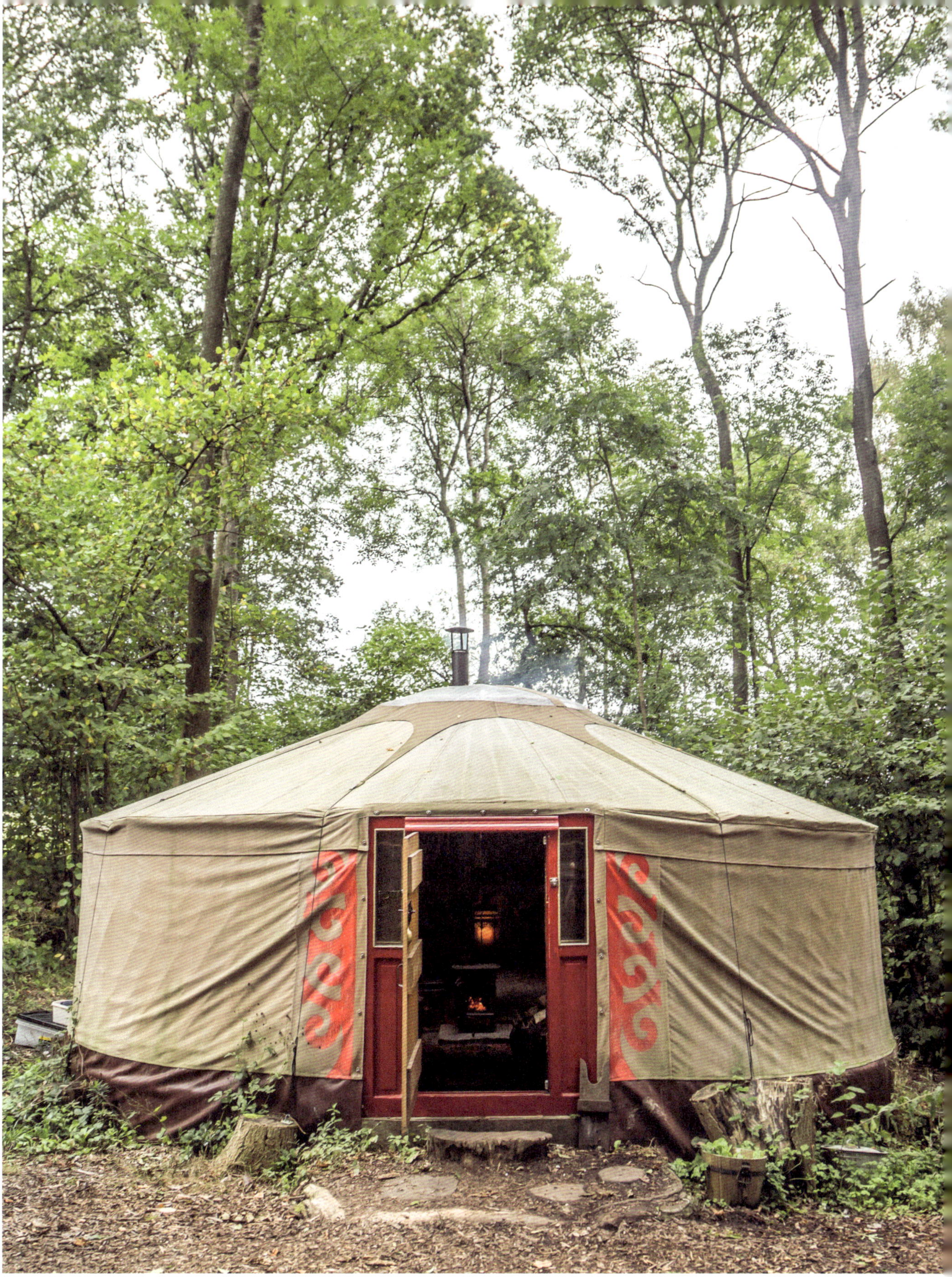

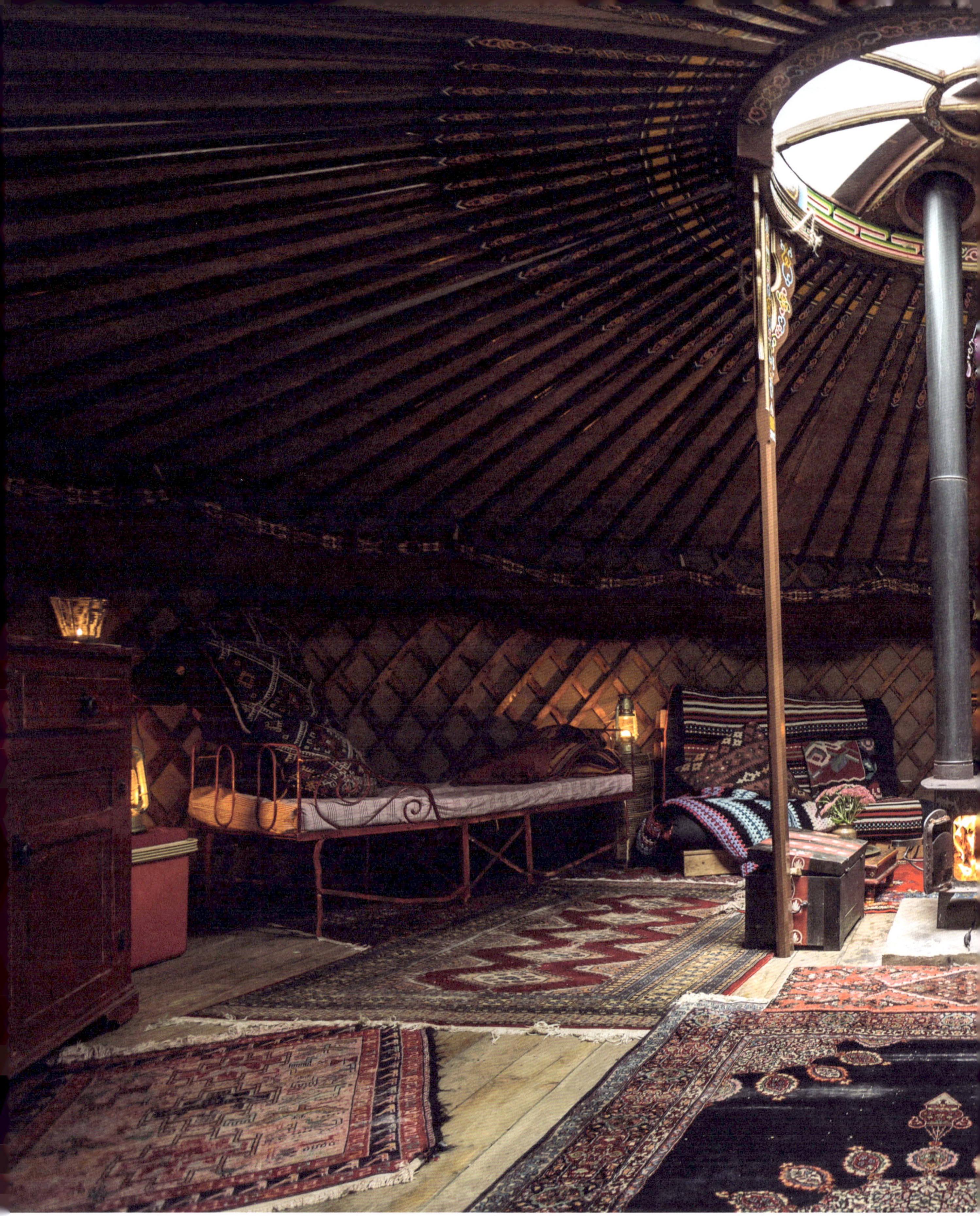

KUSHTI

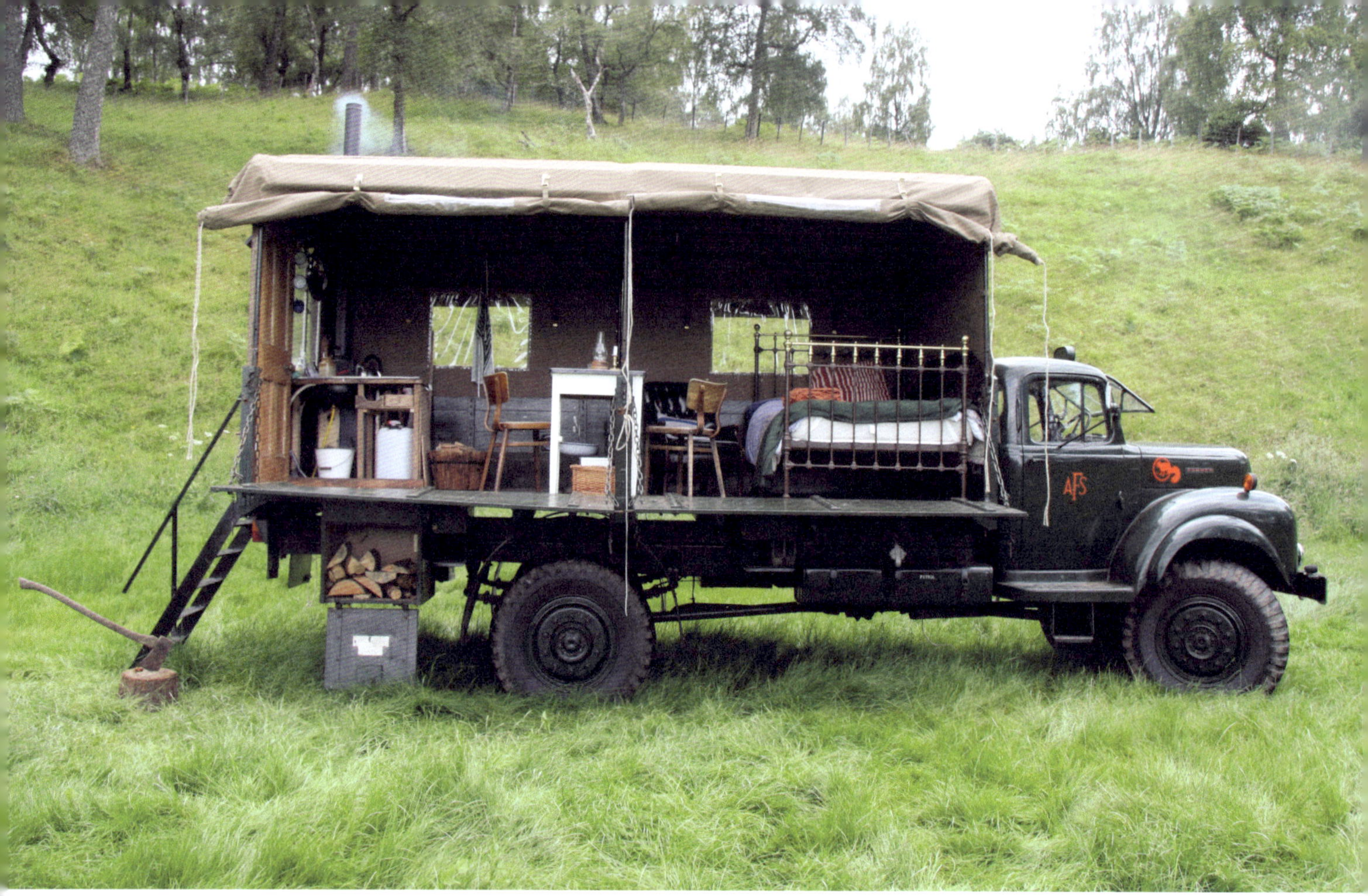
AFS

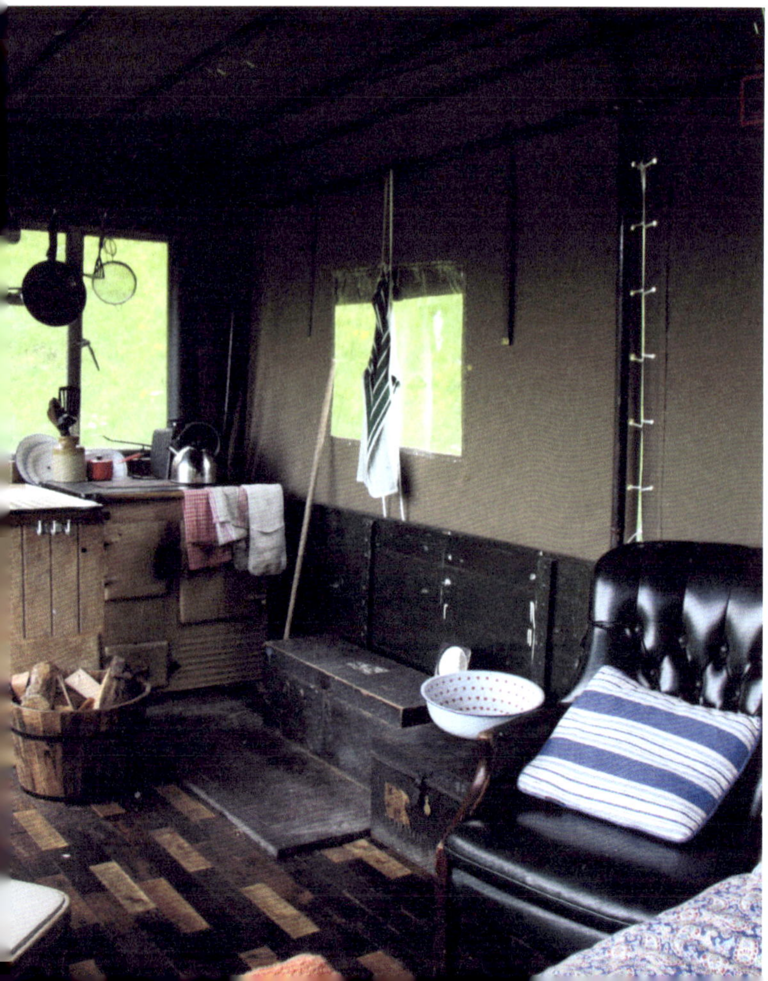

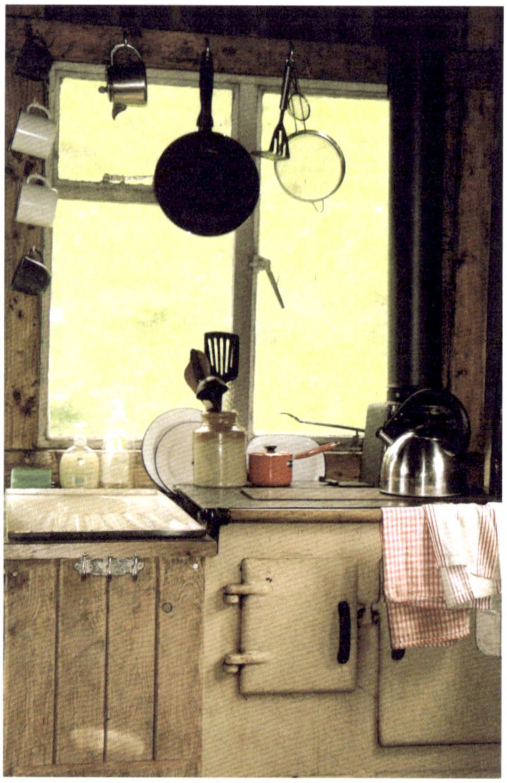

An Al Fresco Home on Wheels

Roll up the canvas, lower the sides, and take in those glorious Highland views

THE BEERMOTH
THE CAIRNGORMS,
SCOTLAND

Not many people return from the Scottish Highlands having slept in a 1950s fire truck. Fewer still get to sweat it out in a horse-box sauna. But that's the charm of the Beermoth on the Micklethwaits' Inshriach Estate. Treated to a renovation of the quirkiest order, the cosy truck has oak parquet flooring salvaged from a Tudor mansion, and a wood burner at one end and an elegant Victorian bed at the other. It makes for a fantastic, rough-and-ready base from which to enjoy the estate — a haven for wildlife — as well as numerous activities further afield, including white water rafting and pony trekking.

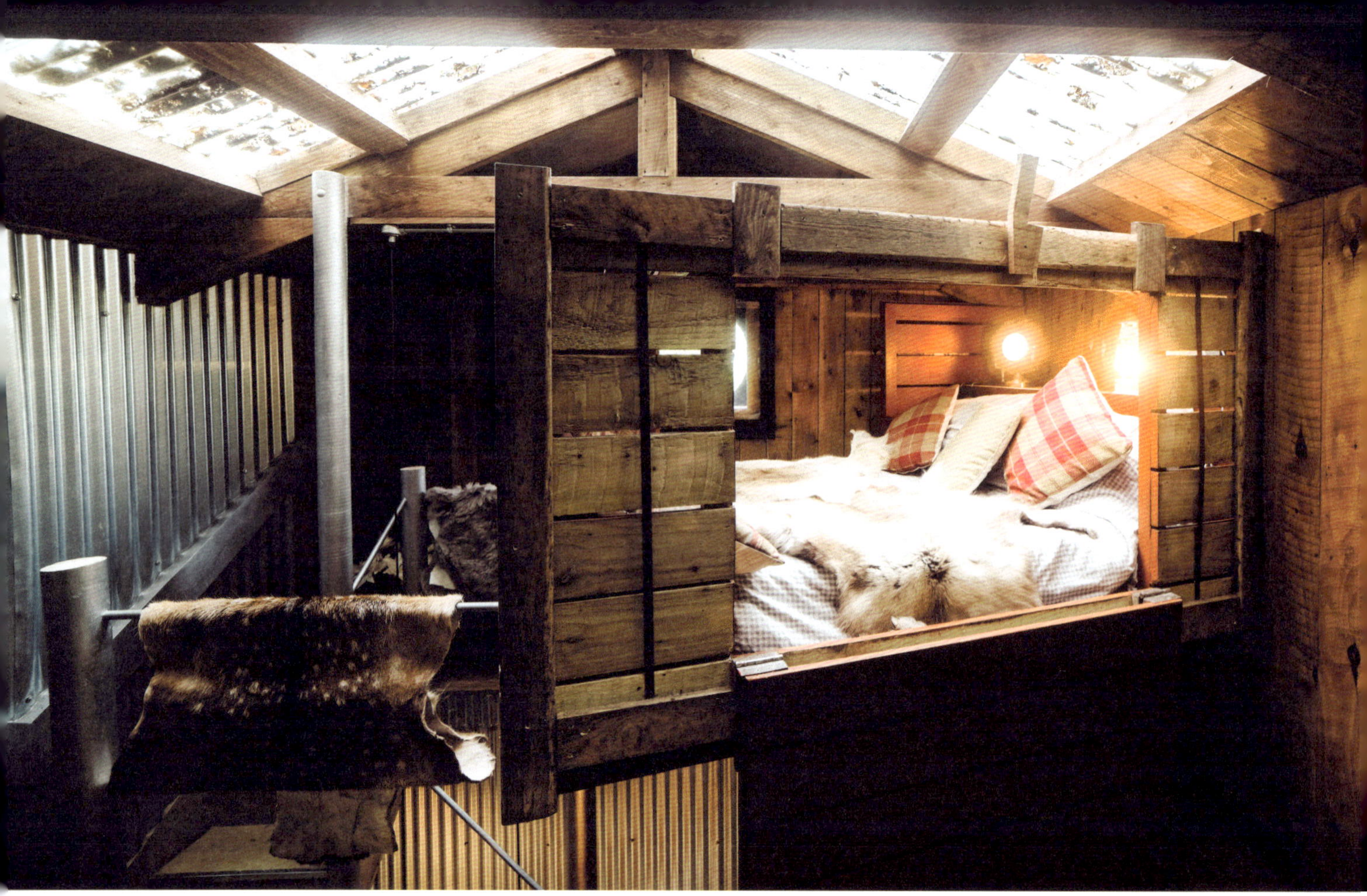

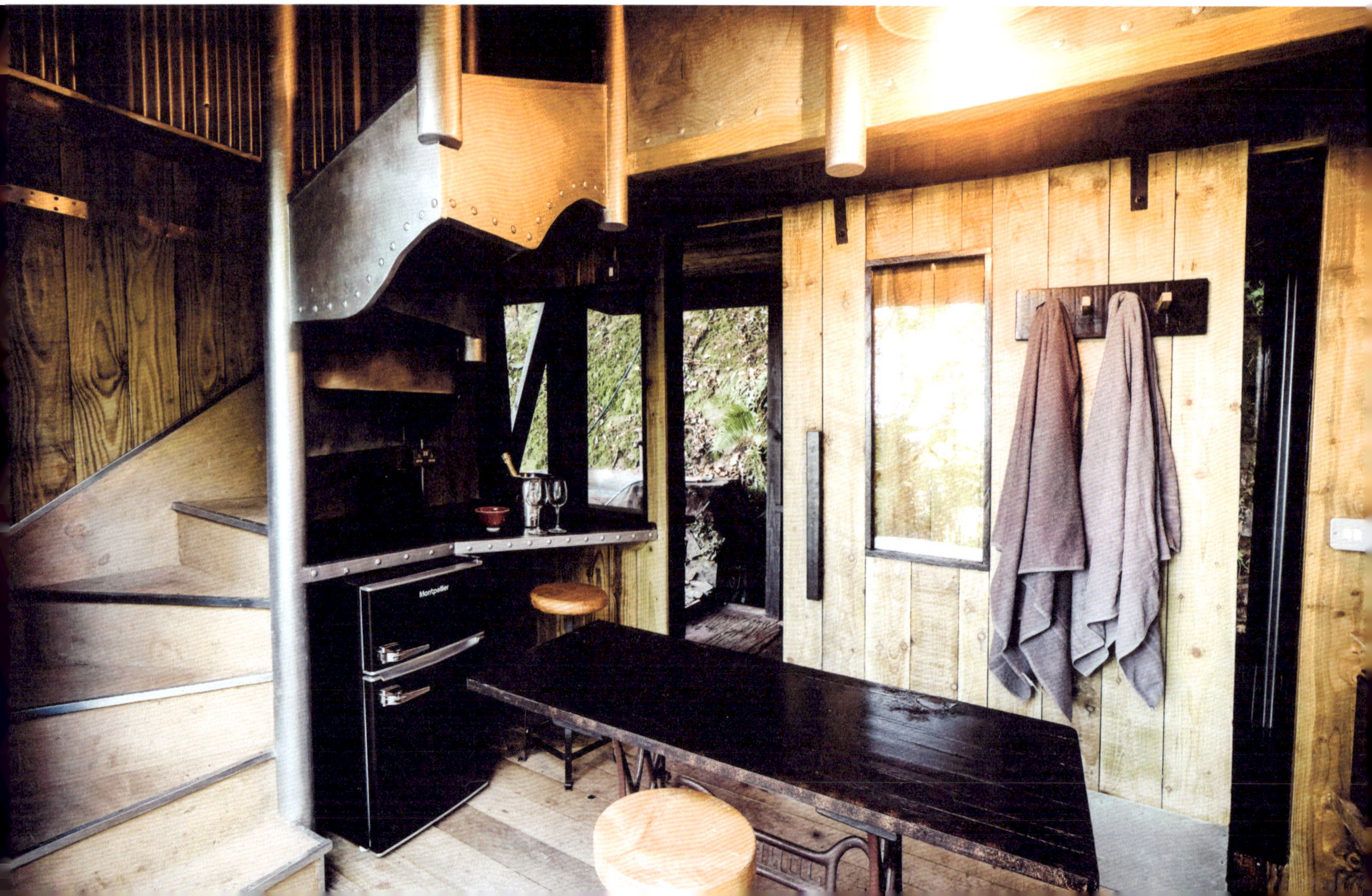
Montpellier

The Taste of Honey

Life really is sweet in this human-sized beehive in a Devonshire woodland setting

HUMBLE BEE
DEVON,
ENGLAND

Within reach of Dartmoor National Park and its trails across open moorlands and through river valleys, forests, and wetlands, the Humble Bee is a beehive-shaped three-level cabin. Right at the top, a king-size bed hovers above the main space, while the landings below are kitted out with a kitchen area and a fireside corner for lounging. Dark wood panelling, a honeycomb feature wall, and thick furs provide a cosy hive vibe, but guests can also open the large doors and windows to let the stunning woodland scenery in. Best of all, a stone bath for thermal bathing is carved into the rock outside.

Embracing Life in a Cornish Wilderness

A rustic frontier-style cabin with a natural 'jacuzzi' for chilly open-air dips

LOG JAM CABIN
CORNWALL, ENGLAND

Log Jam Cabin is raised on a platform in a little pocket of Cornish wilderness. Furnished with a leather sofa, a wood-burning stove, and a king-size bed in a room accessed through a secret door, it doesn't run short of creature comforts, and there's a refreshing frontier vibe about the place too. Relying entirely on sustainable energy, life is geared towards the slow pace of the wild surroundings. Guests linger on the cabin's generous decking or gather around the Dutch oven as it cooks food over an open fire. For adventurers, a wild 'jacuzzi' pool has been cut into the river that flows nearby.

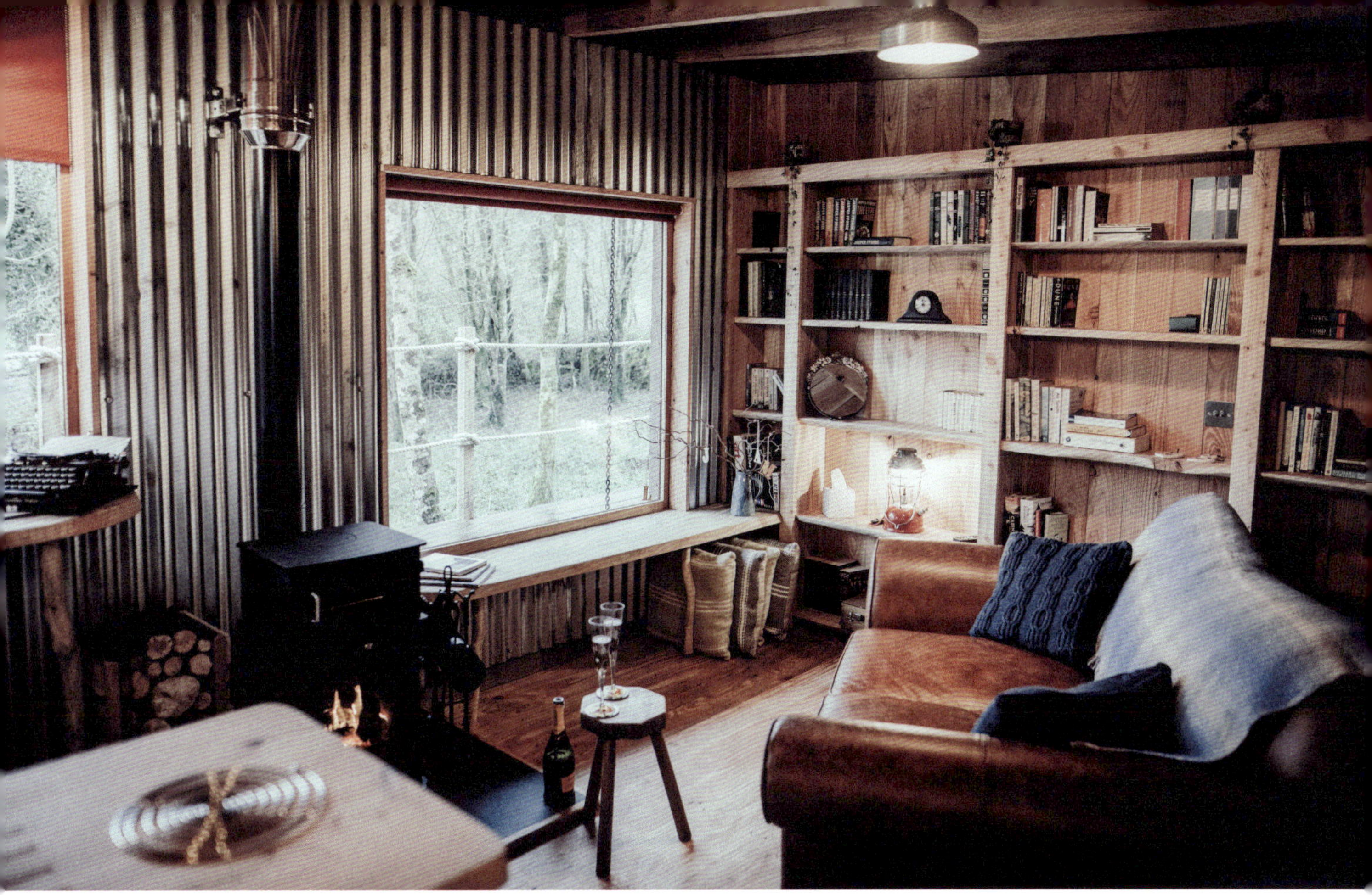

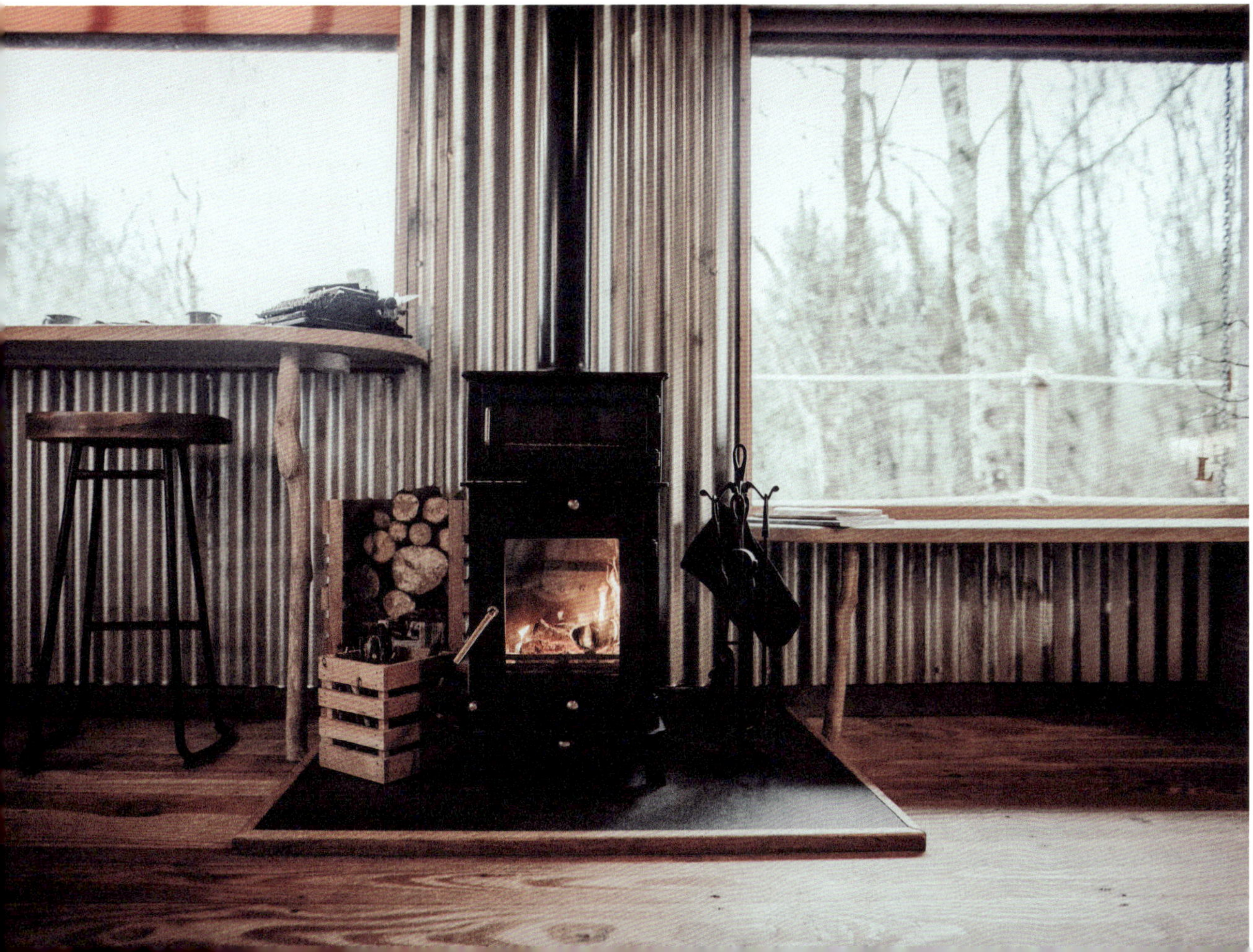

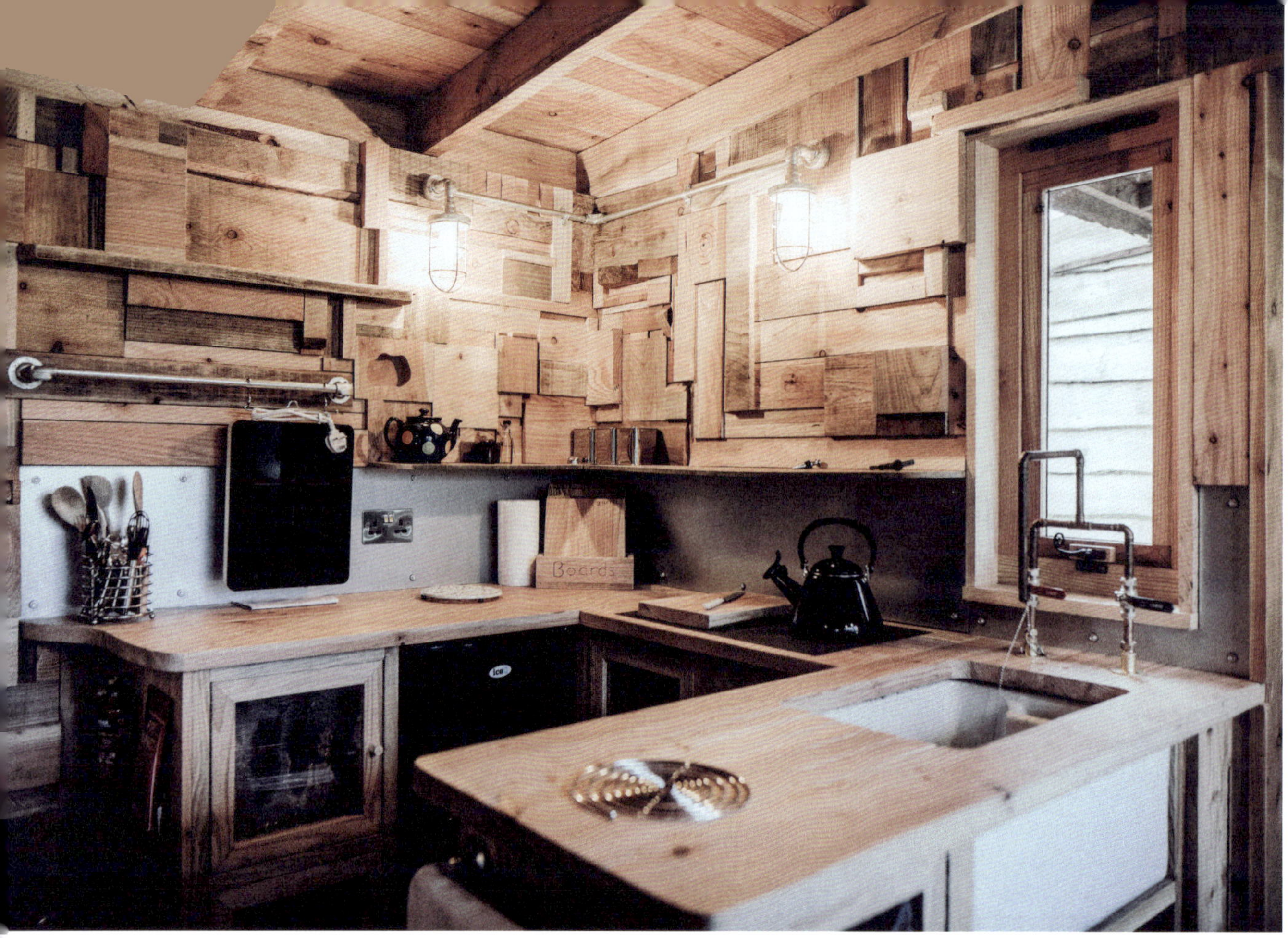
Boards

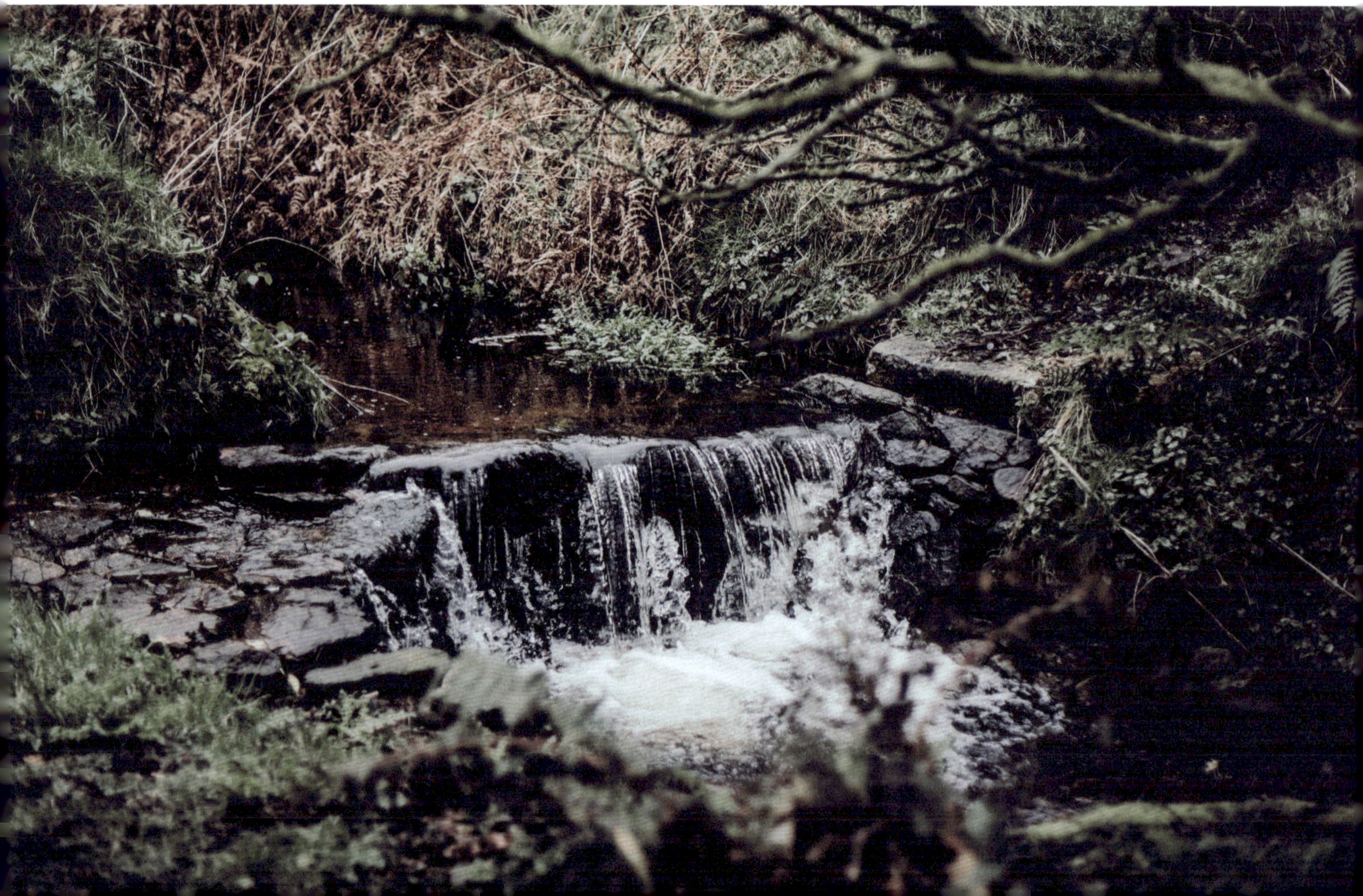

LOG JAM CABIN

A Hideaway Deep in the Woods

A fairy-tale castle within easy reach of the spectacular North Yorkshire countryside

RUFUS'S ROOST
YORKSHIRE, ENGLAND

From the wealth of wildlife right outside the windows to the fairy-tale fun indoors, this treehouse wows on every level. Rufus's Roost is the creation of Barney Smith, whose family has owned the Baxby Manor estate in Yorkshire for four generations. With the utmost care and respect for the environment, Smith has built this treehouse on principles of sustainability, installing a biomass boiler, heat-recovery ventilation, and LED lighting to minimise on light pollution. On the surrounding estate, extensive conservation work has led to the return of masses of small bird and wildflower species. Deer and badgers roam amongst speckled light in the woods, and bats flit across the sky come nightfall. Then there is the 'roost' — a spectacular wood-shingled, turreted two-storey castle with a bedroom in the attic, a slide that accesses a secret reading nook, and a veranda complete with hot tub and pizza oven.

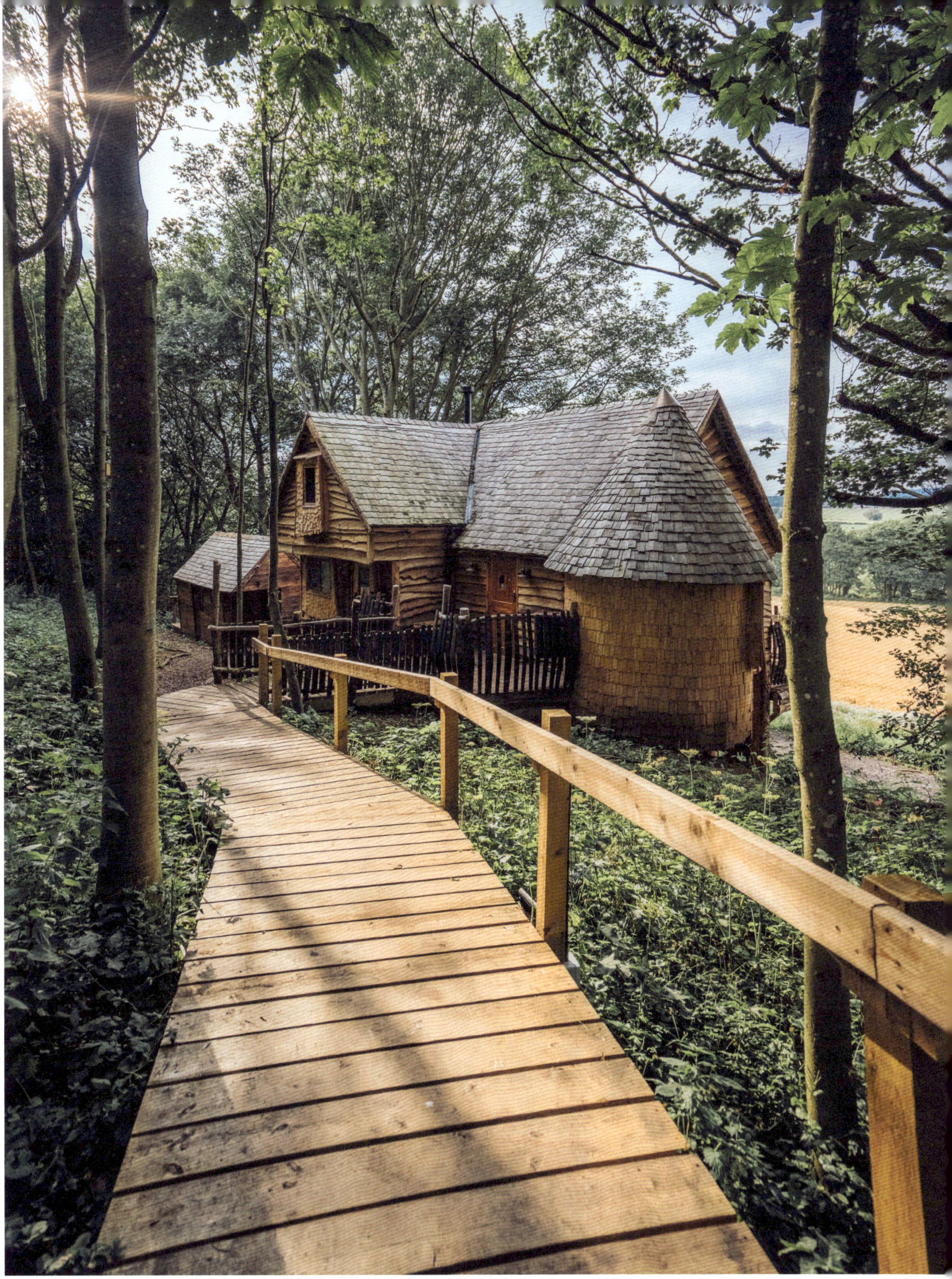

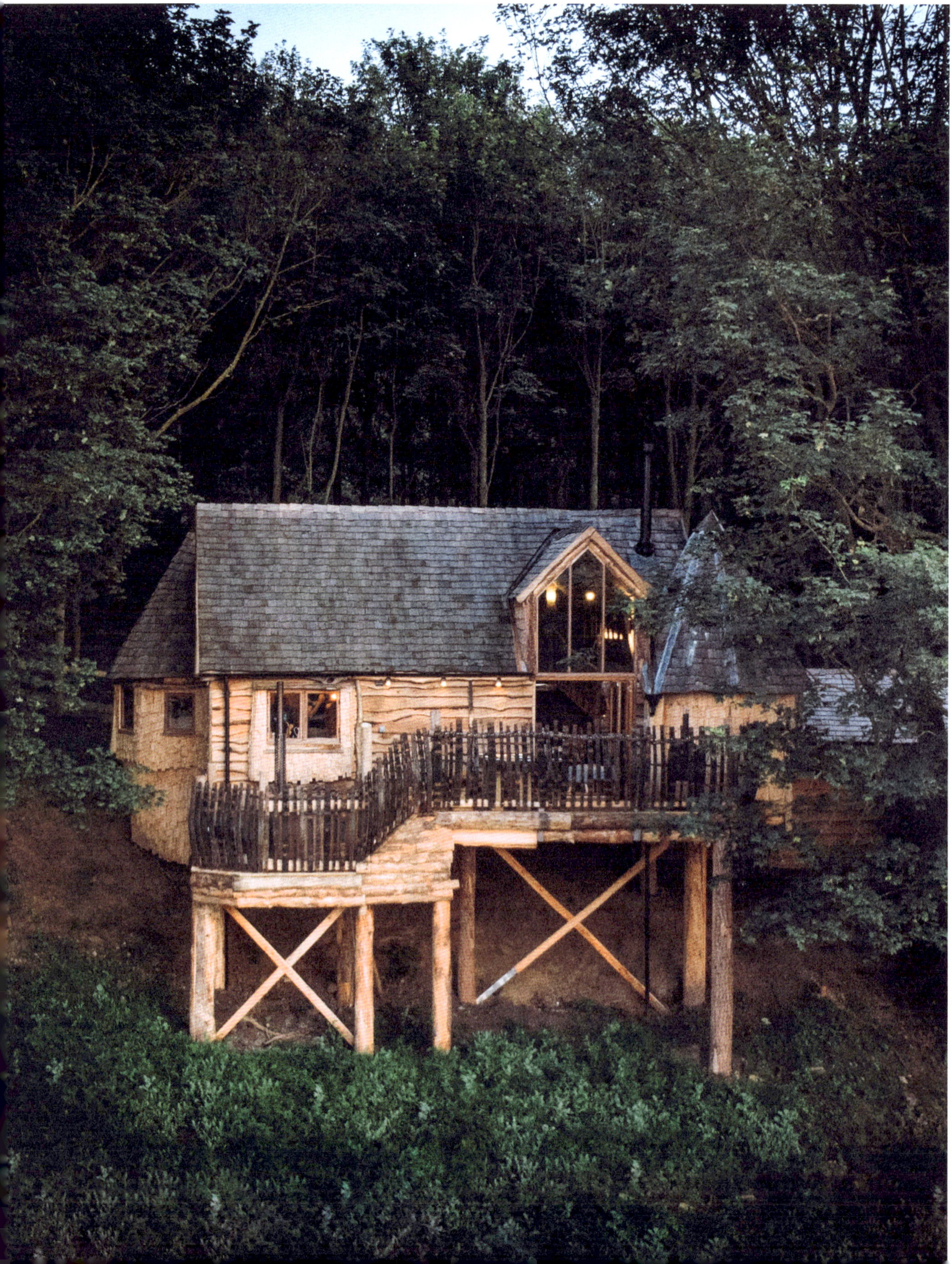

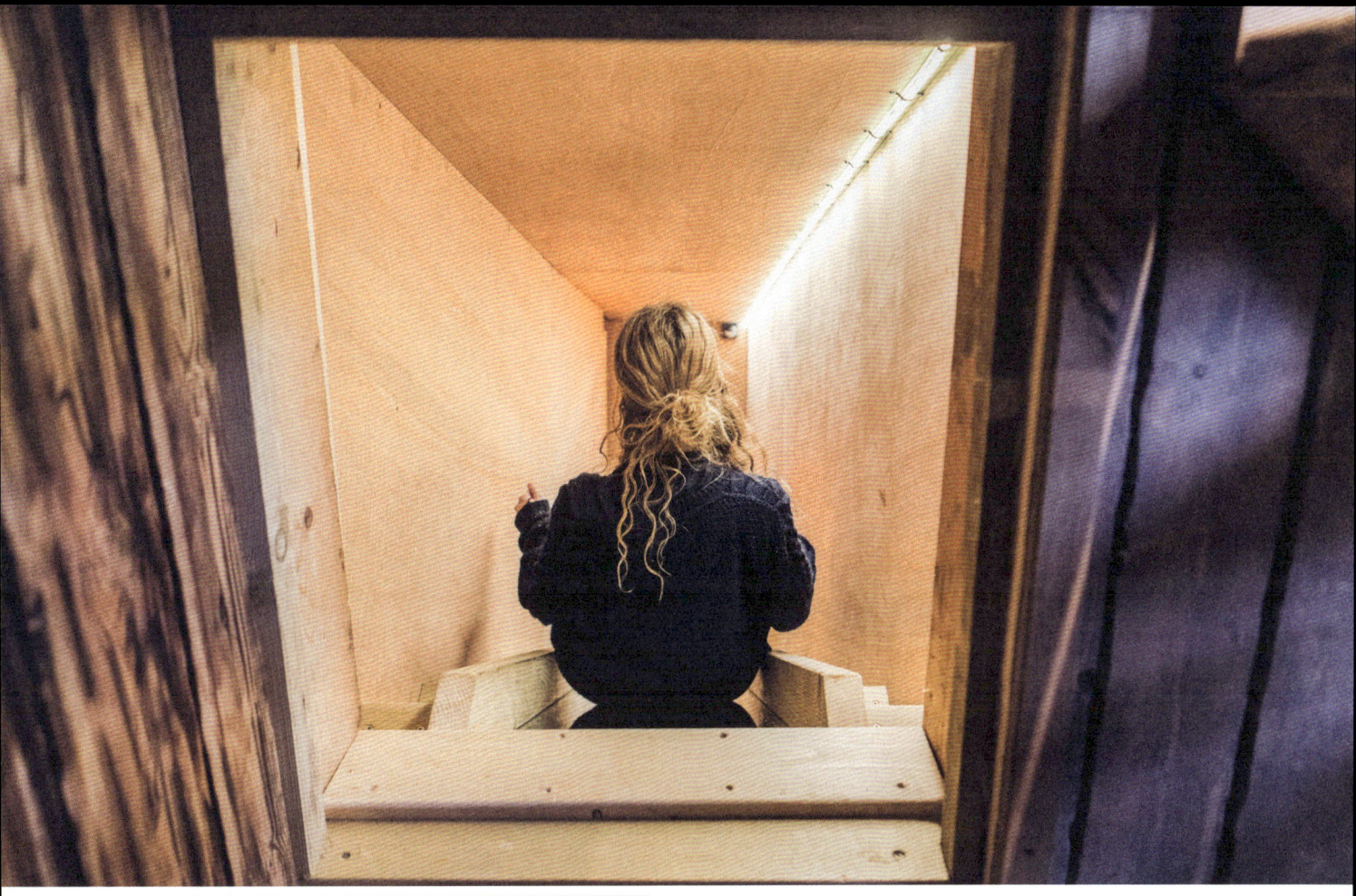

RUFUS'S ROOST

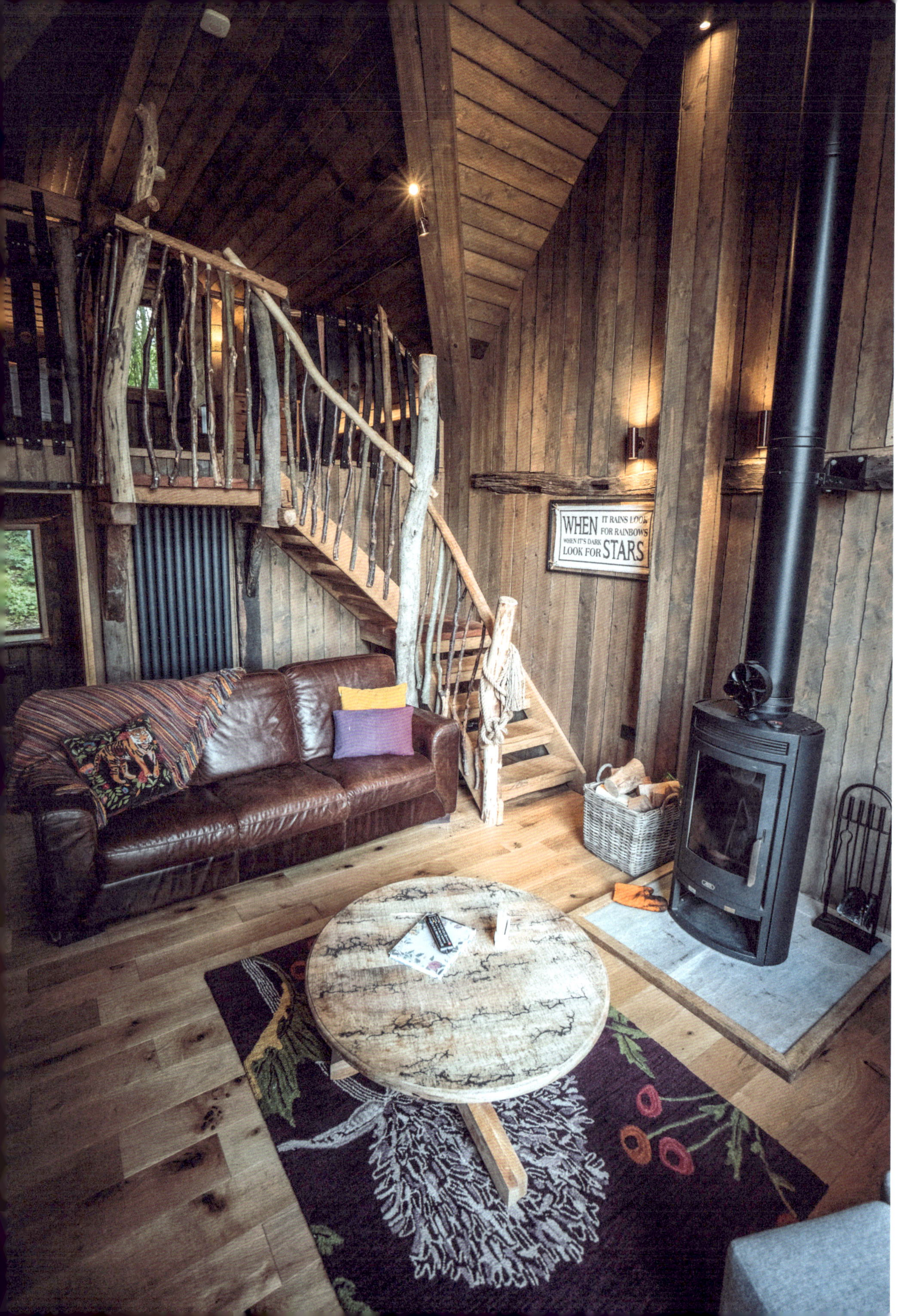
WHEN IT RAINS LOOK FOR RAINBOWS
WHEN IT'S DARK LOOK FOR STARS

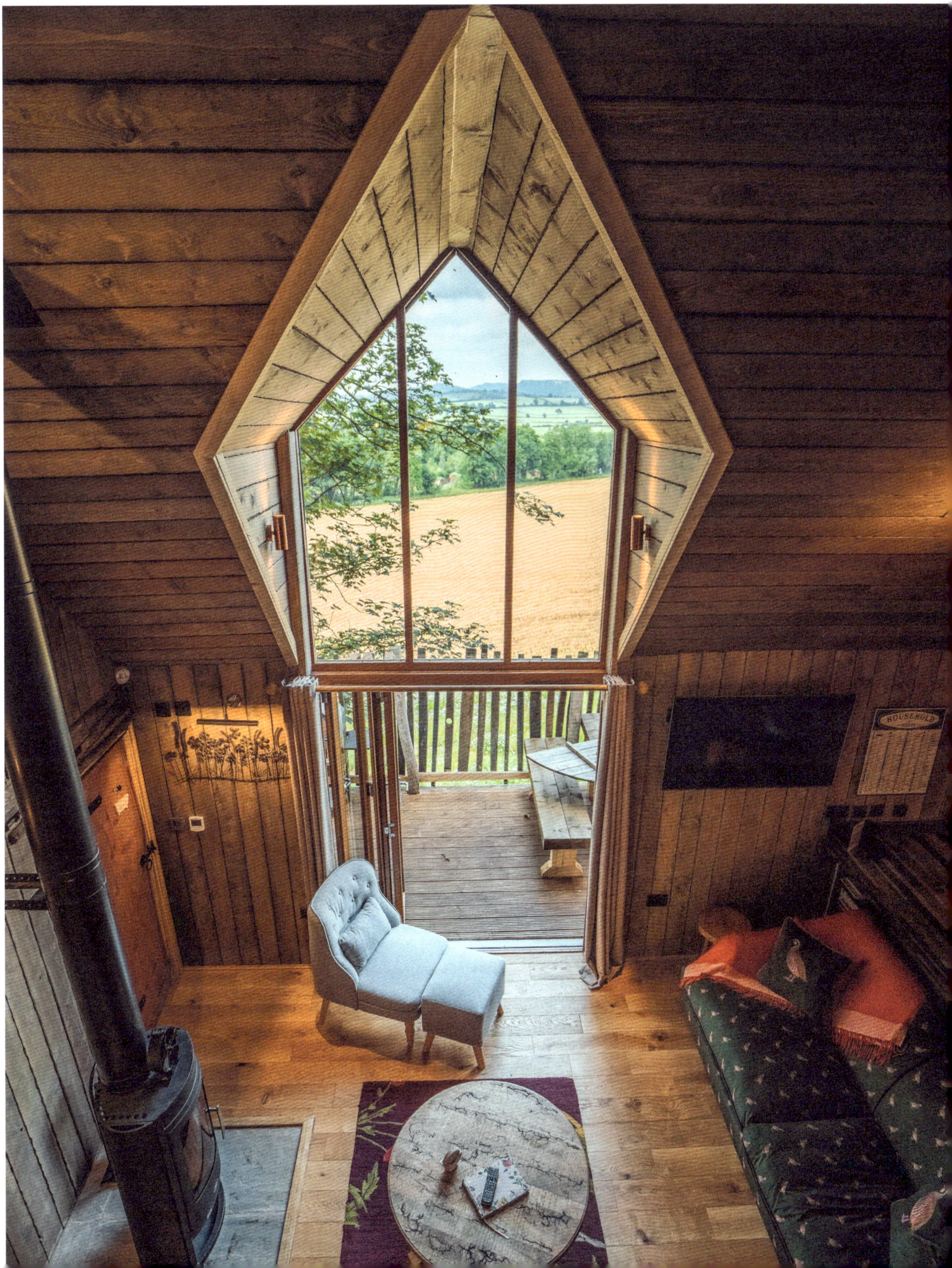

Our Wild Future

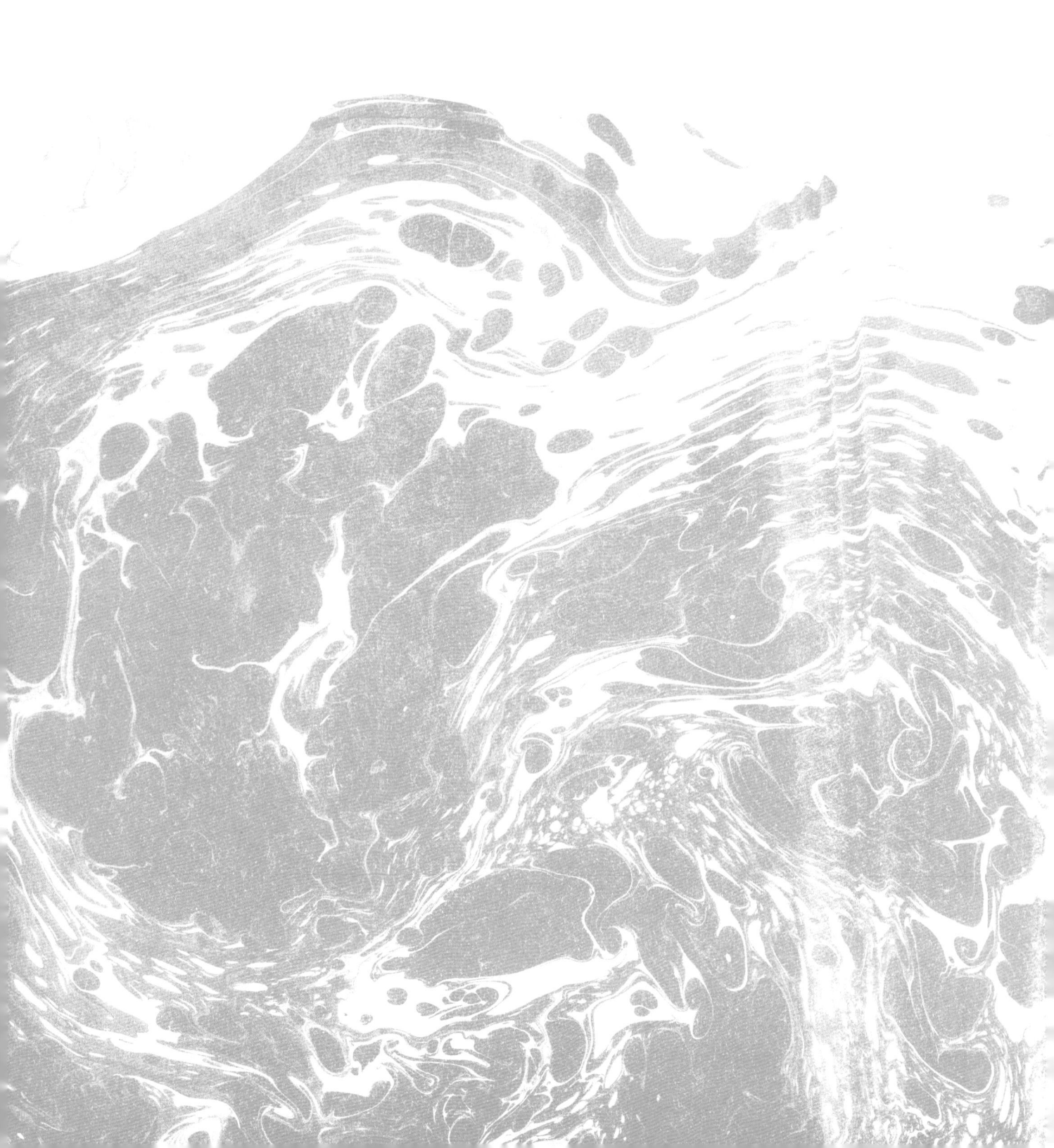

How to inspire yourself and the next generation to discover, value, and protect the natural world

— by campaigner and environmentalist Mya-Rose Craig

As someone who had a childhood bursting full of nature and wilderness, it has been painful to watch the erosion of our access to the natural world. It would be seen as cruel to keep any other animals in places that resemble the cities we have created for ourselves, away from nature and the true outdoors. While it might seem an impossible task to drag people out into the elements, away from their screens and their comforts, we can and should find the wilderness of our past, and a way to build it back into our future. We need to expand the natural community, fostering a greater sense of ownership and care. It's something I dedicate my life to, but we can all make a difference every day.

In the past 30 years we have lost over 400 million birds across Europe, a number that is only increasing. Bird watching is my particular passion, and this loss is a grim motif being repeated across the natural world. We are doing our best to dominate every inch of our countryside, even beating back wildlife in already man-made but nevertheless essential habitats like farmland. In the process, we are constantly losing more of our wildlife.

Meanwhile, the environmental movement that is fighting against issues of habitat and biodiversity loss is struggling to keep up with the times and is still frighteningly homogenous — still full of the white and middle-class who became the stereotype of the movement nearly half a century ago. It is a movement that desperately needs to engage with people outside of the usual. Environmental issues are some of the most important of this century, and environmental activism is hurting itself critically by not broadening its voice. To save our wildlife and our planet we need everyone working together, not just the traditional few. Even dragging a friend or your children outside for the weekend is a valuable contribution.

> We can and should find the wilderness of our past, and a way to build it back into our future. We need to expand the natural community, fostering a greater sense of ownership and care.

The biggest hurdle you'll have to overcome is the fact that people cannot truly care about something they know nothing about. Nature is no exception. However, as wildlife and nature decline, so do the opportunities to form a connection with them. Spending time in the outdoors and in the countryside is increasingly becoming a pastime for the privileged. Access is very difficult, and many people don't have the time, money, or energy to seek out something that is often completely alien to them. This is particularly an issue in the ethnic minority communities of the United Kingdom.

If we are to make a difference, this situation needs to change.

You will hear many times that there are some people who just aren't interested in nature, who are unable to engage with it, but I know for a fact that this is not true. My organisation, Black2Nature, runs camps for children from minority ethnic groups to give them an opportunity to spend time out in nature in a way they never have before. I have never had a child who hasn't enjoyed themselves and engaged with nature on these camps, and I suspect I never will. The key is to provide them with knowledge.

At the first camp I ran, I persuaded five teenage boys to join a group of young bird watchers. When we arrived at our beautiful destination, they looked around for a moment and took in their surroundings, then sat down and asked what they were meant to do. What they were asking was, 'How do we enjoy this place?' A young volunteer took the initiative and immediately started talking to them about the speed of a peregrine falcon as it drops through the air to the kill. However, he instinctively knew this was not enough, and so he went on to compare that speed, the speed of a small bird, with the speed of a Formula One racing car. Immediately, instantly, all five boys were mesmerised, standing up and asking a roll of questions. It was like seeing another world — my own, but through the eyes of ordinary teenage boys.

What I learnt from that first camp was that all you need to do to engage someone with nature is find out what will give them that buzz. One boy loved bird ringing and checking out the mammal traps, becoming terribly disappointed when they were all

As wildlife and nature decline, so do the opportunities to form a connection with them. Spending time in the outdoors and in the countryside is increasingly becoming a pastime for the privileged.

empty except for some shrew poo. Another was interested in art and drew a swan wing from a real wing that an artist volunteer had brought with him. A third got into pond dipping and found a newt. A fourth fell for mothing, spending ages holding a large hawkmoth and looking at it in the darkness with just the light from his phone. Each of their faces lit up, with the brightness of the natural world reflecting in it.

None of these boys went on to become bona fide naturalists, but that wasn't the aim of the weekend away, and nor should it be if you take your kids or friends out into the wild. They later told me that they noticed sparrows when they walked to school and birdsong when they played football in the park. They were finally seeing nature rather than muting it out. They told me that they suddenly understood why so many people cared enough about nature to fight for its future. That was from only one day.

Our planet and our nature have been slowly dying for decades now due to humanity's own self-destructive behaviour, and for many people it has been endlessly frustrating to watch this, knowing that it was entirely preventable. This is the feeling that is being harnessed by the youth movement of today as they march in the streets for their future, but this is also a feeling that cannot exist without having that ever-important engagement to nature in the first place.

The youth movement has been created by both urgency and desperation, but it is also the potential key to unlocking a green planet. Unlike the generations before us, it feels like there is little other option than to fight for that idea, and to be absolutely unflinching in doing so. I see a strength and a passion in young environmentalists all over the world that I, and others, should find both emboldening in terms of our own campaigns and hopeful when discussing a potentially wilder future. What we need now is for everyone, not just the young or the middle classes, to begin exploring and enjoying nature. So next time you go outdoors, see who you can take with you. Show them what's out there, find the part of it that calls to them, and make them one more voice speaking out for the preservation of our precious, fragile wild.

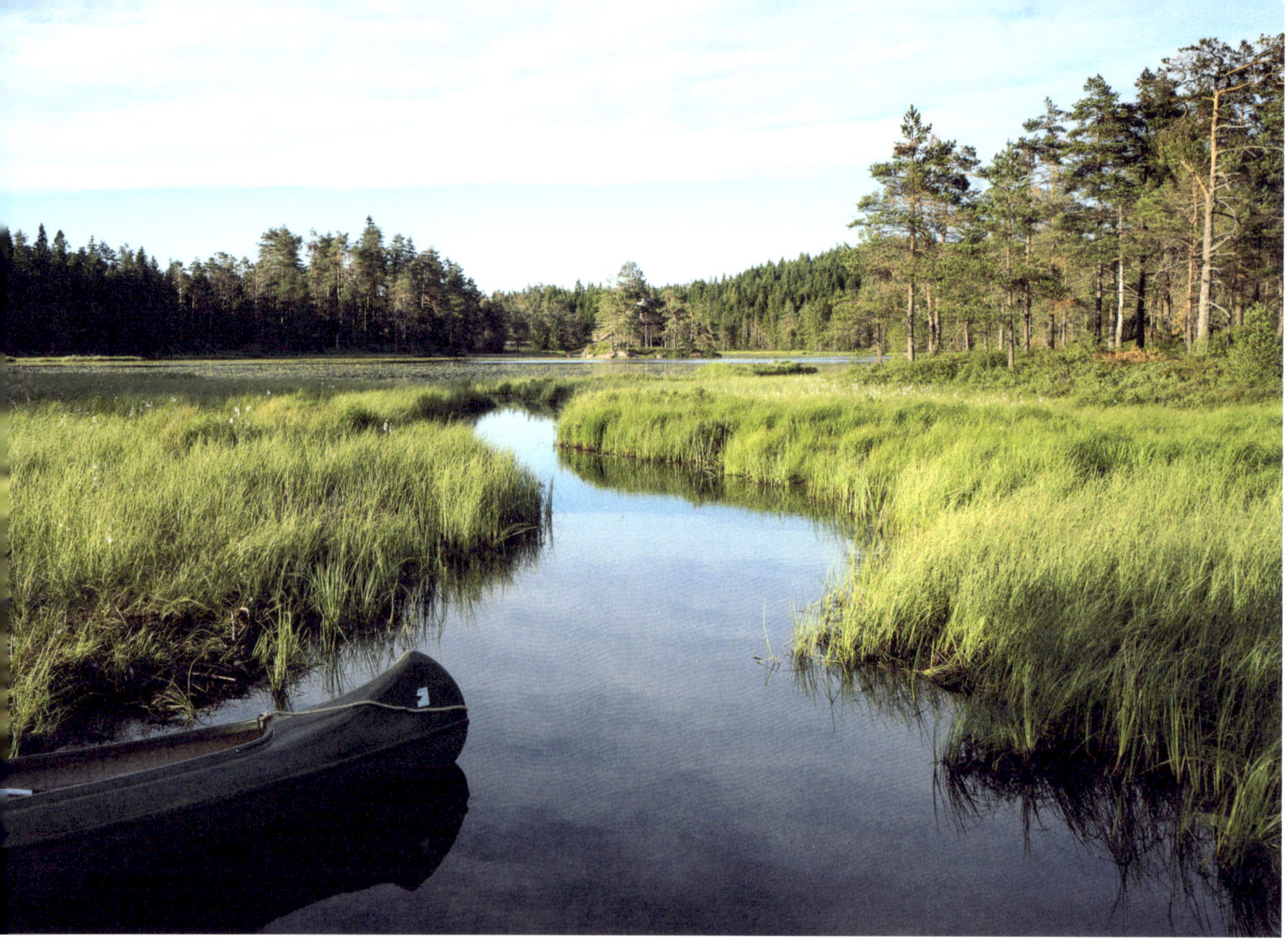

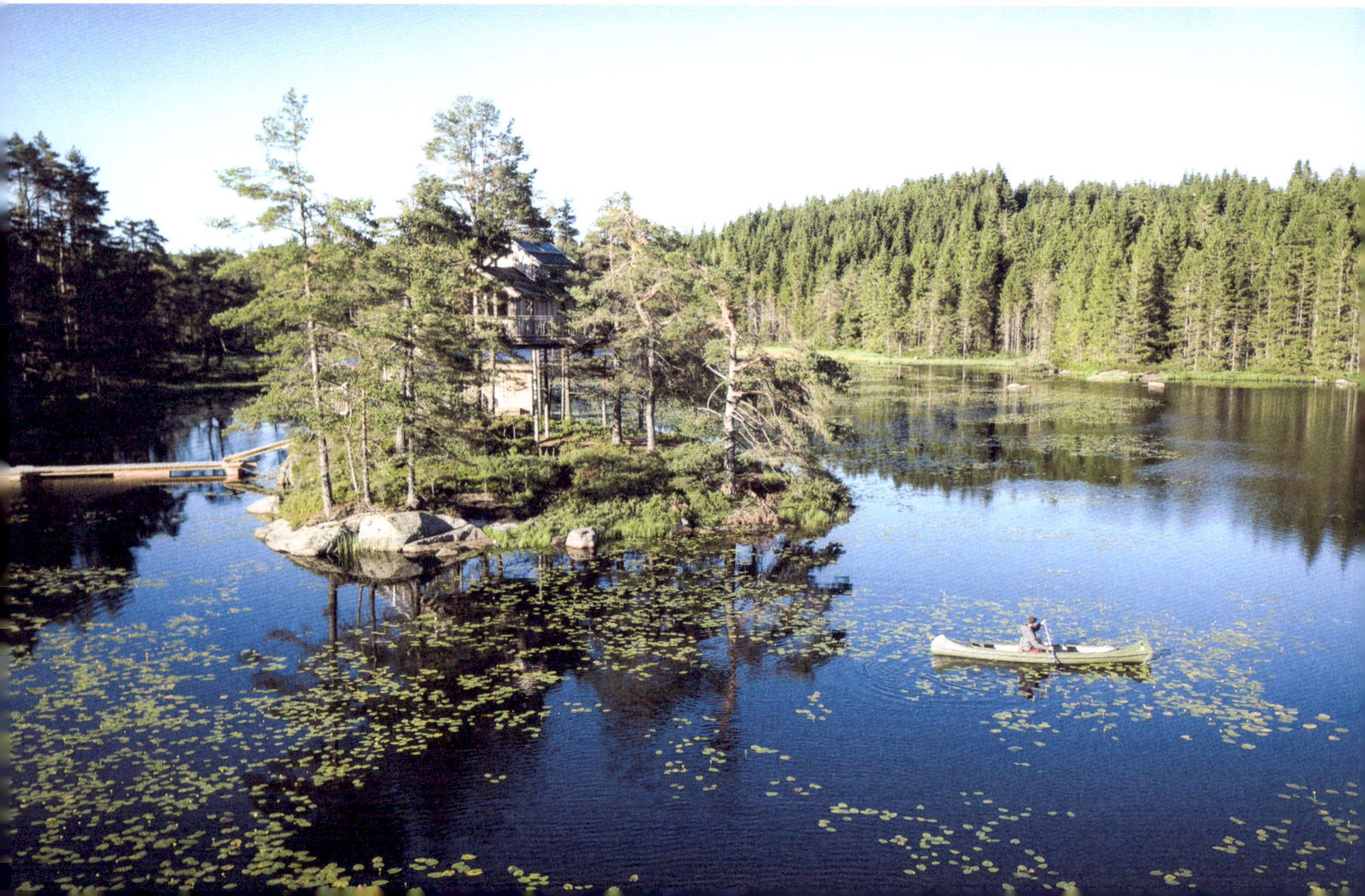

Up a Tree, on an Island

Embracing life's simpler things in a treetop cabin deep in the forests of Norway

THE ISLAND CABIN
AGDER,
NORWAY

Wedged between three old pine trees on an island in the wilds of Norway, this stunning log cabin is the stuff of children's adventure stories. After initially approaching on foot through the surrounding woodland, guests make their way to the island by crossing a floating bridge or by rowboat; in winter, though, the lake freezes and it's possible to simply walk over. Settling in is akin to freeing the spirit. For one thing, there are the views from the deck, all big skies and treetops for miles. Then comes the simplicity of day-to-day living. Visitors have some 200 hectares (500 acres) in which to splash about in the lake, go foraging for wild berries and mushrooms, or to fish for trout to cook up over hot coals in the firepit. A creation of two neighbours named Knut Eivind Birkeland and Knut Andre Fiddan, the Island Cabin sits in the middle of private farmland and is totally off-grid. It's the ultimate spot for getting back to the basics of a hunter-gatherer lifestyle in natural surroundings that haven't changed for centuries.

THE ISLAND CABIN

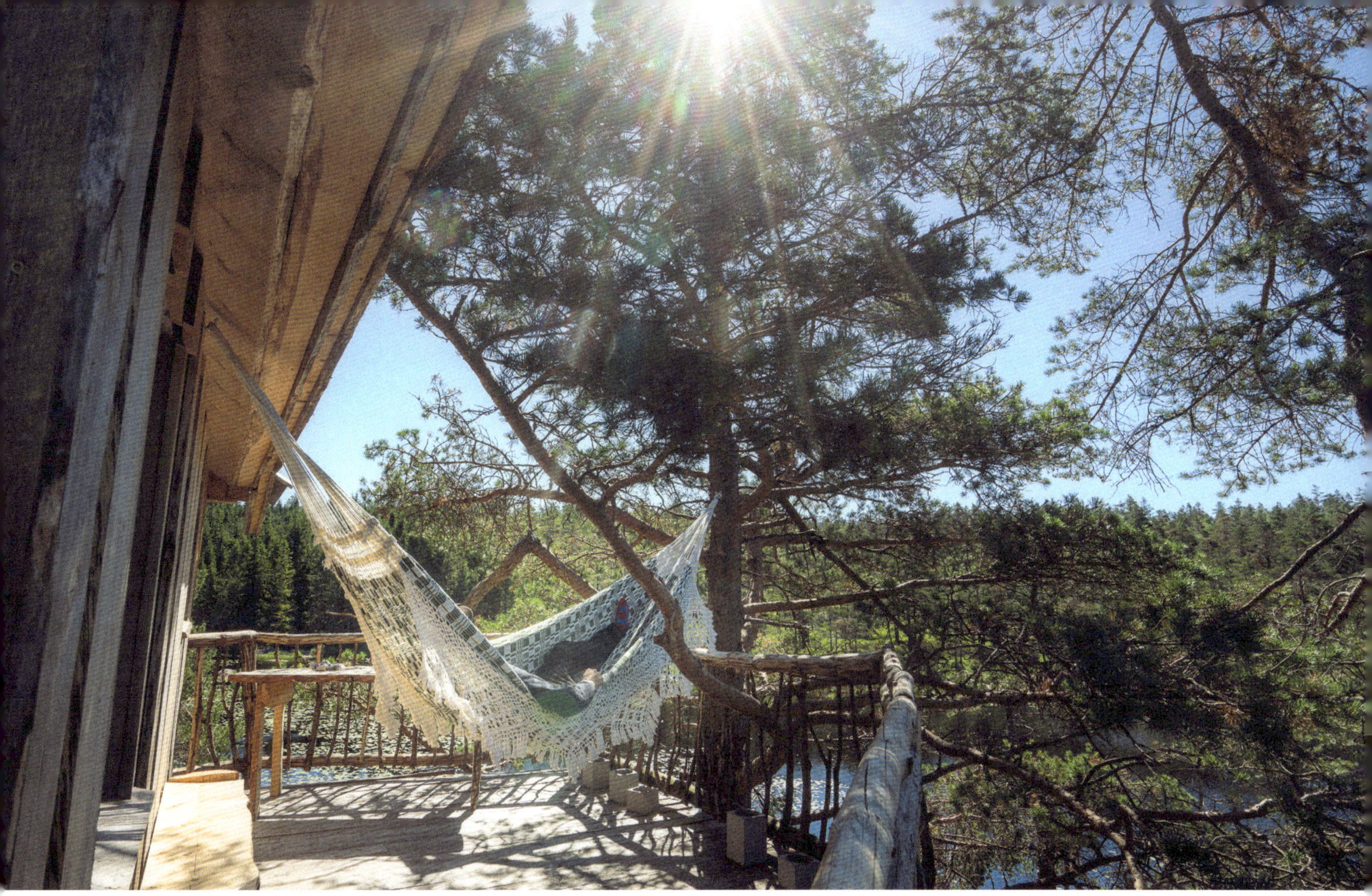
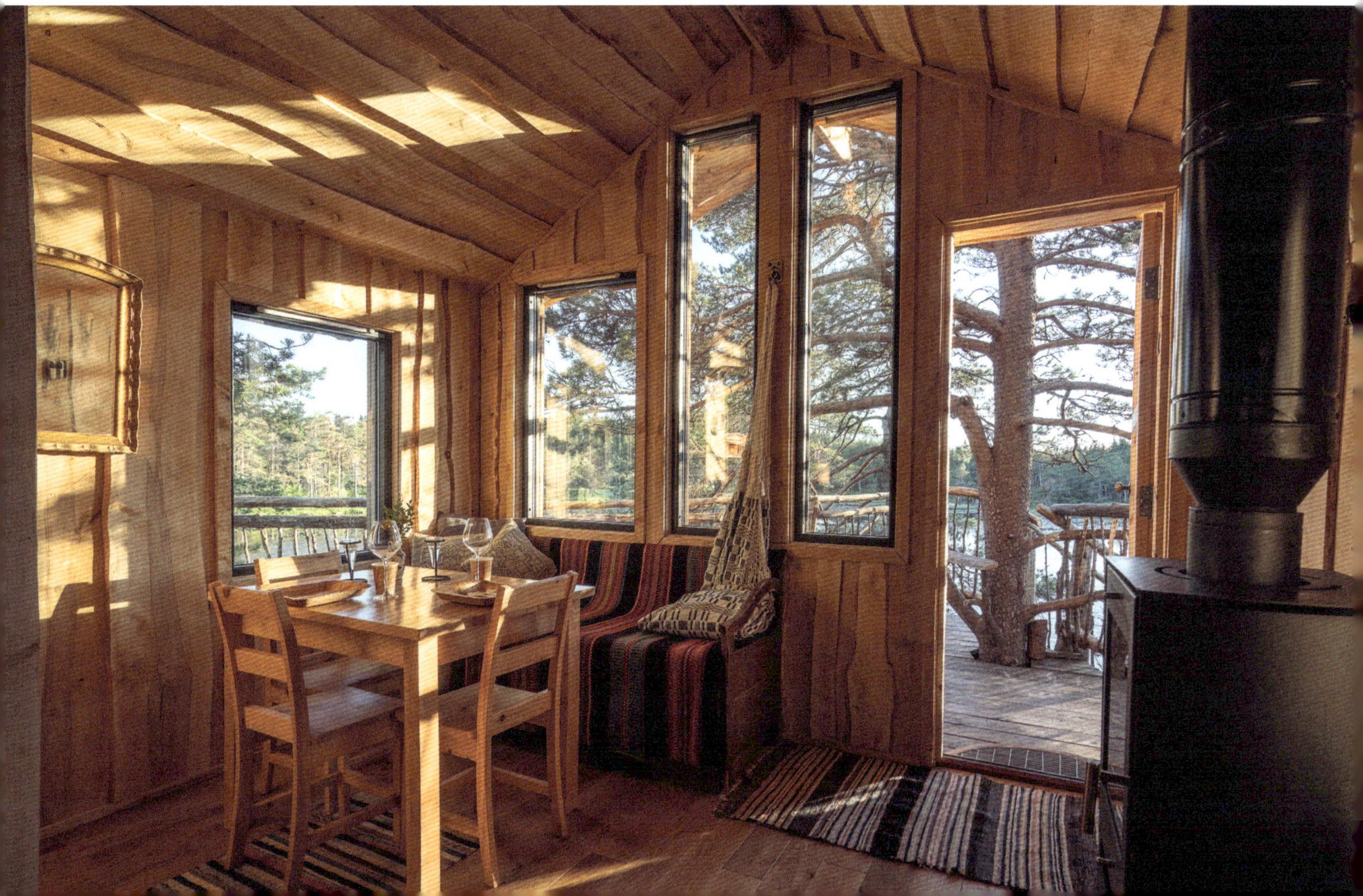

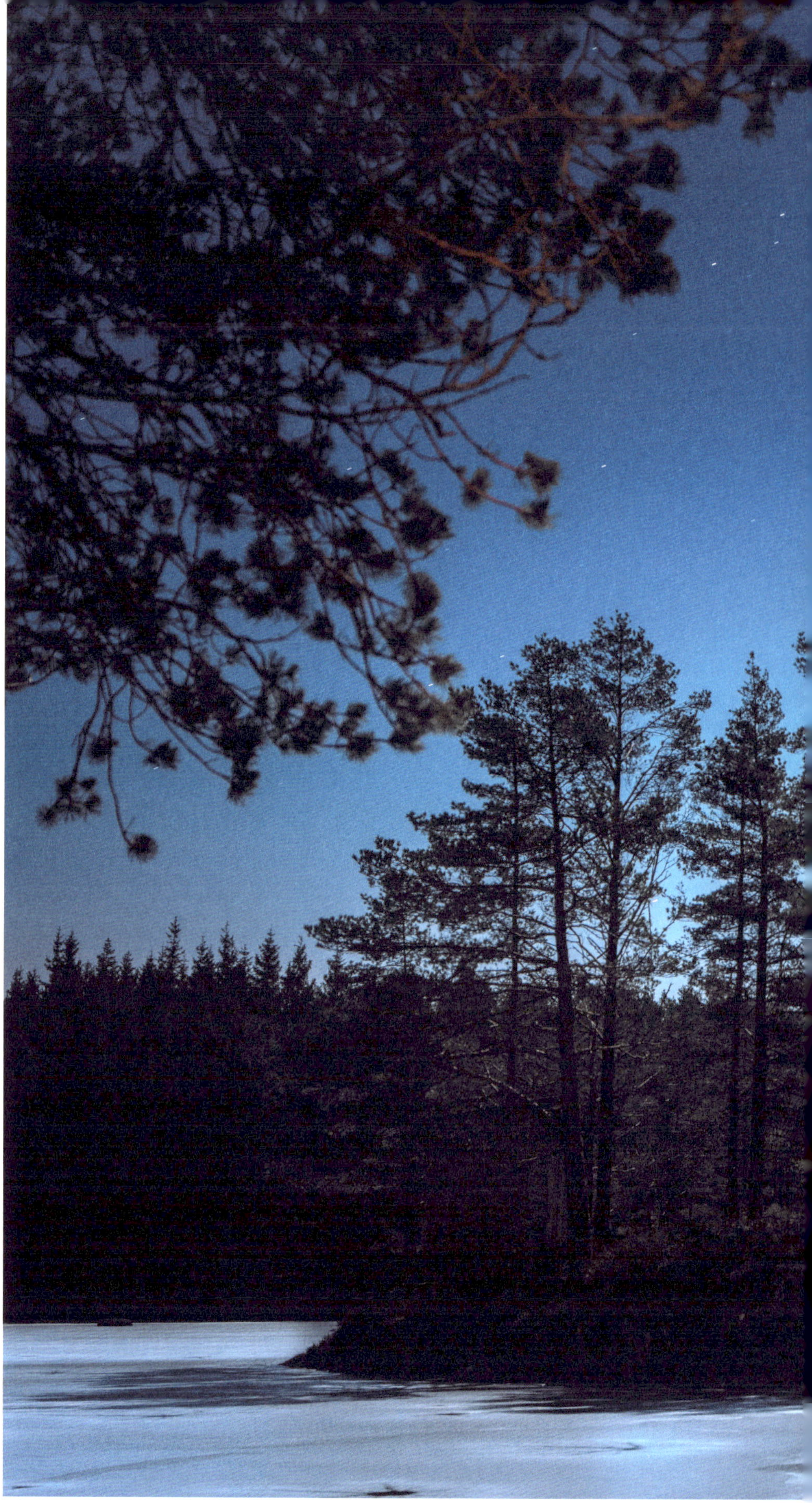

THE ISLAND CABIN

A Scandinavian Seventh Heaven

This burned-wood treehouse with wraparound views lies deep in a Swedish forest

7TH ROOM
NORRBOTTEN,
SWEDEN

Suspended 10 metres (33 feet) above the ground, with a tree growing right through its centre, the 7th Room offers one of several unique forest stays at Sweden's Treehotel, not far from the Arctic Circle. All of the cabins sit high up amongst the branches of the pines that grow in the area. Those gazing upwards as they approach the 7th Room will notice that its underside features a life-size photo of the treetops as they looked before the treehouse was built. From there, an external staircase leads to a generous living space, at the heart of which an immense outdoor hammock lies primed for nighttime stargazing — during daylight hours, guests find lying on their bellies to stare down at the forest floor equally mesmerising. With room for six, this treehouse is larger than those that may typically be called to mind. Indoors, the colour spectrum is neutral and, thanks to a wood-burning stove and plenty of fleecy throws, the rooms are cosy and warm. Huge north-facing windows and bedroom skylights offer the perfect opportunity to watch the play of the northern lights.

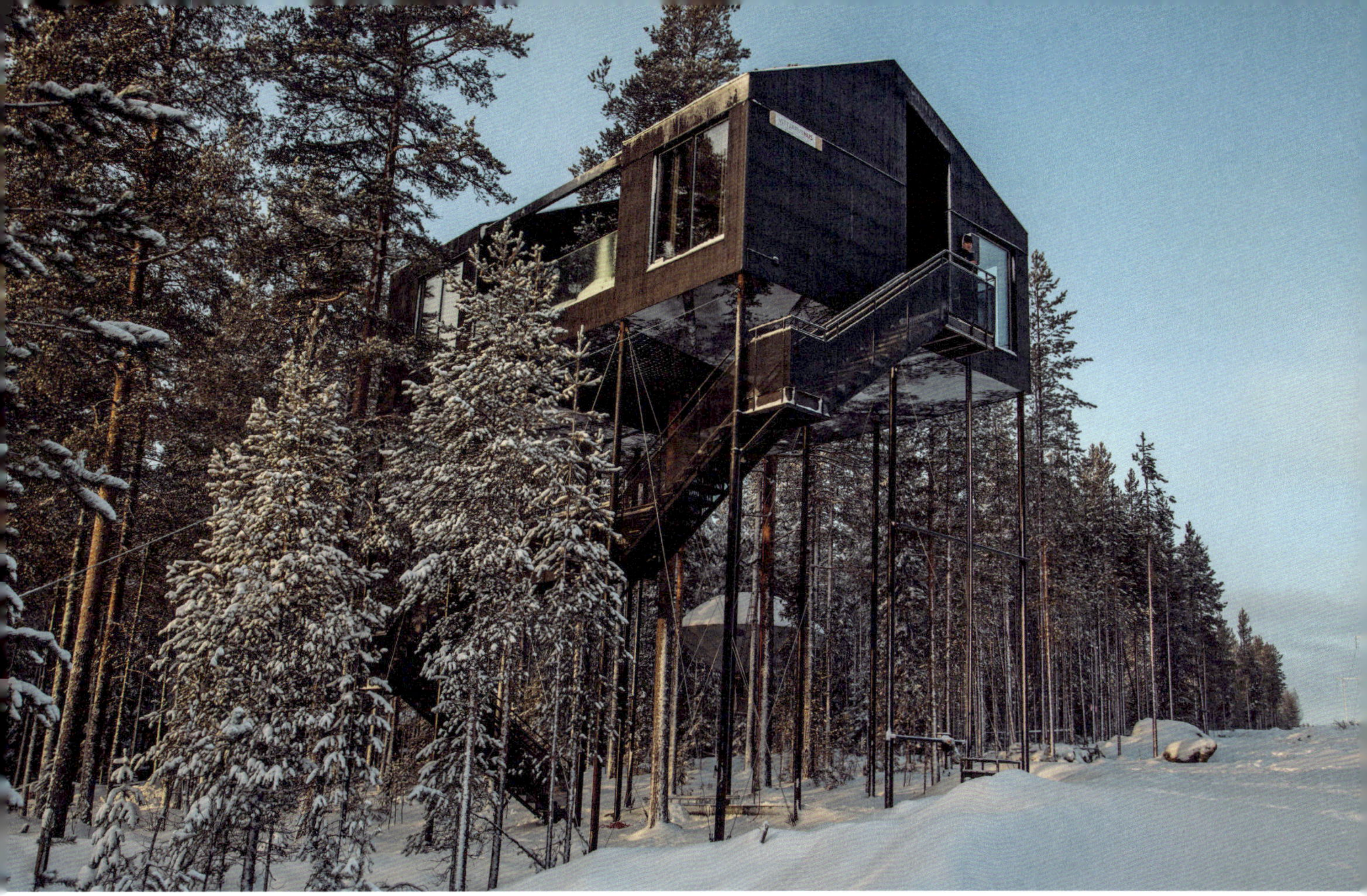

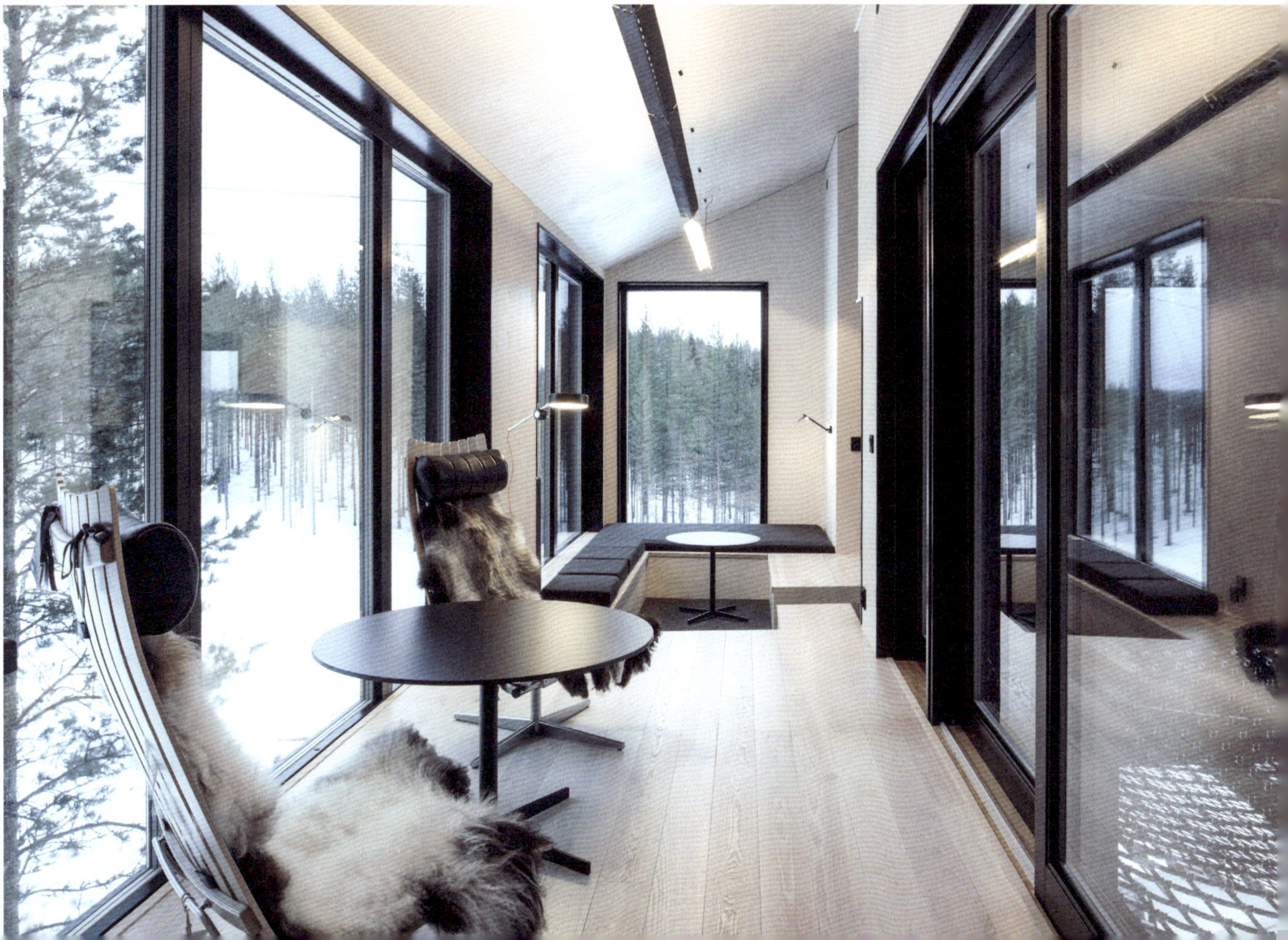

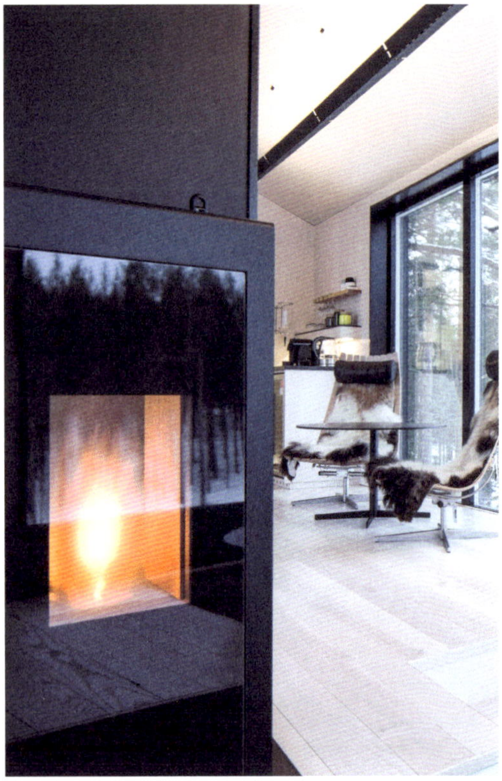

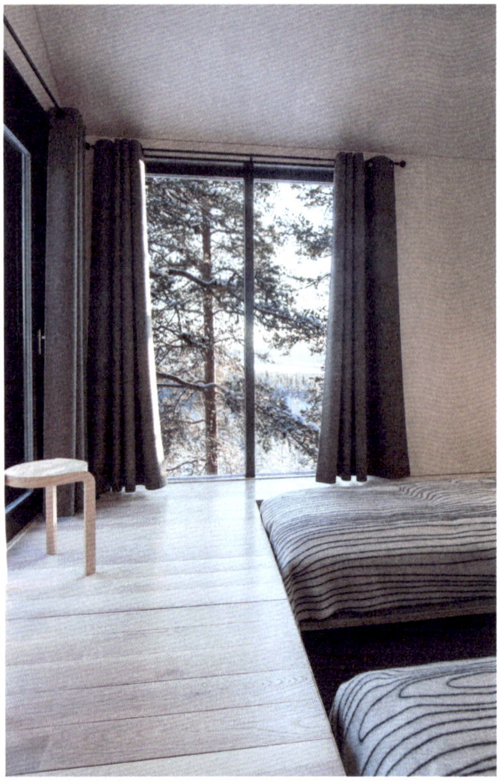

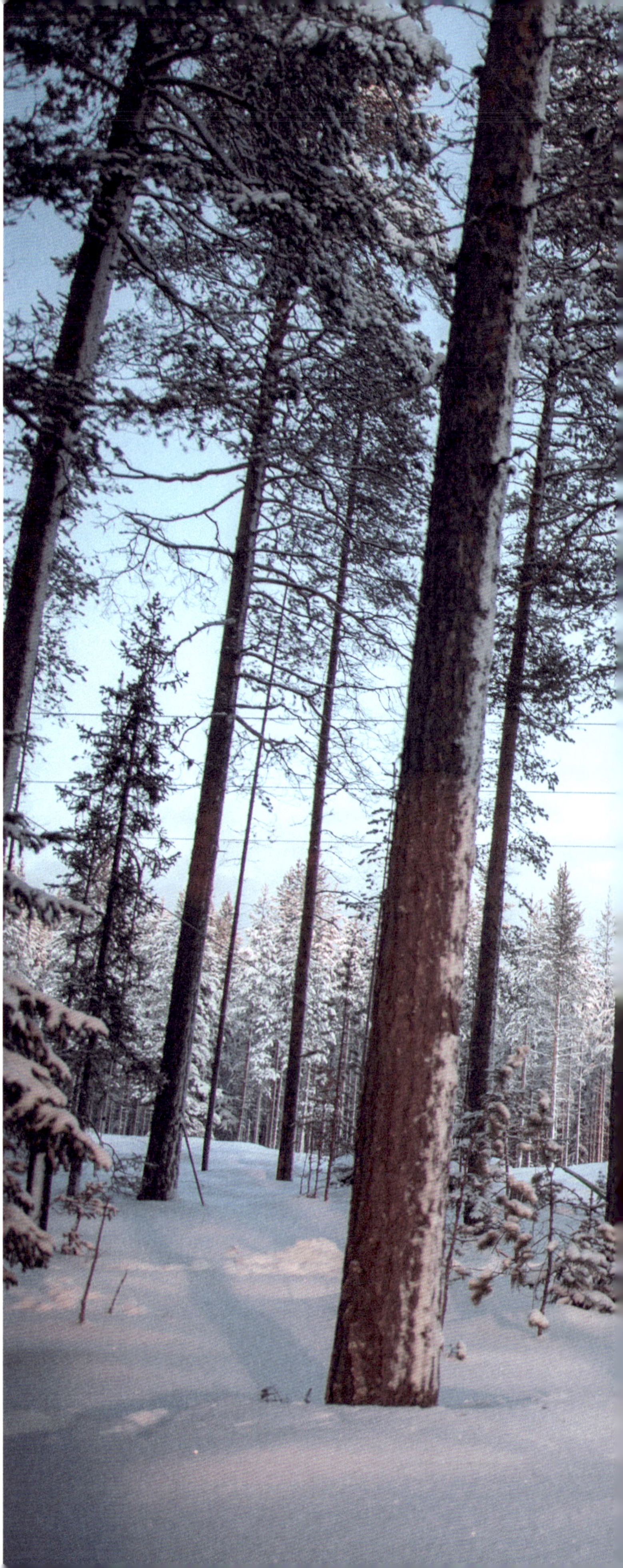

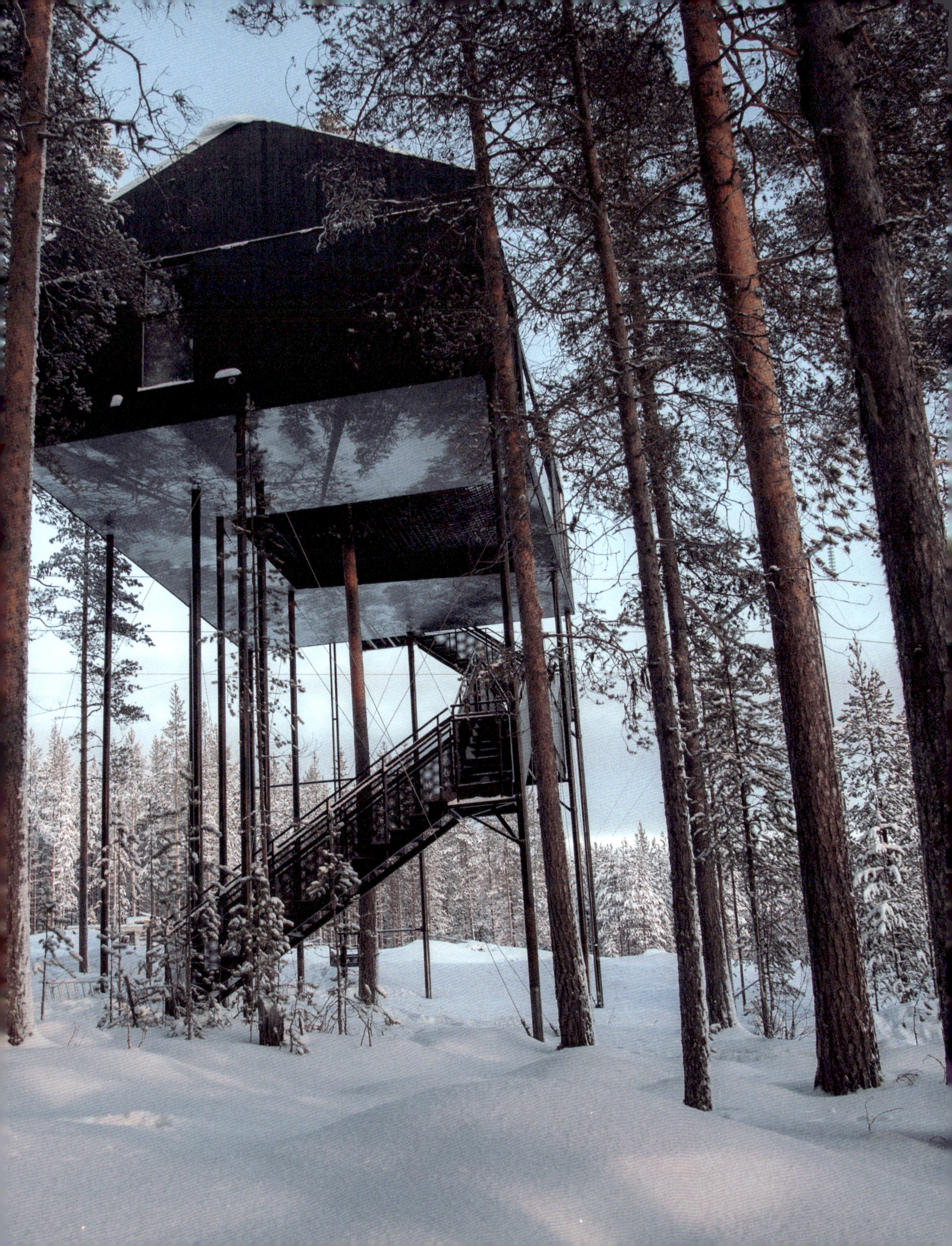

Luxury in the Shape of an Igloo

A lakeside geodome in Finnish Lapland promises cosy Arctic sky-gazing through its transparent walls

AURORA DOME
LAPLAND,
FINLAND

Pitched between the shores of Lake Toras-Sieppi and the boreal forest of Finnish Lapland, the Aurora Dome is possibly one of the most romantic places to stay at any time of year. Holed up beside a wood-burning stove, guests keep cosy while gazing through a huge transparent wall with wide-open views of the northern sky. Those staying in early September are invited to make pancakes before heading out in search of the magical aurora borealis, and from June through to August, visitors can go wild river rafting under the midnight sun. Run by a family that has been operating in this wild and ancient landscape for almost half a century, the dome hugs the ground at the edge of a reindeer and husky farm, just a stone's throw from Pallas-Yllästunturi National Park. Guests are more than welcome to feed the reindeer and huskies before indulging in traditional, locally produced organic food at the café or partaking in one of Finland's most celebrated leisure activities — the sauna.

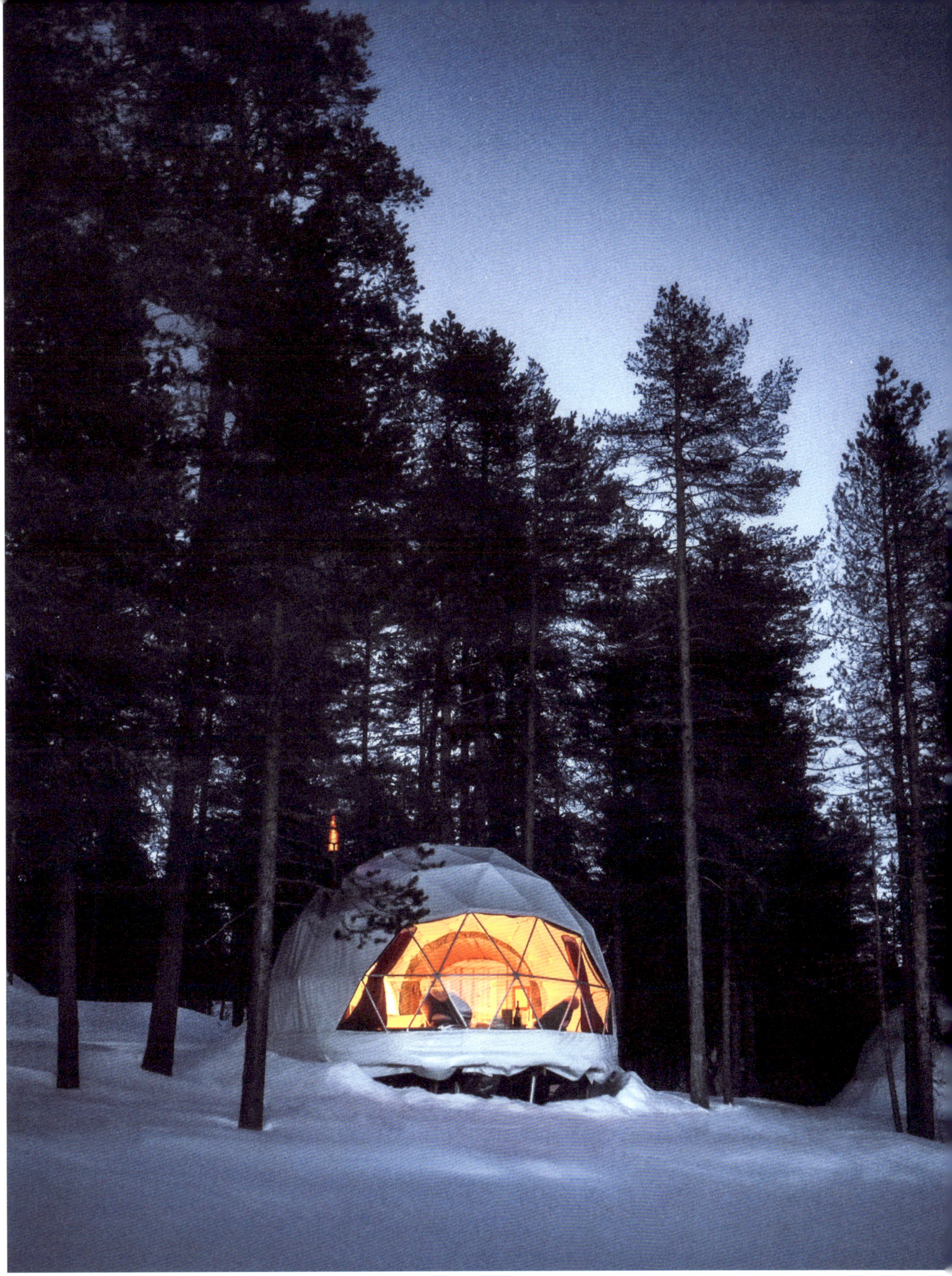

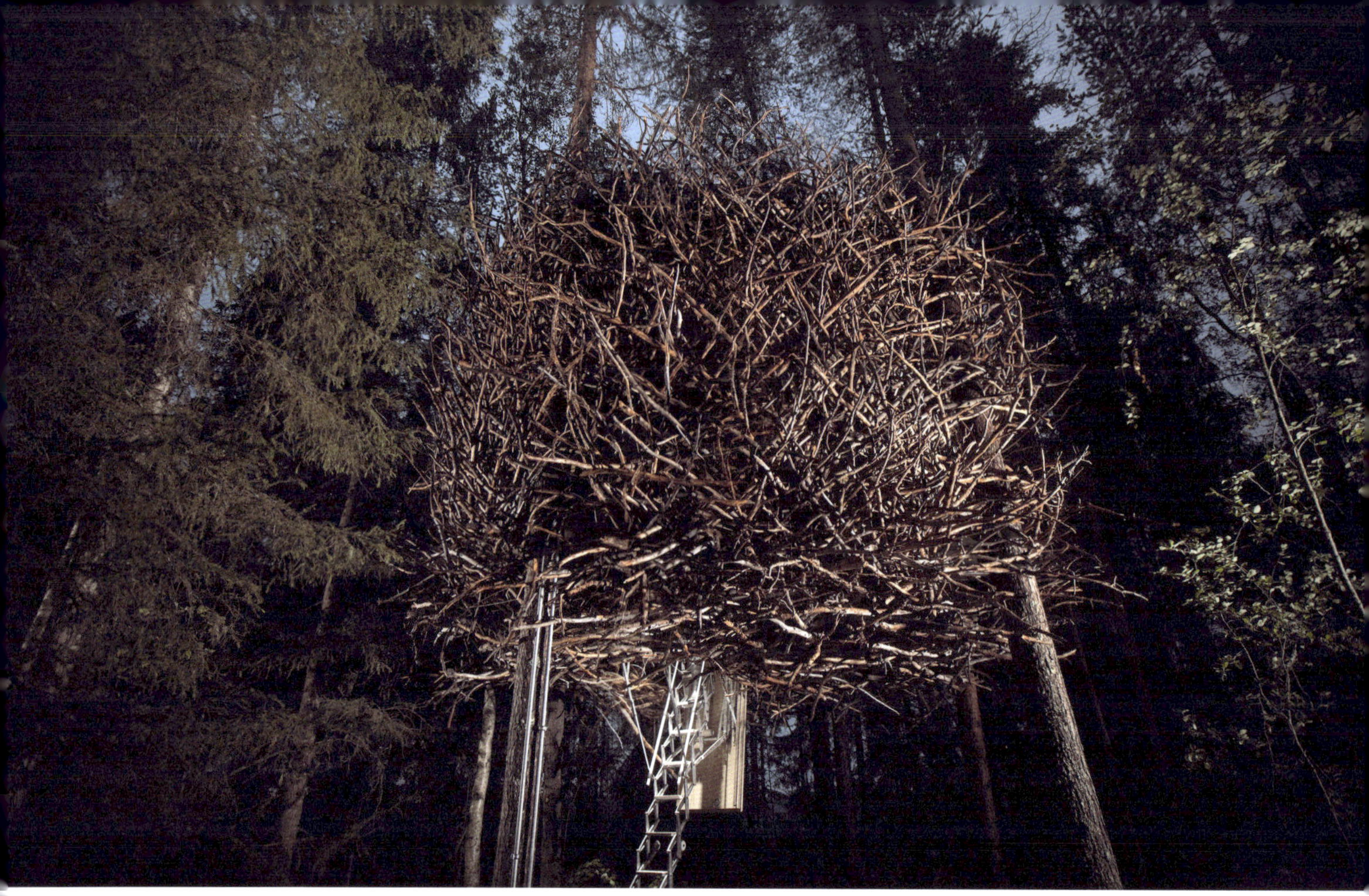

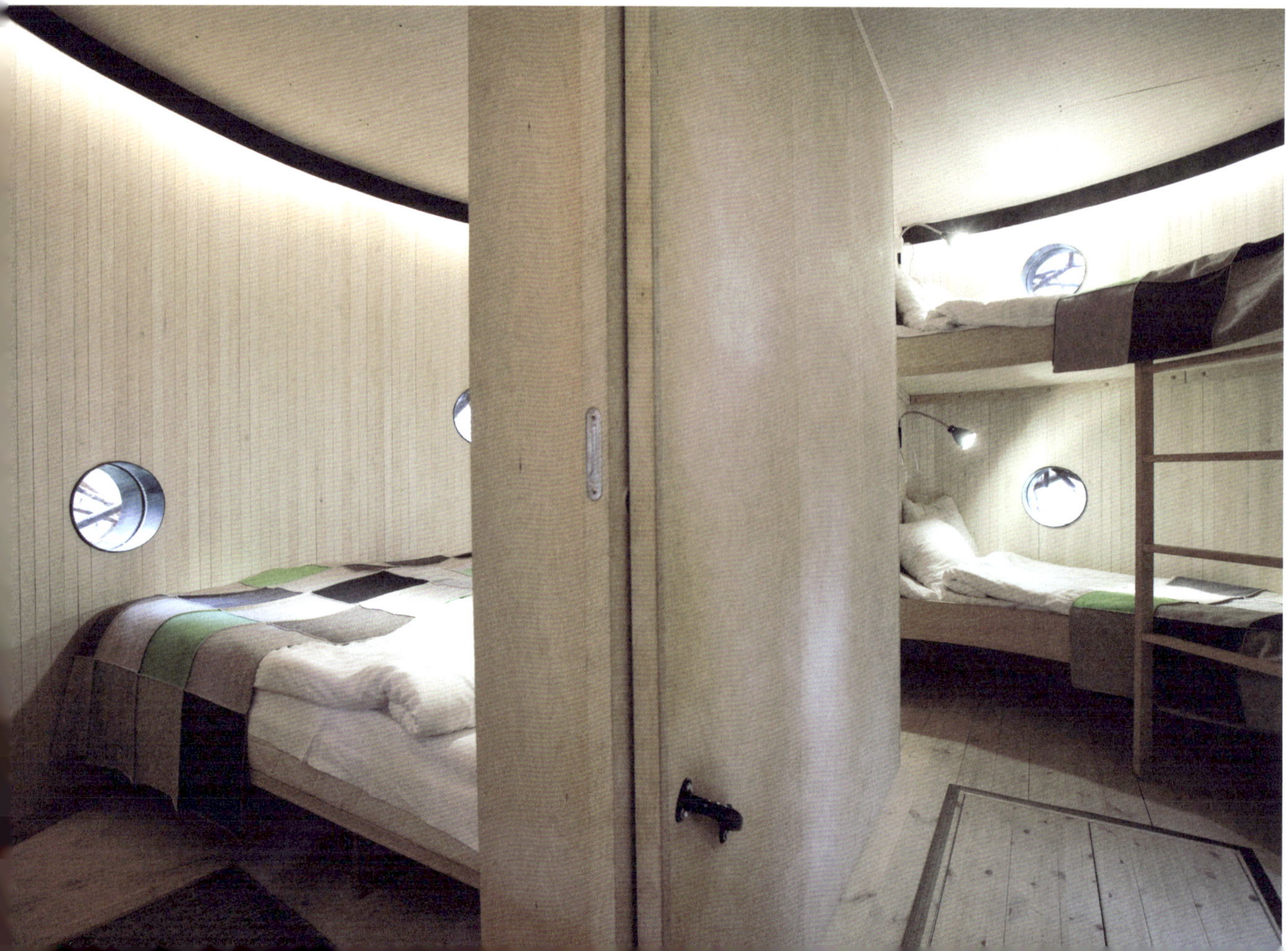

Possibly the Biggest Bird's Nest in the World

A treetop den inspired by the twiggy nesting creations of giant sea eagles

THE BIRD'S NEST
NORRBOTTEN,
SWEDEN

Amongst all the cabins at this glamping site in the forested wilds of northern Sweden, this is the one that merges most successfully with the surrounding landscape. Retract the electronic stepladder and it's not recognisable as a cabin at all, but rather as a gigantic bird's nest amongst the branches of the trees. Inspired by a nest the owner spotted on a fishing trip, the Bird's Nest offers the ultimate space for feeling totally at one with nature. From inside its compact, curvaceous interior, strategically placed windows allow for bird's-eye peeking across the forested world outside.

Time to Reflect in Sweden's Boreal Forest

Now you see it, now you don't: a 'mirrorcube' treehouse that melts into the landscape

MIRRORCUBE
NORRBOTTEN, SWEDEN

Guests staying at Sweden's Treehotel zigzag their way up a gently inclined walkway to arrive at the perfect forest hideaway: a treehouse wrapped in reflective glass. Inside, six windows offer stunning views across the boreal landscape — but, to be sure, no one can see in. Measuring just 64 cubic metres (2,260 cubic feet), the Mirrorcube is perfect for two, cocooning them in rooms lined with birchwood ply and complemented with underfloor heating and stylish woollen rugs. At night, visitors can climb a ladder to a rooftop terrace to gaze up at the starry skies. The cabin is one of several treehouses in a pine forest owned by Kent Lindvall and Britta Jonsson-Lindvall, and the couple also operates a homely 1950s-style hostel just a 10-minute walk away, where guests dine and have breakfast during their stays. The woodland location is a great spot for solitary treks or riding husky-drawn sleds through the snow, and if your mood is more reflective, it also presents ample opportunity to simply stare out of the window at the tranquillity of the Arctic landscape beyond.

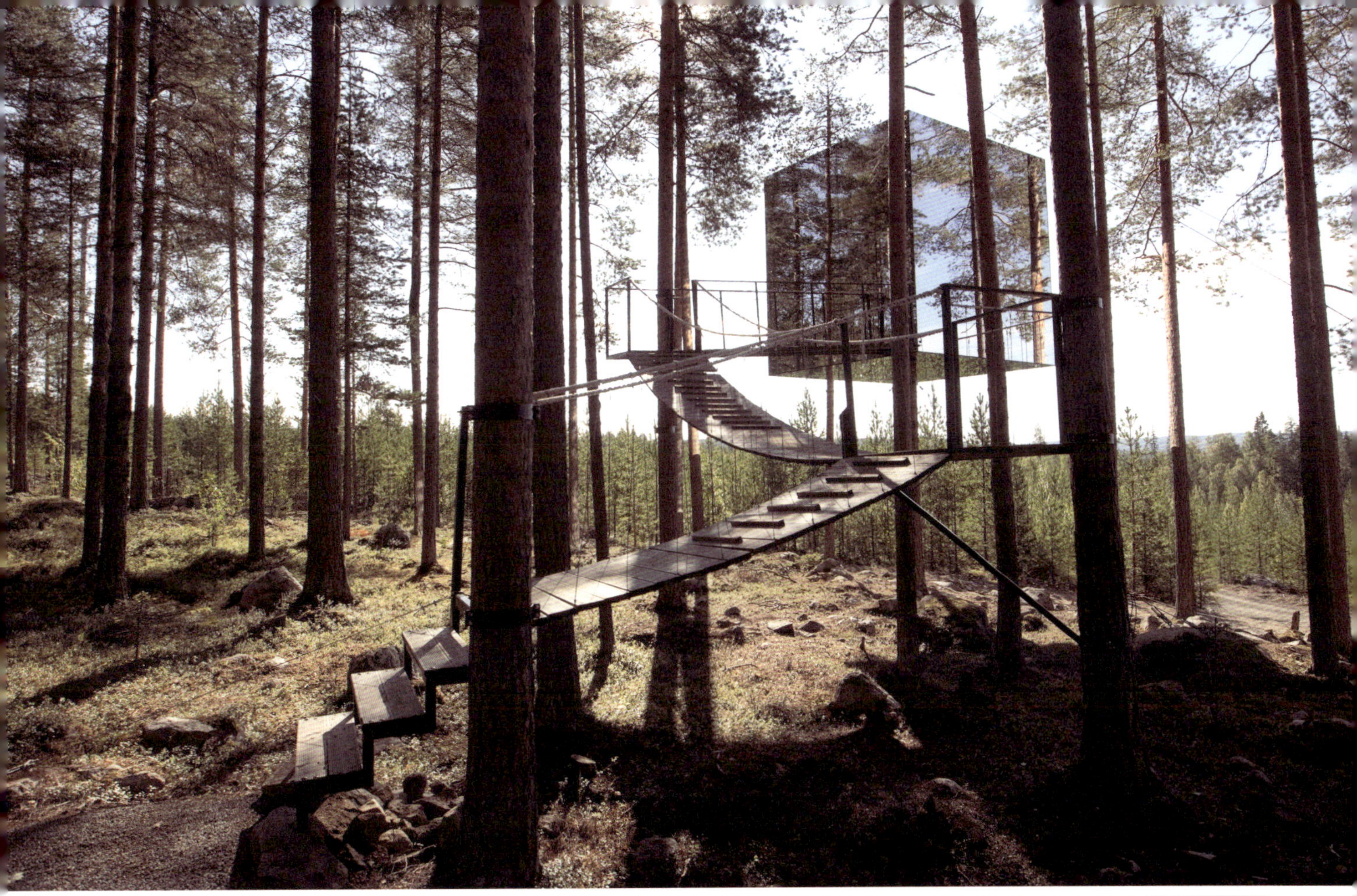

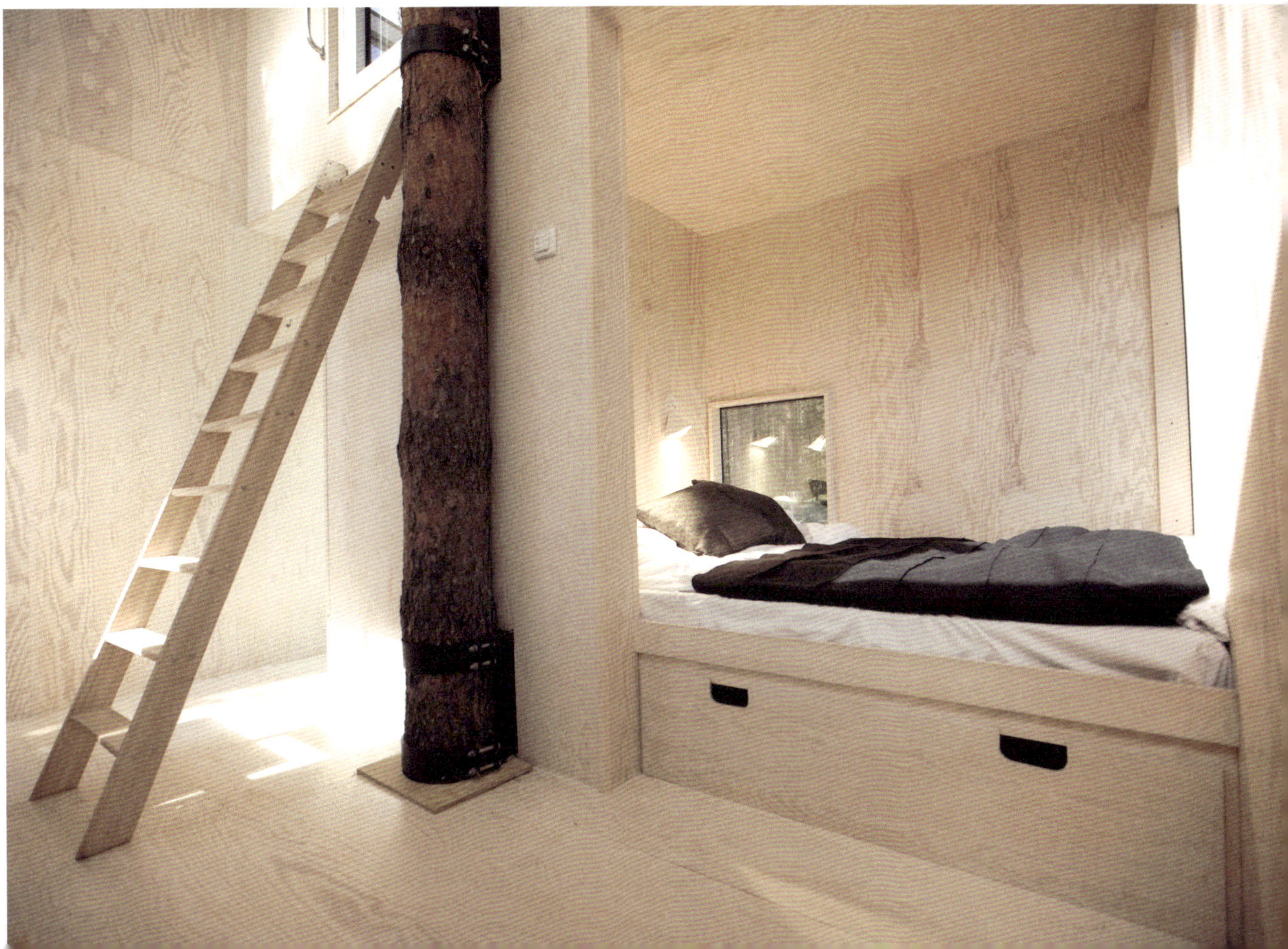

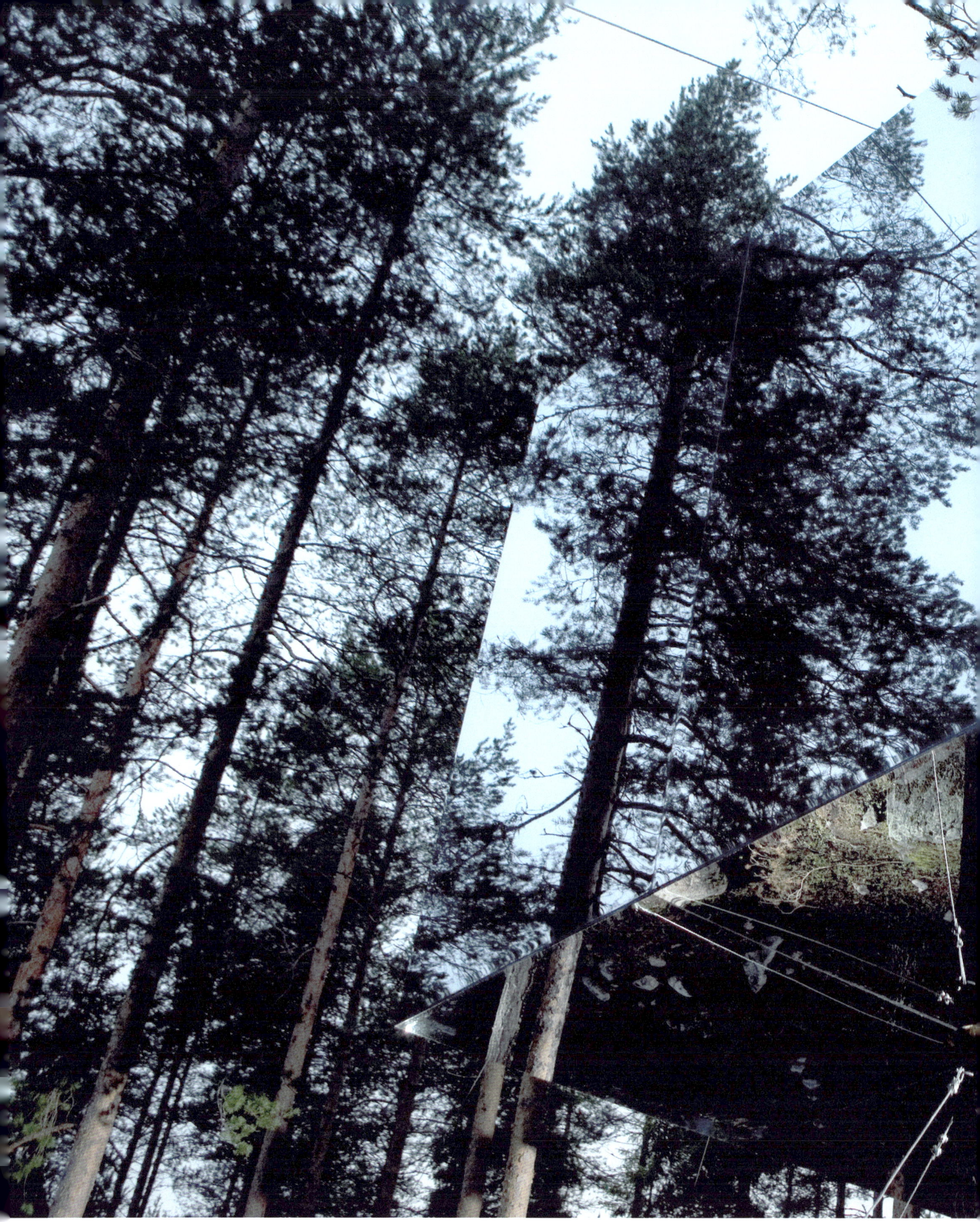

MIRRORCUBE

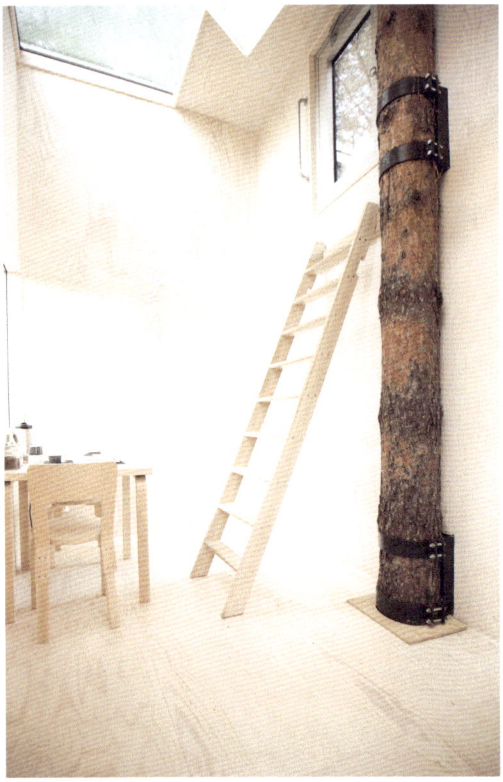

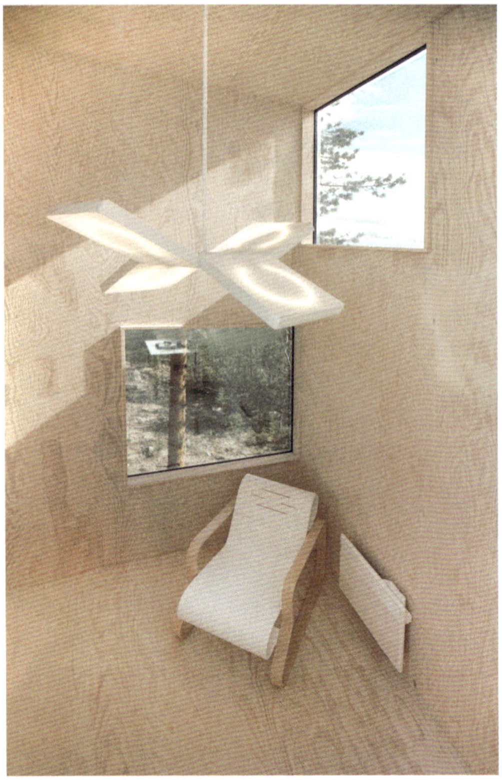

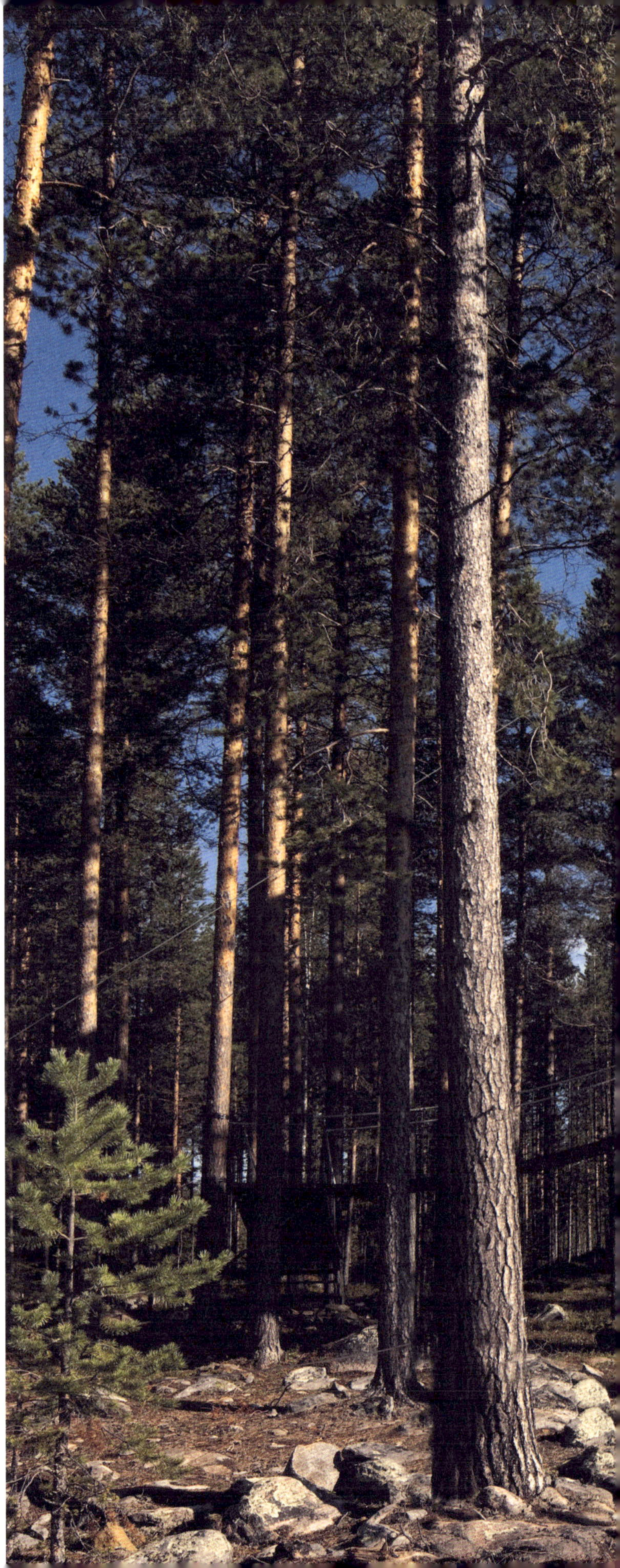

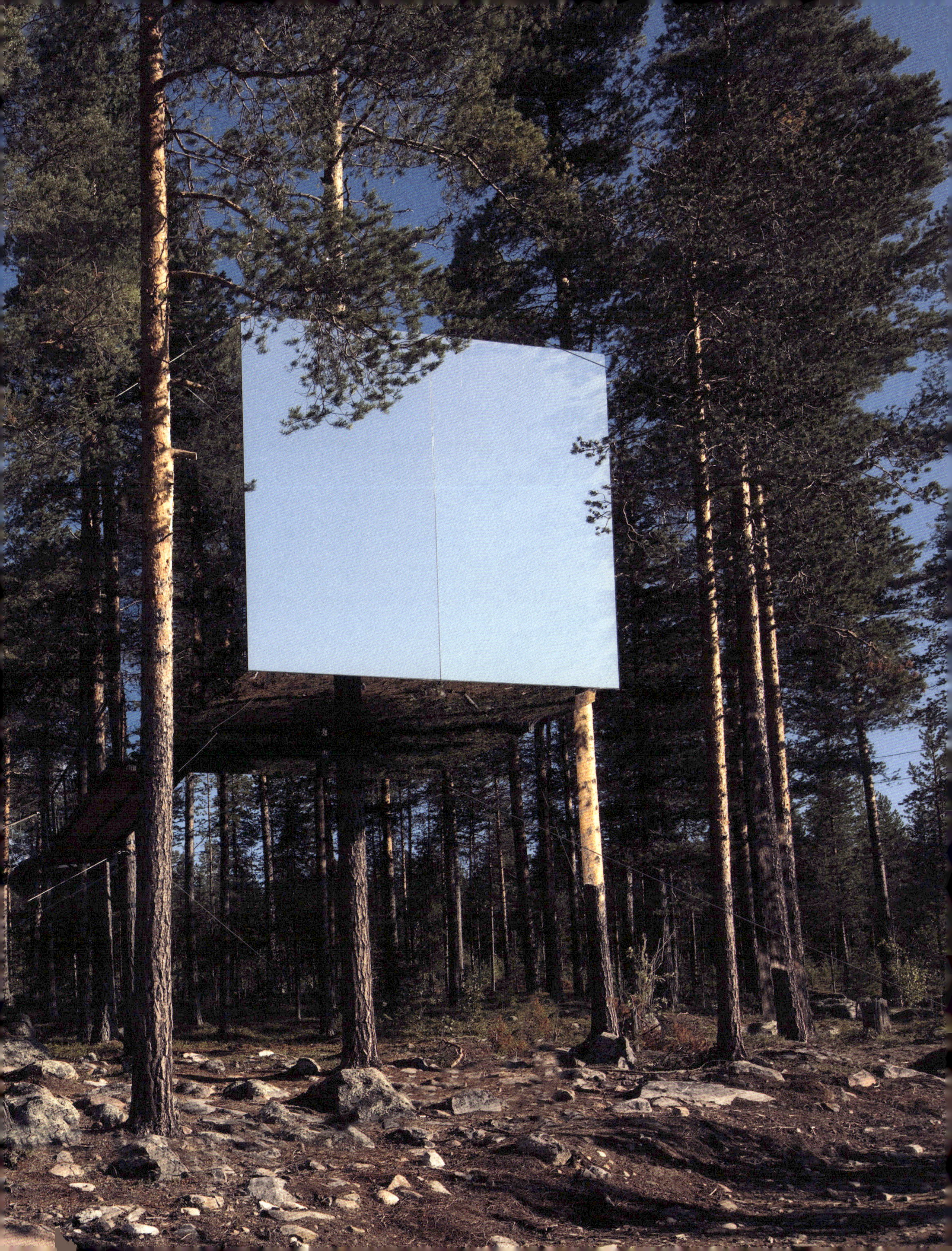

A Dazzling Night Out in the Arctic

Staring into vast starry skies from the comfort of a Ski Doo-drawn sleeping pod

ESKO'S CABIN
LAPLAND,
FINLAND

Guests staying at Esko's Cabin are towed by snowmobile to the middle of a frozen lake, where they spend the night in cosy comfort with nothing but each other and the dark sky for company. It's a truly unique experience, made all the more magical by the chance to see the northern lights dance across the sky above Inari, a cluster of islands where the water freezes over in winter. Added extras include soaking in a wood-fired hot tub, taking a husky sleigh ride across the frozen landscape, dabbling in a little ice fishing, and partaking in a feast of fish and reindeer around a cosy open fire.

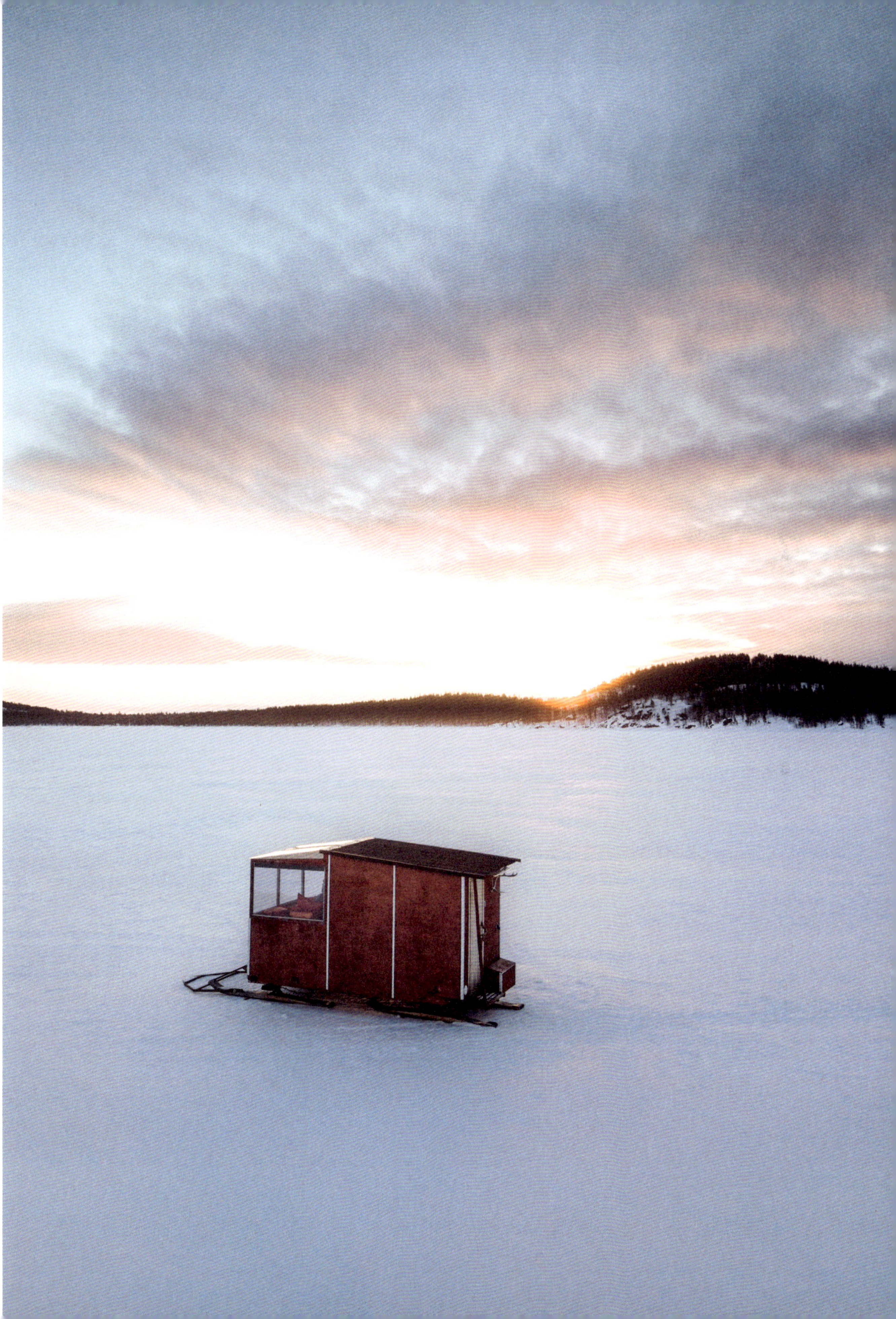

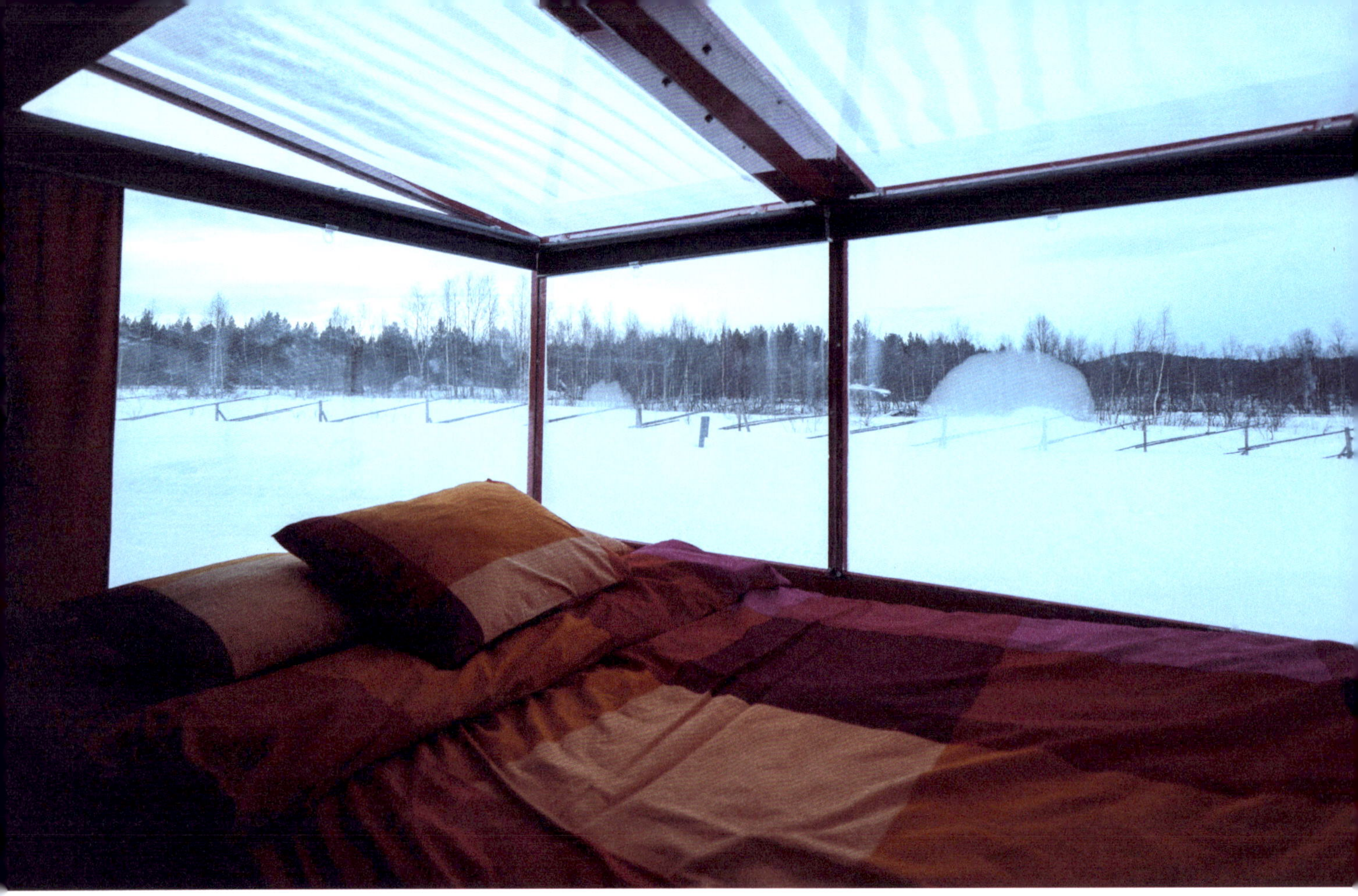

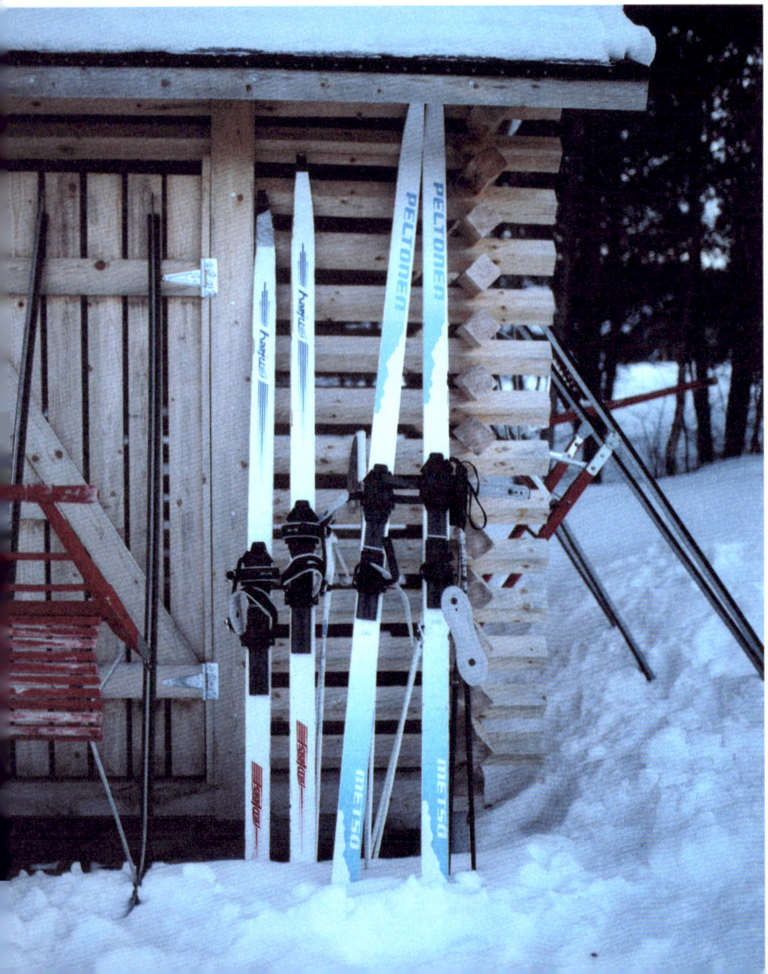
PELTONEN
PELTONEN
METSO
METSO

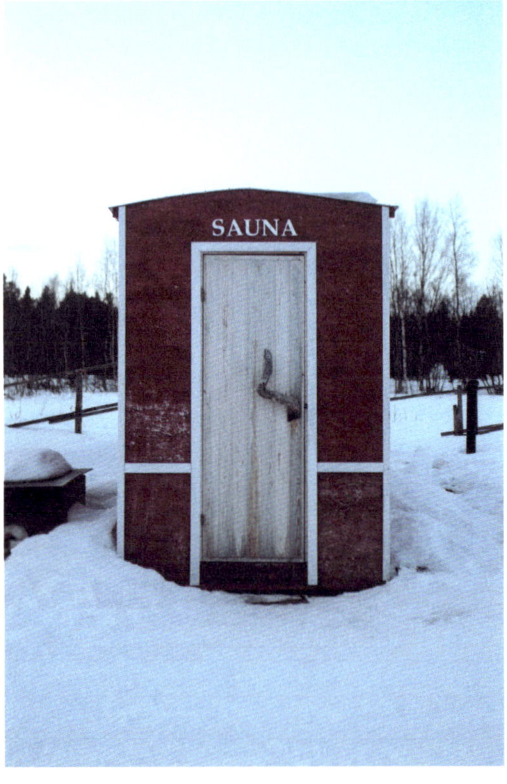
SAUNA

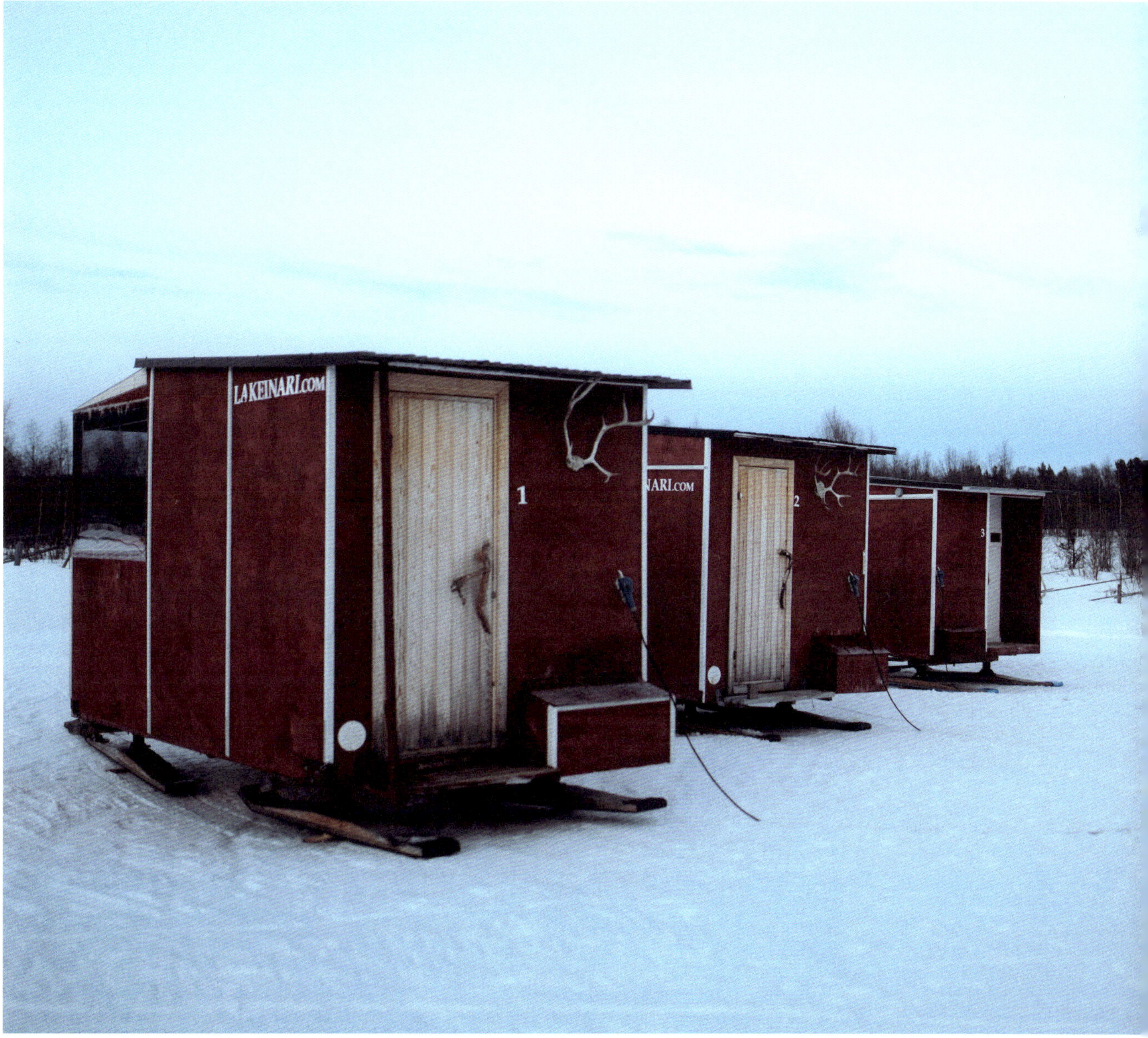
LAKEINARI.COM
1
2
3

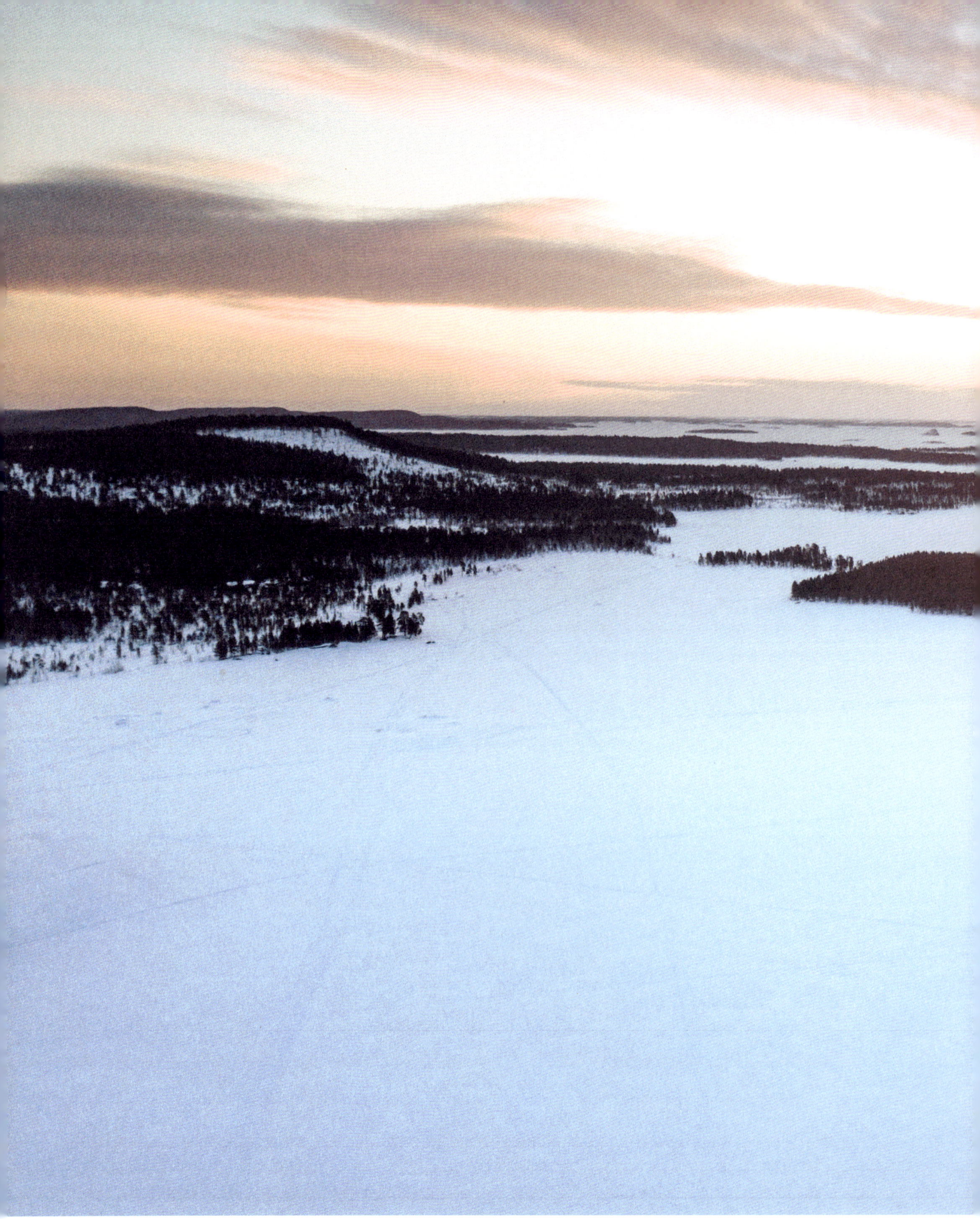

ESKO'S CABIN

Our Outdoor Pantry

How finding and picking our own food gives us nourishment far beyond the physical

— by chef, writer, and forager Gill Meller

What do we think about when we think of foraging? We think about our early ancestors roaming the forests. We think about a wilder wooded world, long before agriculture, far away from our lives today.

The truth is, looking for wild food isn't such a far-flung idea, and it can still have a part to play in our lives. I bet there's something edible growing in the wild a stone's throw from where you're sitting right now.

Foraging is about so much more than the food we hope to gather. For me, it's about the whole journey, from the beginning to the end. It's about where I'm going, how I got there, and getting lost on the way. It's about the black mud on my hands, the blood drawn from brambles, rain-soaked boots, and the owl feathers I collect below the shade of a pine. Foraging is about looking and actually seeing; it's about listening and actually hearing. It's about the uncorrupted silence of the crying winds. Beyond all this, foraging is about the reward, or the hunt, if you like, because sometimes, but not always, there's a prize at the end: a gift from Mother Nature, a fragment of wildness, a comforting whisper from our ancestral past — something to take home and share with your family or eat alone.

Take the humble blackberry, for example. This little wild autumn fruit has a special place in my heart, and not just because of the sugary crumbles and cobblers I like to bake it in. When my daughters were little, we used to all take off together to gather blackberries from the wrangles of thorny briar that line the trackways, meadows, and copses that wind down to the sea. There was an innocence and a purity in those forages. We found a happiness there amongst the squabbling blackbirds, under the soft rain, in the lee of a distant rut. It was a happiness you couldn't unearth indoors, within the pages of a book or in front of a TV show. In that moment, memories were made that I've kept close to me. My family have kept them too, and when I'm out on my own, I sometimes catch the ghosts of these memories as they're carried by in the broad ochre arms of an October wind.

There are two approaches to foraging. The first involves research, detailed guide books, Latin, magnifying glasses, and a full day in the field. The second involves grabbing a basket, going for a walk, and maybe finding something good to eat along the way. I personally prefer the latter approach. I'm not a mycologist or a botanist or any kind of '-ist', but I've learnt, over the years, to identify a handful of delicious wild foods that can be picked, taken home, and eaten in one way or another. They're not always there, because nearly all our edible plants and other wild foods are seasonal, but this is what makes them special. Turn away and they're gone with the wind.

I pick the things I love and know to taste good. I'm not on a quest for obscure grasses or rainbow-coloured fungus. Most of the things I like to gather will be as familiar to you as they are to me: nettles, wild garlic, and common seaweeds; blackberries, crab apples, and sloes. These are wild plants and fruits that are not only plentiful but, for the most part, easy to identify and wonderful — and safe — to eat, even if it takes a little work.

Let's take the stinging nettle as a case in point. To some, it's a prolific weed whose sole intent is to cause us all pain. To others, it's a superfood and one of nature's most underrated medicinal plants. The nettle seems to be feared and revered in equal measure, but those who fear it have probably never experienced the simple joy that a bowl of vibrant emerald-green nettle soup can bring to both body and soul.

When I'm picking nettles, I tend to don a pair of gardening gloves, because until this barbed little plant is cooked, it will sting you. I always pick the new, tender growth, which is why spring is the right time to harvest. I only take the tip of the plant, or the crown, which is made up of the first six to eight leaves and is usually the tastiest part. One of my favourite ways to cook nettles, apart from in a wonderful soup, is to blanch them in salted water, just like you would any of our more familiar cultivated greens. Once drained, I toss them in an ample amount of butter and a trickle of extra virgin olive oil, and season them with plenty of flaky sea salt and freshly ground black pepper. I could eat this every day. Buttered nettles make an ideal accompaniment to roast chicken, a piece of grilled fish, or some decent pork sausages, and they can make the most marvellous stand-alone meal too: simply turn the buttered, seasoned nettles through a bowl of freshly cooked pappardelle pasta and serve with a generous grating of pecorino or parmesan. Another sublime way to use the stinger is to replace the spinach in creamed spinach with this iron-rich leaf. I like to serve this gratinated, hot and bubbling, alongside slices of moist garlic-and-rosemary roast lamb or a piece of oak-smoked trout. It's absolutely exceptional.

In late spring, I can look out my window and see elderflowers in full bloom. It's an incredible — and very common — plant that can be utilised in all sorts of ways. In June, I use its flowers to flavour citrusy cordials, refreshing sorbets, and luxurious possets. A bit later, I use the hard green berries to make a quirky alternative to pickled capers, and then in late summer, I use the dark-red ripe fruit to make jams, syrups, and infused vinegars.

I believe the best way to tune into nature is through the food we eat, since the way we grow, rear, and harvest is fundamentally connected to the state of the natural world. Something as simple as shopping locally and cooking seasonally can help change the way we think about food and where it comes from. It can help us forge connections with the people who live and work within our rural communities, and it can help us understand and appreciate the cyclic rhythms of our four seasons. Foraging goes even deeper into the earth, and the more we understand about our environment, the easier it will be for us to do some good at a time when our world is crying out for help.

As long as we look after our environment there will always be wild food to be found, whether it's gleaming mussels the colour of pearlescent coal picked from the salted, craggy rocks of the shoreline, or sprays of deeply scented ivory elderflower cut next to the train line in June. We must remember, however, that nothing ever comes for free. We reap what we sow, and although we don't sow the seeds of wild food directly, it is all entwined in a global ecosystem that is wholly reliant on and at the complete mercy of us — people. It is our responsibility, as custodians of these lands, to preserve and uphold them. We haven't been very good at this in recent years, but there's still time to change the way we live and reverse some of the negative effects our society has on the natural world. Foraging for a few simple wild ingredients can bring us far closer to nature than we might actually think, and with that comes a deeper understanding of the struggle the earth faces. As with so many things, the balance is precarious, and it's tipping and tilting all the time. We can't expect to feed our families day in, day out on wild foods. There are simply not enough edible species growing wild, and besides, it would be completely unsustainable. Foraging is a question of moderation and respect, and is born more of giving back than it is of taking away. The watch words must always be 'take what we need and no more'. This way we'll waste less, and we'll be leaving a portion where it belongs. Careful, sensitive harvesting will ensure that next time you, your children, or your children's children return, there should still be plenty to go around.

```
Foraging is about so much more than
the food we hope to gather. For me,
it's about the whole journey, from
the beginning to the end. It's about
where I'm going, how I got there, and
getting lost on the way. It's about
the black mud on my hands, the blood
drawn from brambles, rain-soaked
boots, and the owl feathers I collect
below the shade of a pine. Foraging
is about looking and actually seeing;
it's about listening and actually
hearing. It's about the uncorrupted
silence of the crying winds.
```

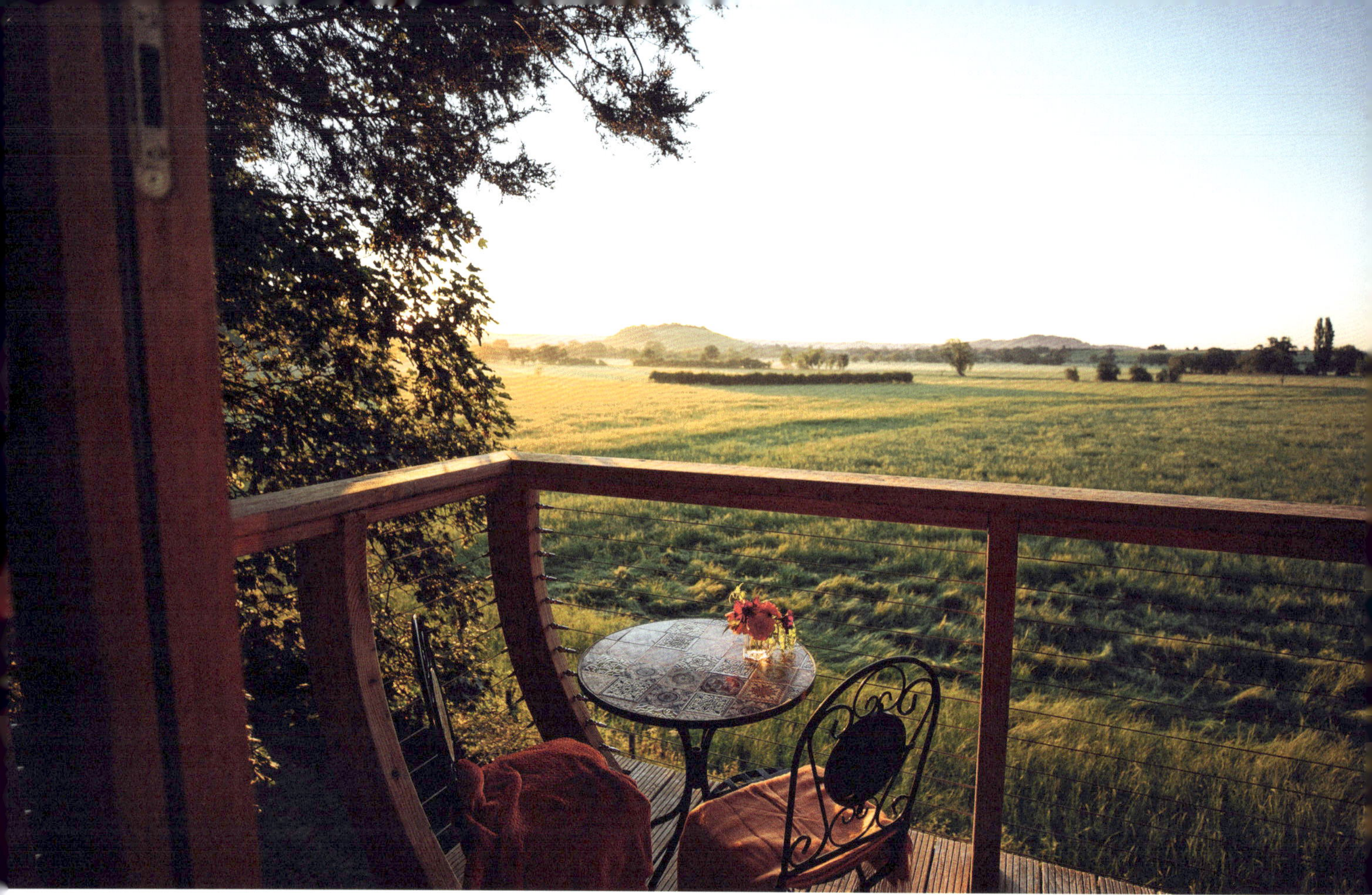
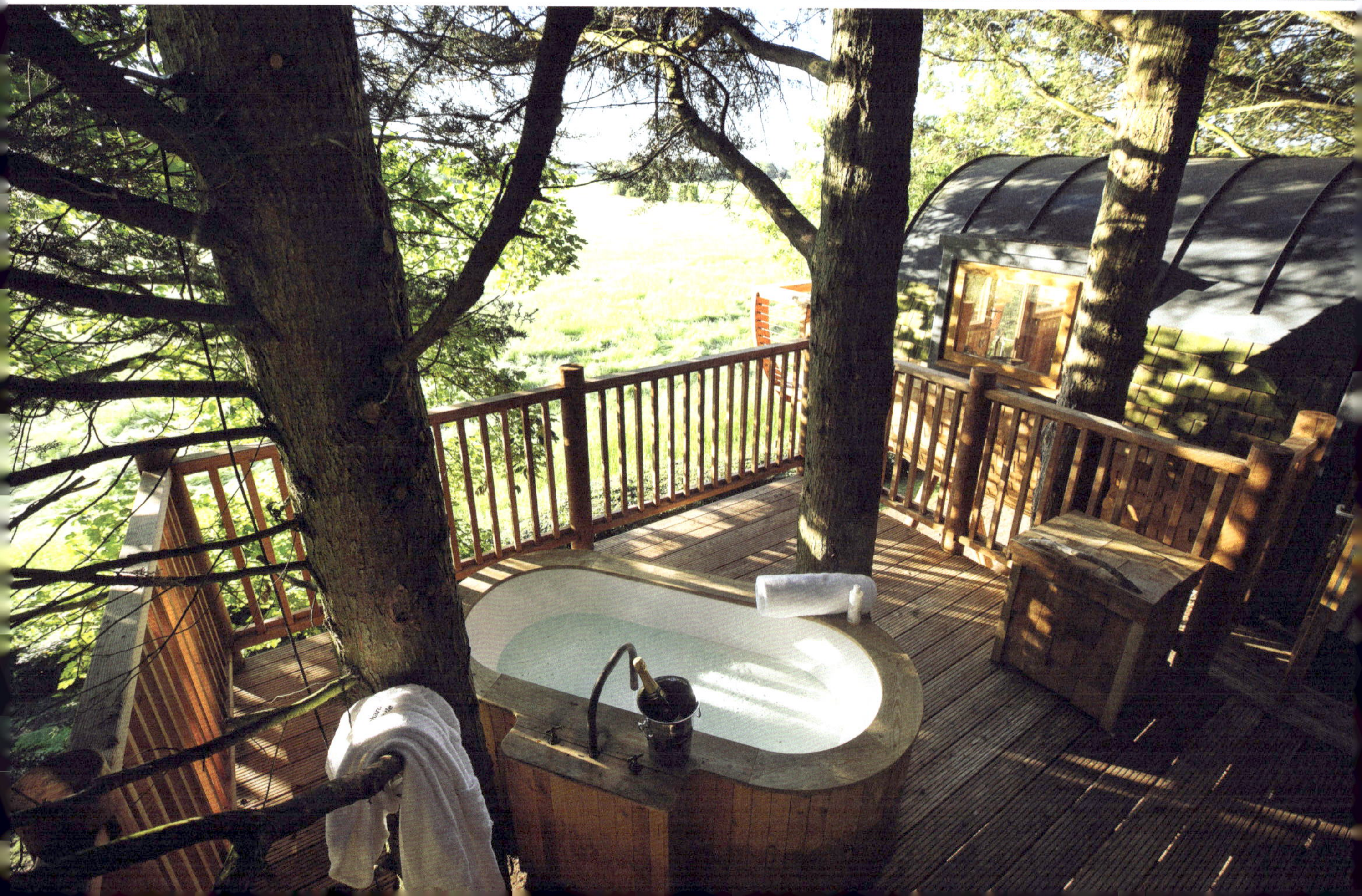

A Lofty Room with Wraparound Appeal

Totally immersed in the quiet of the countryside, amongst the treetops of the south-west of England

DABINETT TREEHOUSE
SOMERSET,
ENGLAND

This beautifully crafted cocoon of a treehouse stands aloft on a tripod. Beside it, a generous deck is home to an inviting wood-panelled bathtub beneath low-slung branches that offer just the right amount of privacy. Lights twinkle in the trees at night as magically as the stars shine up above, and, come morning, the air fills with birdsong. The interior of the stylish cabin comes complete with a king-size bed, luxury bathroom, mini kitchen, wood burner, and sofa. Guests can idle away the hours admiring views across Somerset while they plan no end of hearty walks in the Mendip Hills.

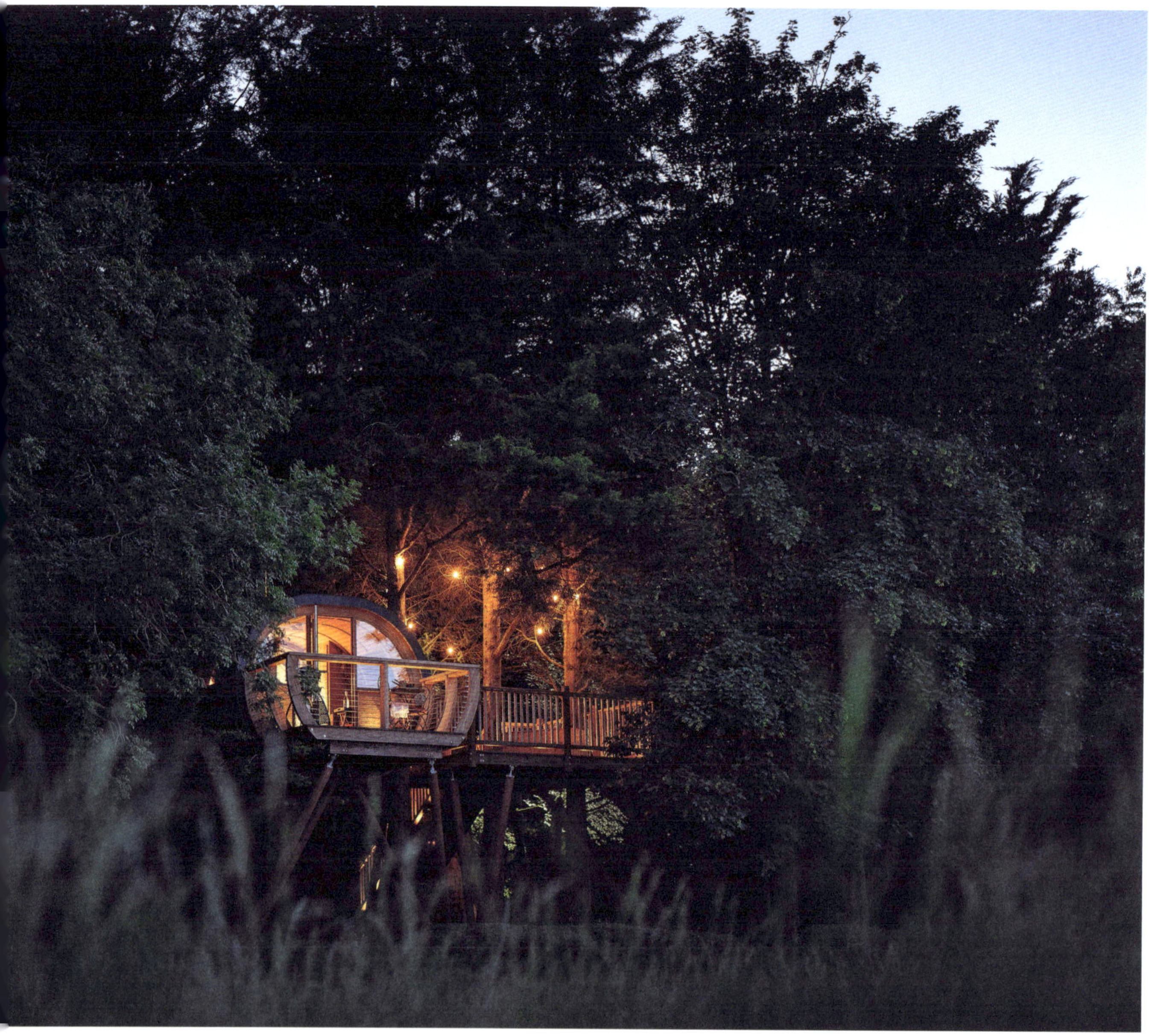

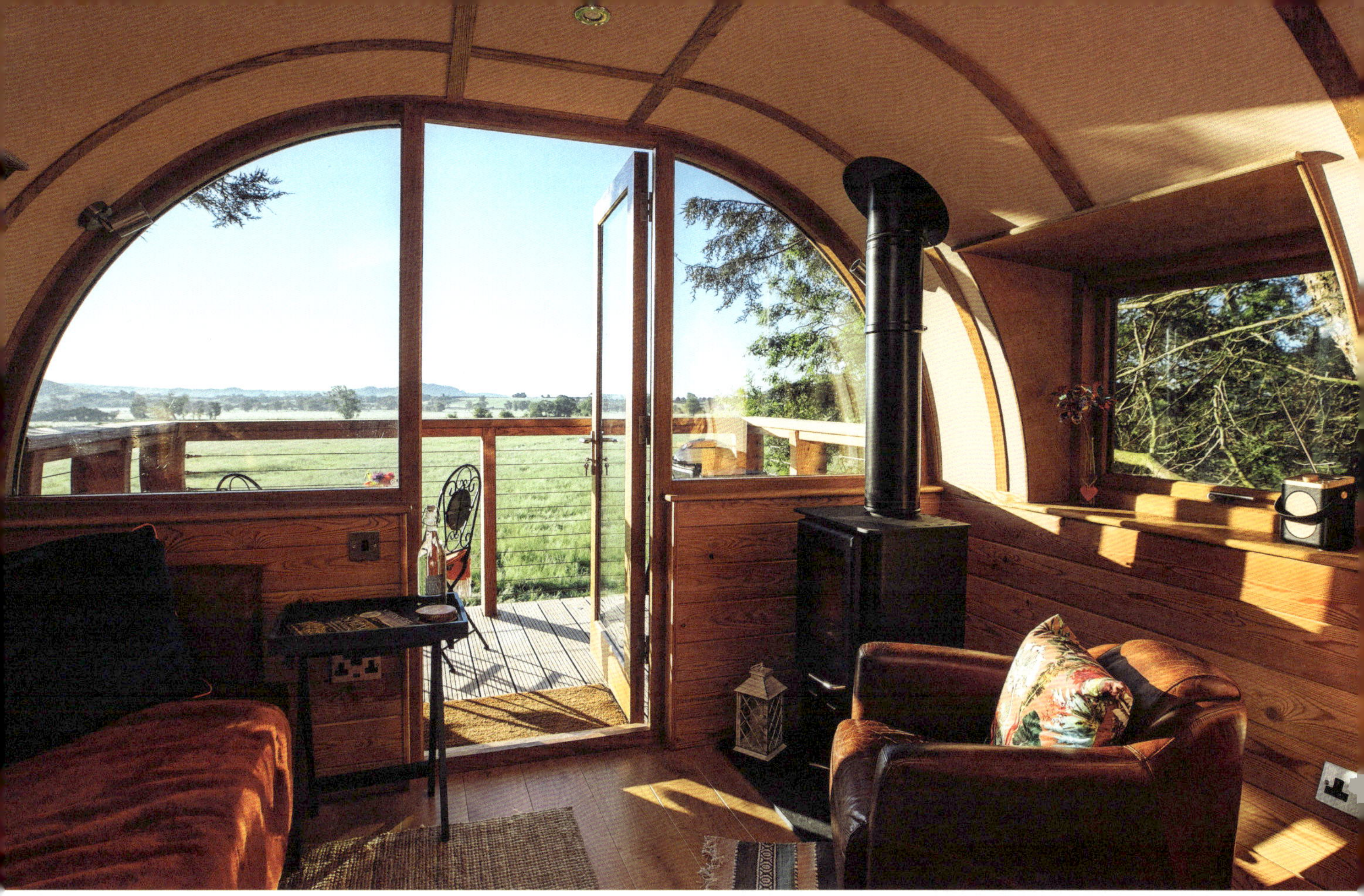
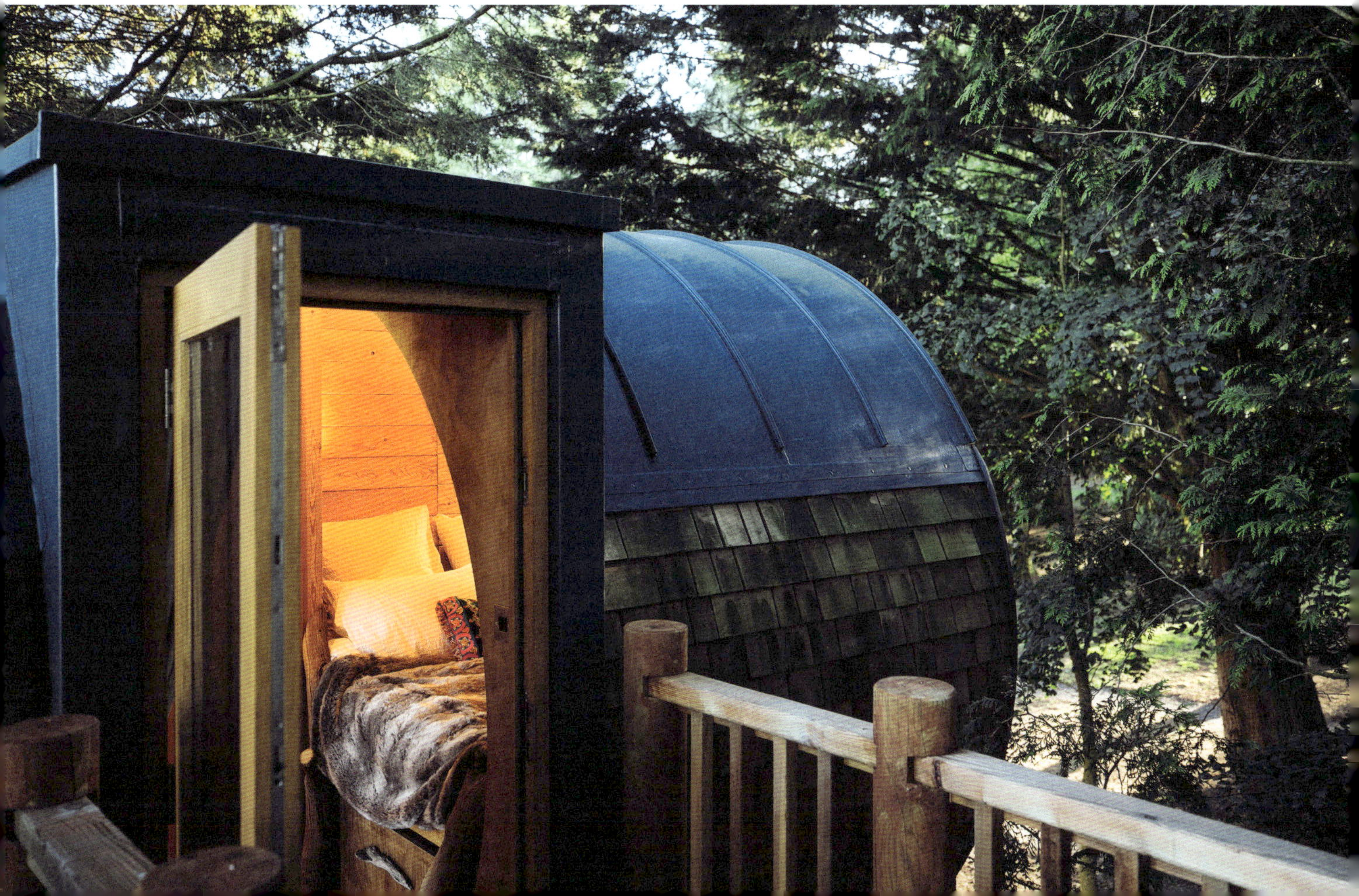

Raising the Roof in Northumberland

A quirky treehouse set within a landscape teeming with wildlife and outdoor activities galore

SKY DEN
NORTHUMBERLAND,
ENGLAND

In an amazing feat of design and engineering, Sky Den's roof opens up to the heavens, allowing those who bag the master bedroom a chance to sleep cosily and securely under the stars in this Dark Skies-designated spot. The den was built by William Hardie Designs in collaboration with George Clarke of Channel 4's *Amazing Spaces*, and the openable roof is not the only gimmick here. Downstairs, Clarke has maximised the space by incorporating foldaway furniture that includes two single beds. This unique holiday home is set within the vast Kielder Water and Forest Park, home to 50 percent of the United Kingdom's red squirrel population and an amazing outdoor activity centre. Visitors are spoiled for choice, with water sports, rope courses, orienteering, and countless woodland trails on offer. Back at Sky Den, guests can slide back the glass doors to sit on the balcony and take in riverside views, or head to a circular lookout wrapped in corrugated iron for a cuppa brewed the old-fashioned way, over a wood-burning stove.

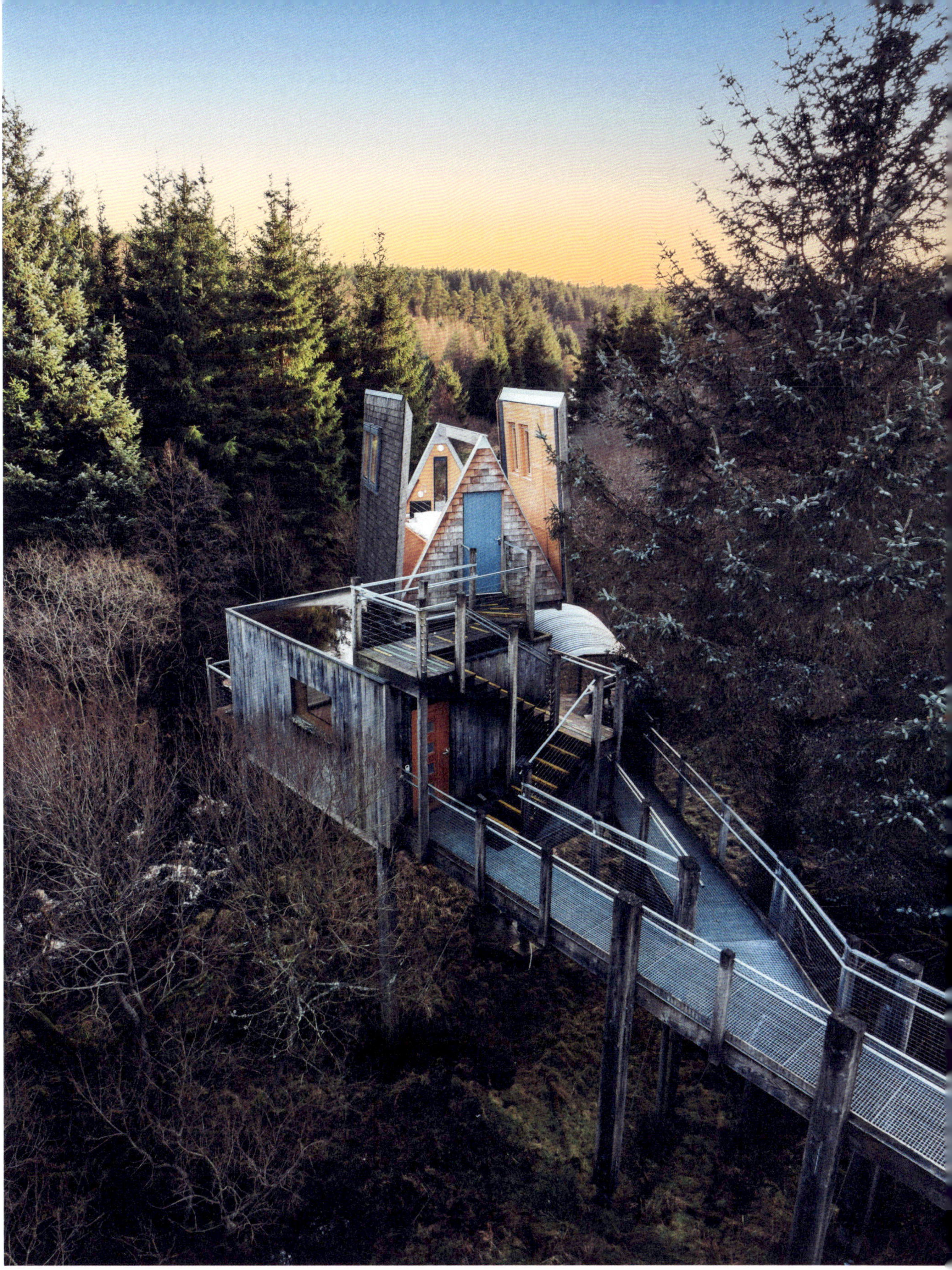

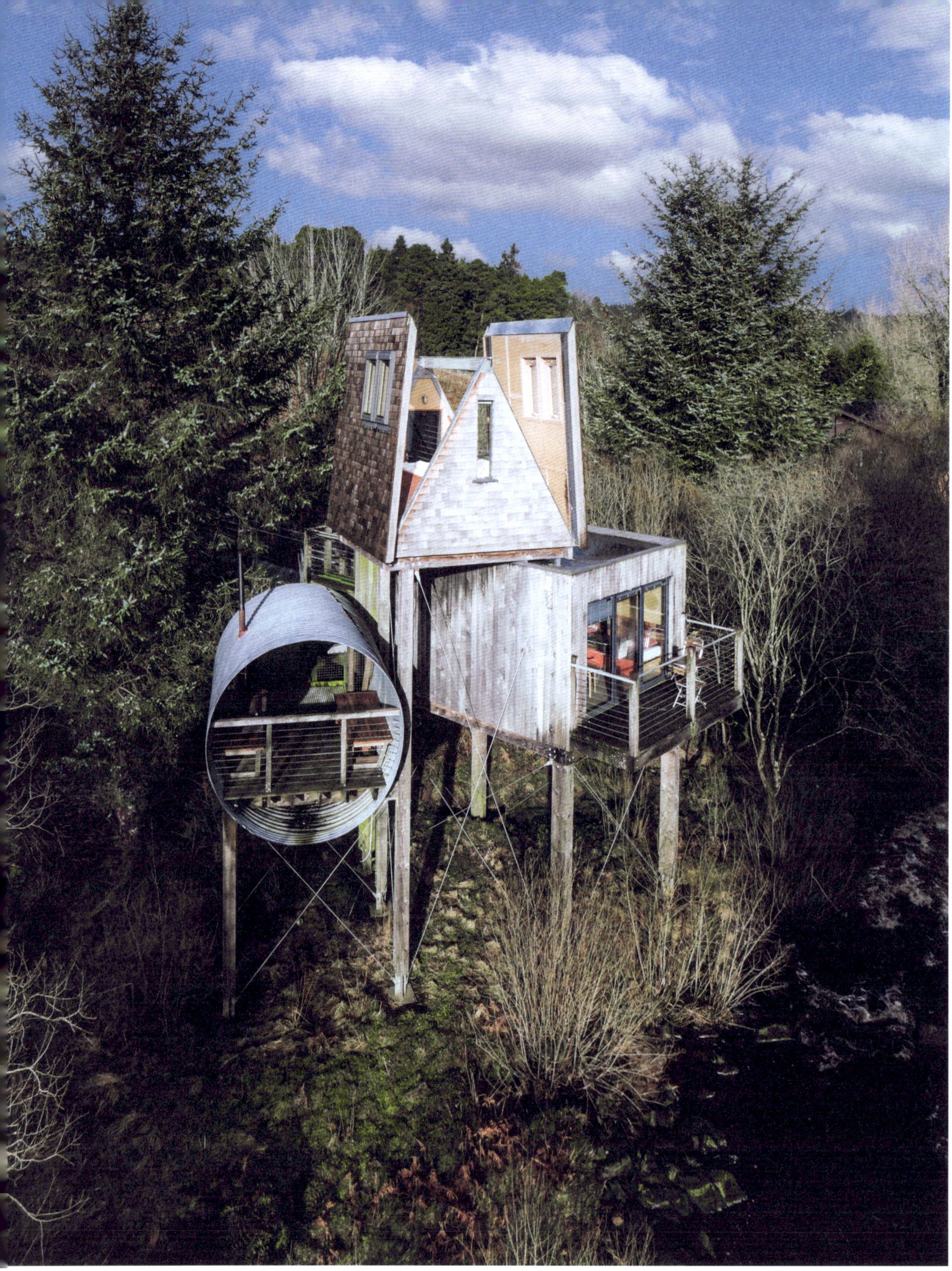

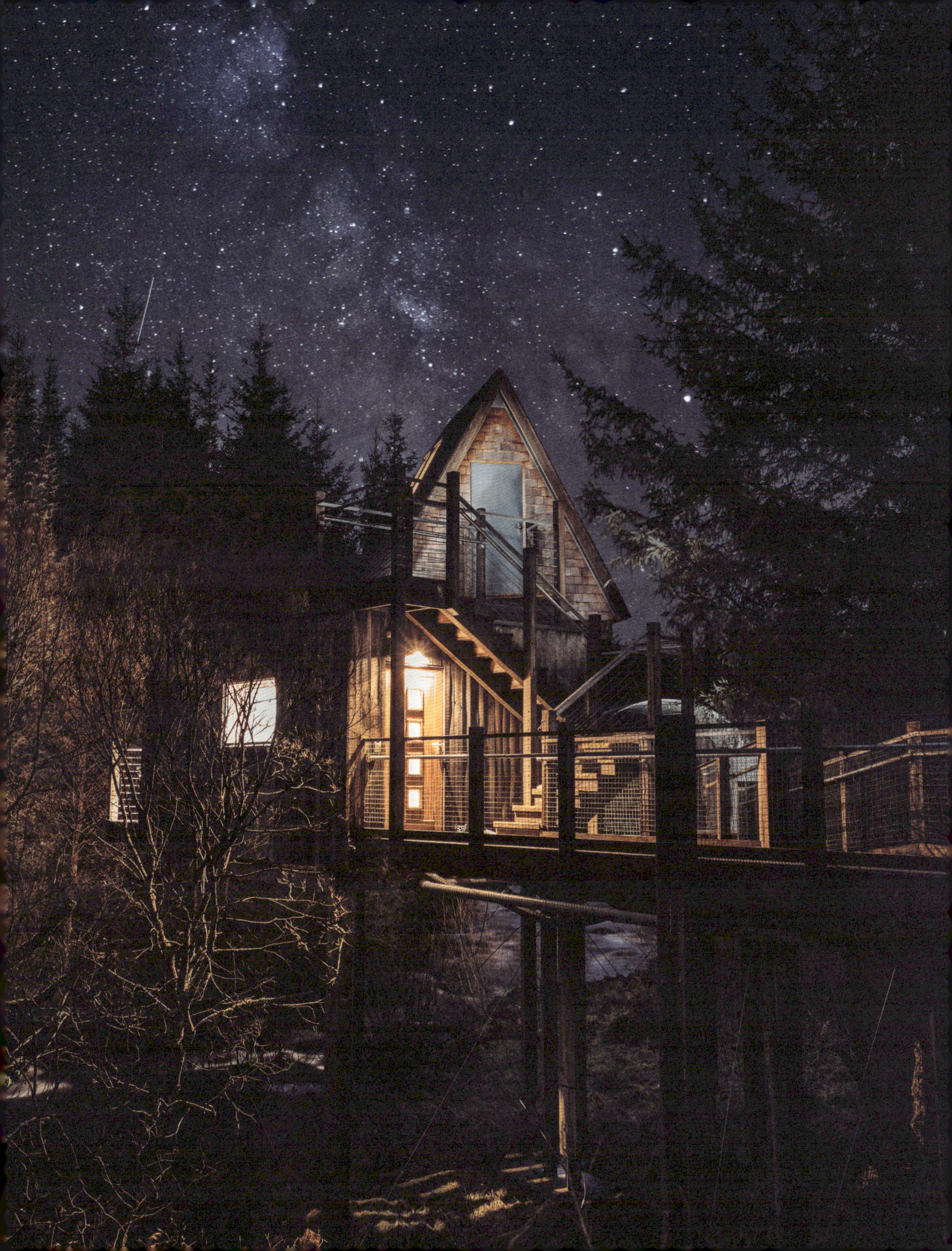

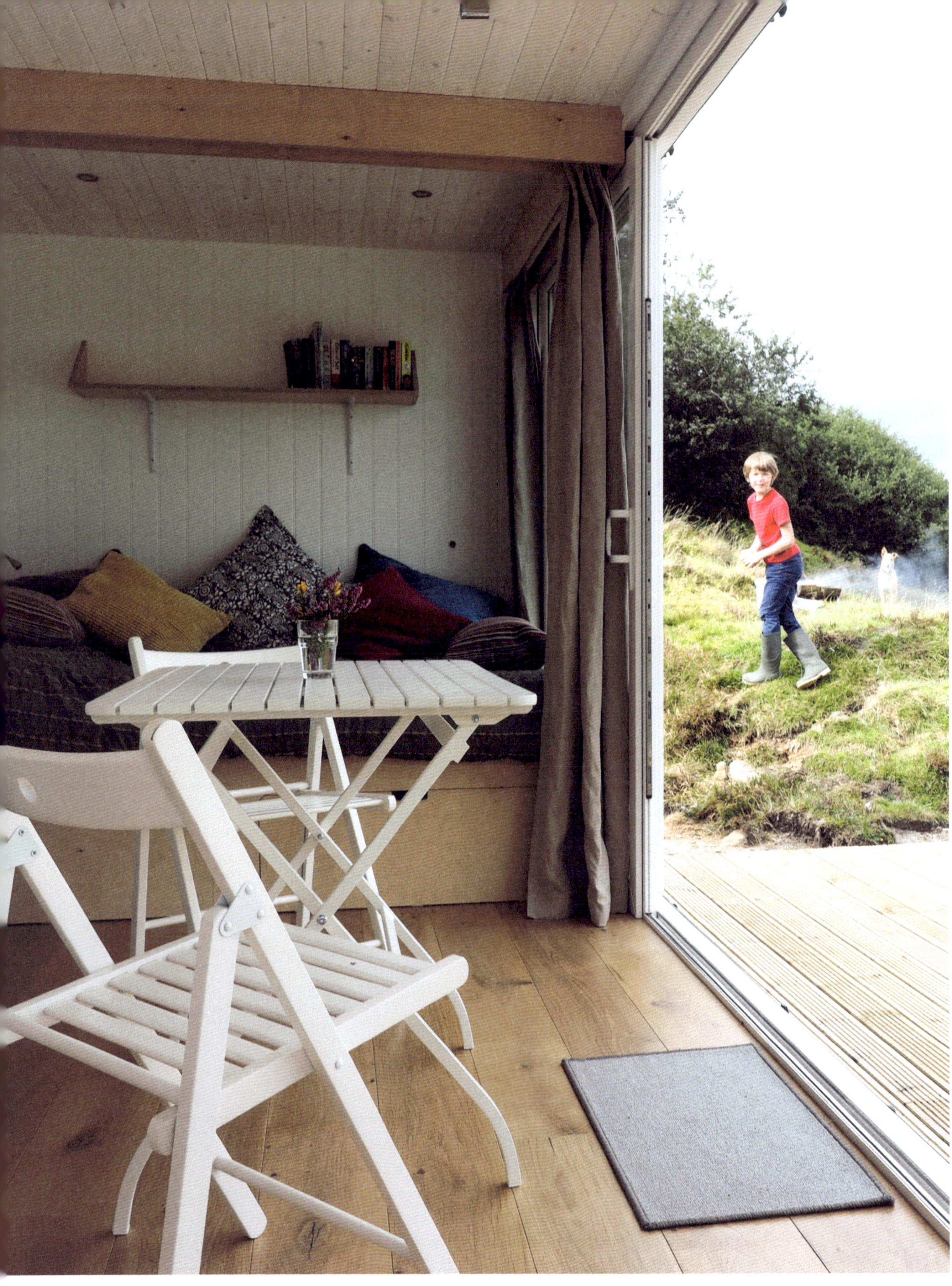

Living Off-Grid on Bodmin Moor

Time stands still in this remote spot of Cornish moorland, with no life but wildlife for miles

THE LAKE
CORNWALL,
ENGLAND

Skirting the edge of a flooded former quarry in a little pocket of Cornwall's Bodmin Moor, a converted industrial container provides the ideal base for exploring 486 hectares (1,200 acres) of open moorland, and beyond. But just staying put can be good for the soul, as guests are invited to take in the earthy tones of these vast wetlands and the blue skies that reflect off of the lake's mirror-still surface. Accessed via a half mile or so of rough track, the simply kitted-out container is completely off-grid, with solar panels powering the lighting and a wood burner keeping things cosy. Water for cleaning is pumped directly from the lake, and there's a piping-hot supply in the showers behind the main space. Life could not be simpler.

For those who do venture further, on offer are miles of walking trails to nearby tors, day trips to the Cornish coast, or outings to local pubs in sleepy villages. At night, guests can relax into the evening and await the spectacular show of stars above the moor.

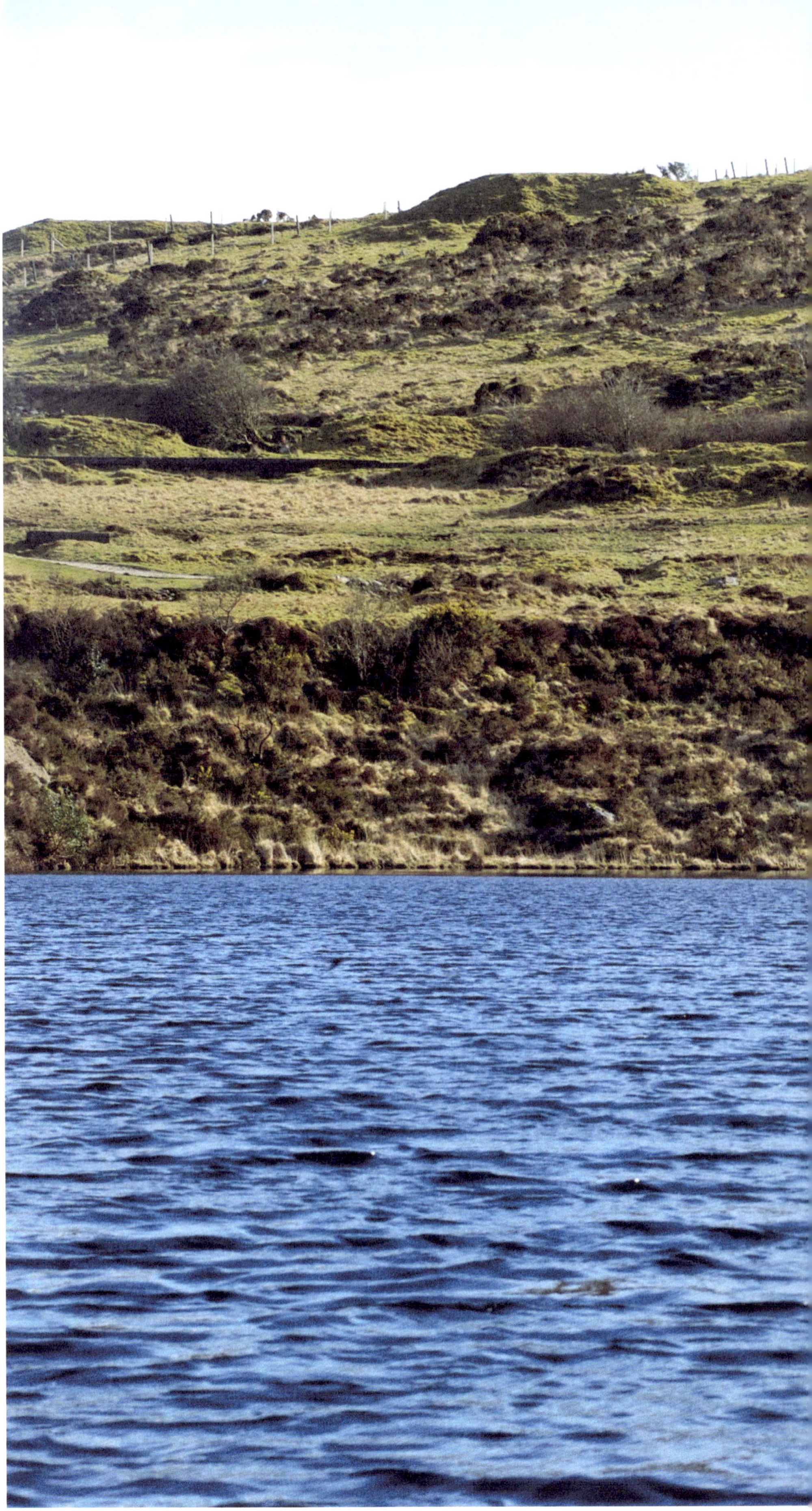

THE LAKE

Slowing the Pace

Why and how to make the journey part of the fun and fight against our modern tendency to rush from place to place

— by Canopy & Stars' Chris Elmes

Slow travel isn't actually about speed. Whether you're going for a week of relaxation or packing everything you can into a weekend of adventure, it's an attitude that runs through every decision you make — the opposite of the destination box-ticking mentality. It's going with an open mind and no fixed plans, letting yourself feel the land and the weather instead of running to the next scenic viewpoint, snapping a photo, and moving on. It's the philosophy that travel isn't about how much you see, but about how you connect with what you encounter. Nature, so blissfully empty of the things that pressure us to rush, makes slow travel easy. Its beauty is simple, accessible, and often a lot closer than you think. A few small changes to your thinking on destinations, transport, and time can add up, with ironic speed, to a gentler, richer, slower way to go.

Slow travel starts before you've even gone anywhere. Think about what it is you get from being away. If it's the reinvigoration that comes from stepping out of life for a bit, you might not even need to travel that far. We all love exploring exotic corners of the world, but sometimes the things right on our doorstep can give us the same invaluable sense of release and reconnection. A long walk in the woods near your home can be as invigorating as a round-the-world adventure, and it doesn't cost you or the planet nearly as much.

If you can't resist the lure of far-off lands, then avoid flying, not only to reduce your environmental footprint, but also because of the mindset it represents. Flying is all about getting to your destination as quickly as possible, whereas slow travel is about enjoying the journey, taking detours where you feel like it, following a river, and literally going with the flow. Taking a slower form of transport makes the trip part of the experience, not an inconvenience to be minimised wherever possible. Leave early if you need to; leave ridiculously early, in fact, and revel in the feeling of having plenty of time, stopping for coffee or to paddle in a river just because you can. It's the first step in getting away from the mindset of cramming things into the time you have, rather than doing the things you have time for.

Slow travel also lets you feel the place you're moving through. When you appear in an airport, surrounded by glowing yellow signs and global coffee chains, you have no sense of where you are or how far you've travelled. You don't see the scenery gradually change as misty blue hills appear on the horizon, or as you come blinking out of a forest into sudden bright sunshine. It's so much more meaningful to see the context of where you are, whether that's a winding river and the plains that surround a vibrant city, or the beautiful forest that you never knew was so close to home.

It's the philosophy that travel isn't about how much you see, but about how you connect with what you encounter. Nature, so blissfully empty of the things that pressure us to rush, makes slow travel easy.

However you get where you're going, unpack as soon as you arrive if you're spending more than a day or two in one place. It seems absurdly simple, but it makes a powerful statement. Unpacking means that you've committed to settling in. It says that you're not moving on the next morning. You've chosen to see fewer places and experience them in more detail. If you're always ready to hit the next hotspot, you're not thinking about where you actually are. You'll spend more time looking at bus schedules than scenery. So stash your clothes, tuck your bag away, and act like you've just moved in. Get to know the people at the local shop, and quiz the park rangers about trails only residents know or the best place to see the sunrise.

Although it isn't all about pace, take slow travel literally and walk wherever possible, rather than taking public transport. When you walk, you can explore at random, letting

We all love exploring exotic corners
of the world, but sometimes the things
right on our doorstep can give us the
same invaluable sense of release and
reconnection. A long walk in the woods
near your home can be as invigorating
as a round-the-world adventure.

paths, smells, and sounds guide you. It's a physical slowing down that leads directly to a mental slowing down and a remarkable sense of freedom. You'll climb instinctively to hillside viewpoints, or follow the ripple of a waterfall to a moment of perfect, natural solitude. You'll begin to understand a place as you feel its weather and sense its rhythms. Without a rigid timetable or 'Ten Unmissable Sights' to get to, you'll be more likely to stop and chat in the shade instead of stomping through the heat of the afternoon only to find yourself turning for home because the sun's getting low.

The essence of slow travel is making time to appreciate everything about where you are. Stop as often as you want, and not just when you reach a milestone. Take mental snapshots: moments of stillness when you soak up the sounds and the sights. Fill your water bottle from a spring and hear a hawk cry overhead; hold your breath and listen to an animal's soft footsteps rustle in the woods; or sit by a fire and watch a spark drift off into the night — these might not be things you'll read about in guide books, but that's the point. Travel is about so much more than the highlights.

When you experience that pure, simple connection to where you are, it stays with you. You come home feeling as if, however briefly, you lived somewhere else and experienced the world differently. It might seem a bit lofty to say that slow travel changes you, but it certainly gives you souvenirs you can't buy. There's the sensation of tiny fish nipping at your feet as you paddled in the river, the trail with no name that ended at your own private waterfall, the taste of crisp spring water, and the lingering smell of woodsmoke on your clothes.

```
When you walk, you can explore at
random, letting paths, smells, and
sounds guide you. It's a physical
slowing down that leads directly to
a mental slowing down and a remarkable
sense of freedom.
```

Perhaps 'slow travel' is a misnomer. Maybe 'aimless travel', 'free travel', or 'thoughtful travel' better imply the desire to get out from behind the camera, ditch the app-rated recommendations, and become a part of where you are. But, in times when we're constantly sold the virtues of speed and technology at the cost of connection and happiness, 'slow' feels like a term of defiance — a definite and heartfelt stand. It's not a refusal to embrace modernity, nor a blinkered nostalgia. It's just an acknowledgement that, as much as the world might like to tell us, faster isn't always better.

```
The essence of slow travel is making
time to appreciate everything about
where you are. Stop as often as you
want, and not just when you reach
a milestone.
```

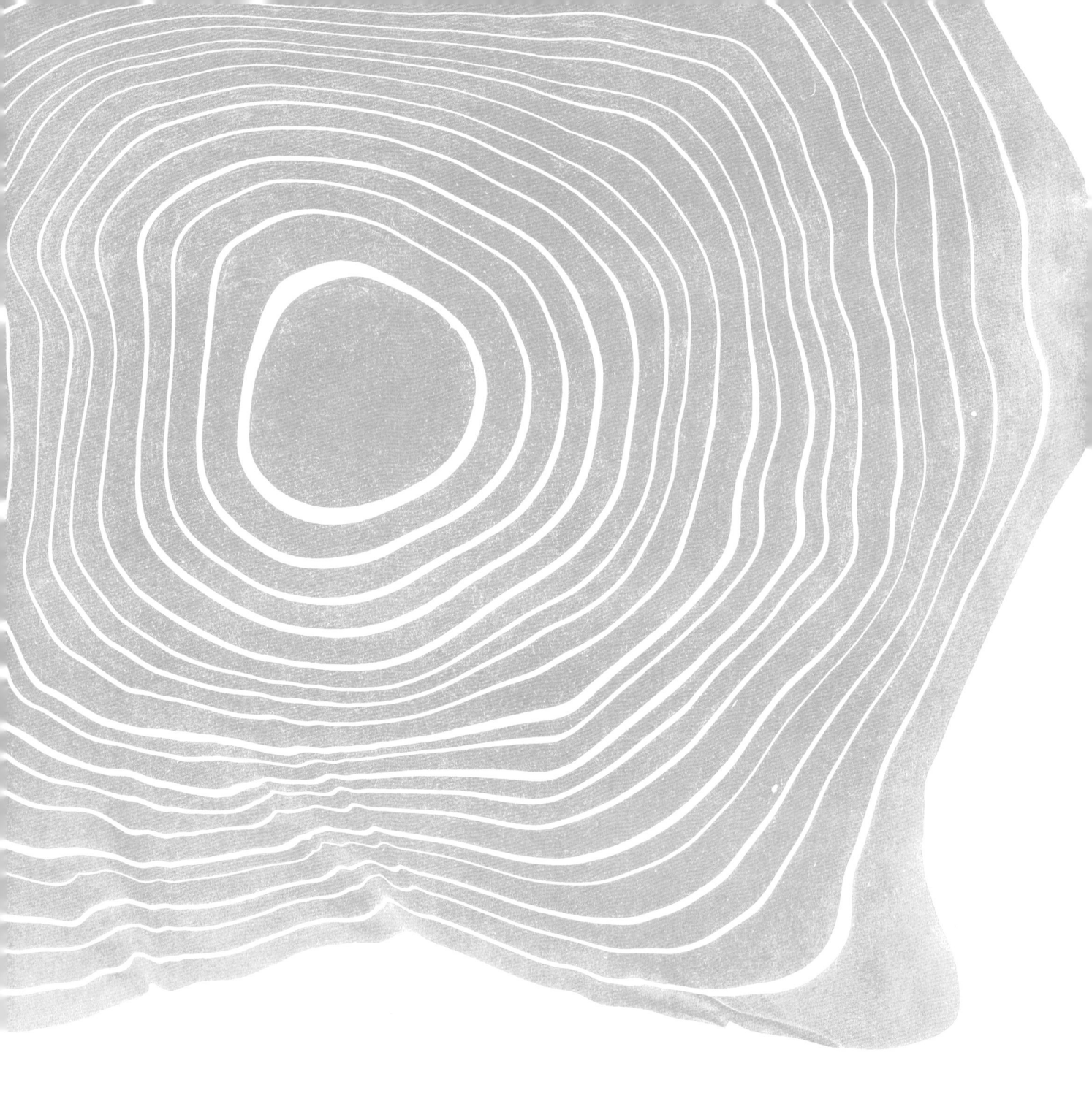

The Meaning of (Cabin) Life

How the simplicity and setting of a woodland cabin bring out the best of our childlike wonder and joy

— by cabin lover Jack Boothby

It's hard to say where my love of cabins started, because I didn't even know it was there until later in life. When it finally revealed itself to me, it brought a youth I'd almost forgotten flooding back. There was something in the freedom of the wilderness that not only reminded me of what I'd loved about the outdoors as a child, but called to me even as an adult. I realised that what nature offered me now was the same thing it always had. All I had to do was throw myself into it, just like I used to when I was a kid.

When we were young, we went camping like most families did, cooking on wobbly stoves, going on hikes, and shouting at mum to put the camera down for once. I was a Scout, so I spent great weekends out in the woods building bridges, making slingshots, climbing trees. I barely noticed the places we

As life got more complicated, I found myself, as most of us do, spending less time in nature and less time doing things just for fun. On some level I knew I was missing something, and I started to get drawn to the beautiful outdoor imagery I'd see on social media.

stayed in. If you give a 10-year-old the choice between appreciating a cabin's rustic aesthetic and jumping into a muddy ditch, you know which one they're going to choose.

As life got more complicated, I found myself, as most of us do, spending less time in nature and less time doing things just for fun. On some level I knew I was missing something, and I started to get drawn to the beautiful outdoor imagery I'd see on social media. The memories of those days of freedom and simple joy started trickling back. With an adult eye, I could see how the cabin was at the heart of that lifestyle, how the structure and the setting could give

THE MEANING OF (CABIN) LIFE

us the space to be children again. I became obsessed with finding the places that would make that possible, and with tapping back into a time when I was happy almost because I never stopped to think whether I was happy or not.

My very first trip in search of that feeling was to Glencoe in Scotland, where I found a cabin surrounded by the trunks of looming pines. The silence, the sunlight, and the sweet smell of damp earth were all instantly evocative. It felt incredible, but it was about to get even better. In the early hours of the morning, I woke up to find a strange, bright light filling the room. Whilst I'd been sleeping, a foot of snow had fallen and the rising sun was shining off of it. It felt like a mythical Christmas morning, or like those days when you woke up and knew there was a good chance school would be cancelled. I gave in to my inner child completely and ran outside to spend hours taking pictures of the pristine snow. There was that thick silence you get when every edge is softened — the snow was sparkling and I didn't notice the cold. From that moment on I was hooked.

My childlike enjoyment of cabins would come as no surprise to the people who build them. They're tapping in to the same feeling when they set out to create their incredible spaces. In the Kielder Dark Sky Reserve, in Northumberland, I visited a place that was described as having a folding roof so you could watch the stars. As I made my way there, I imagined something like a giant skylight, but I've never been happier to be wrong. Two whole sides of the triangular building lever gently back like a drawbridge and reveal the stunning clarity of the night sky. Any sensible adult who wanted to stargaze would just put some good reclining chairs out on the deck, but this was the kind of thing a child would draw. It felt like a spaceship, and I couldn't believe someone had actually built it.

On another trip in Yorkshire I celebrated my 25th birthday in a treehouse that had a slide down into a games room. Again, this was the sort of thing you'd have found in a drawing stuck to my mum's fridge with 'Jack, age 10' scrawled at the bottom, but here I was arriving feet first at high speed into a room full of, let's be honest, toys.

On another trip in Yorkshire I celebrated my 25th birthday in a treehouse that had a slide down into a games room. Again, this was the sort of thing you'd have found in a drawing stuck to my mum's fridge with 'Jack, age 10' scrawled at the bottom, but here I was arriving feet first at high speed into a room full of, let's be honest, toys. On that trip I happened to be with a group of my oldest friends, and I could see them responding the same way I was.

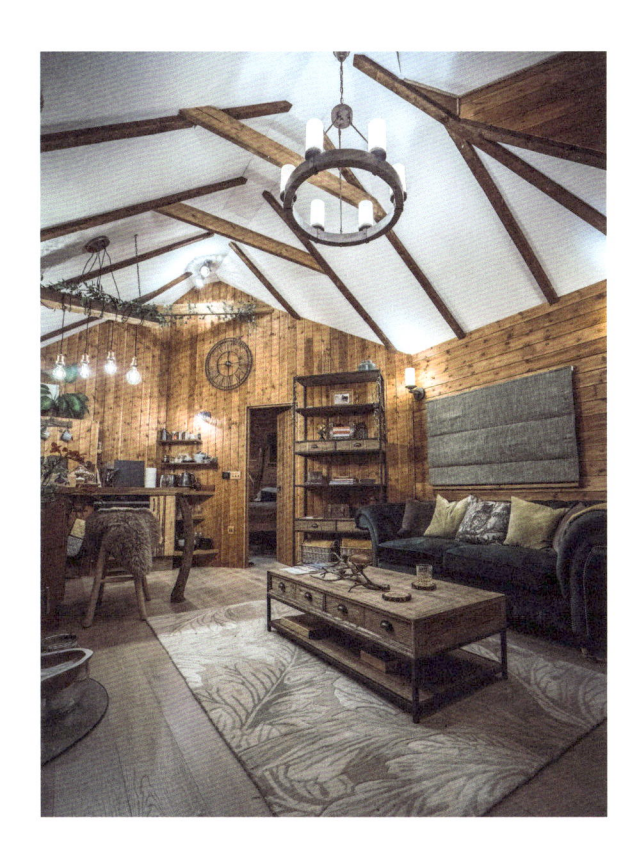

a kid in the woods. So many of us experience that so rarely these days, and there are some who, for various reasons, never get out into the countryside at all. I want to re-awaken the child in those people and inspire them to explore that part of themselves further.

My dream is to own a huge piece of land and build cabins that touch on every style, from the clean Scandinavian to the old Western frontier, so people can see how innate that desire for a simpler life is in all of us. That's a long way off, so for now I'm doing what I can to tell the stories that cabin life inspires.

I feel like it would be a much better world if we could all ditch some of our precious adult seriousness and rediscover the childlike joy of running wild.

On that trip I happened to be with a group of my oldest friends, and I could see them responding the same way I was. We all regressed, in the best possible way, to our 10-year-old selves as nature and a touch of creative magic blew away all the structure and worry that life slowly surrounds you in.

I'd noticed a similar effect to that before, no matter who I took with me on my cabin stays — friends, family, even people I'd only just met. We talked more than we normally would but were also happier to spend time in silence, enjoying our surroundings. There was an almost visible relaxation as we all connected with something either nostalgic or possibly even more primal, a sense of wildness that was deep and powerful. It was a feeling that had been the unseen background of my fondest moments as a child, and I felt enormously grateful that it was now becoming a part of my favourite experiences as an adult as well.

I'm not the first person to say there's much we can learn from children, but I totally believe it. What I try to do with my photography isn't just to take beautiful images, but to capture that spirit of adventure so effortlessly reified by

```
We all regressed, in the best possible
way, to our 10-year-old selves as
nature and a touch of creative magic blew
away all the structure and worry that
life slowly surrounds you in.
```

Taking a Break from Divisive Devices

A countryside cabin in which the best things in life are free — digital-free

DIGITAL DETOX CABIN
ESSEX, ENGLAND

Just an hour's drive from London, this small cabin sits overlooking the open Essex countryside. The quiet, secluded hut, kitted out in a back-to-basics style, has a ban on digital devices — guests have to lock away their smartphones upon arrival. To help city dwellers cope with withdrawal symptoms, there's a 'Digital Free' box of goodies that includes a Polaroid camera, a retro cassette player, and postcards to send to the device-dependent friends and relatives they have left behind. With more time on their hands, visitors are free to roam their rural surroundings, to stroll to the village pub for a slow pint, or to simply sit on the bench outside the cabin and do absolutely nothing. The charming retreat is the creation of startup duo Hector Hughes and Ben Elliott, who believe you can only truly escape the manic pace and long working hours that come with city living when you take a break from digital devices. The ultimate in disconnecting from the trappings of modern life, there's no better place in which to idle away your time.

DIGITAL DETOX CABIN

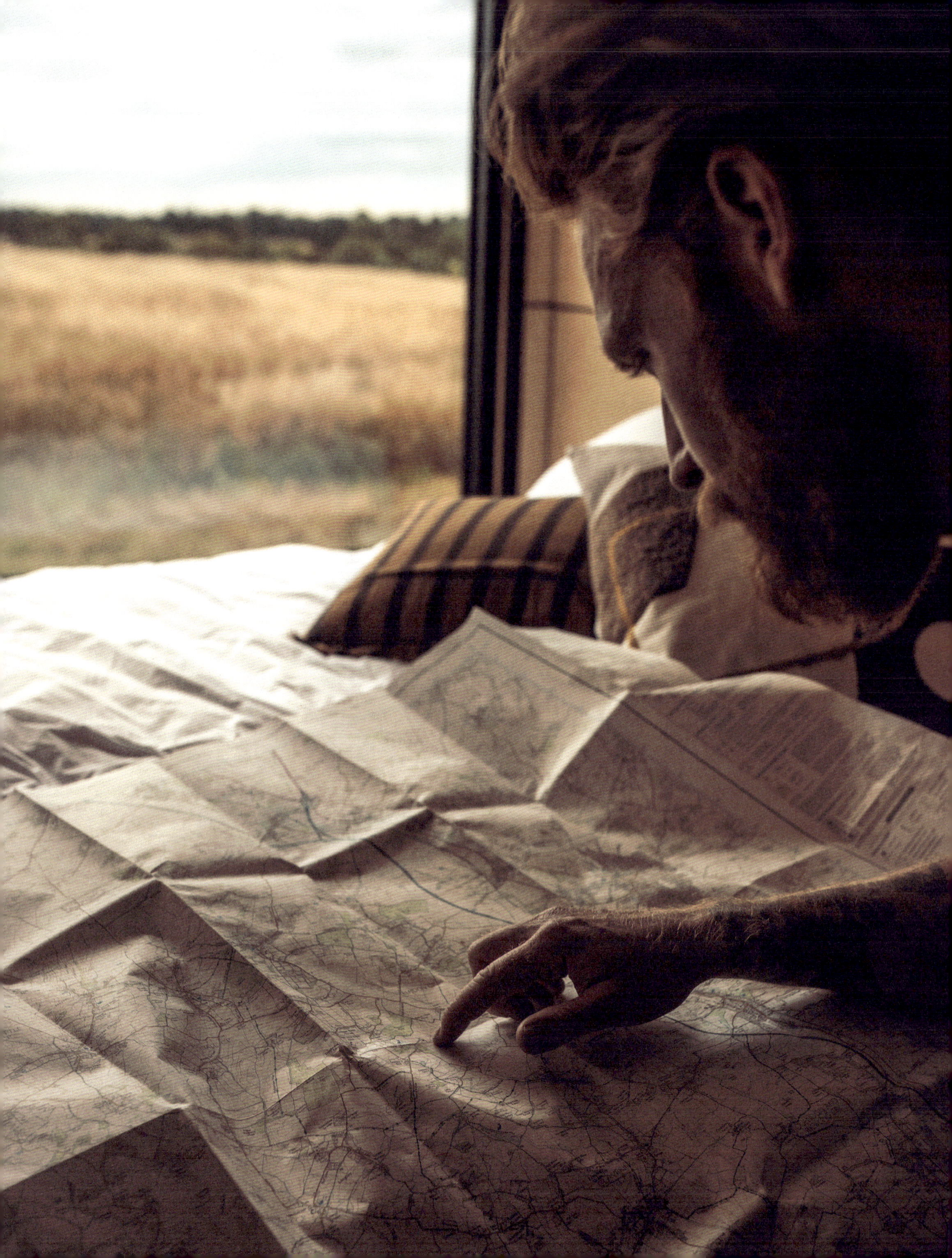

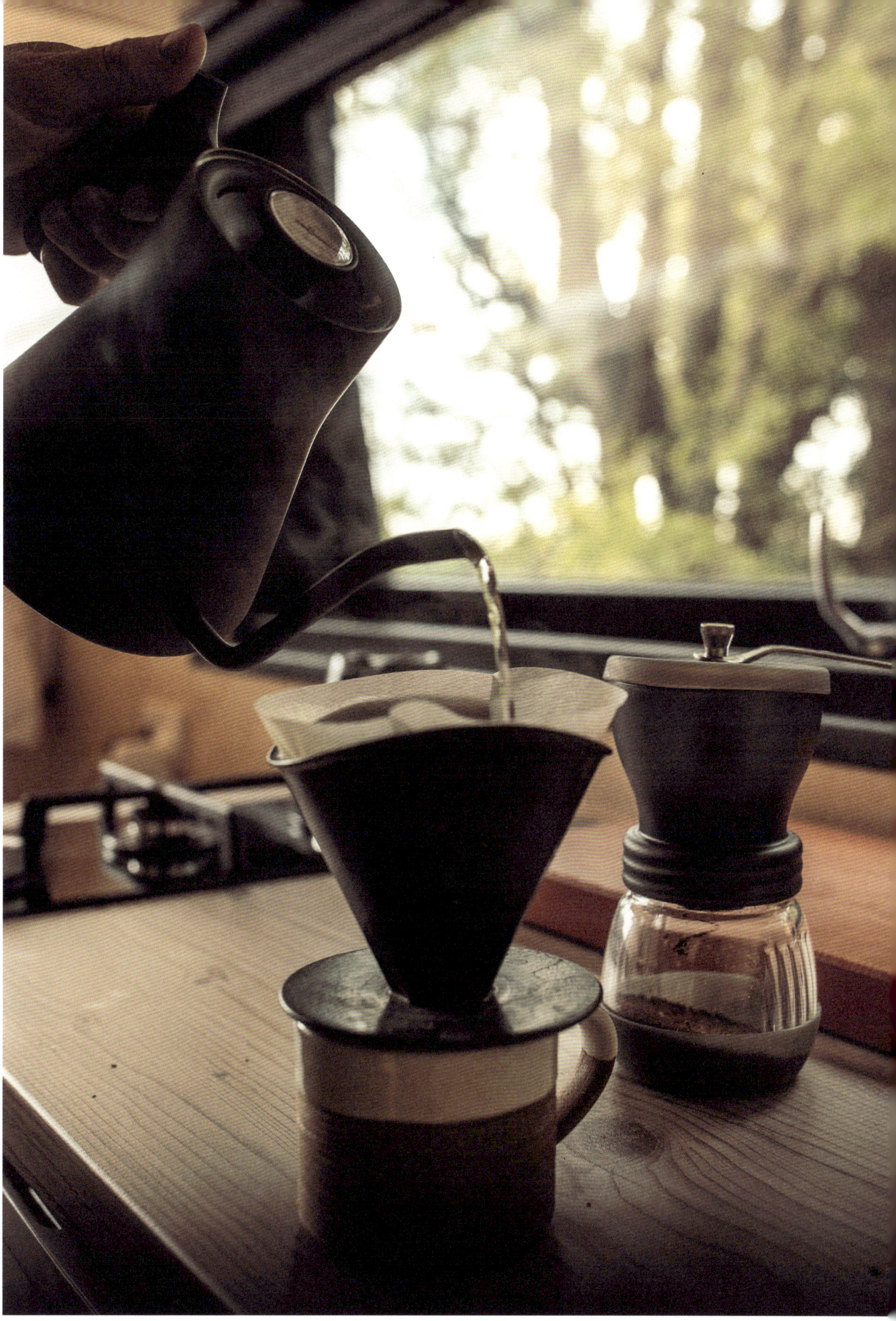

Taking Flight Amongst the Trees

A metal-clad cabin in the pine tree forests of Sweden's Lule River valley

DRAGONFLY
NORRBOTTEN, SWEDEN

Weighing in at 22 metric tonnes, this cabin may seem on the hefty side for a dragonfly, but don't let that deceive you. The stunning structure is suspended amongst the trees of a Swedish pine forest, hovering elegantly in mid-air. Accessed via a 15-metre-long (49-foot-long) ramp, and fitted out with Wi-Fi, a modern bathroom, a wood burner, and air conditioning, the multi-use space can serve as accommodation for a family of four, or as a business suite with two group rooms and a conference table. And what a place to hold a meeting — behind large picture windows with vast views across the valley.

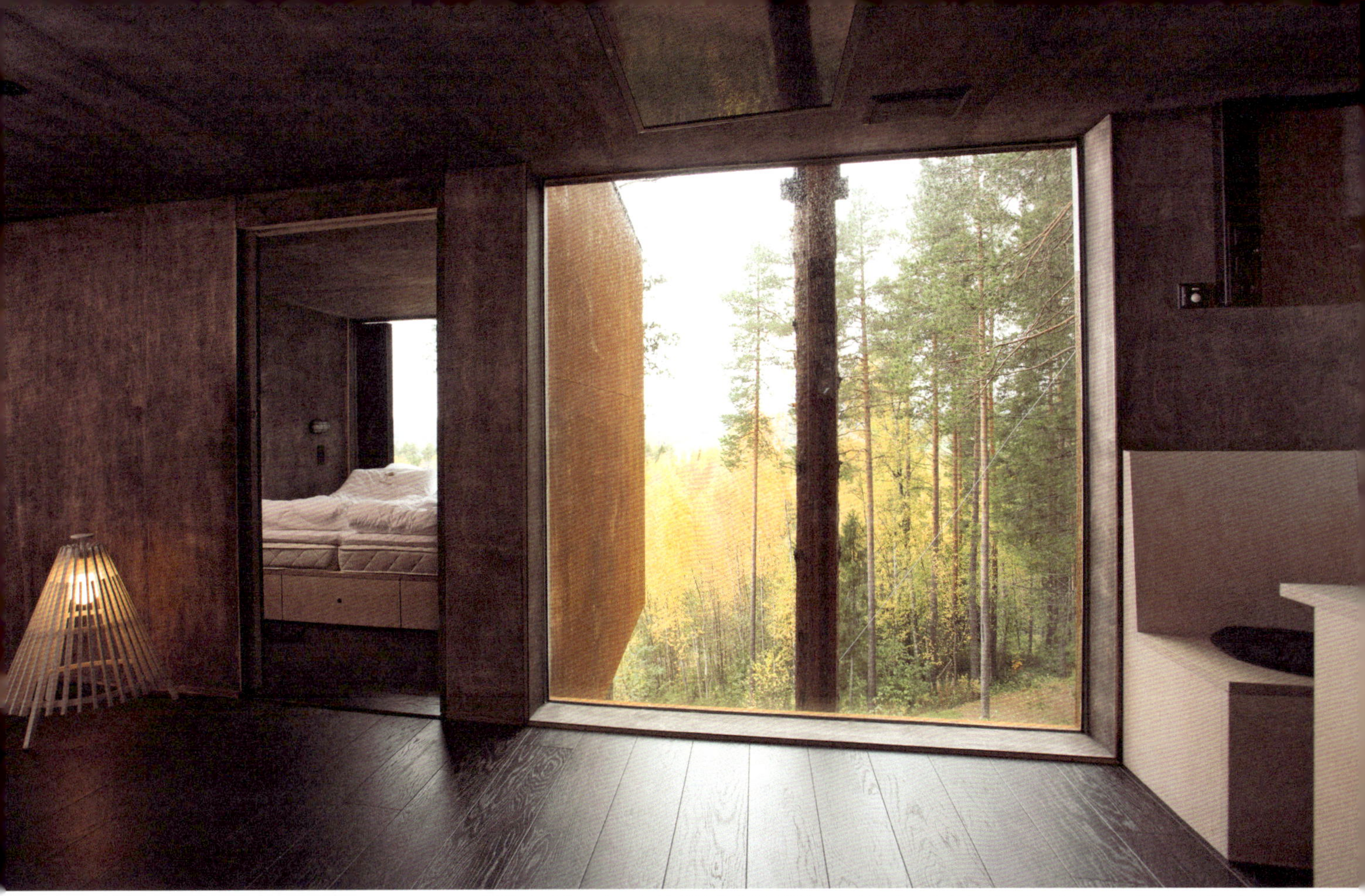

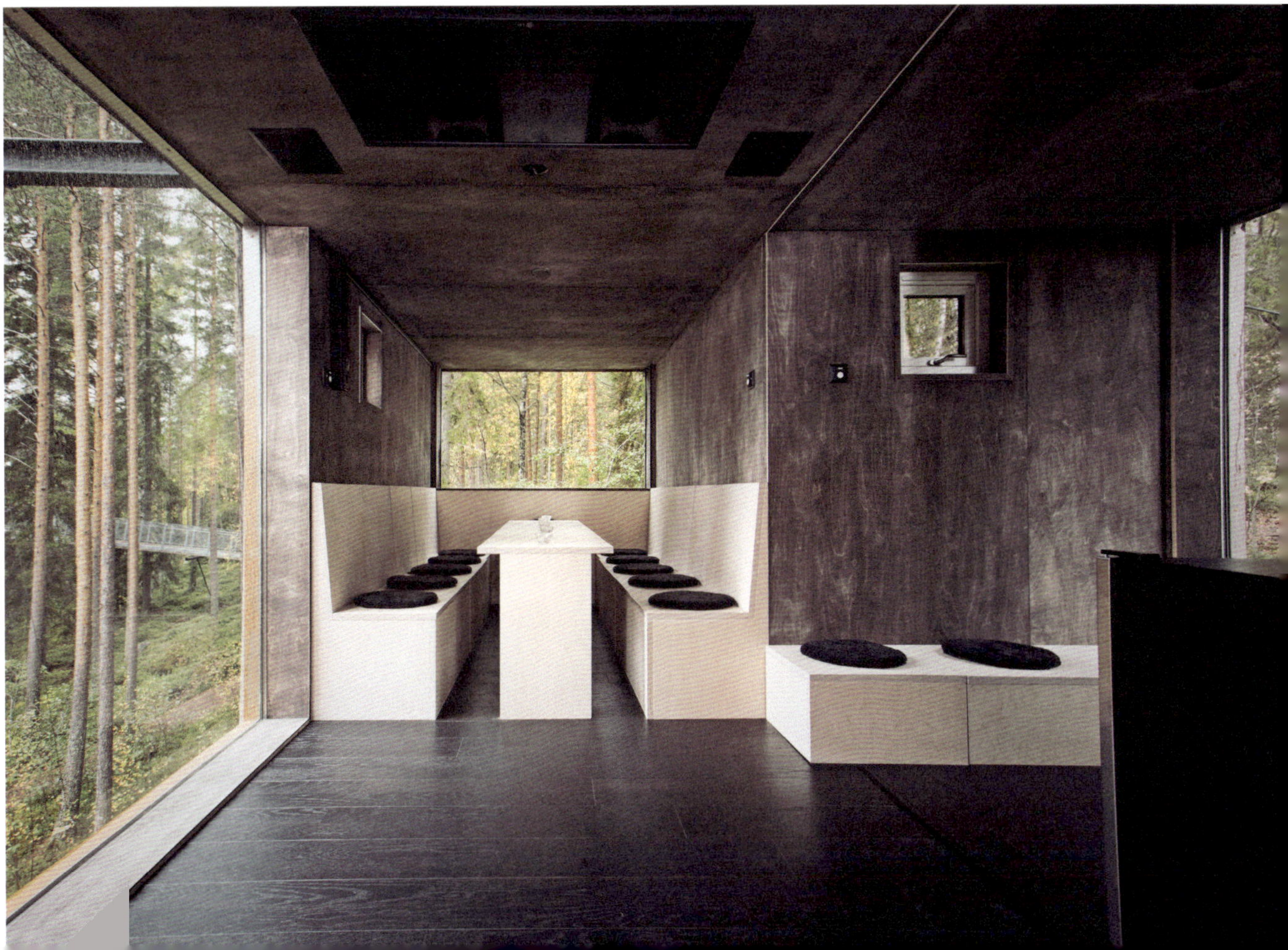

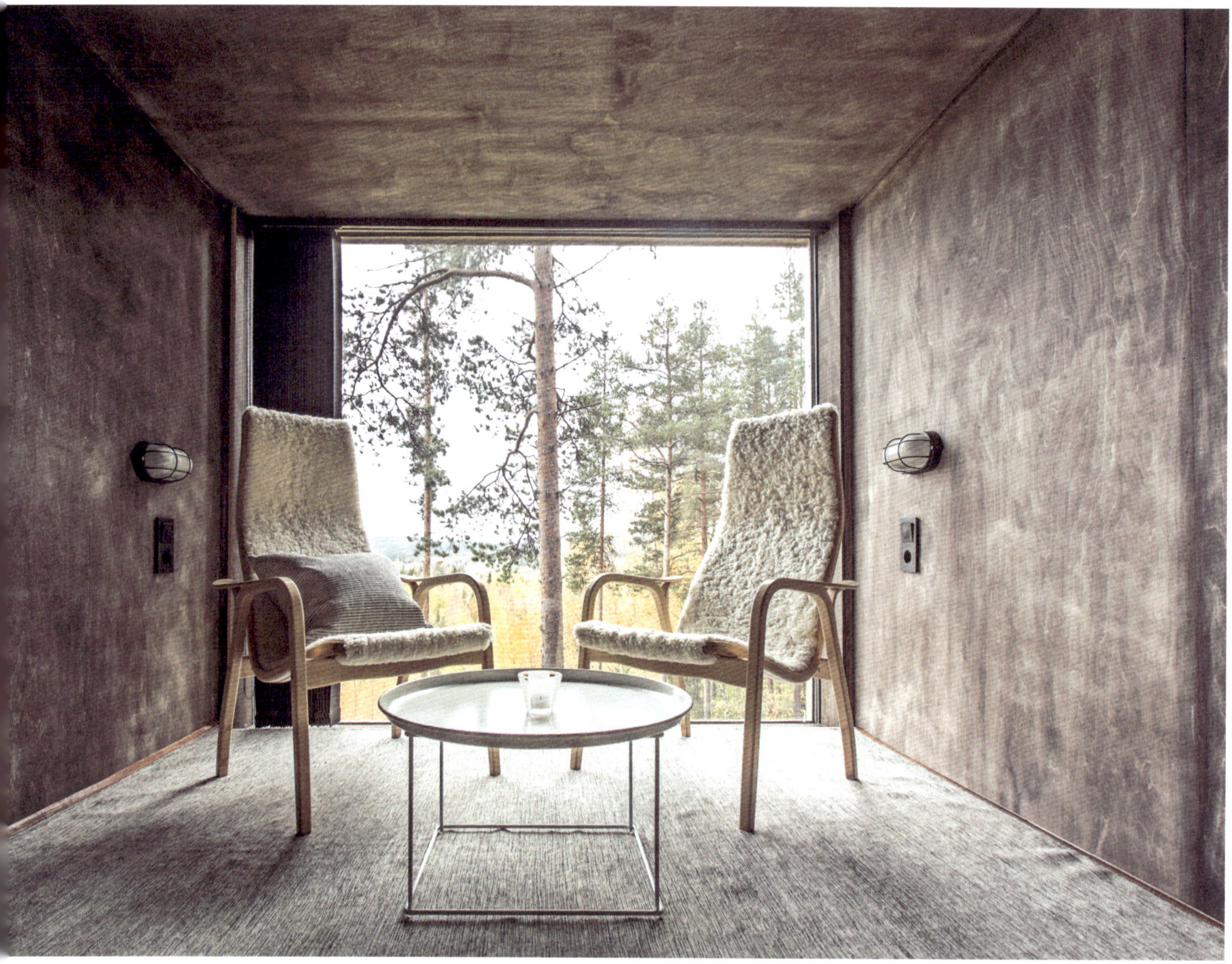

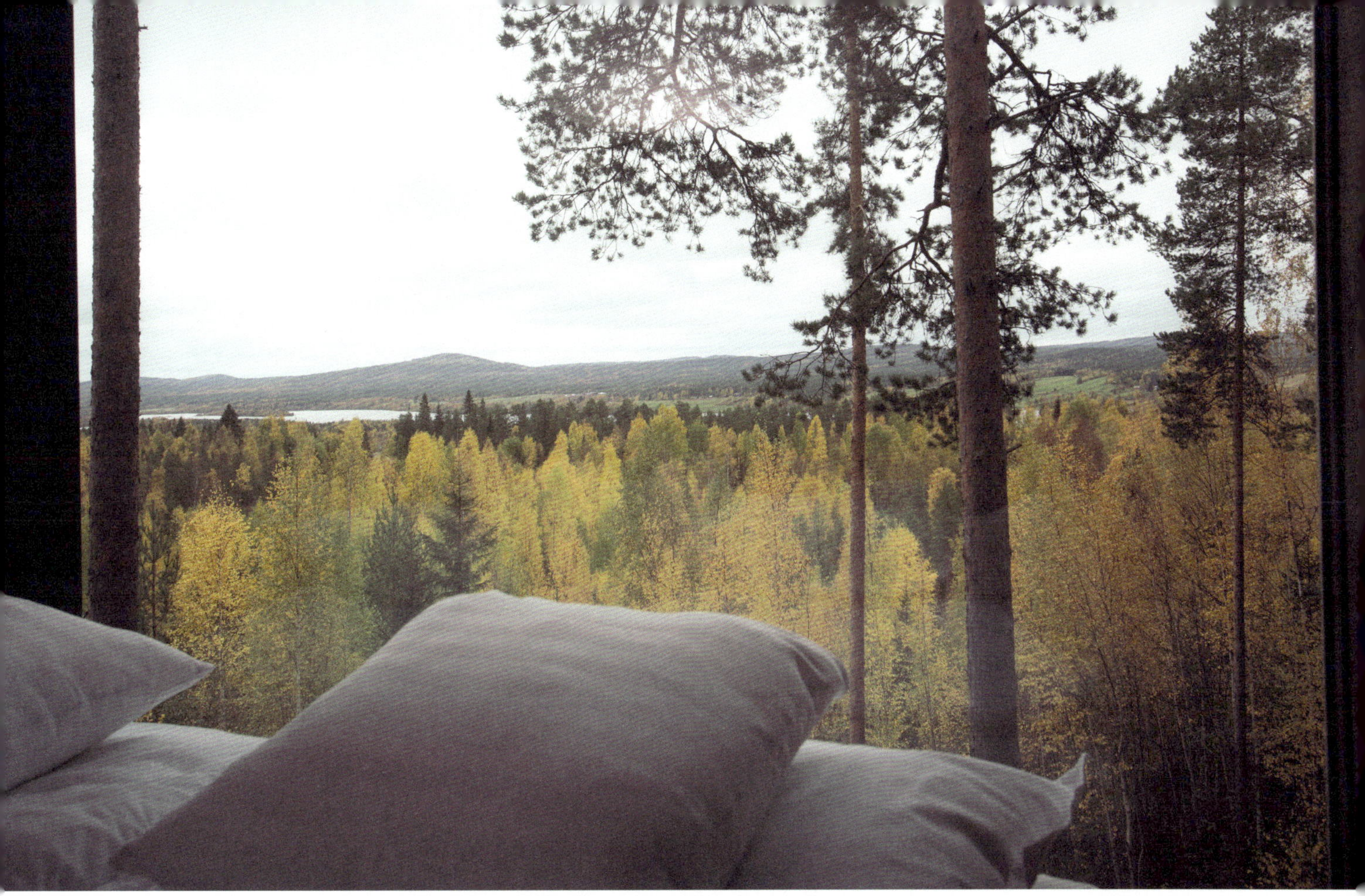
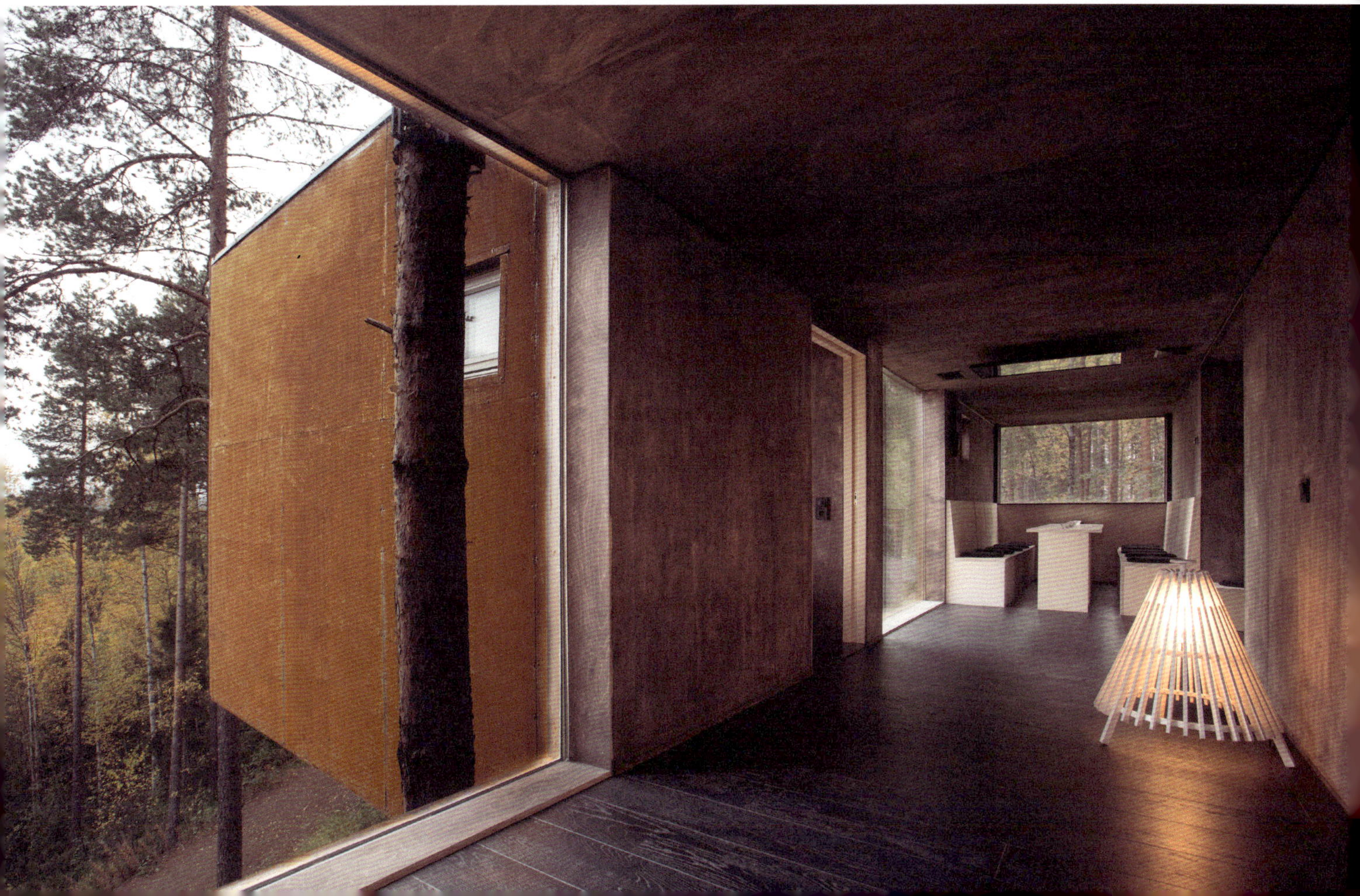

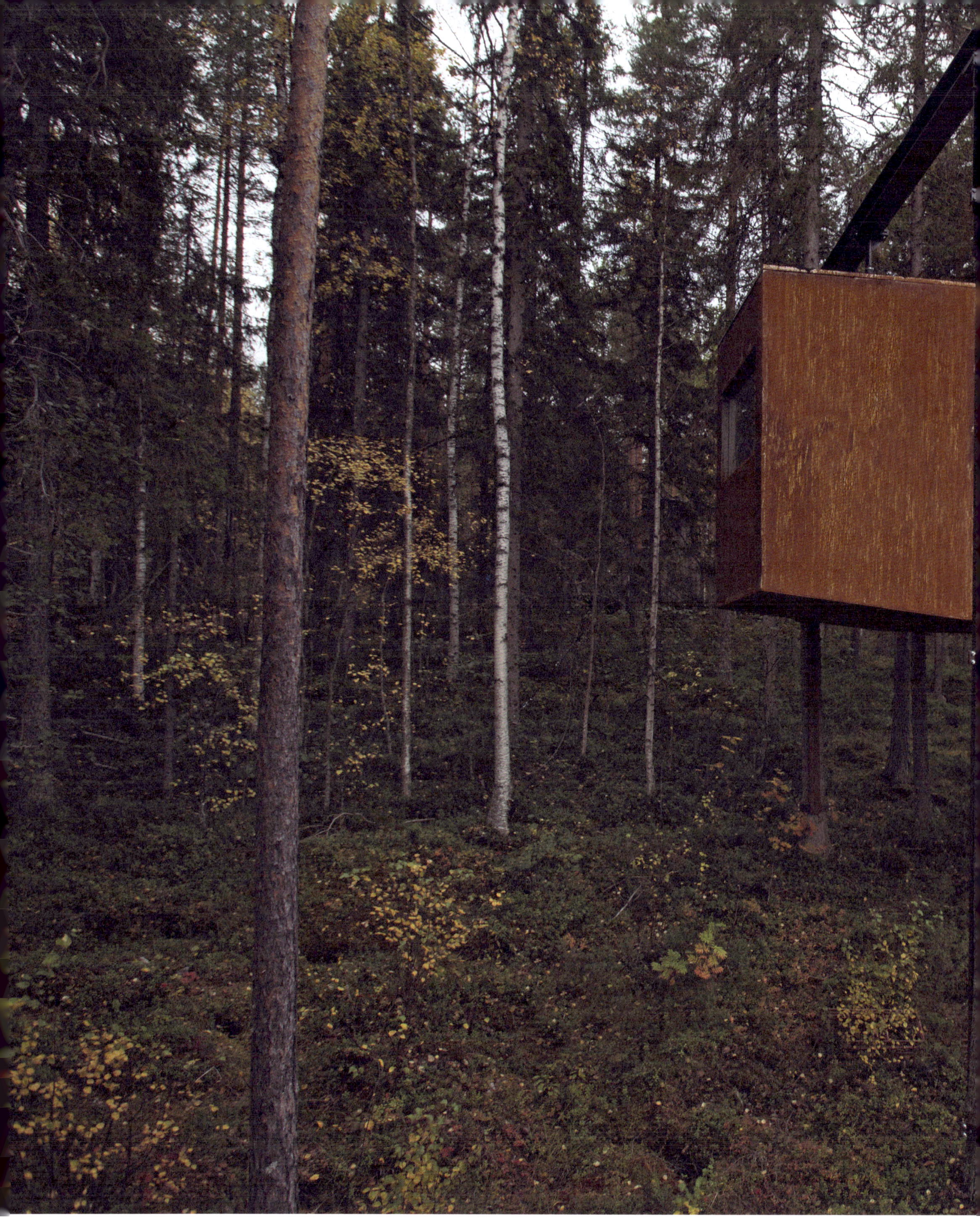

DRAGONFLY

Standing Out from the Crowd

A splash of vibrant colour in an otherwise neutral and wholly natural landscape

BLUE CONE
NORRBOTTEN, SWEDEN

Located in an arboreal forest in Sweden, Treehotel is the most fantastic village of getaway cabins. Conceived by Britta Jonsson-Lindvall and Kent Lindvall, it features a number of unforgettable cabins in which guests can experience life fully immersed in nature, among pine trees and other verdant flora, and perhaps relive adventures from their childhoods, whether remembered or read in stories from their youth. While most of the cabins in the woodland are perched up high among the branches, blending into their surroundings, Blue Cone does quite the opposite. For one thing, it is raised only slightly above the rocky forest floor, on a ridge with wide-open views across the treetops. For another, it is not blue. Still another, it is not quite a cone. Instead, this fun cabin for four is a bright-red cube with a steep-pitched roof. Inside, all is neutral, with whitewashed walls and pinewood furnishings, and a huge picture window from which to admire the chilly Nordic landscape.

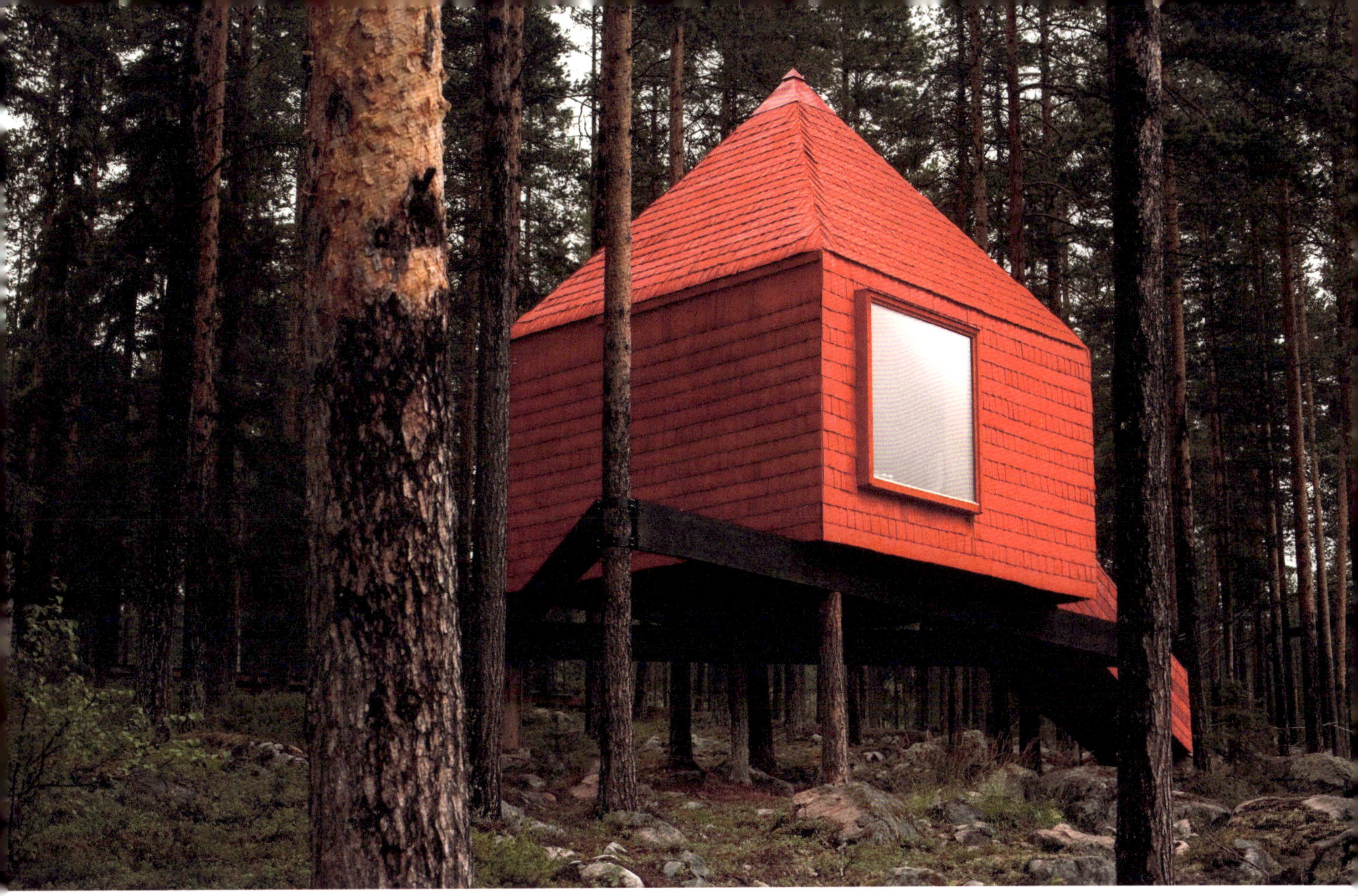

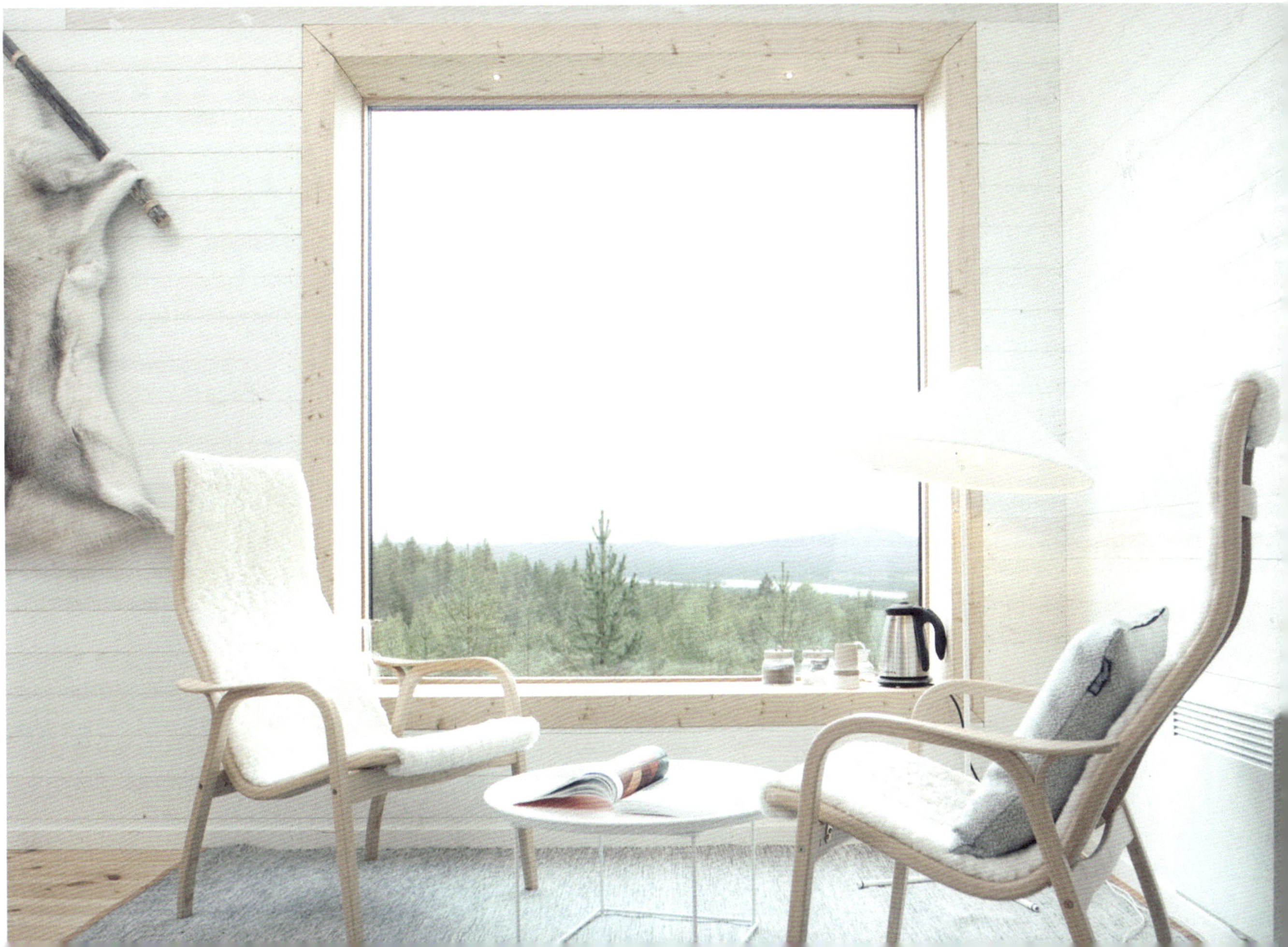

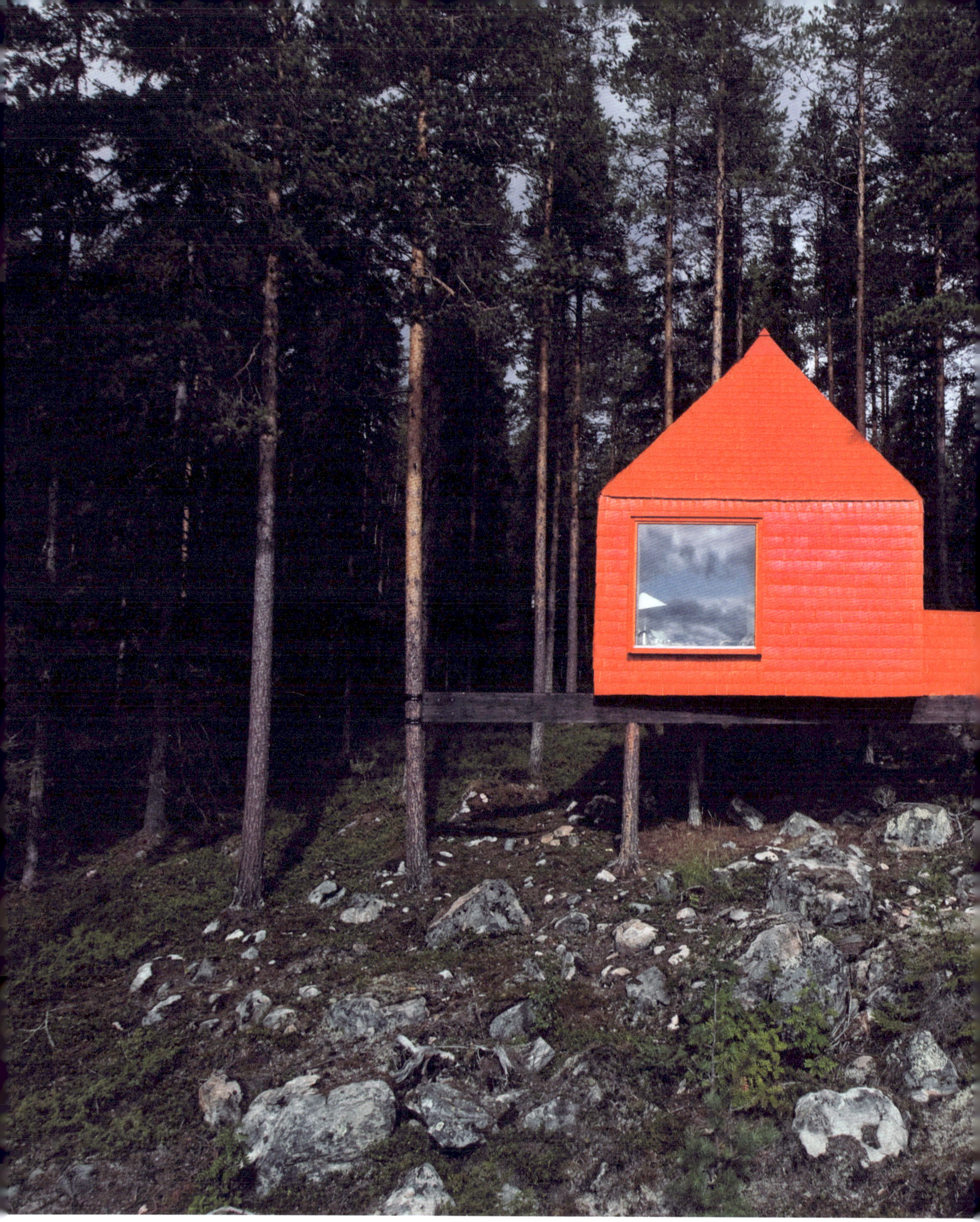

BLUE CONE

A Room with a Treetop View

Sleeping up high in a Swedish pine forest mere miles from the Arctic Circle

THE CABIN
NORRBOTTEN,
SWEDEN

One of several Treehotel accommodations to feature in this book (see Mirrorcube, 7th Room, Dragonfly, the Bird's Nest, and Blue Cone), this snug capsule is suspended from four trees and, from some angles, appears to be floating in mid-air. Located at the top of a steep slope, the cabin is accessed via a long bridge strung up high between the trees, at the end of which the front door seems to almost hover in place, before revealing an outdoor deck with seating and stairs to the shelter below. The bed takes centre stage inside, in a room with a wall of windows and plush cushions on which guests can lounge and gaze out across the forest landscape and the Lule River valley beyond — not for too long, though, as hearty meals at Britta Jonsson-Lindvall's Guesthouse await, as do silent treks through the forest. Those visiting from September to March can also take local fishing trips and pleasant berry-picking forest walks. Come nighttime, they may also get to see the northern lights illuminate the dark sky.

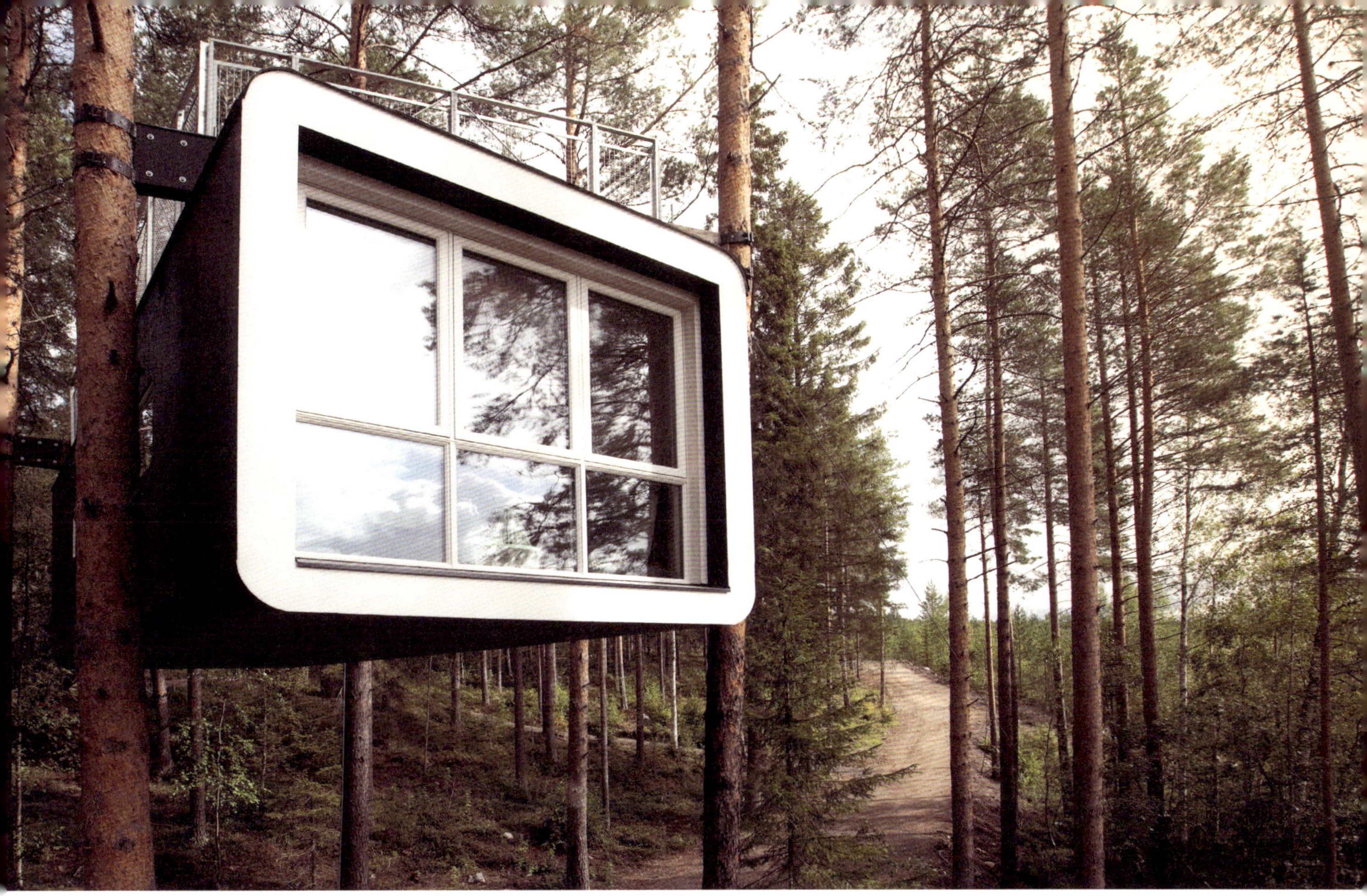

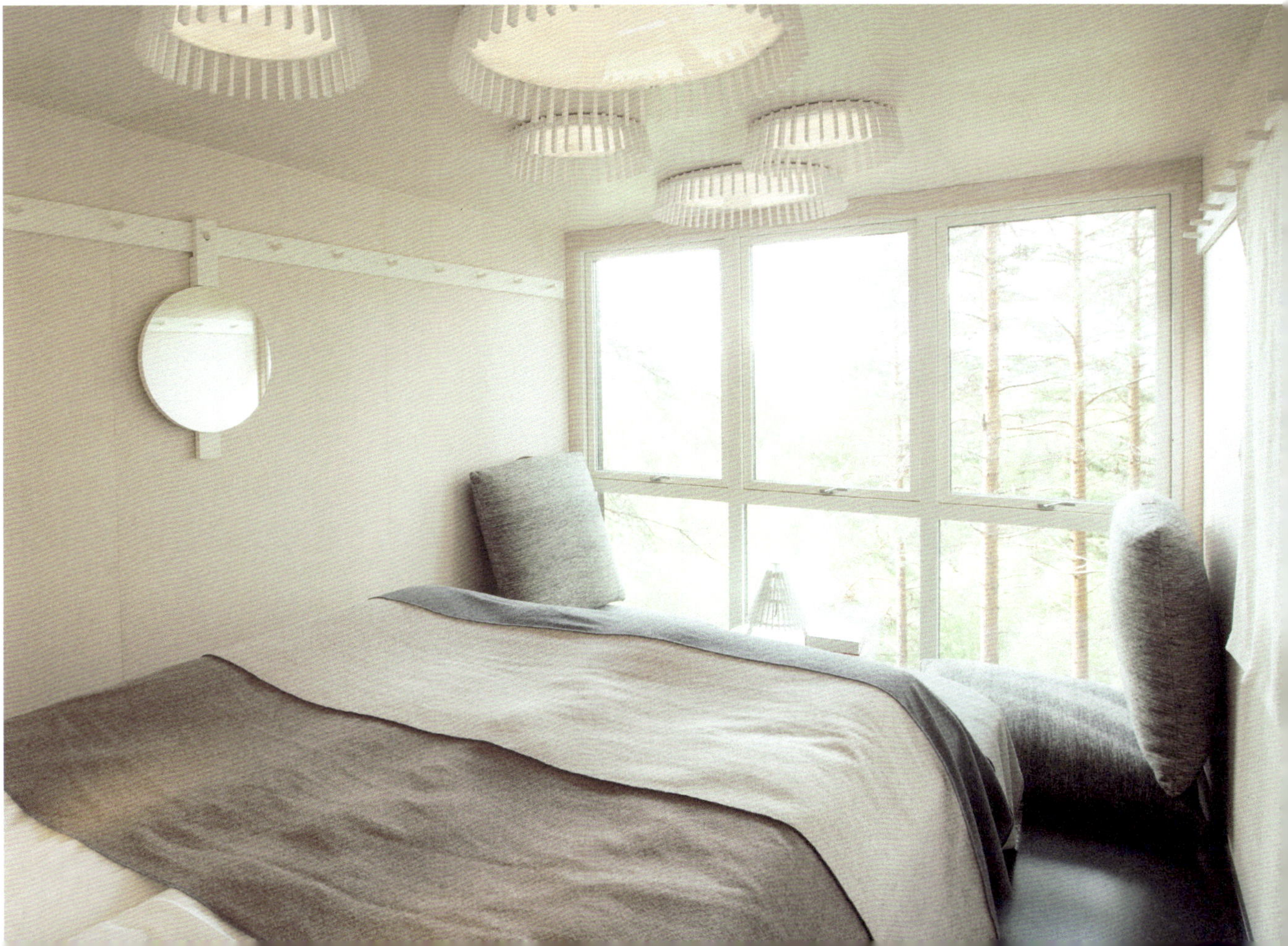

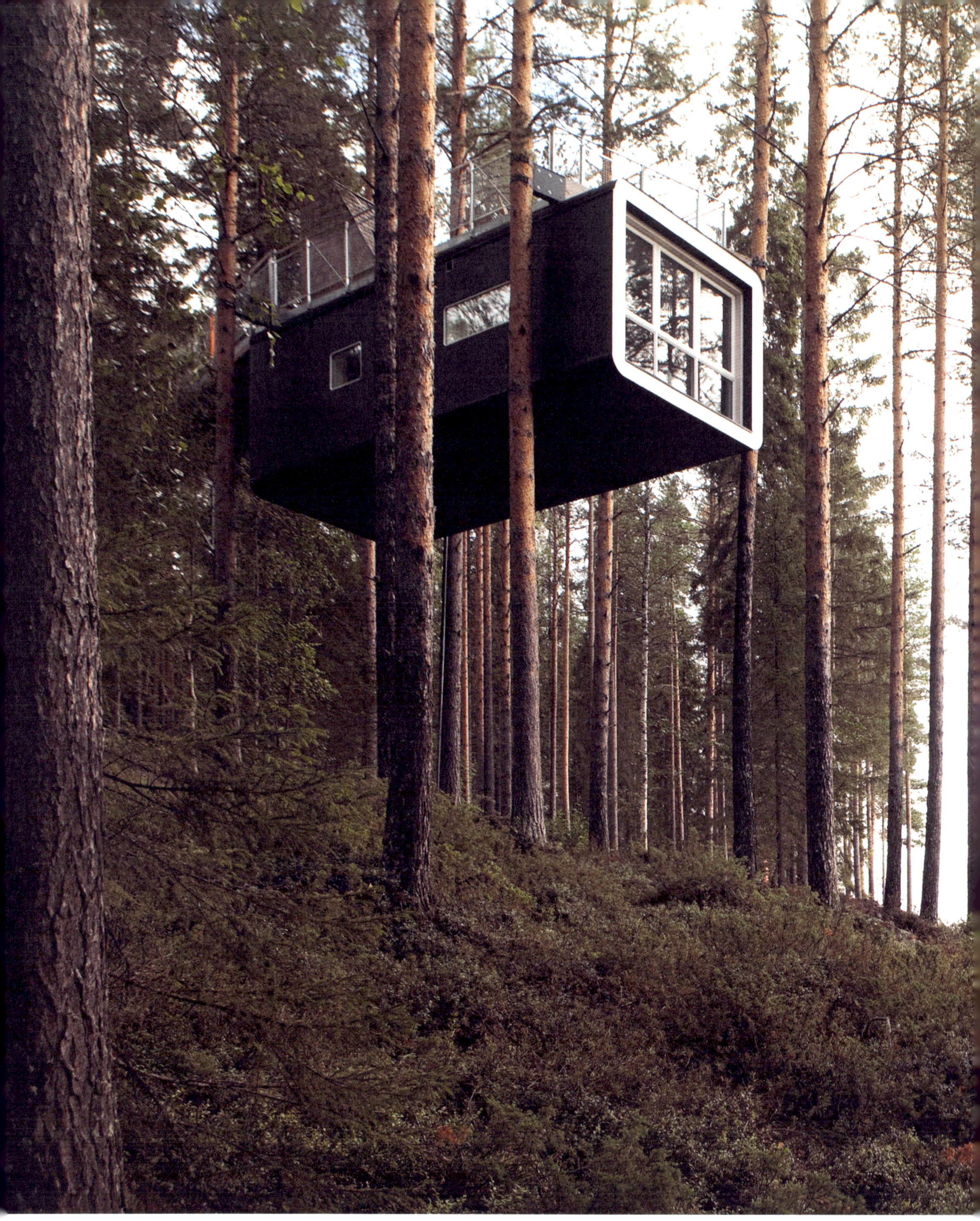

THE CABIN

A Treehouse with a Modernist Edge

This stylish, contemporary treehouse in a French woodland setting has all the comforts of the modern home

LE CÈDRE BLANC TWO
CORRÈZE,
FRANCE

This striking tree cabin makes the ideal getaway for city types who love to escape to the country for some well-earned R&R, but without having to give up too many of their home comforts. Though minimalist in design, the space has all the mod cons, from a chequer-tiled shower room and a little kitchen unit to a TV and Nespresso machine. But that's not to say these modern touches come at the expense of the cabin's naturalness, as the neat design nestles comfortably among the treetops with minimal impact. For its part, the interior is lined with timber in harmony with the branches just outside, and an immense glass wall floods the space with greenery, allowing guests to feel fully immersed in the woodland landscape. Le Cèdre Blanc Two is one of several such cabins set in 40 hectares (100 acres) of beautiful woodland at Cabanes de Salagnac in Corrèze.

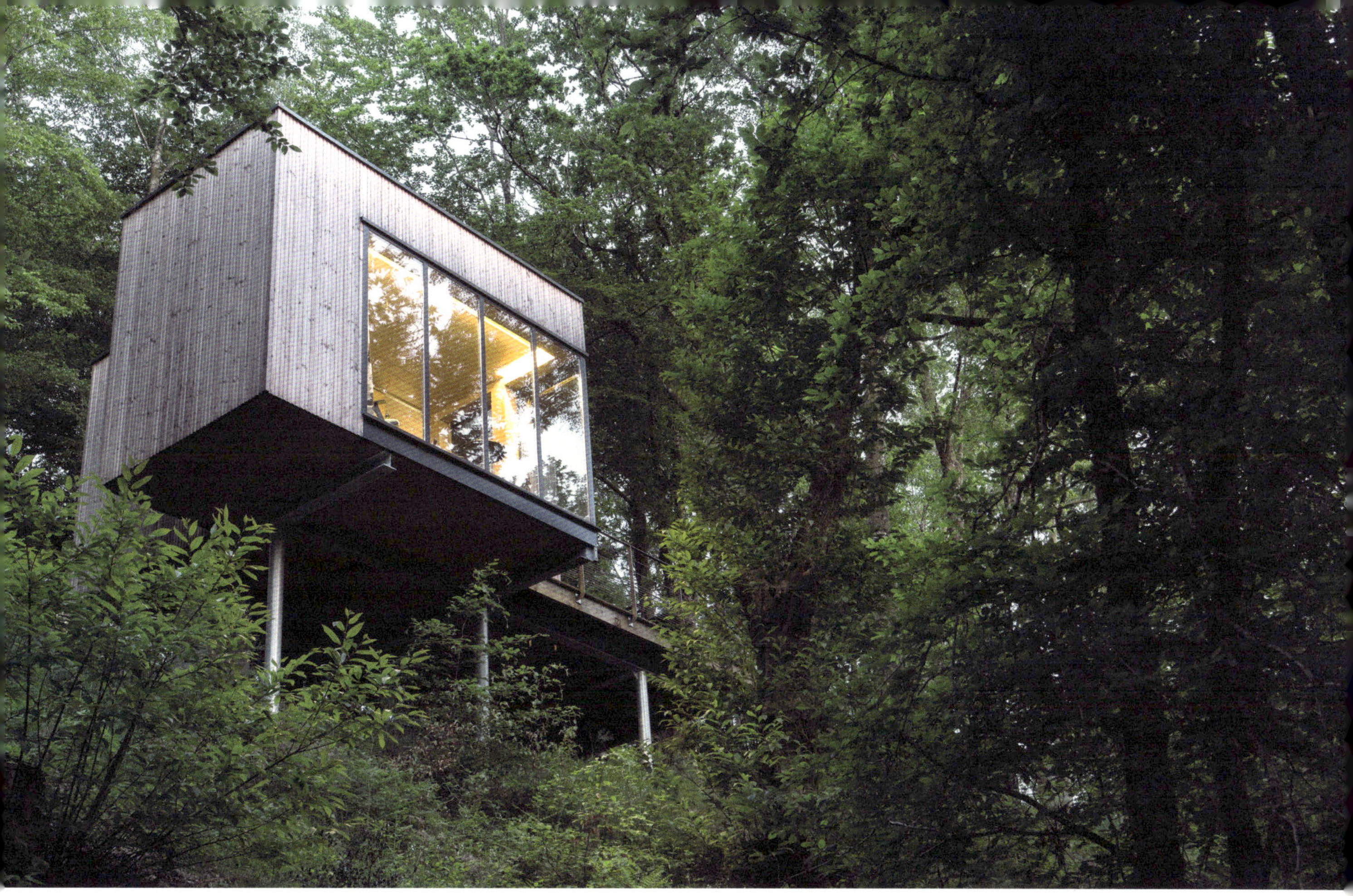

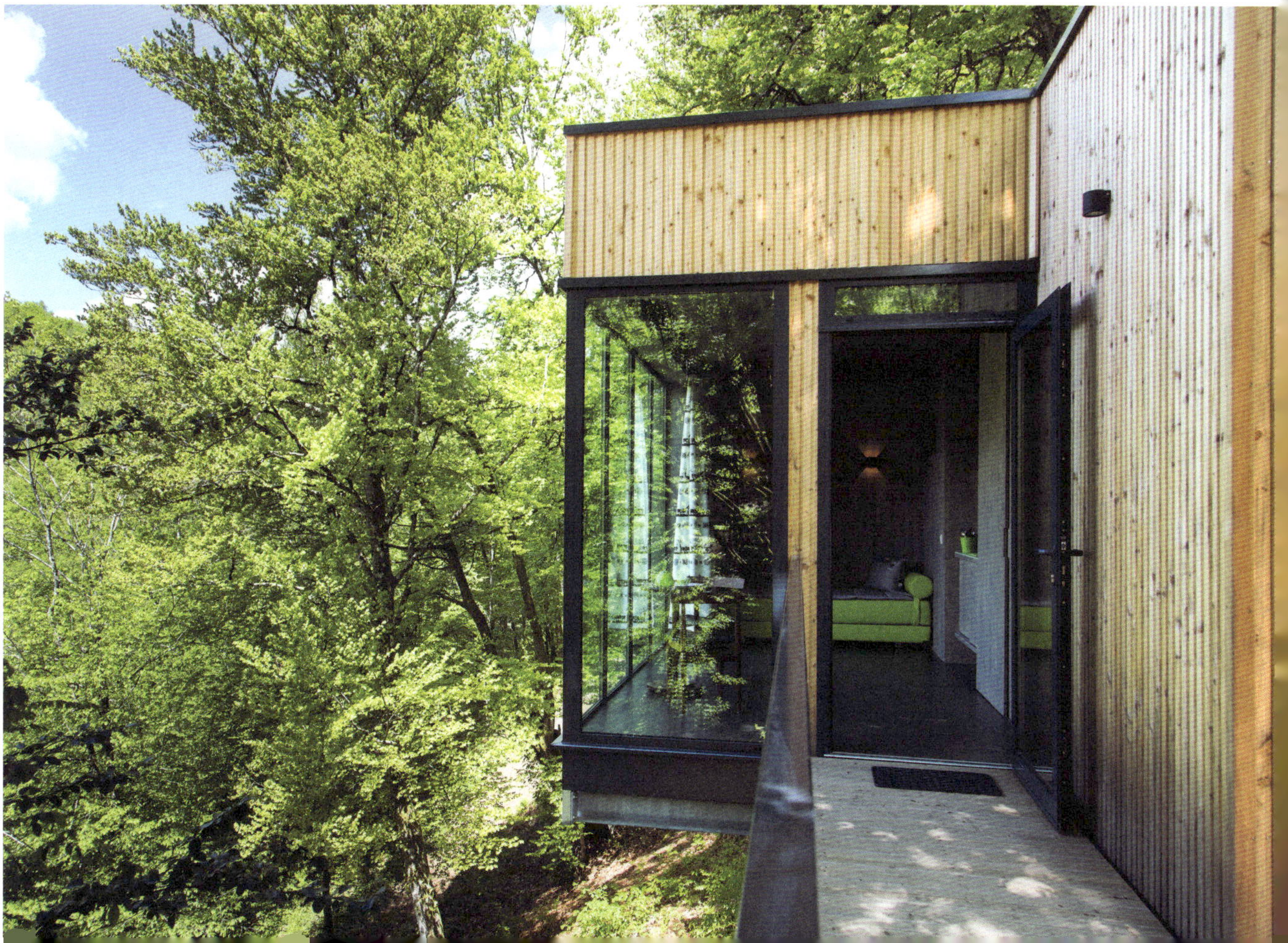

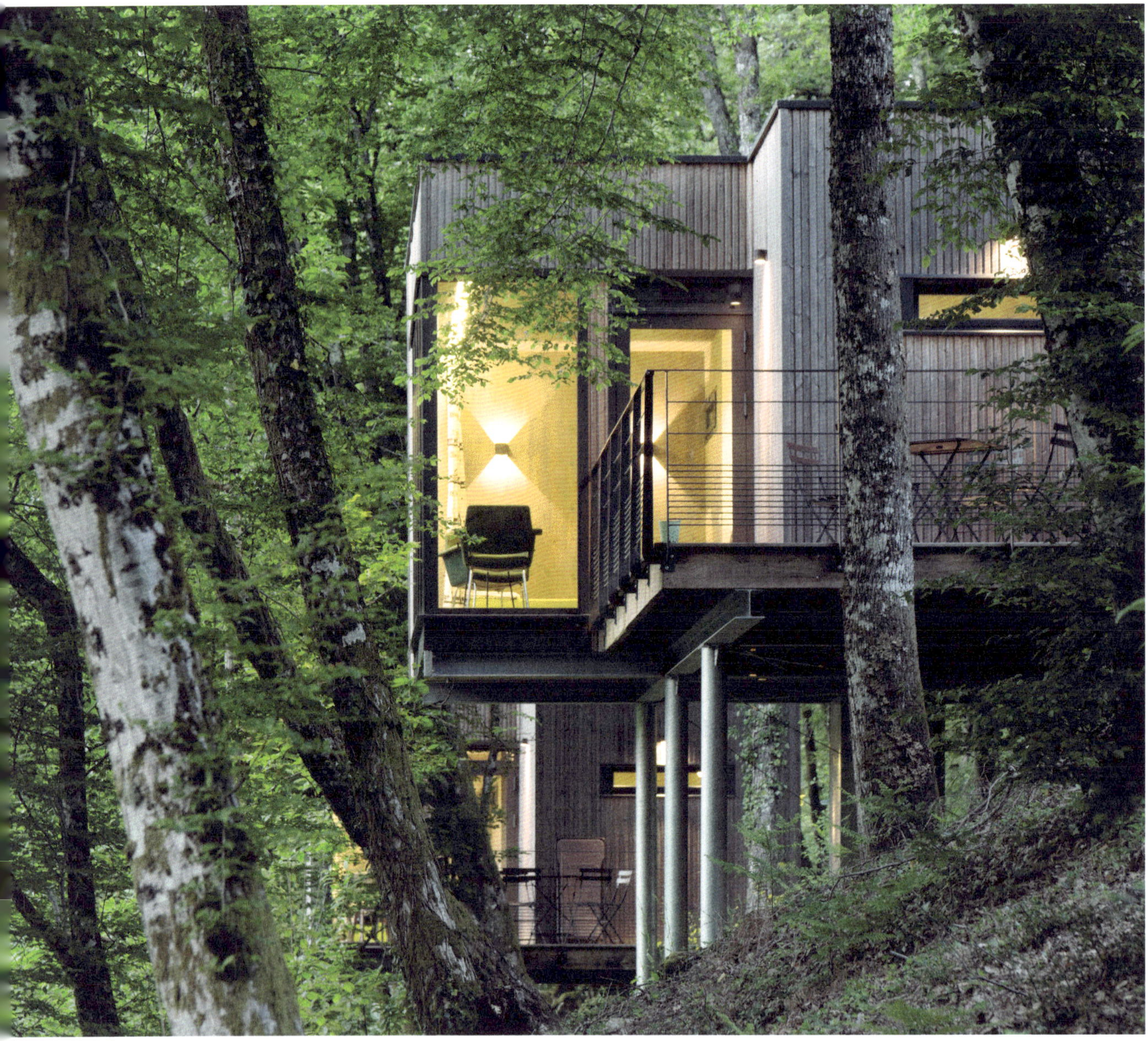

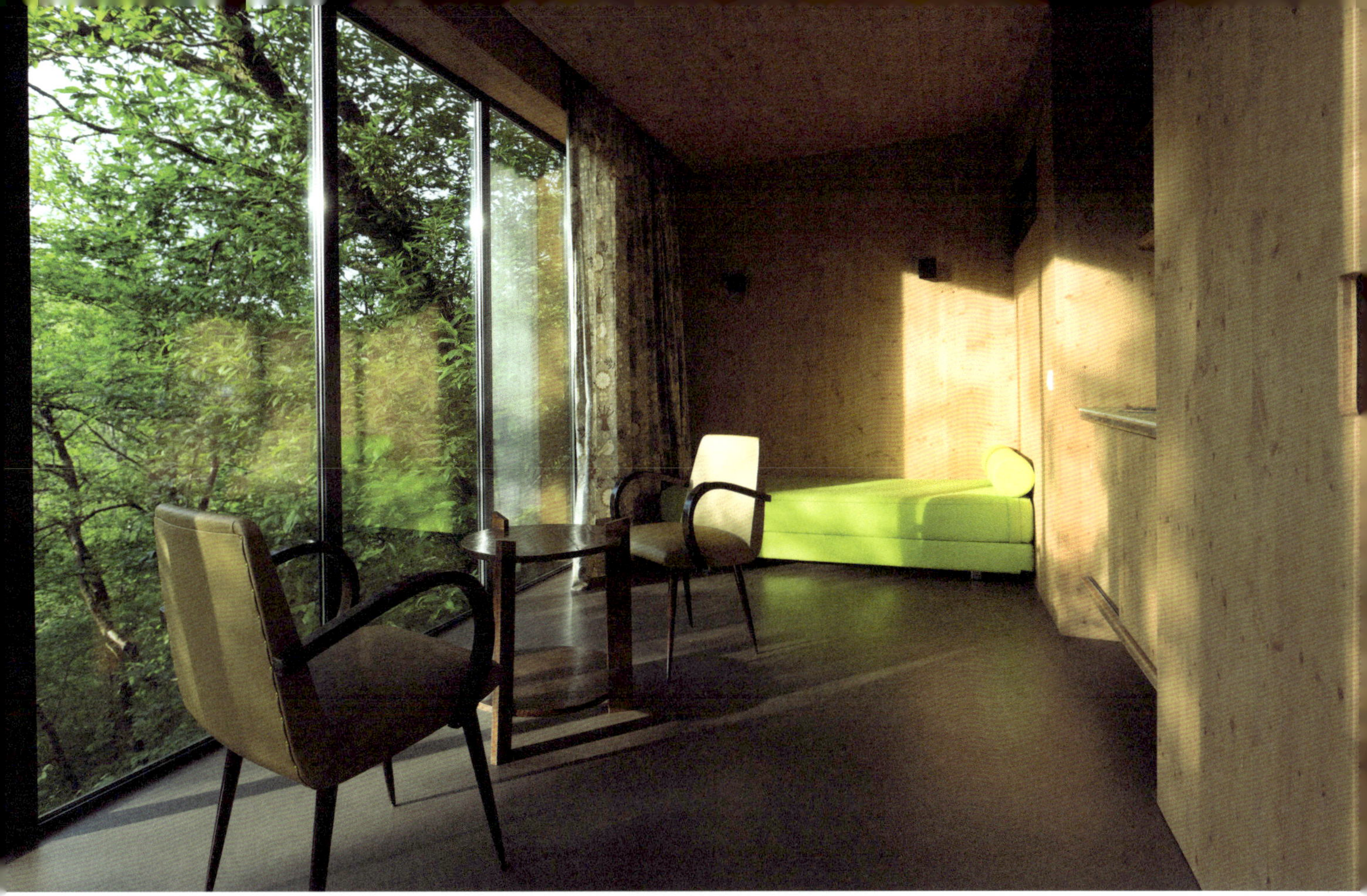

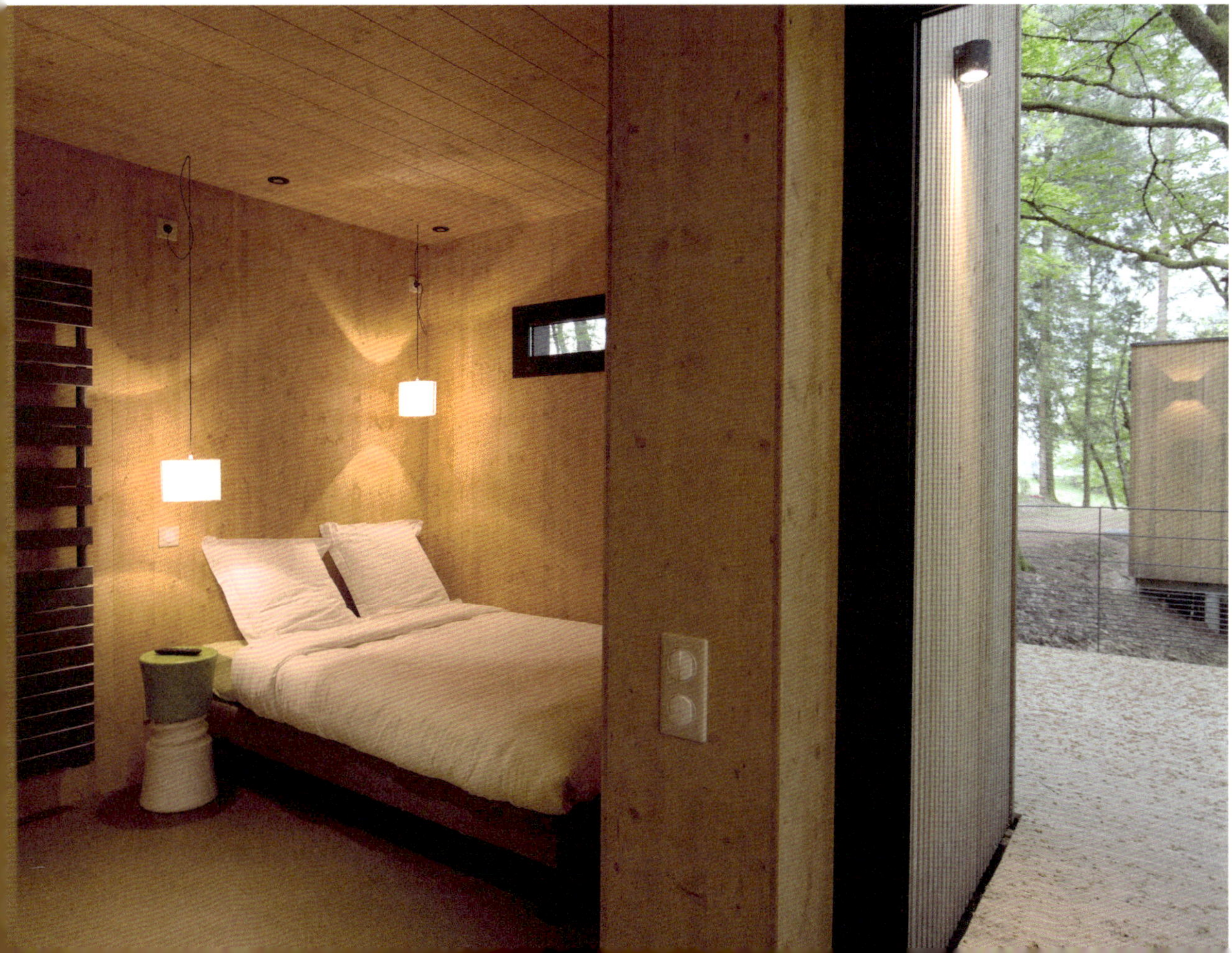

Weekend
Wanderings

Looking at how much you can get from even the briefest time in nature

— by expert microadventurer and explorer Siân Lewis

This is an ode to little adventures. After all, most of us are not round-the-world explorers, Everest summiteers, or full-time forest dwellers. We have jobs to do, children and cats to feed, and bins to put out. Epic expeditions may be few and far between, but I'd argue that small, accessible 'microadventures' can be just as good for the soul. Small adventures are open to everyone, fit around busy schedules, and focus on the pleasures rather than the privations of exploring the great outdoors, being in nature, and escaping the everyday — no hardships or frostbite allowed.

The joy of a microadventure is that it can take any shape, but I'll loosely define it as taking place over a day or two, and as being an accessible, local, and beginner-friendly way of getting into the wild. Remember that there's no need to cross an ocean for a taste of the wilderness: we all have wild spaces such as national parks nearby, places where you can climb epic mountains, walk lost trails, take a dip in the ocean, and sleep out under the stars. Local adventures also have the added bonus of being more eco-friendly

There's a little adventure out there to suit everyone, but I think there are fewer simpler pleasures than spending a weekend holed up in the wild.

than hopping on a plane, which reduces our negative impact on the planet. And one of the biggest joys of exploring on a small, local level is discovering how simple and cheap it actually is to get outside once you own a few basic bits of kit, such as a good waterproof jacket and decent hiking boots.

There's a little adventure out there to suit everyone, but I think there are fewer simpler pleasures than spending a weekend holed up in the wild. What kind of bolthole you choose — log cabin, cosy yurt, or lofty treehouse — is up to you, but my favourite escapes are always the ones that are off the grid and on their own in the landscape, that allow you to physically step away from your chirruping phone and pinging laptop and really reconnect with the world around you.

I once stayed in an old woodcutter's cottage tucked away in a forest clearing — it had no heating or electricity, so in the depths of winter I had to wear multiple jumpers and constantly bank up the wood stoves to keep cosy. That said, the gentle rhythm of reading books by candlelight, exploring rough tracks in the surrounding forest, chopping and carrying wood, and falling asleep under a pile of blankets to the flickering of a fire was the perfect recipe for a weekend break very different from my hectic city life. The simple pleasures involved in staying somewhere off the beaten track — keeping a fire alive, cooking outdoors, watching the stars before bed — turn a short weekend away into a proper adventure, and one you'll remember for years to come.

It's not really a microadventure if you don't venture out of doors, of course. My favourite way to explore a new landscape is on foot — and half the fun is in mapping out a path beforehand. Planning new hiking routes can seem daunting, but there are plenty of beginner-friendly ways to get started. Wherever you live or wherever you're staying, you're likely to have amazing trails and walking paths very close to you that you've never heard of before. Try downloading a mapping app, such as Ordnance Survey or Komoot, and plotting new walking or cycling routes from your front door. I love to walk along a coast path — as long as you keep the sea on the right side of you, you'll know exactly where you are.

If you're a more experienced hiker, pick somewhere to stay near mountains. I find that there's nothing like a hike into the hills to make you feel like you've really got space to breathe. I also love to time a mountain trek for sunrise or sunset. It's the perfect way to fit what feels like an epic adventure into just a few hours — just don't forget your head torch!

Even living in a city doesn't mean you can't find adventure on your doorstep, and exploring the urban sprawl can make you see your hometown in a new light. You can join a global treasure hunt by planning a geocaching walk, and in smaller cities you might be able to walk or run from the centre right out into the countryside in a few hours, or take a local train to a beauty spot you've never visited before and still be home in

Take a dip in a river, a lake, or the ocean and you'll instantly feel more connected to our little blue planet — swim in every season and you'll soon be more attuned to the wild spaces around you and how they are constantly changing.

Fair warning — microadventuring is addictive. Small-scale exploration makes you see your free time with new eyes. Go local, be mindful, find the potential in every moment. You'll be surprised at how much you can get from even a brief escape, and, when you really get under their skin, at what you can find in places you might once have taken for granted. In the end, the art of adventure is all about perspective.

time for tea. A personal favourite is getting a new perspective by investing in an inflatable stand-up paddle board. Paddling along inland waterways or taking to the coast offers up a totally different way of viewing your home city or your local stretch of seaside.

Although I love a mountain hike and drifting along a canal, it's wild water that I turn to when I want to feel connected to nature. Wild swimming makes a perfect little adventure that you can do in a day, or even in your lunch break, and still feel like you've had a taste of the natural world. Take a dip in a river, a lake, or the ocean and you'll instantly feel more connected to our little blue planet — swim in every season and you'll soon be more attuned to the wild spaces around you and how they are constantly changing. Wild-swimming guidebooks and websites map out spots where you can have a paddle, from secret plunge pools to rocky coves, and if you're feeling brave, a quick skinny dip is a great way to find a sense of freedom. Swimming in the altogether is amazingly liberating — I think it's the ultimate stress reliever, guaranteed to make even the most humdrum day feel special.

```
It's not really a microadventure if you
don't venture out of doors, of course.
My favourite way to explore a new land-
scape is on foot — and half the fun is
in mapping out a path beforehand.
```

WEEKEND WANDERINGS

Spoiled for Choice in Dorset

A luxury woodland treehouse with no fewer than three options in treetop soaking

THE WOODSMAN'S TREEHOUSE
DORSET,
ENGLAND

Just 10 miles (16 kilometres) inland from Dorset's ancient Jurassic Coast, the Woodsman's Treehouse occupies a remote corner of an outdoorsy, village-vibe place that goes by the name Crafty Camping. The house is beautifully crafted, with log, board, and shingle-clad facades that, raised on stilts, nestle among the branches of an ancient oak. With a seemingly simple interior, an abundance of comfort can be found in the leather armchairs that bask in the heat of a central wood burner, and in a giant copper bath with verdant views. Guests can take their pick between rainfall shower on the decking outside or the outside hot tub, or they can climb the spiral stairs to the roof and enter their very own personal sauna. As befits any respectable treehouse, this one comes complete with rope bridge access and a slide for a fun exit. This is just one of several places to stay in the woodland village, which seeks to offer fun and luxury experiences in the wild, in accommodation that is built sustainably, with little impact on the surrounding landscape.

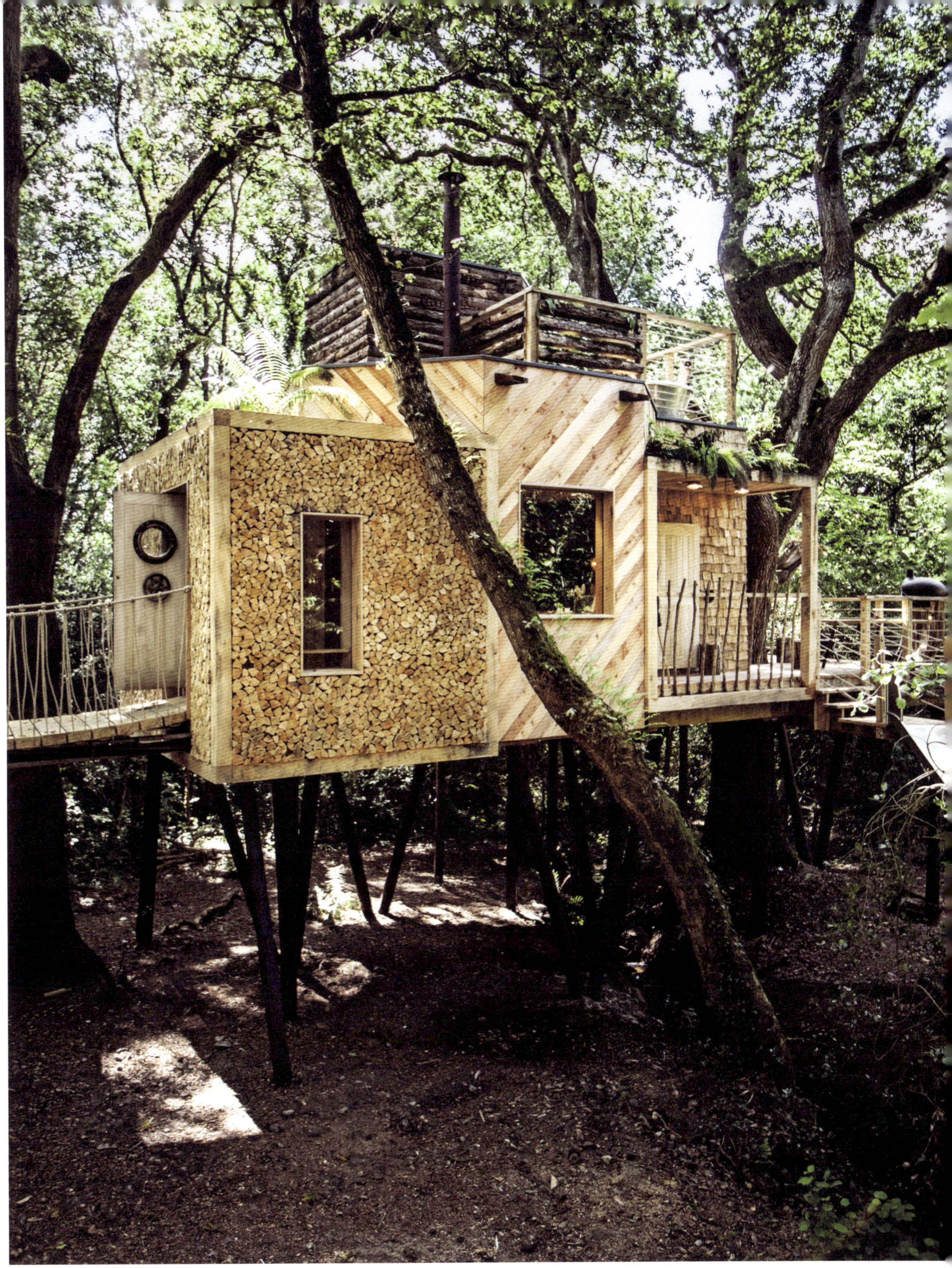

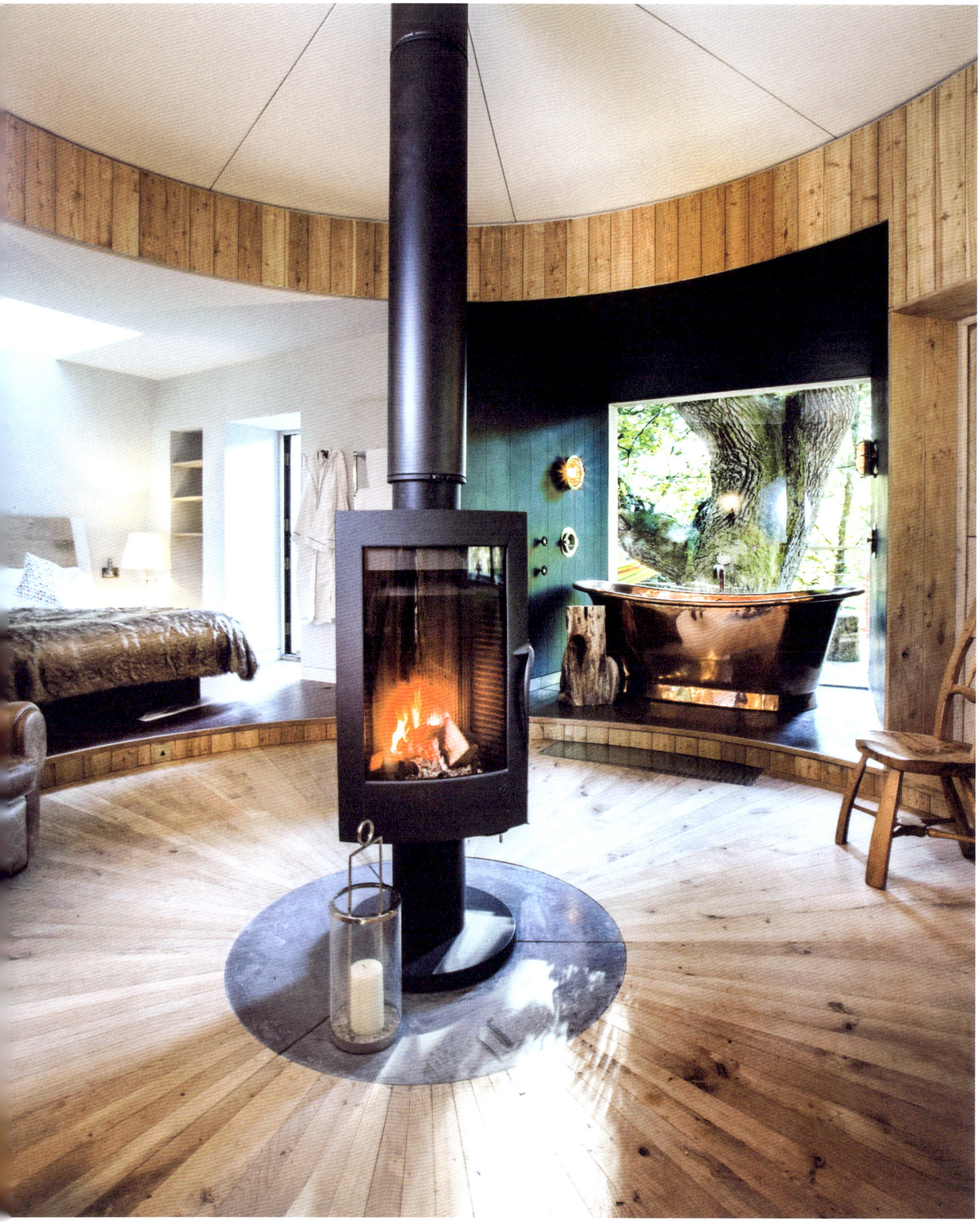

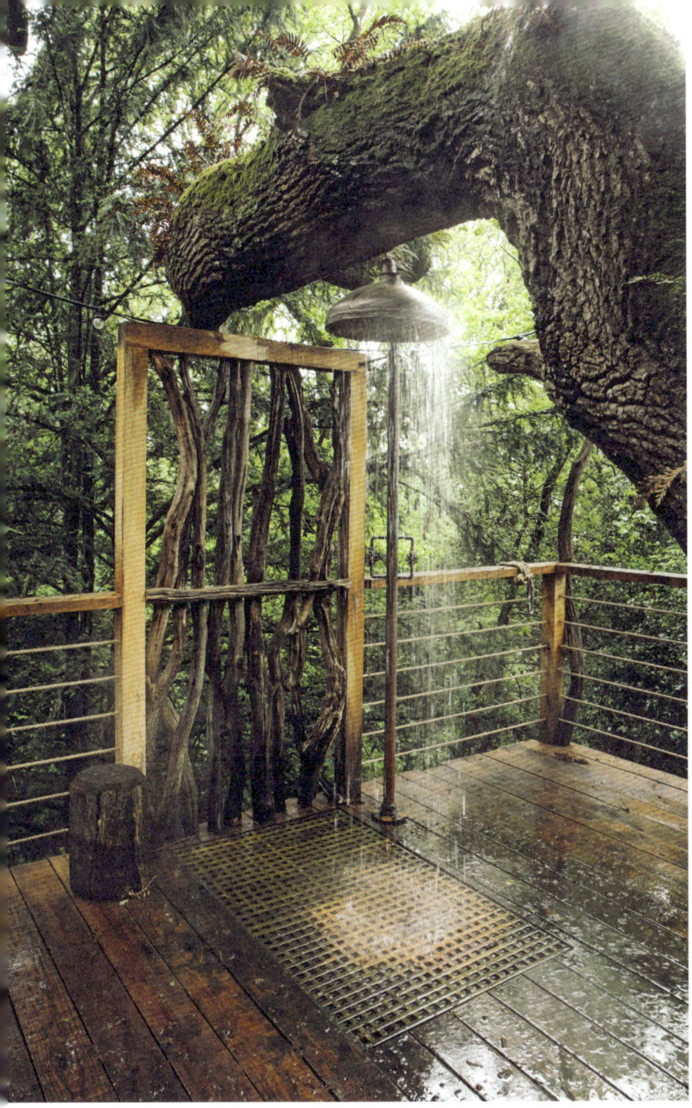

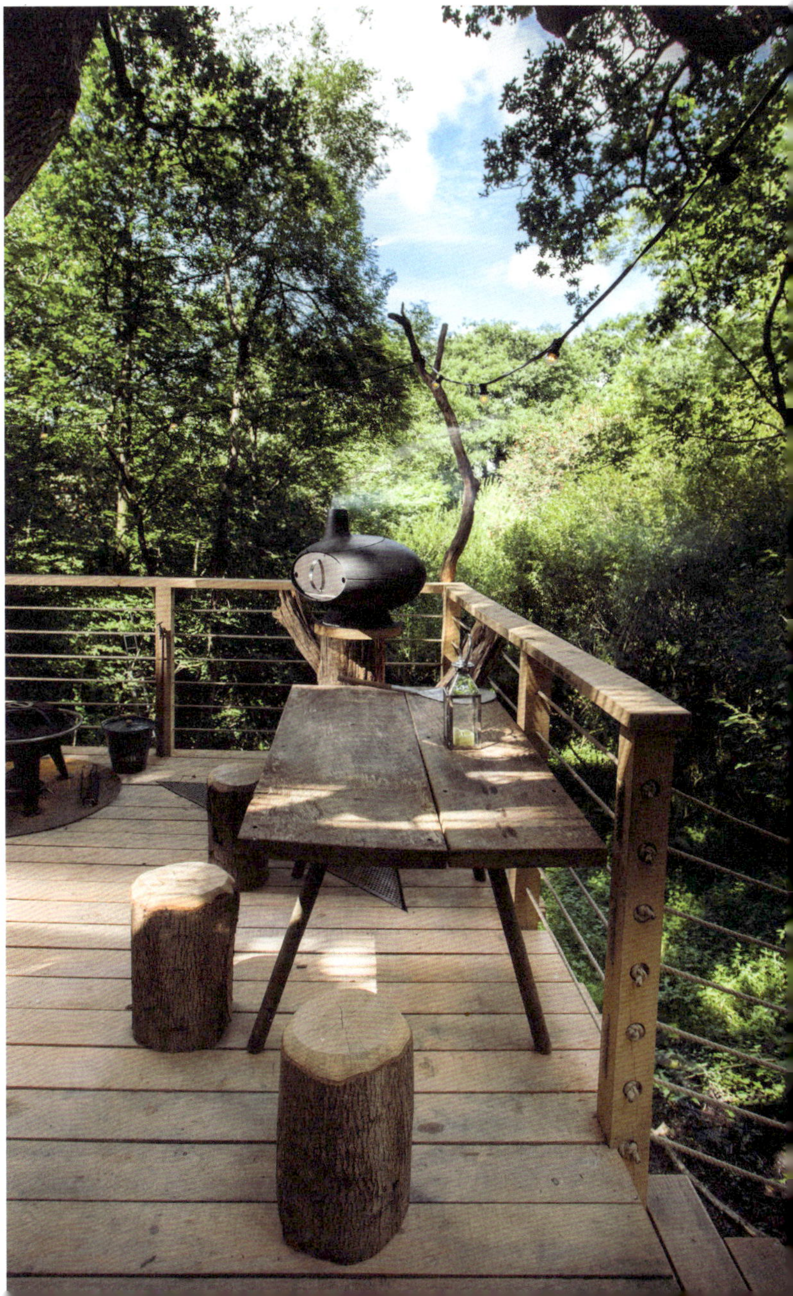

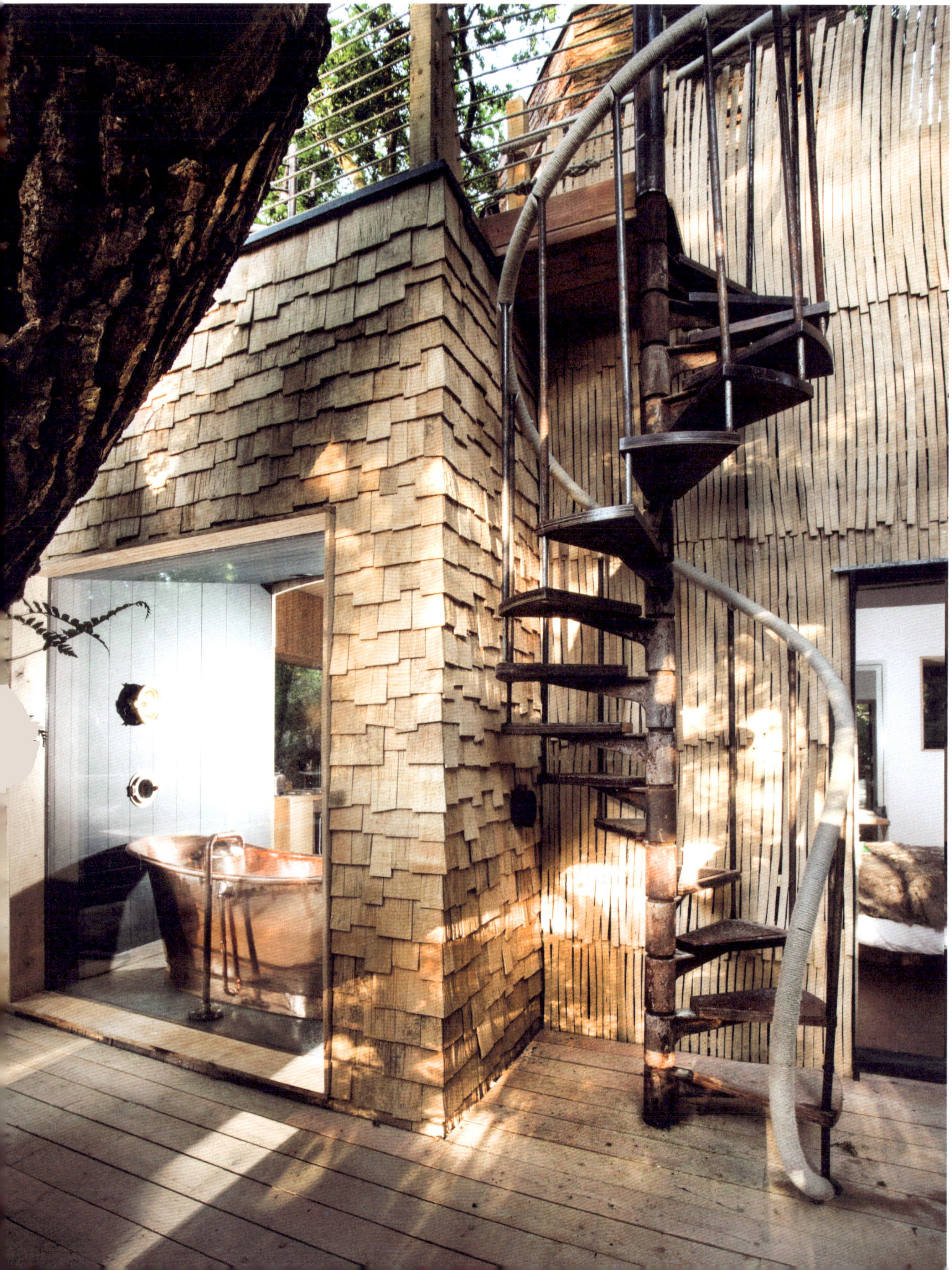

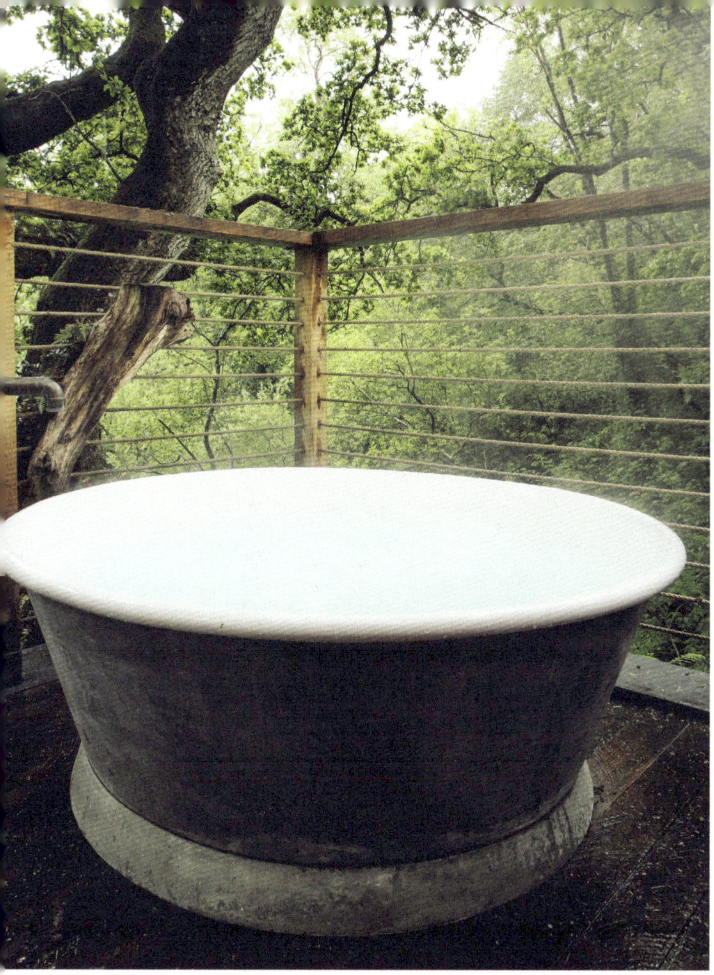
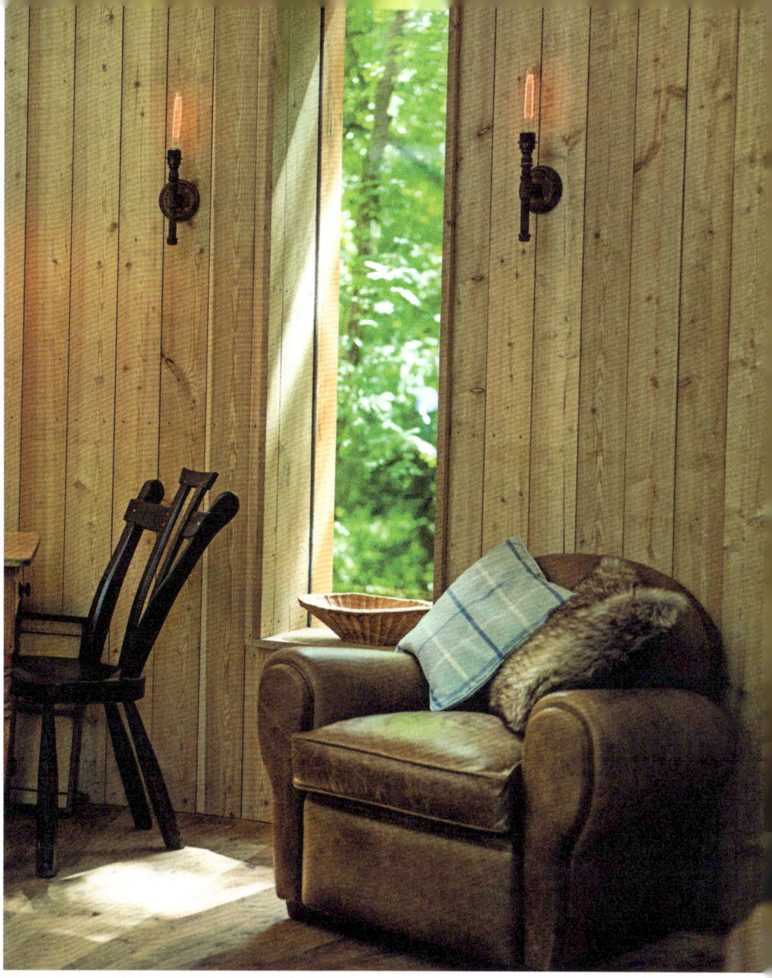
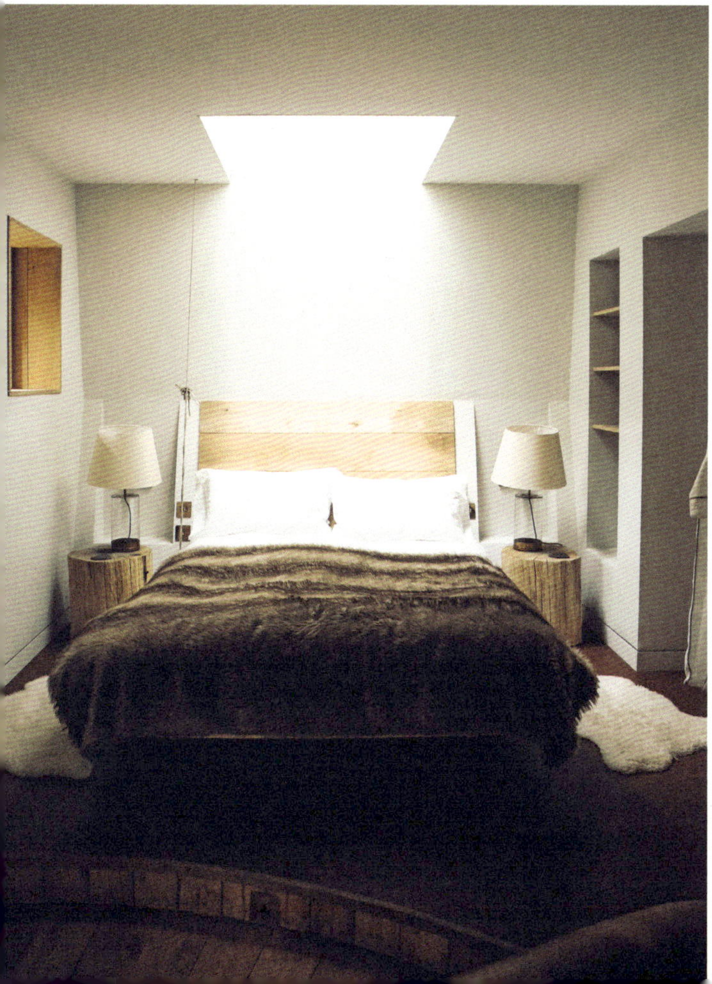
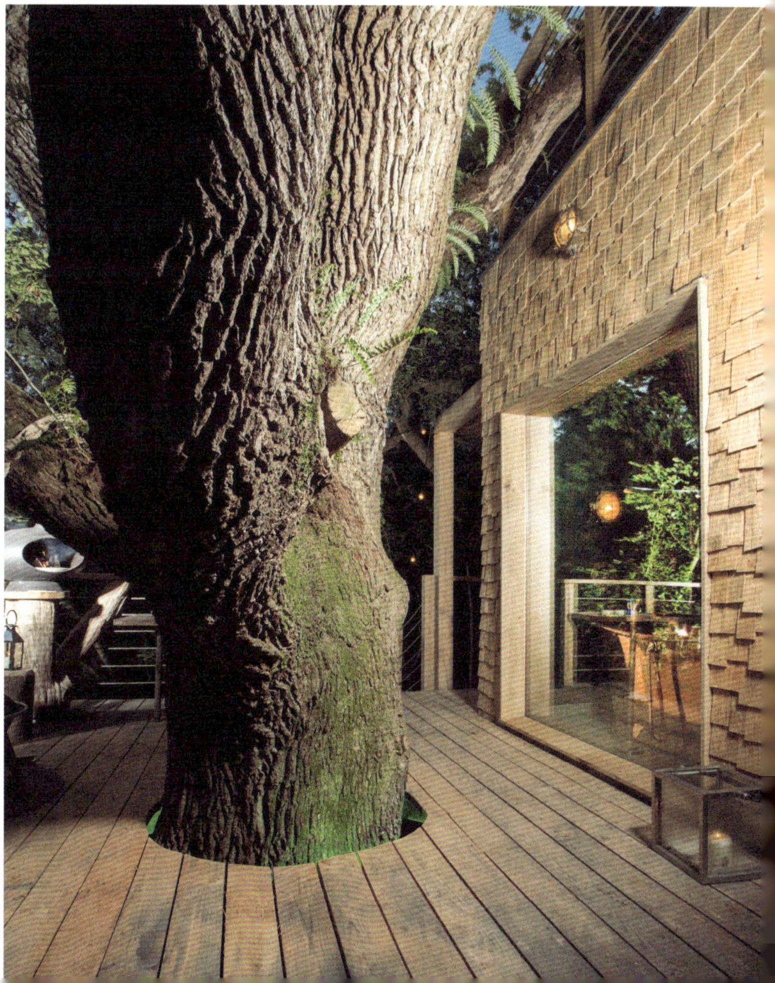

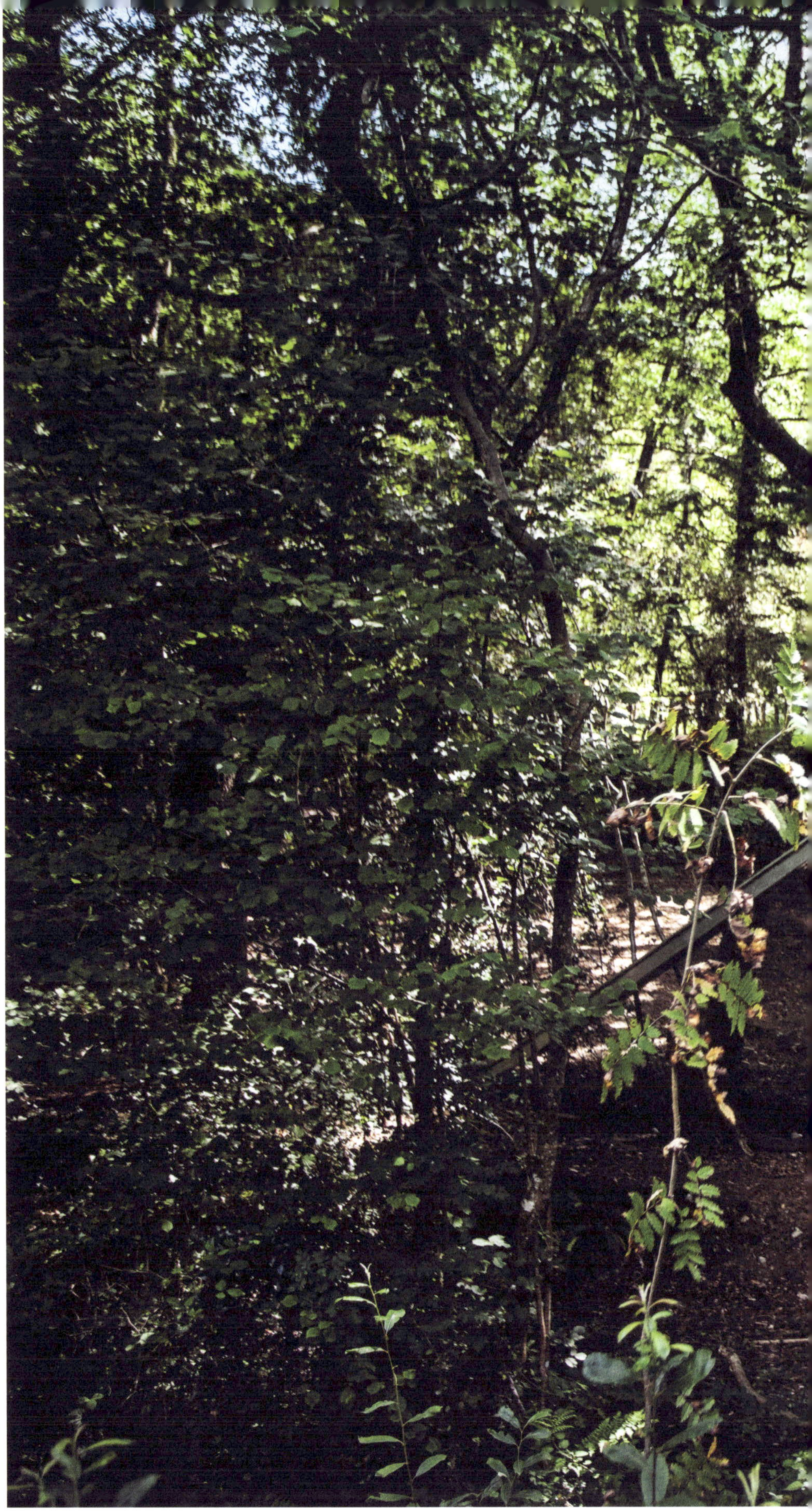

THE WOODSMAN'S TREEHOUSE

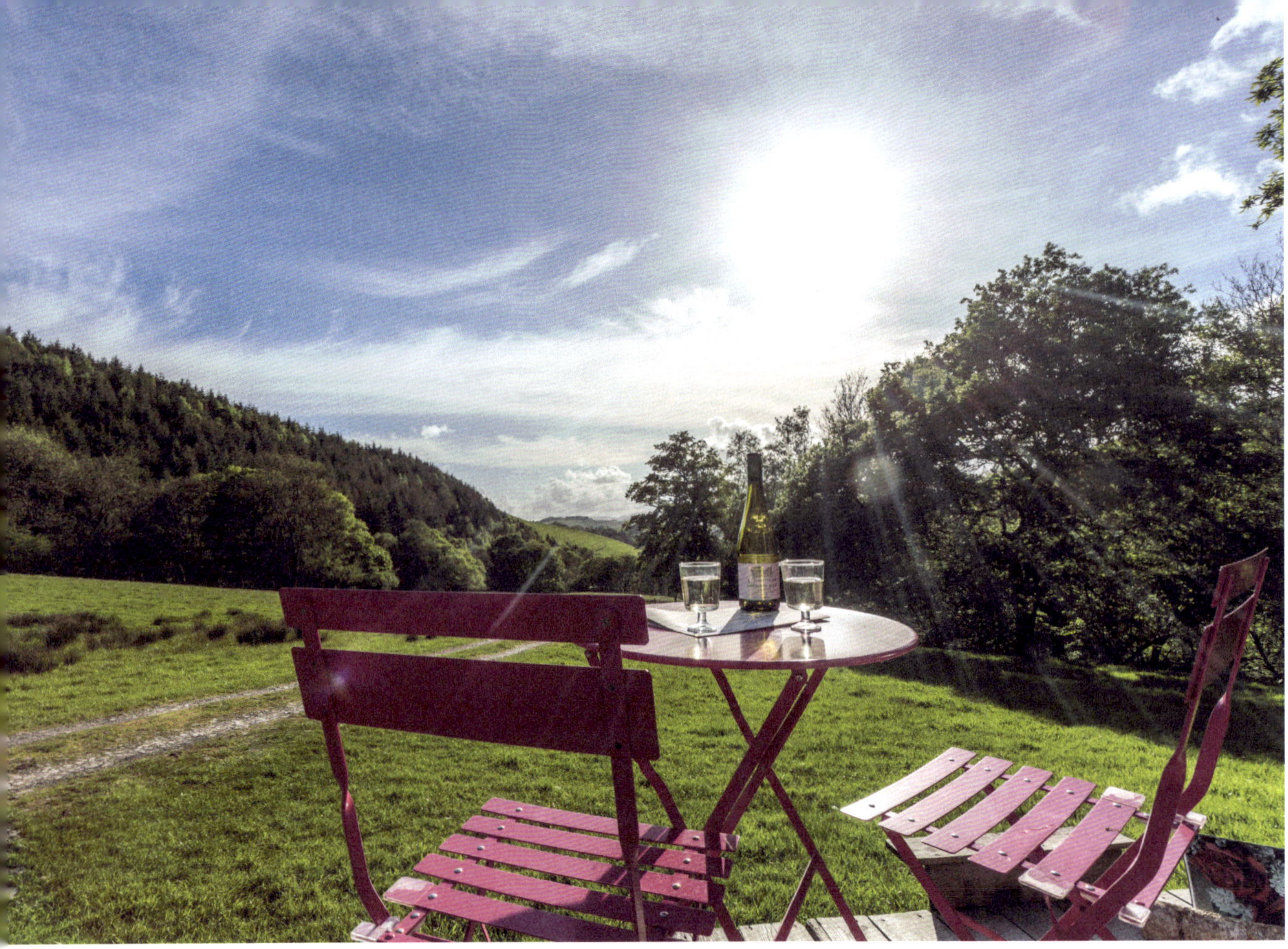

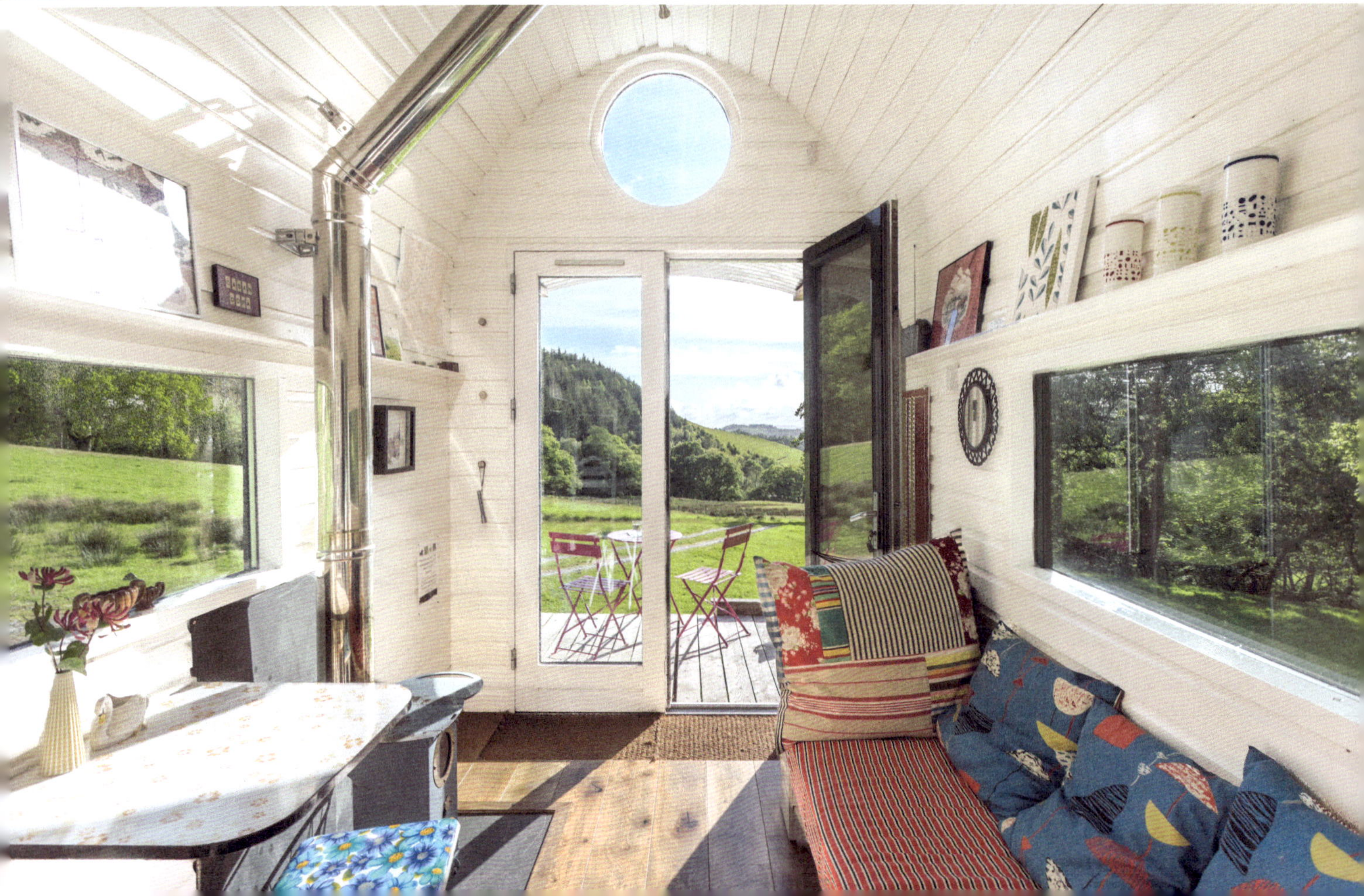

A Small Tin Peak on a Hillside

A compact cabin with a high domed ceiling and greenery all around

CABAN COPA
POWYS,
WALES

Owing to the gracious curves of its domed tin roof, this cabin, perched atop a gentle slope, takes its name from the Welsh for 'summit'. The doors open onto a deck with a fire bowl and stunning views of a landscape traversed by hiking routes and cycle trails, which offer plenty of activities to fill the days with. Back inside the cabin, whitewashed walls are offset with bright, colourful textiles and long picture windows that make the countryside an ever-changing backdrop as each day journeys into night. Come bedtime, guests climb up to a cosy mezzanine to slumber soundly till dawn.

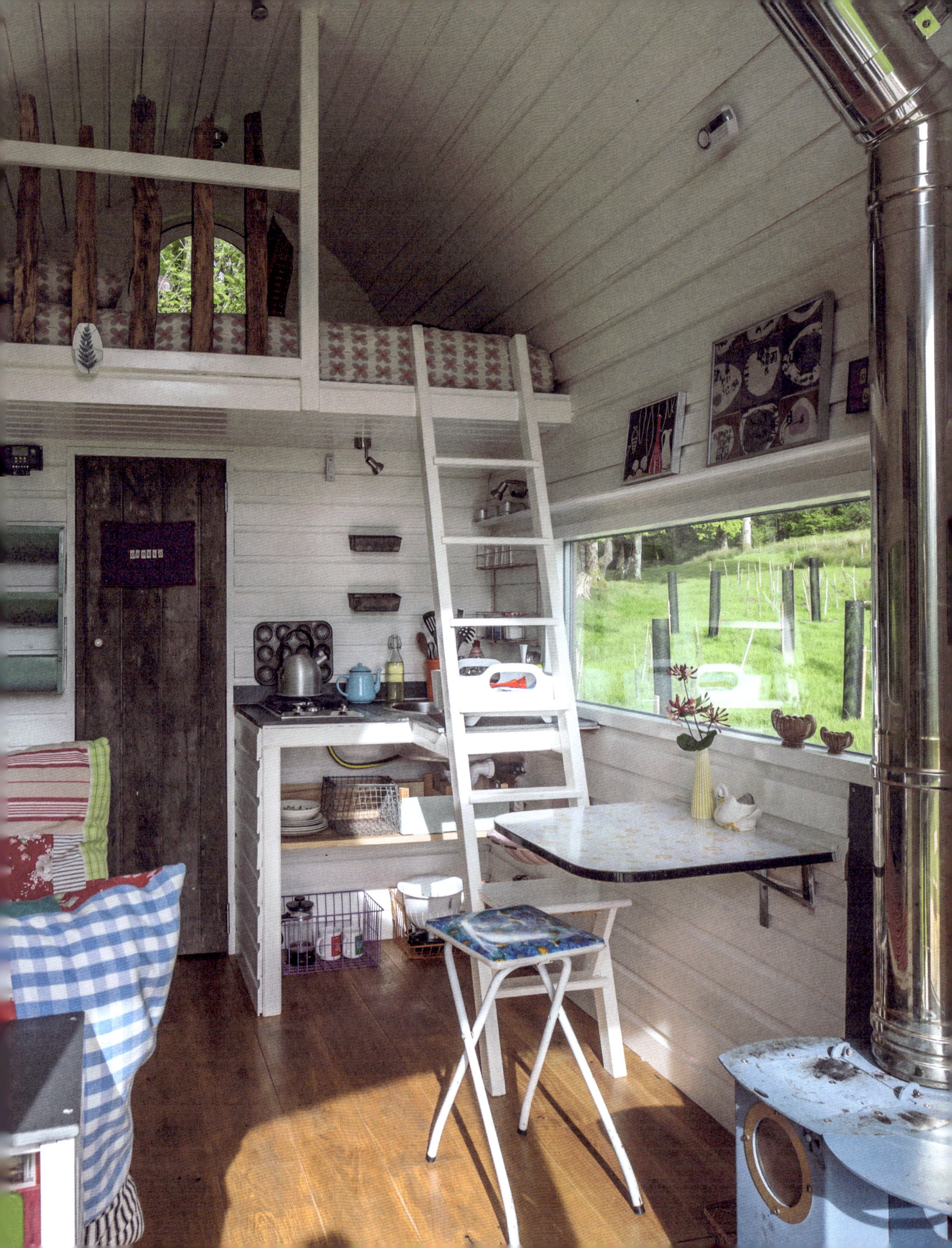

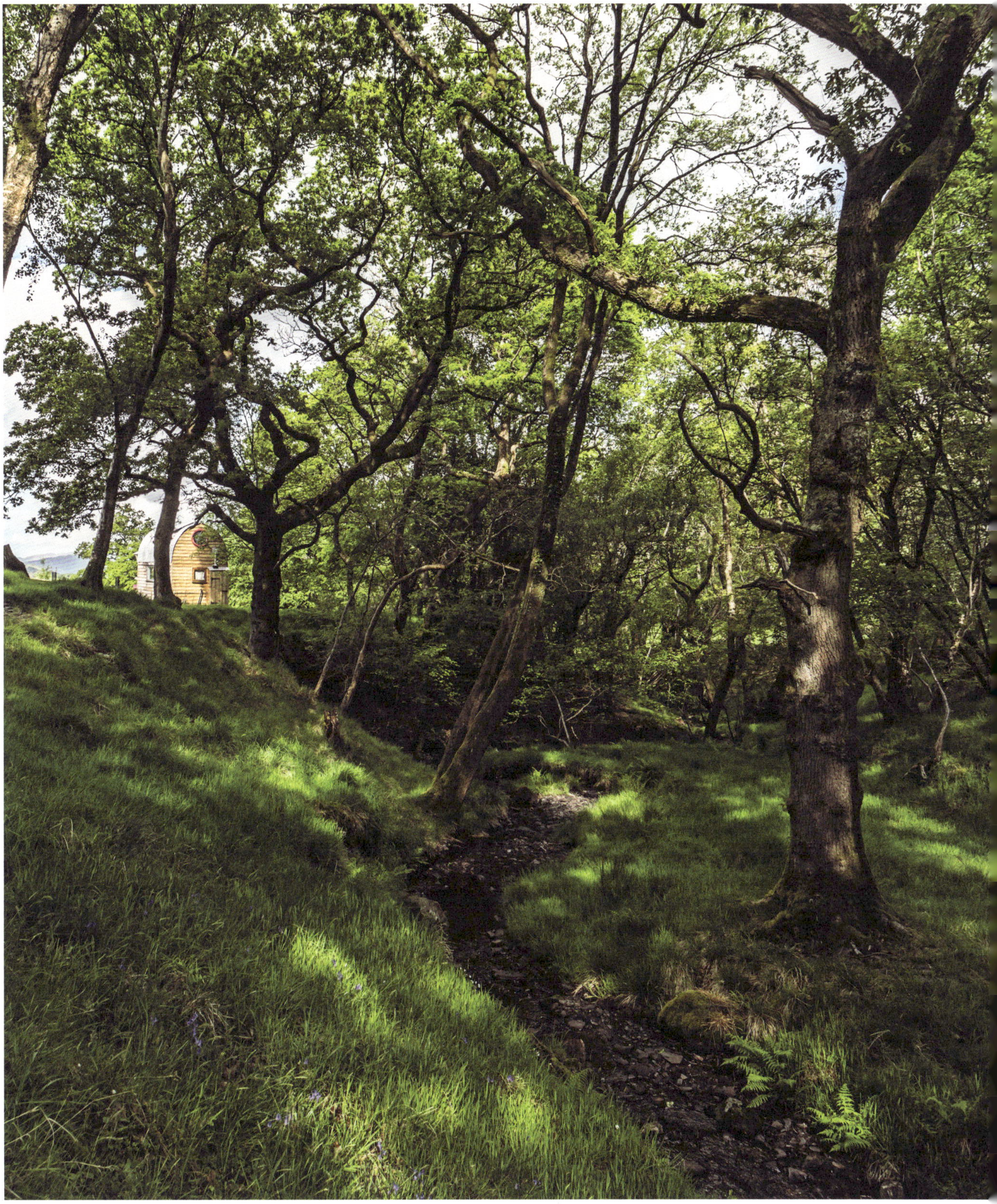

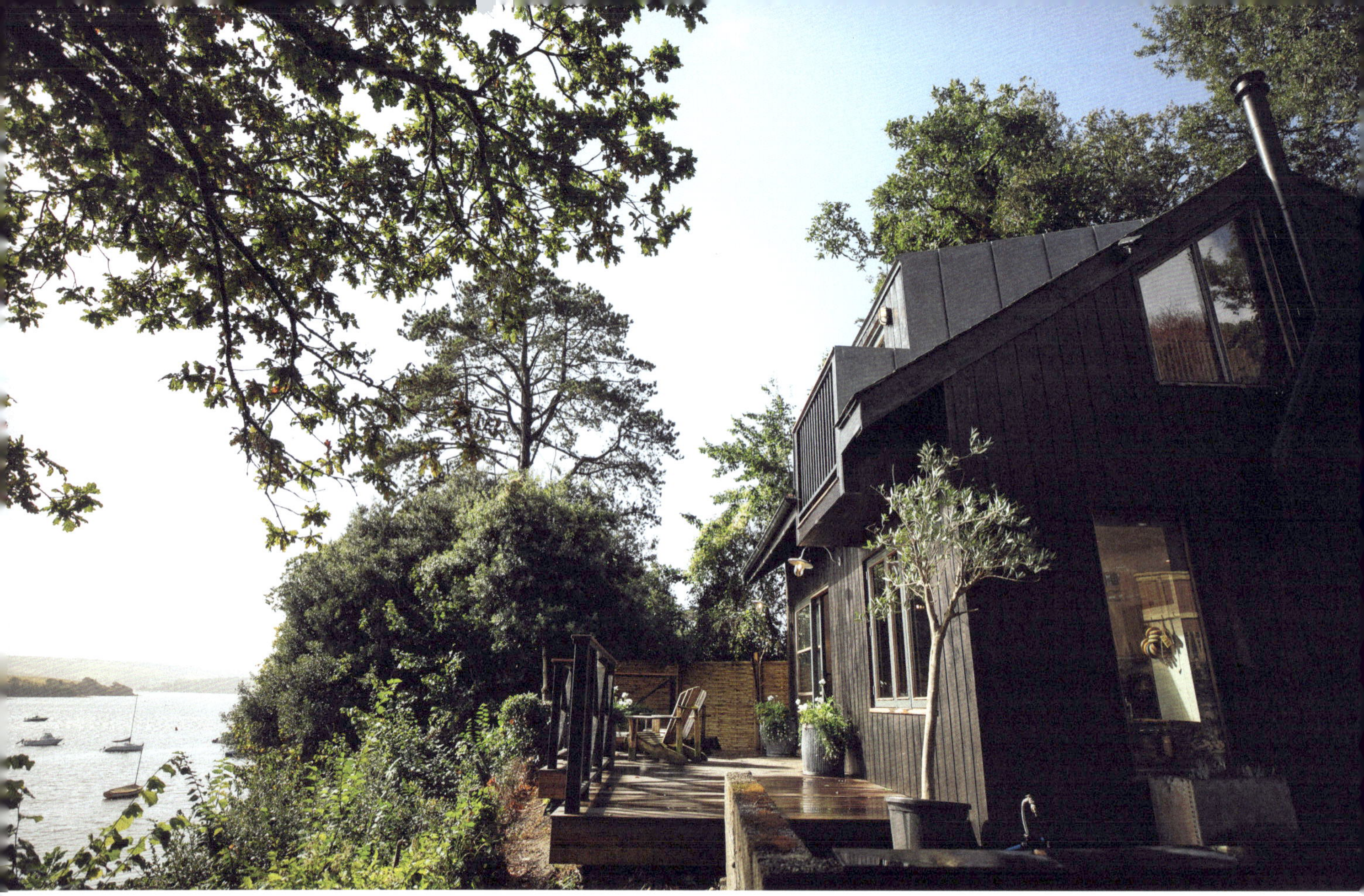
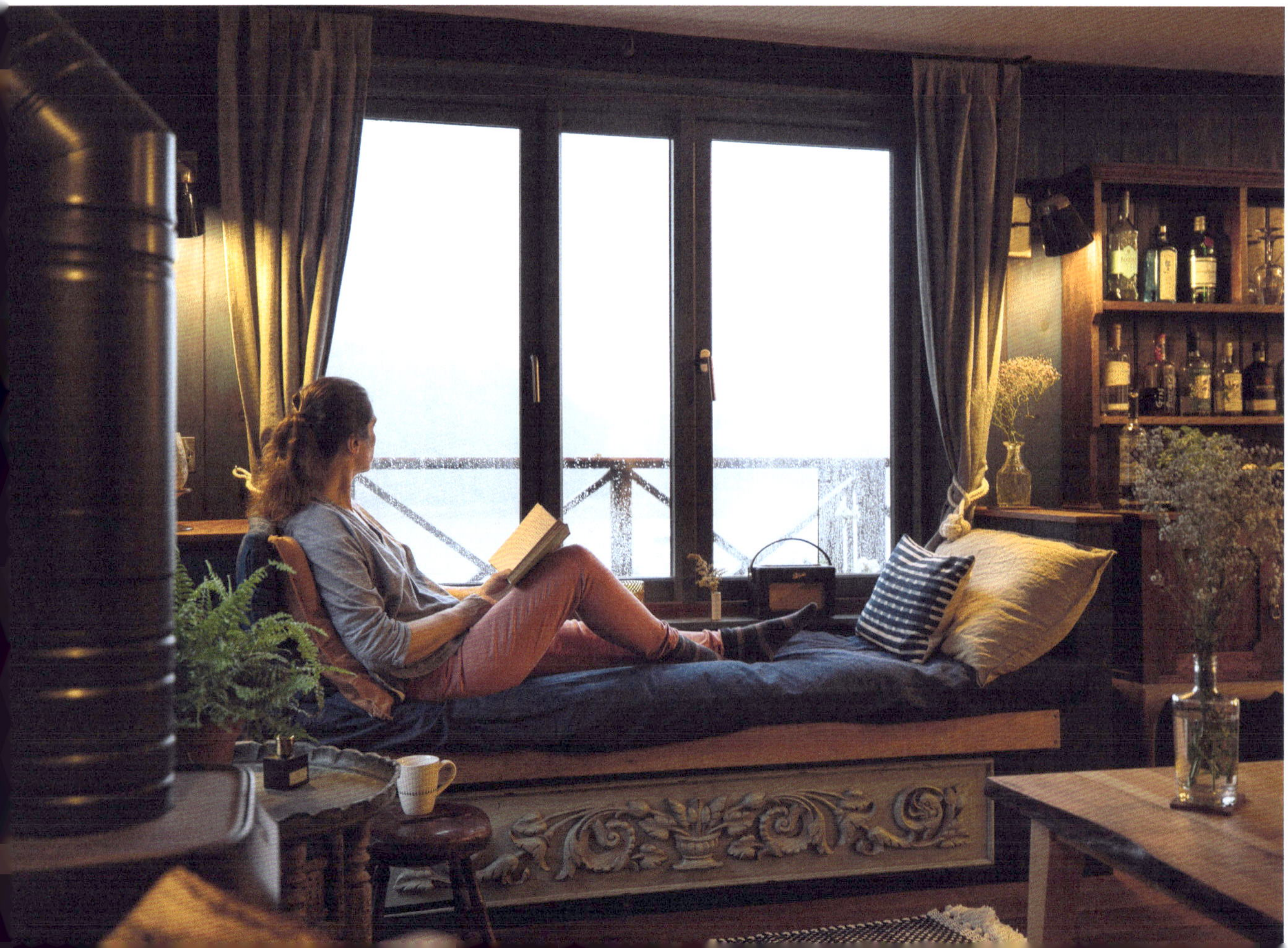

The Most Perfect Waterside Retreat

A beautifully restored boathouse that is both tranquil and luxuriant inside and out

BOWCOMBE BOATHOUSE
DEVON,
ENGLAND

Sitting on the balcony overlooking the water, partially concealed by trees: it's difficult to beat the tranquillity of Bowcombe Boathouse. Tastefully restored by artist and food writer Miranda Gardiner — some of her works hang in the boathouse — this Devon retreat is painted in cool colours, furnished with natural textiles, and has a distinct air of nautical charm. When inside, rather than out on the balcony, guests cosy up on a corner sofa beside the wood burner or lounge on a window seat with river views. And the boathouse even comes with a kayak for messing about on the river.

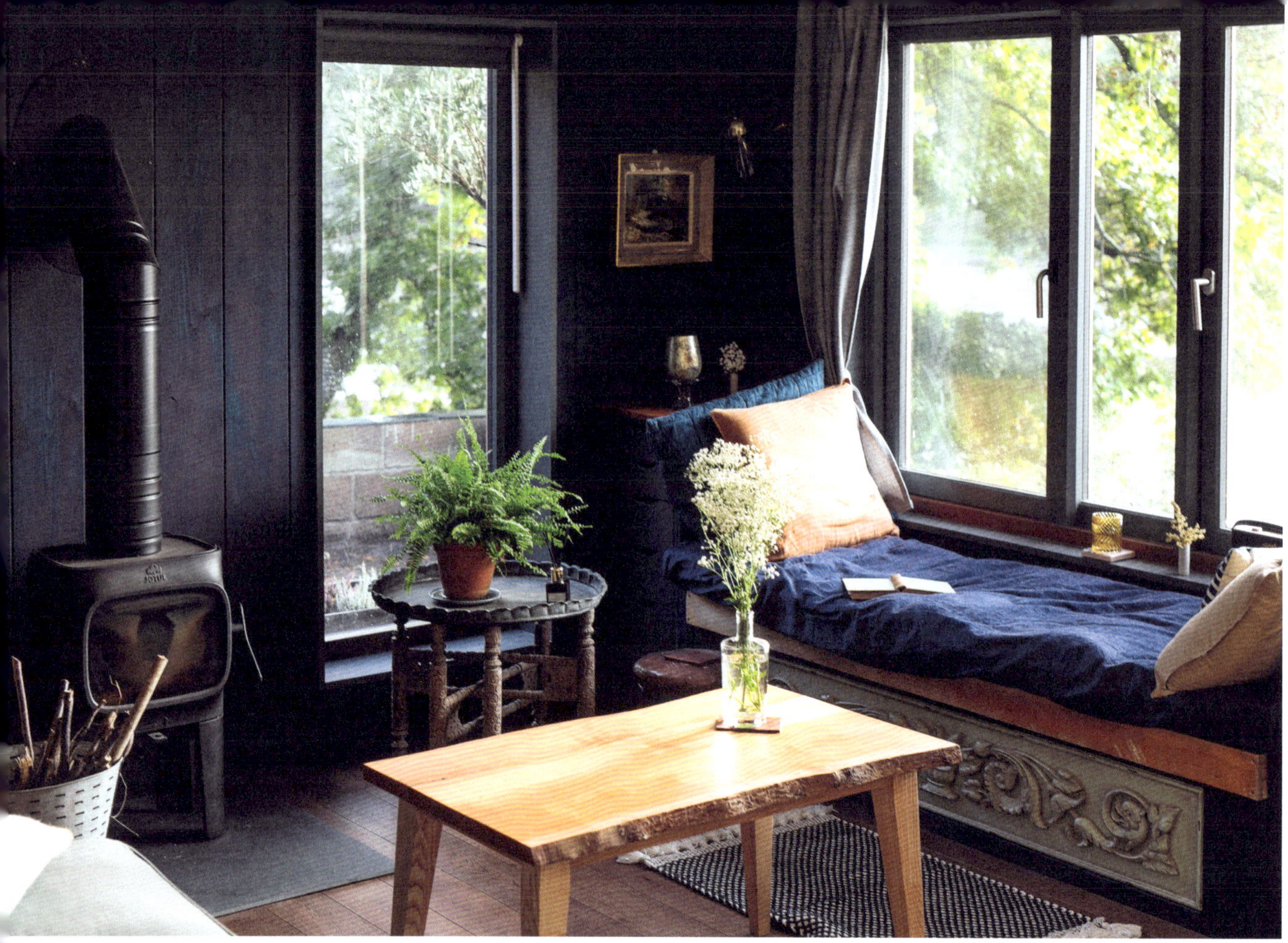

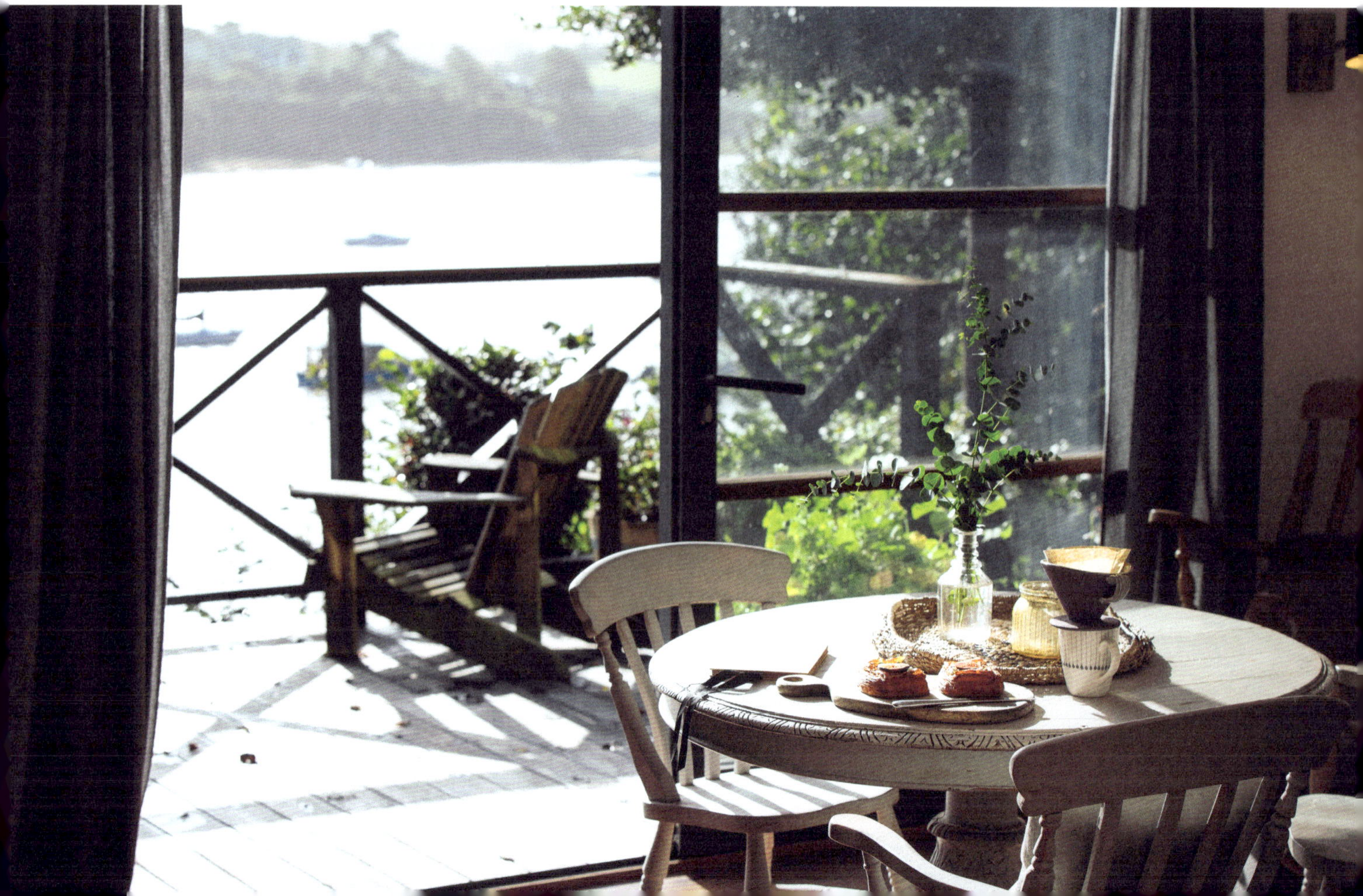

RAIN
CHANGE
FAIR
MUCH RAIN
SET FAIR
STORMY
VERY DRY
BAROMETER

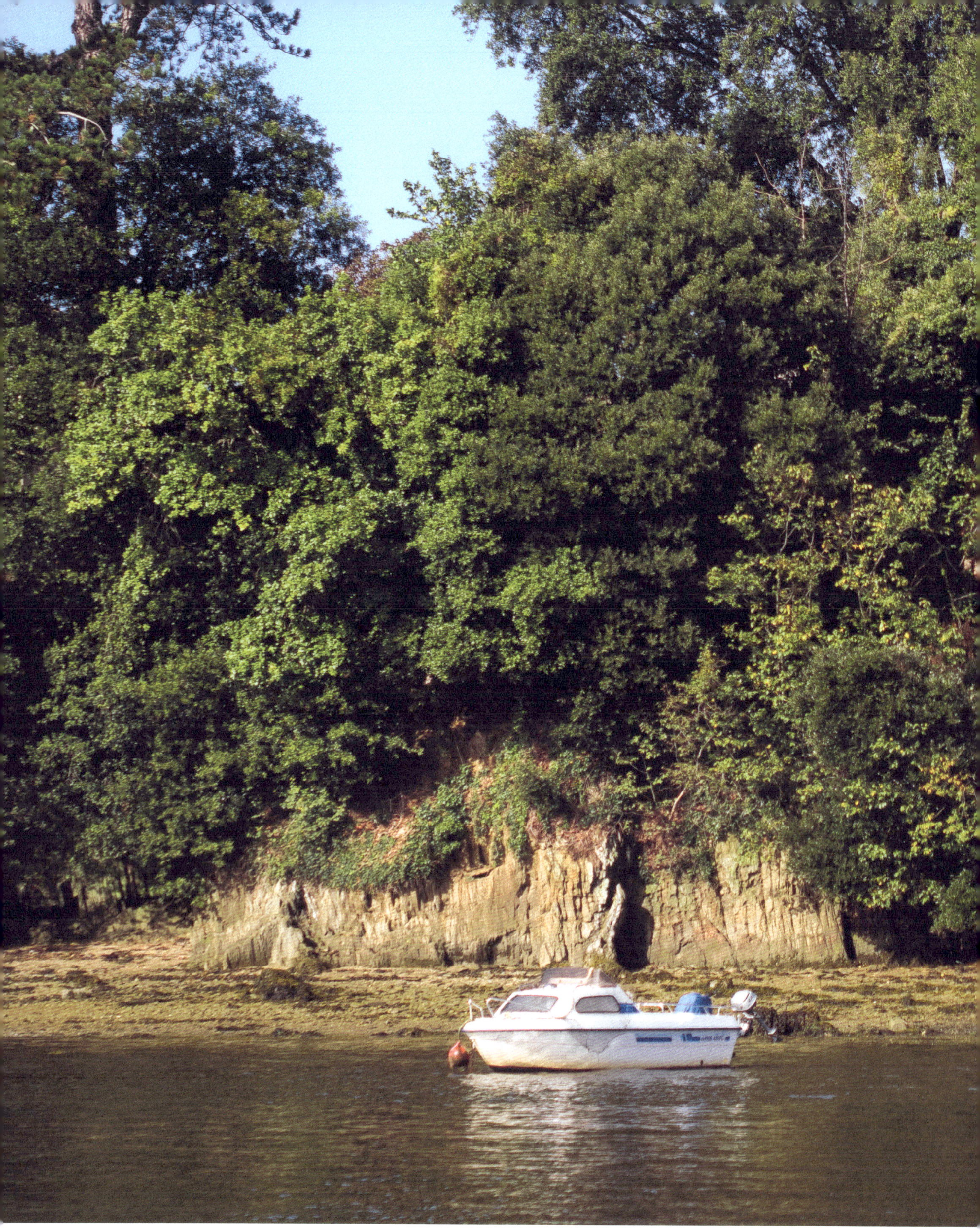

BOWCOMBE BOATHOUSE

Hiding Out in a Cornish Quarry

Where glamping means adapting the site to the landscape, not the other way around

THE DANISH CABIN
CORNWALL, ENGLAND

With a design inspired by the traditional Cornish engine house, this tall, narrow cabin occupies a secluded spot in a disused slate quarry. It's one of several off-grid getaway pads on the 18-hectare (45-acre) Kudhva glampsite, where guests establish a deep connectivity with nature as they hide away from the modern world — after all, 'kudhva' means 'hideout' in the Cornish dialect. The rough-and-ready charm of the place draws adventurous outdoorsy types, as does the rugged terrain. There is a lake, a climbing wall, and, at the top of the quarry, a cave with a 12-metre (40-foot) waterfall. Beyond the site, trails lead all the way to the coast, intersecting with endless paths for scrambling and hiking. The cabin itself stands on a wooden deck raised above a stream and surrounded by woodland flowers, and its intriguing timber-framed structure is made mostly of lightweight polycarbonate walls that fold at the halfway mark, allowing guests to winch them up to open the cabin to the outside world. No matter where you are in this space — sitting at its private bar or having a lie-down on the mezzanine above — it's impossible not to be impressed by the close proximity of the natural world all around.

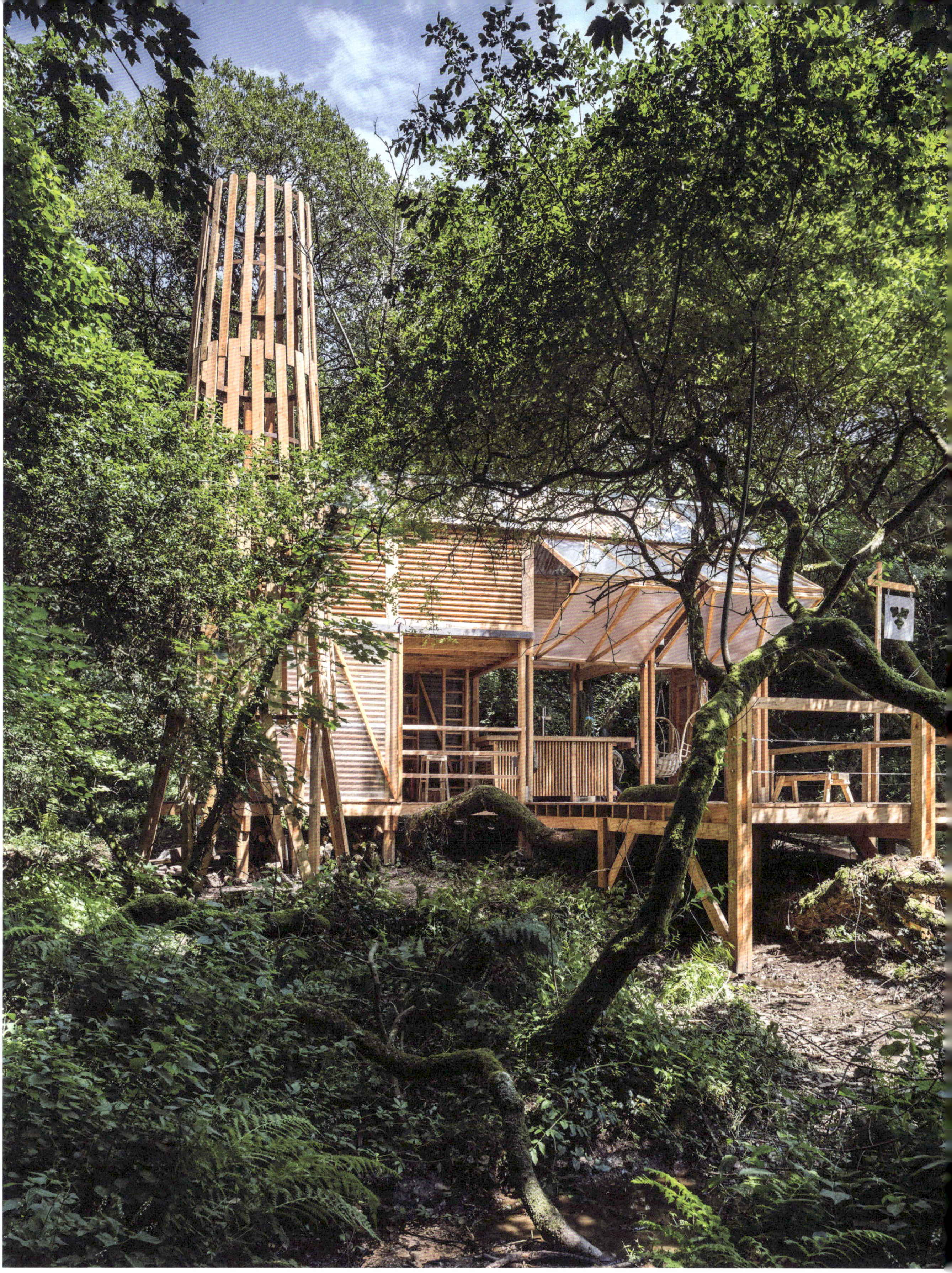

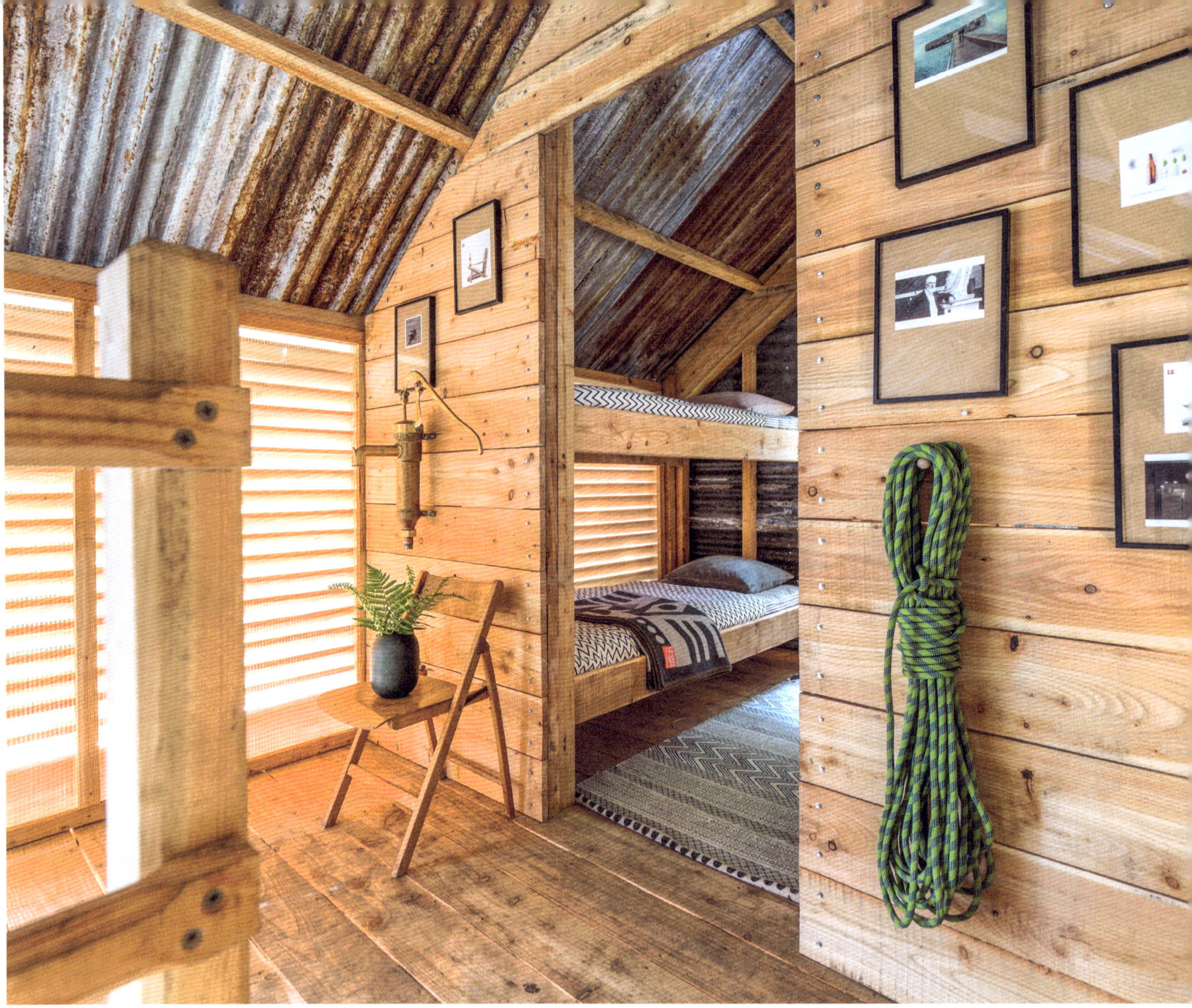

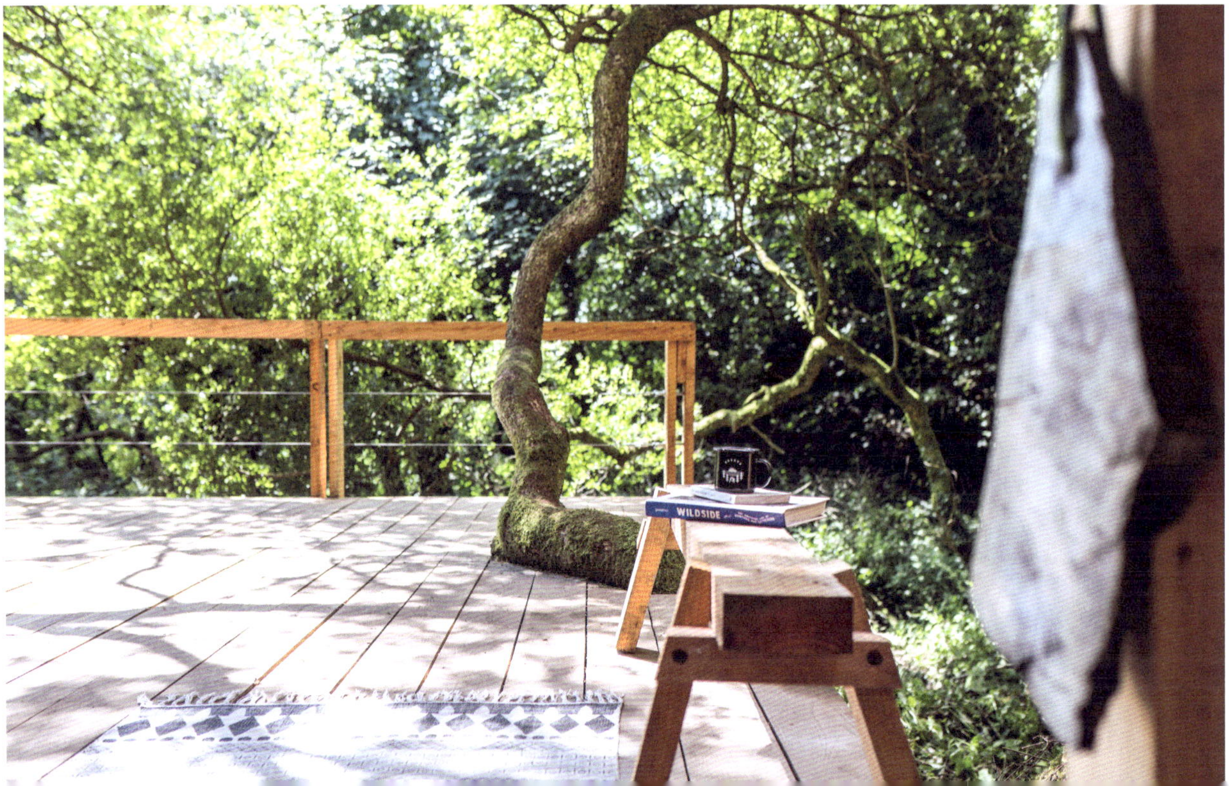
WILDSIDE

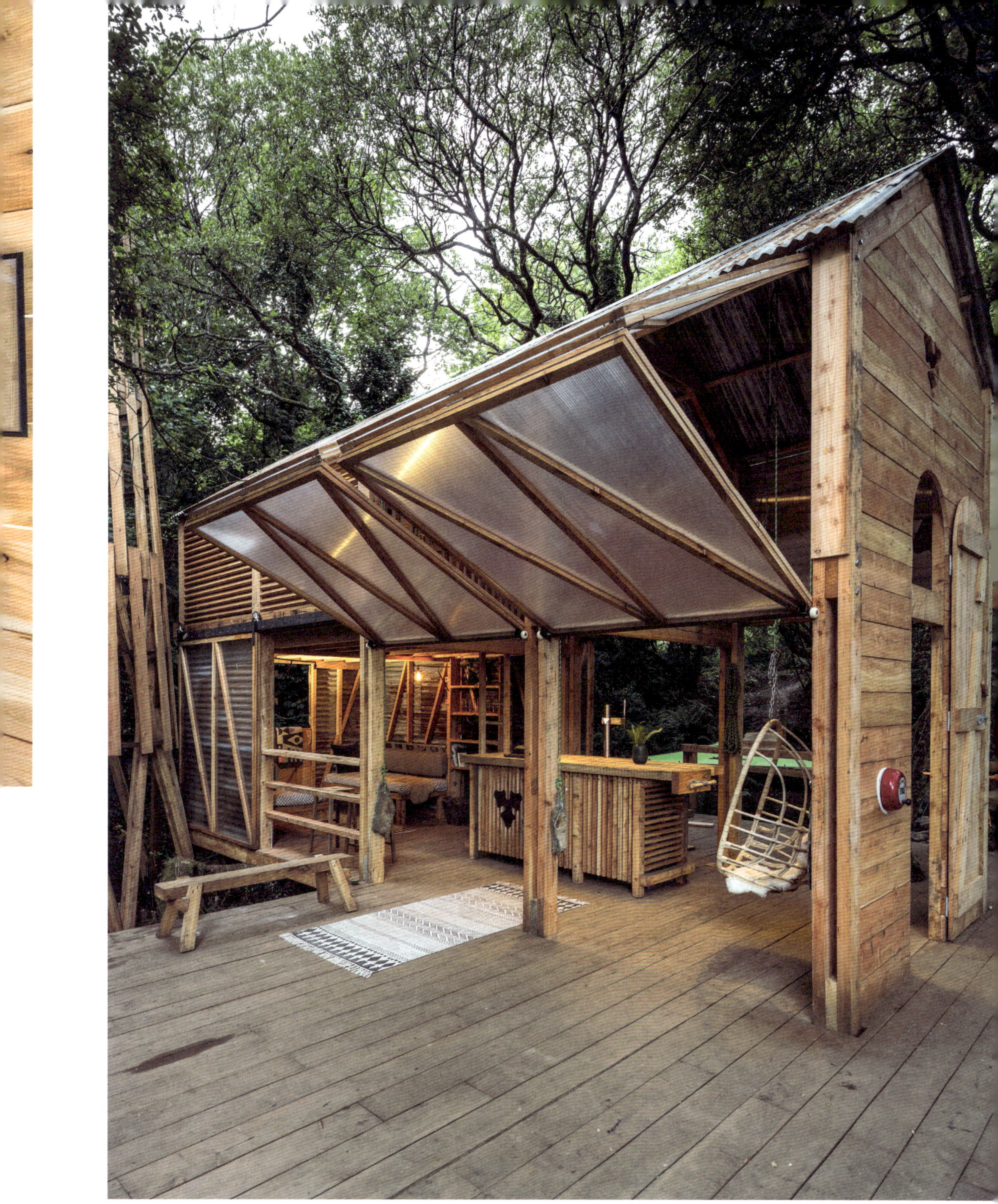

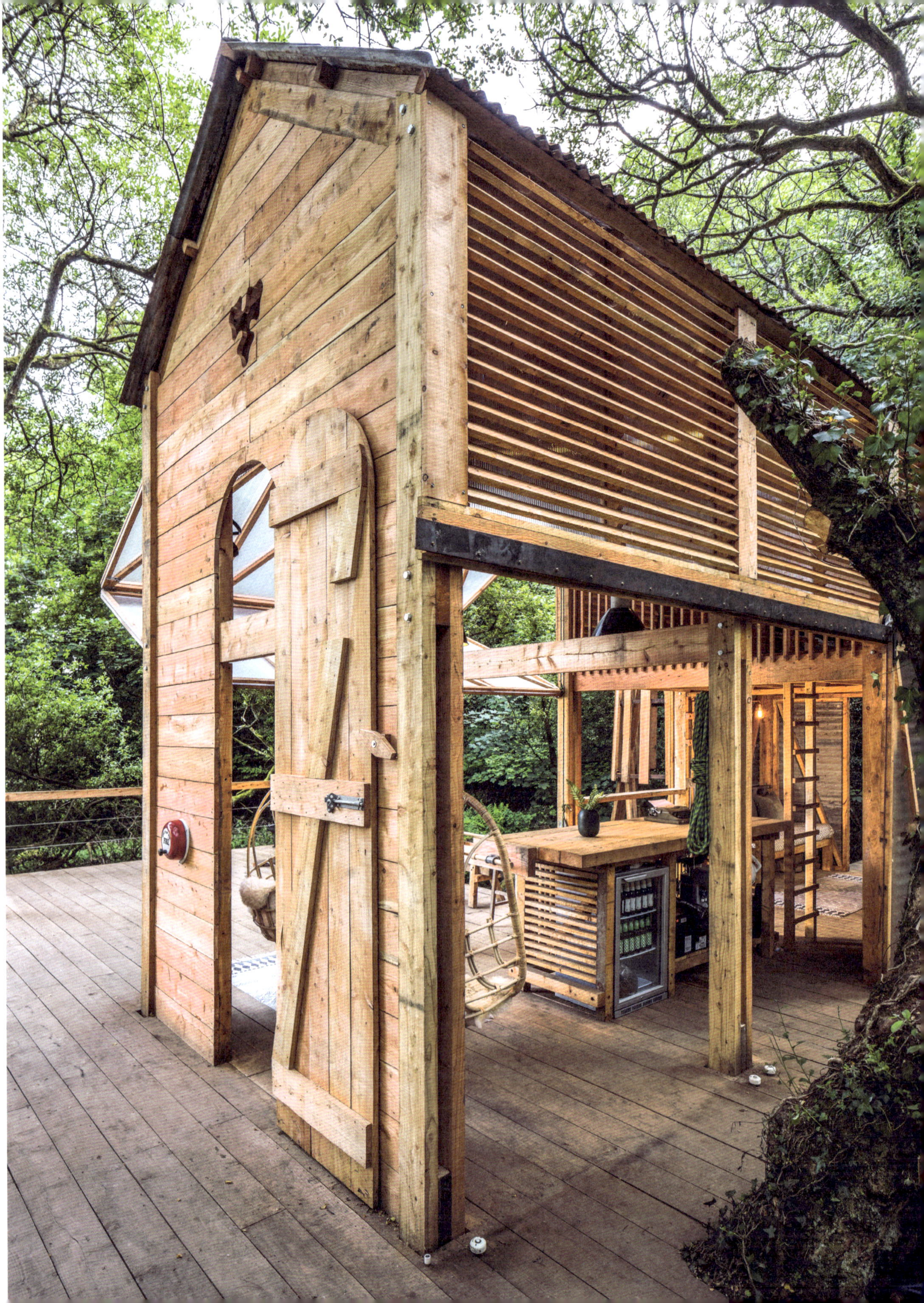

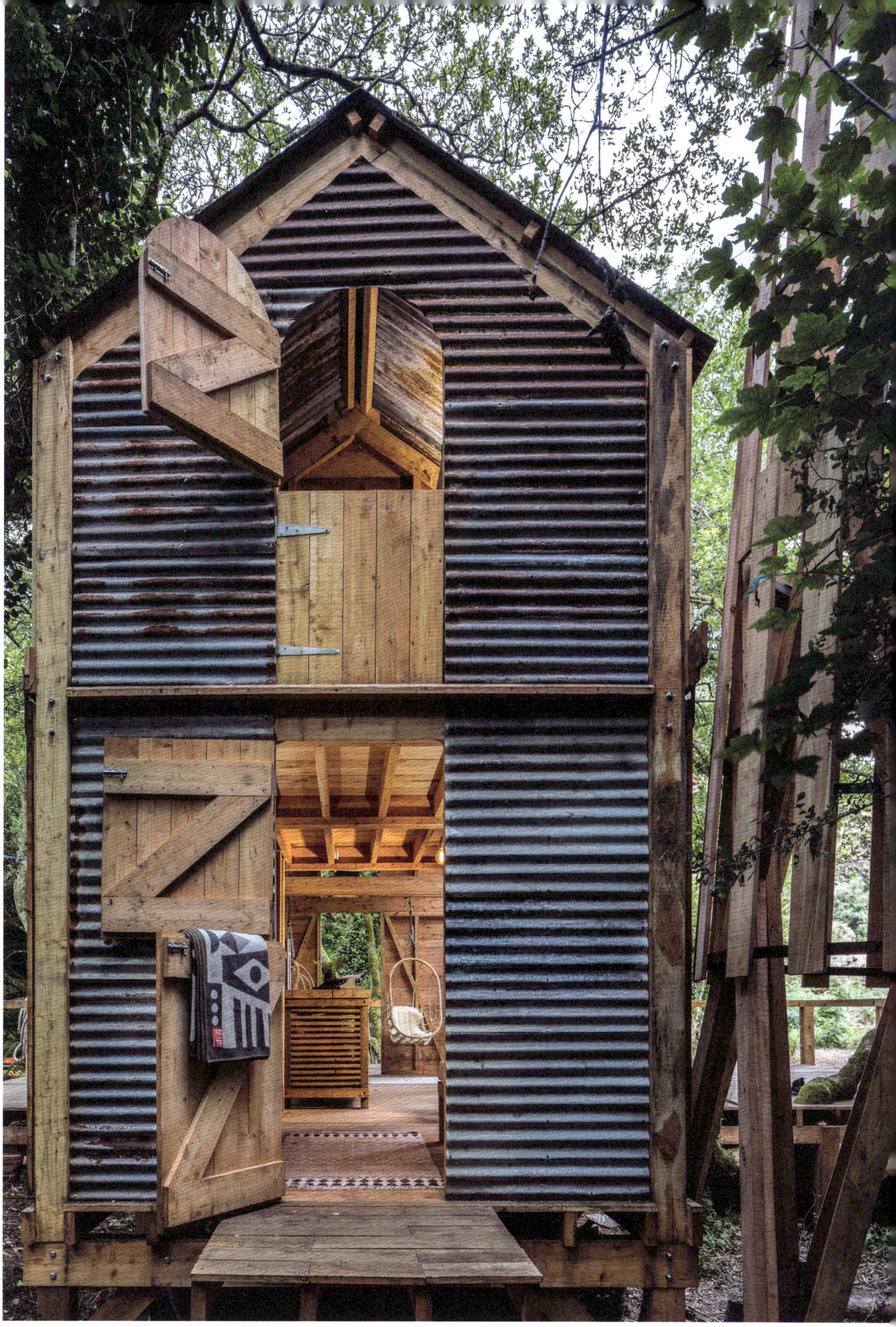

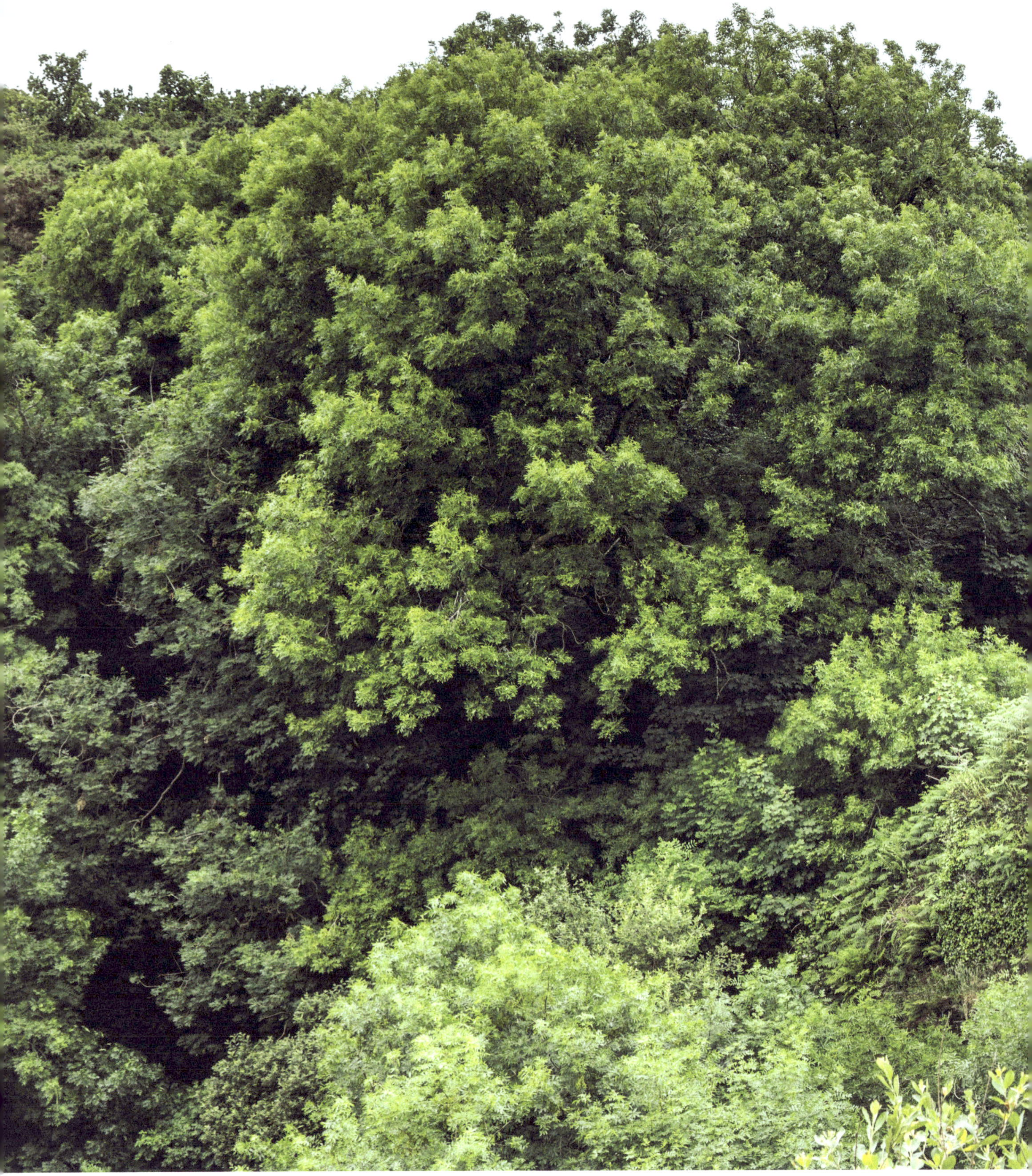

THE DANISH CABIN

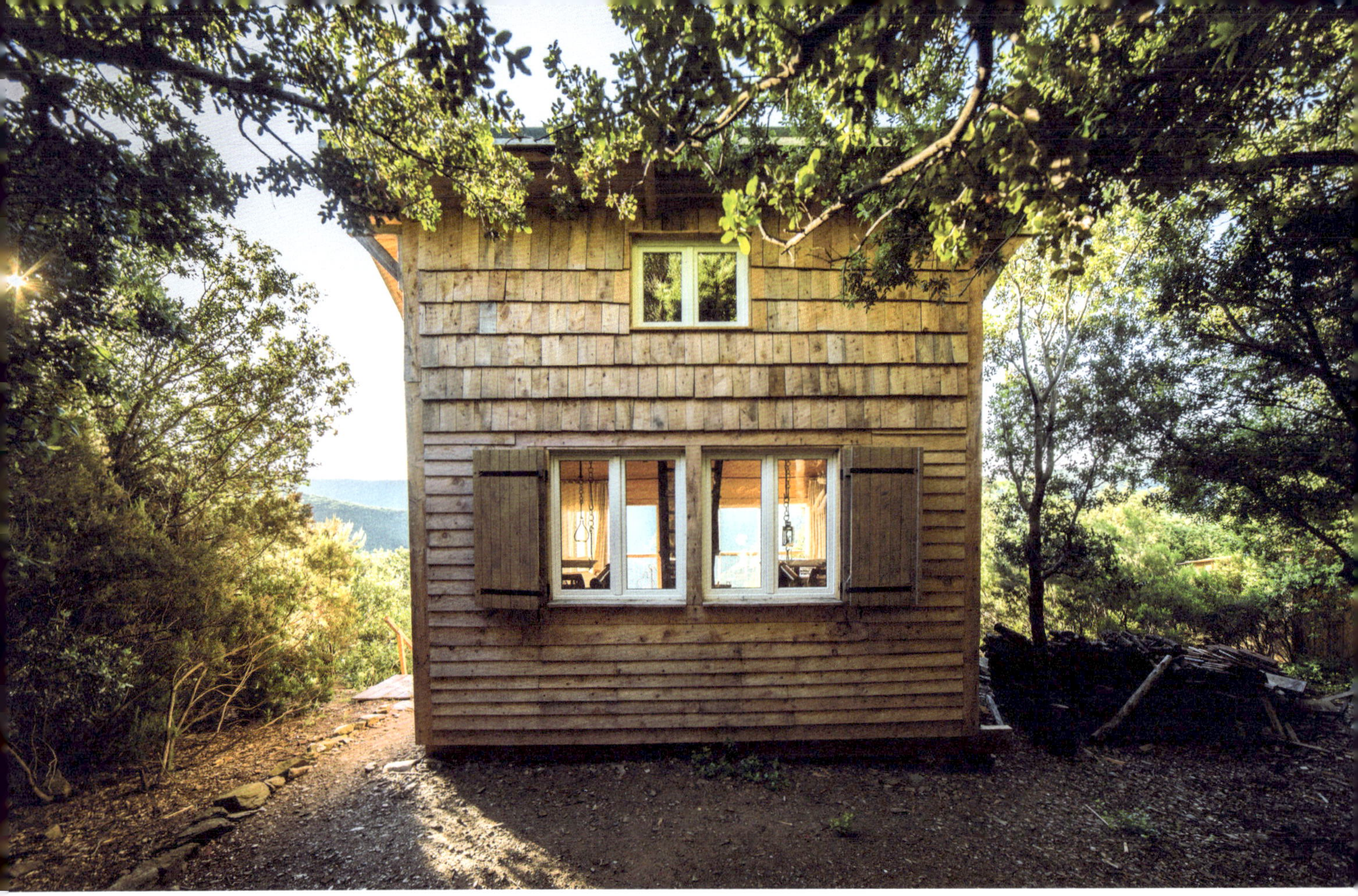
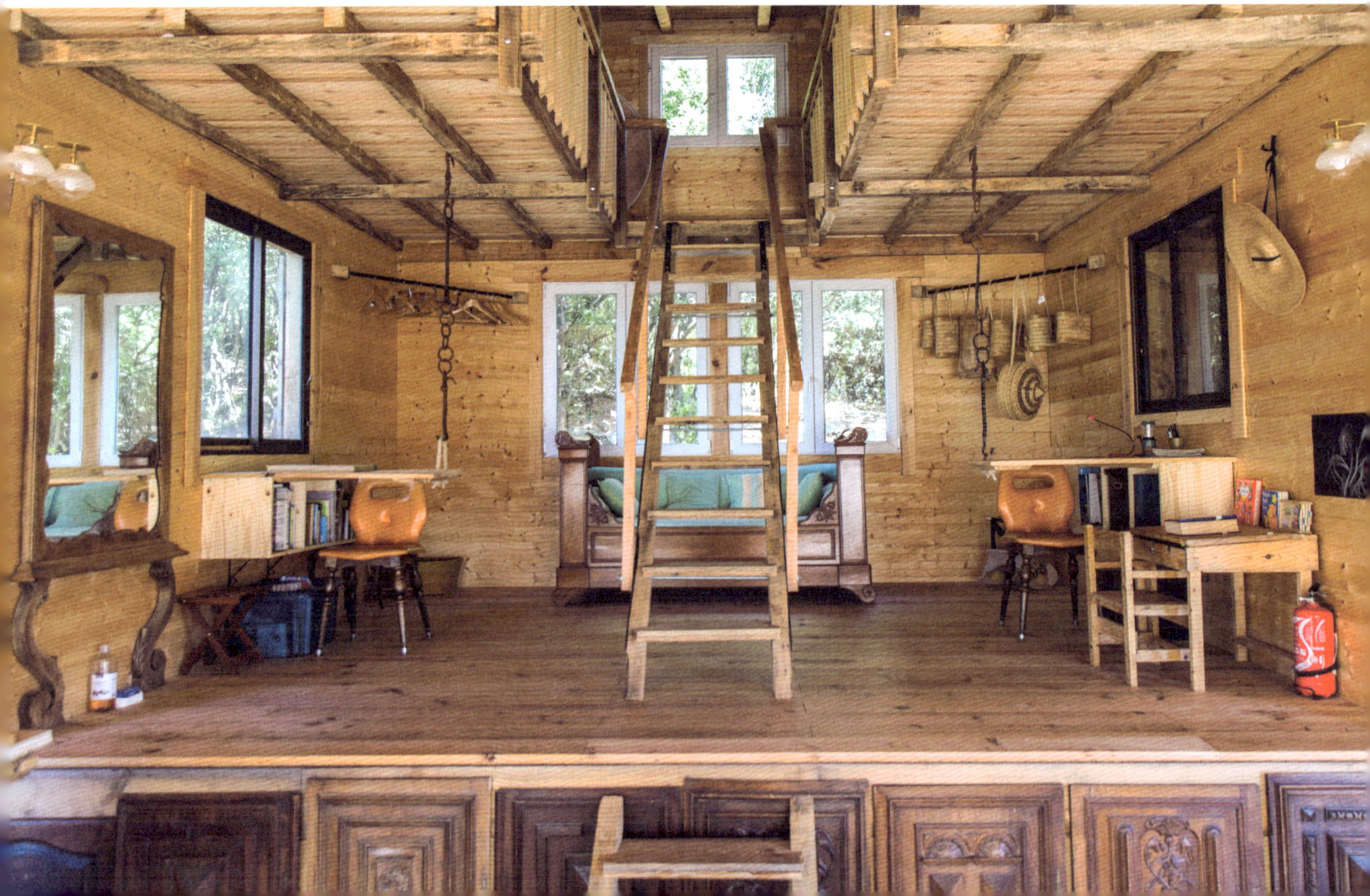

Living Off-Grid in the Hills

A 'house among the oaks': this rustic hilltop cabin promises a simple life in the south of France

CHÂTEAU DANS LES CHÊNES
HÉRAULT,
FRANCE

There's something truly magical about staying at Château dans les Chênes. High up in the heart of the Haut-Languedoc Regional Nature Park, the cabin has incredible views overlooking hills and valleys, oak woods and vineyards — a landscape largely unchanged for centuries. With a rustic vibe that befits such primordial surroundings, the refuge is totally off the grid: rainwater, heated by the sun, is used for showering, and cooking and drinking water is collected from a local spring. Two solar panels provide enough electricity for a few lights, and the loo is of the composting variety. Clad in wood shingles and lined with timber throughout, the cabin has a generous, open-plan interior, with a big country-style kitchen and chunky wooden furniture on the ground floor, and a nest with two canopied double beds on a mezzanine level above. With a wood-burning stove to keep things cosy, this space is the perfect base to return to after a day spent wild swimming, canoeing, or wine tasting nearby.

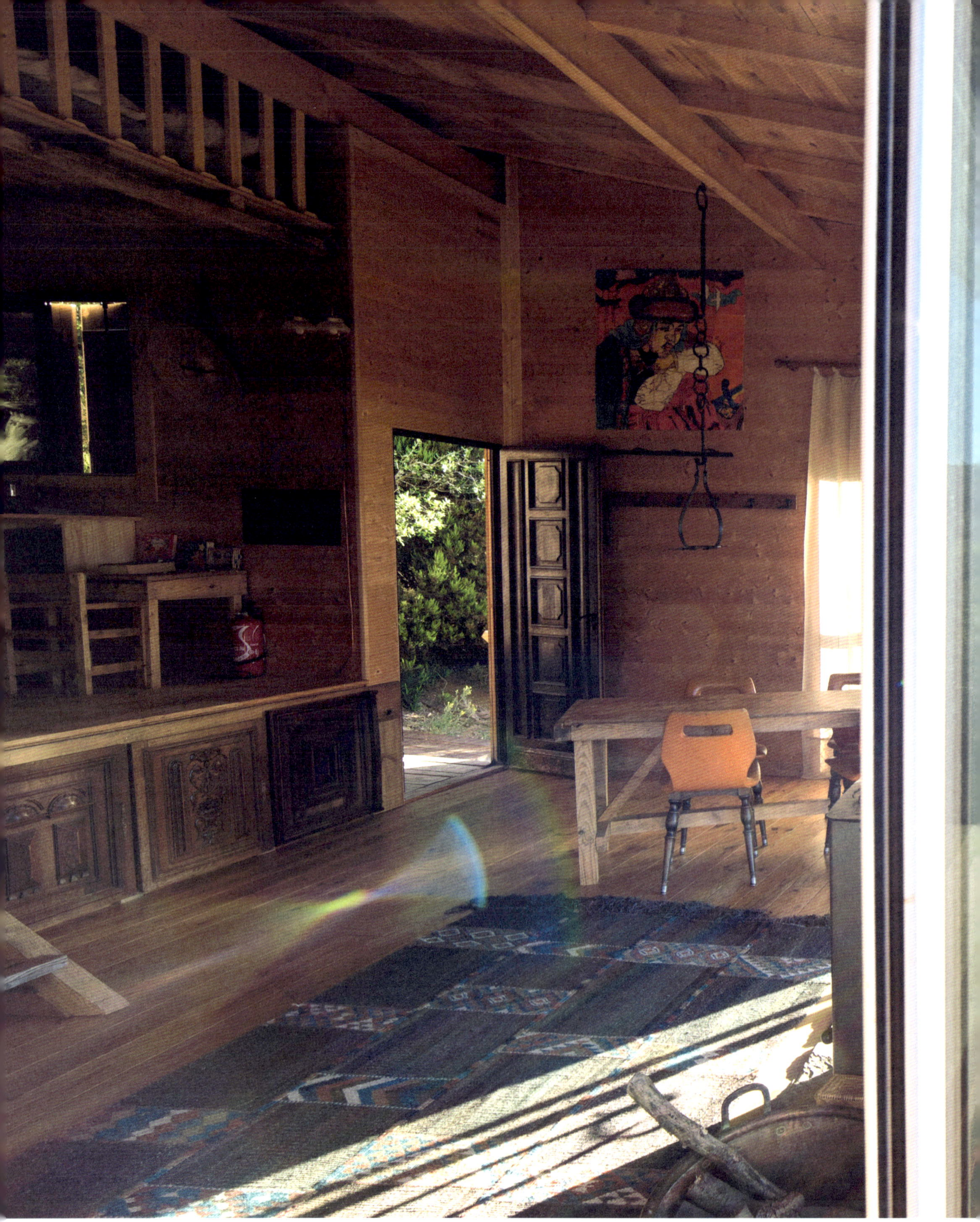

CHÂTEAU DANS LES CHÊNES

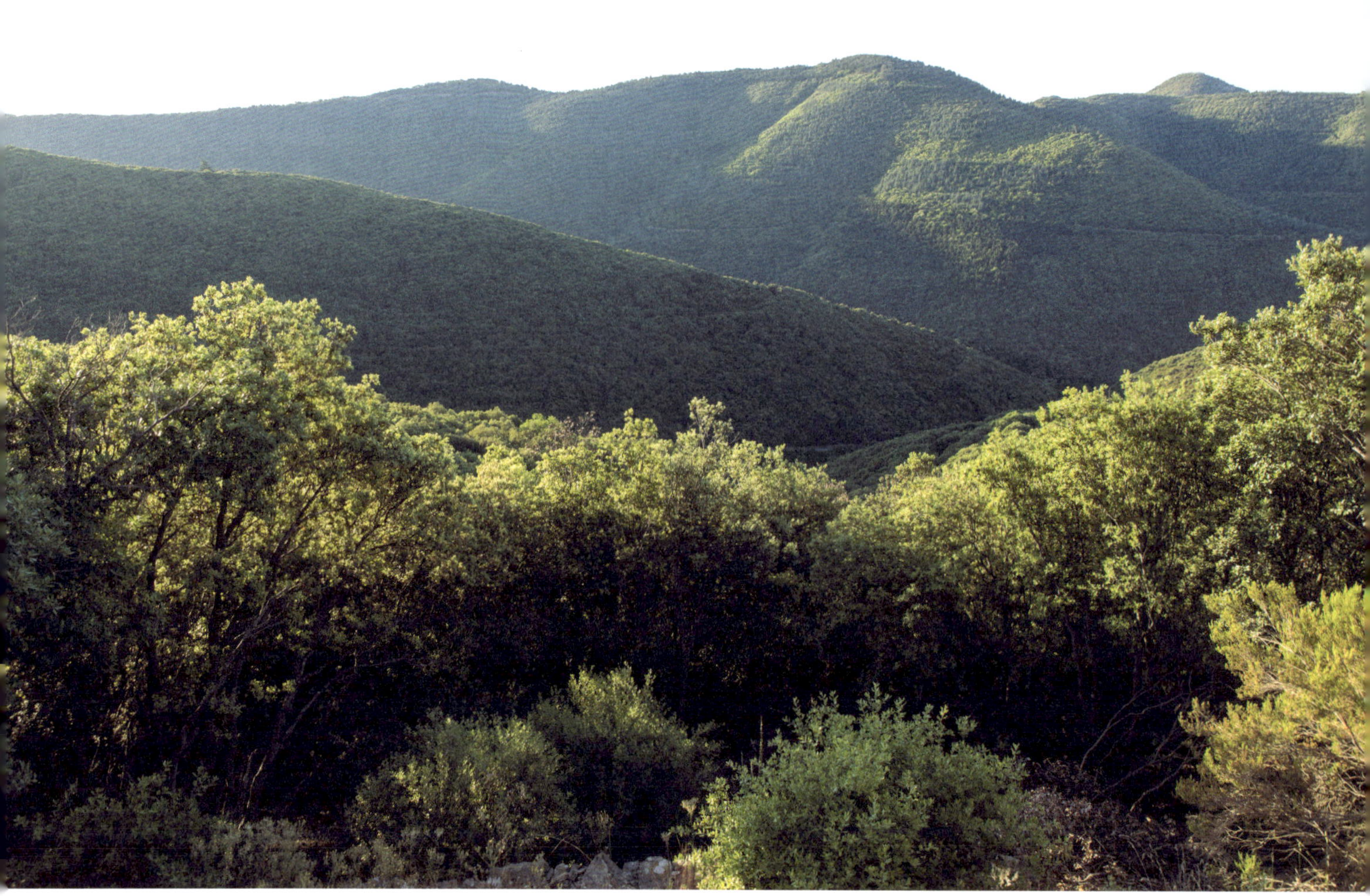

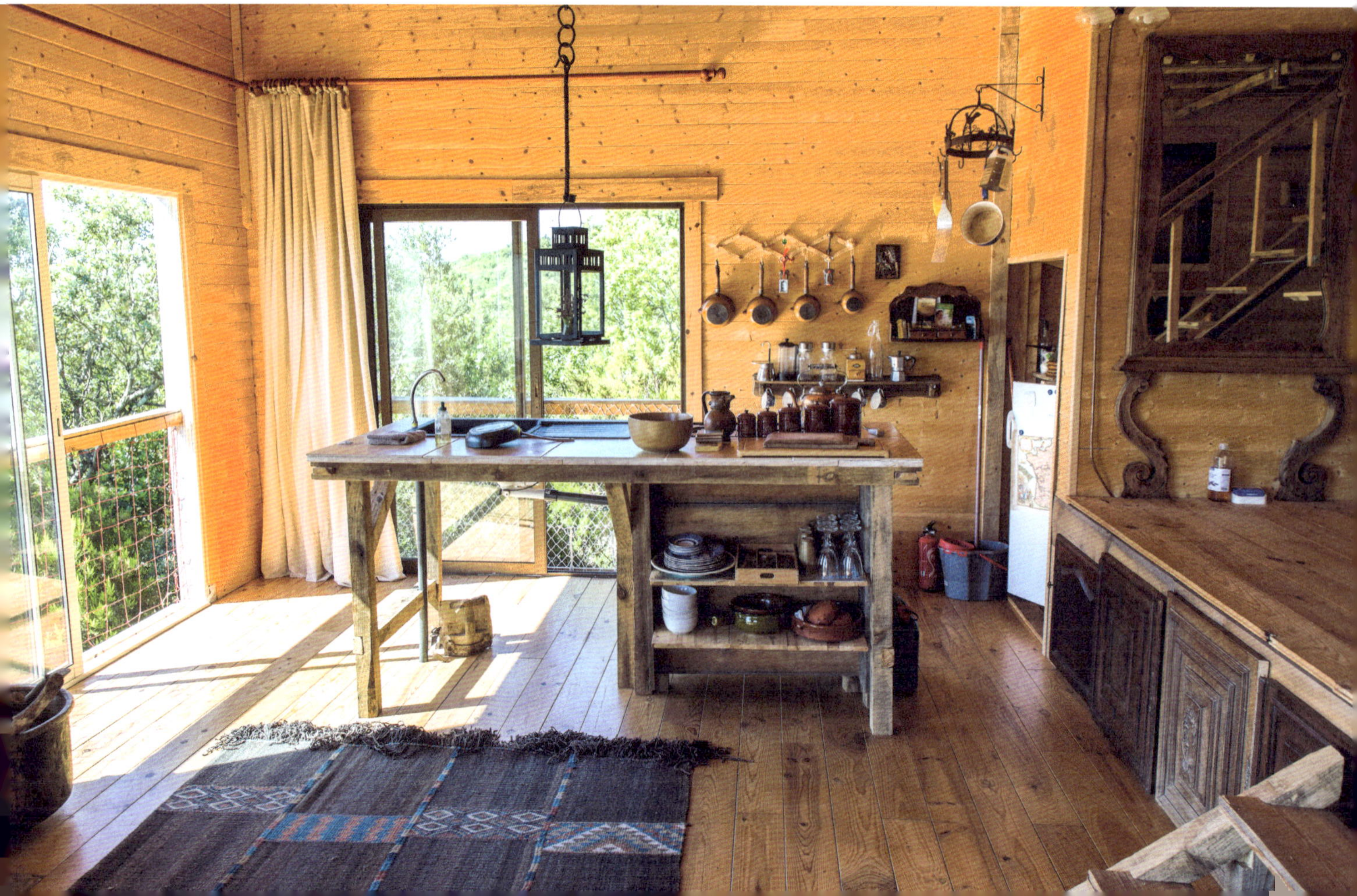

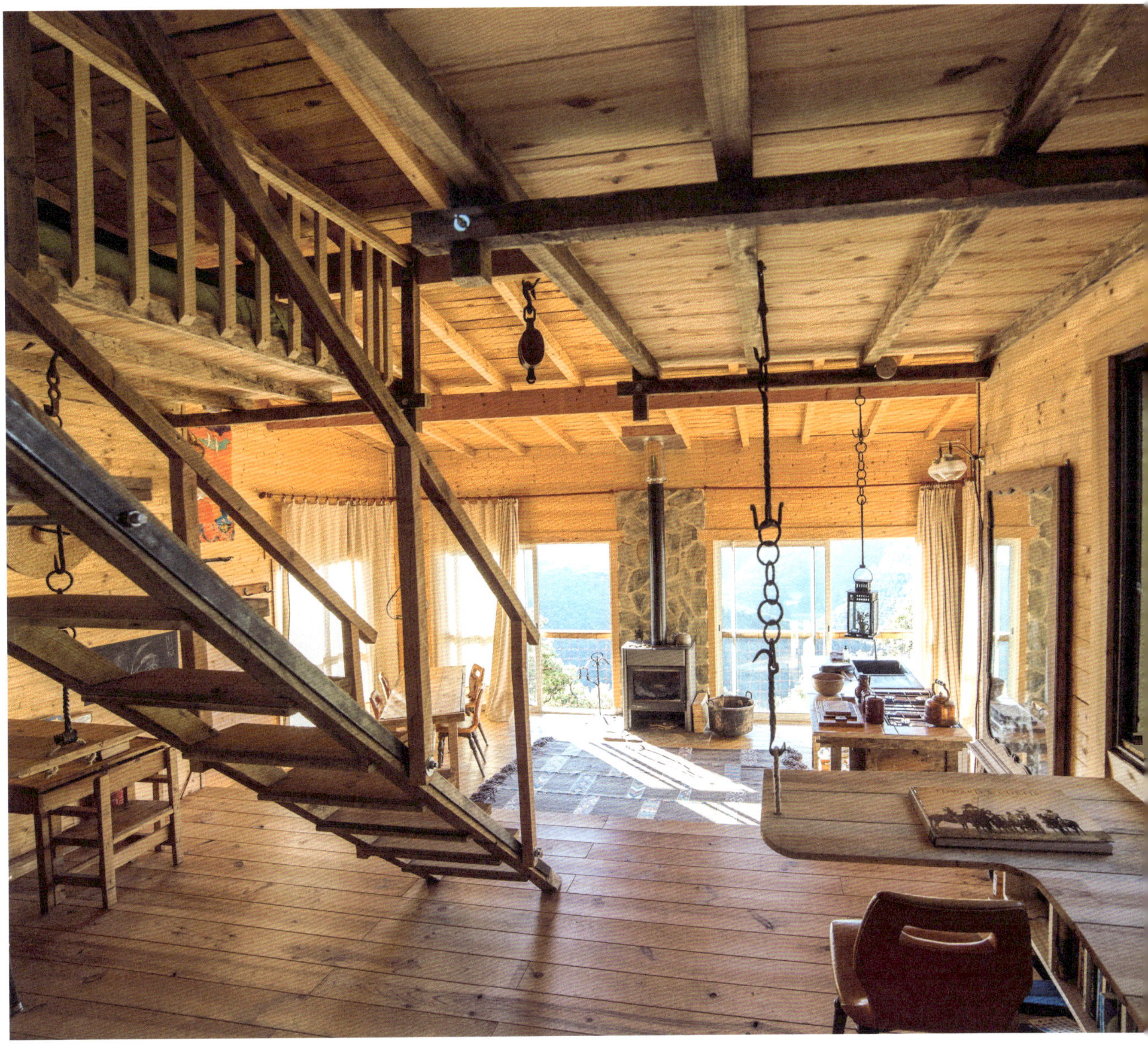

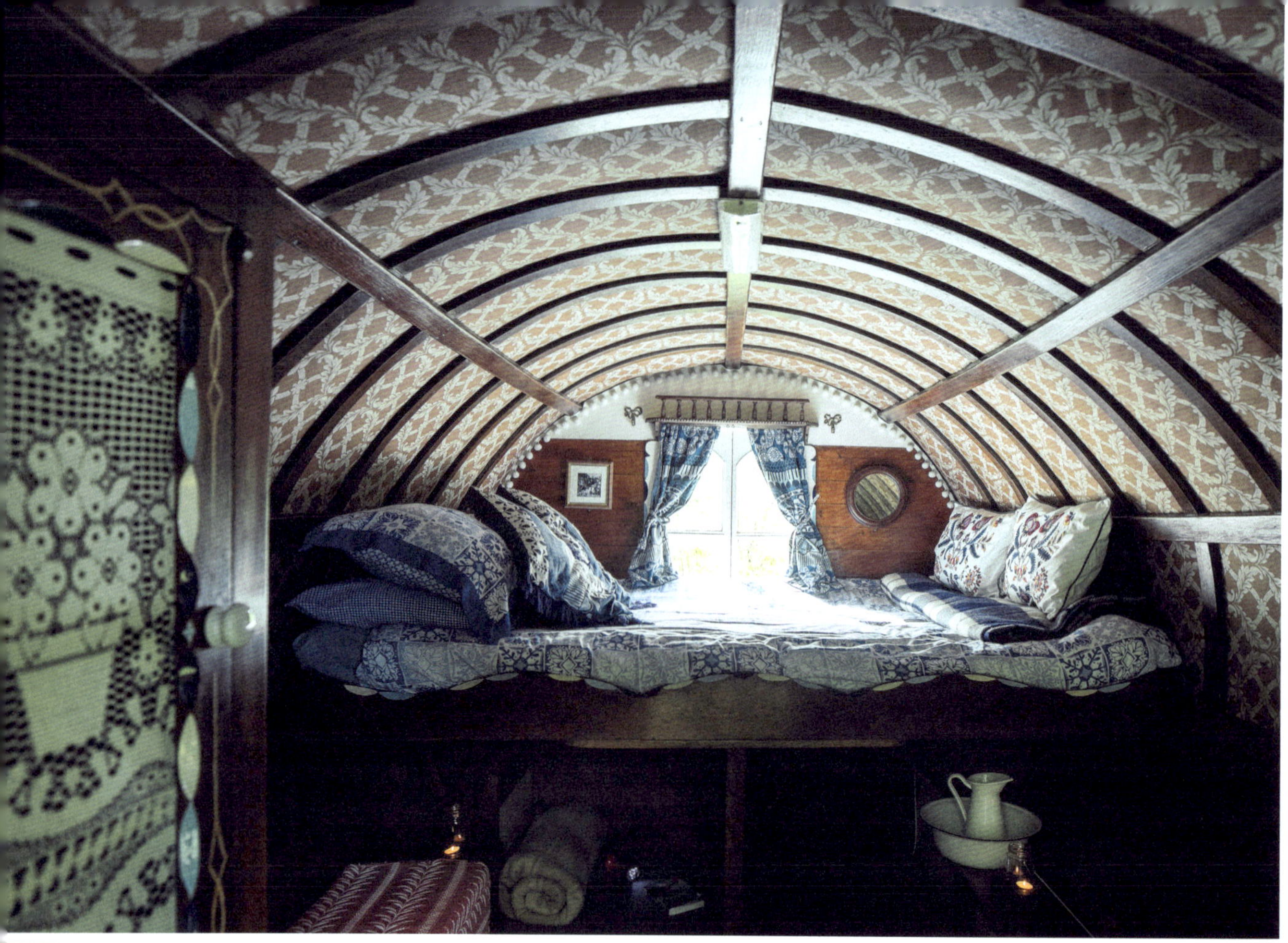

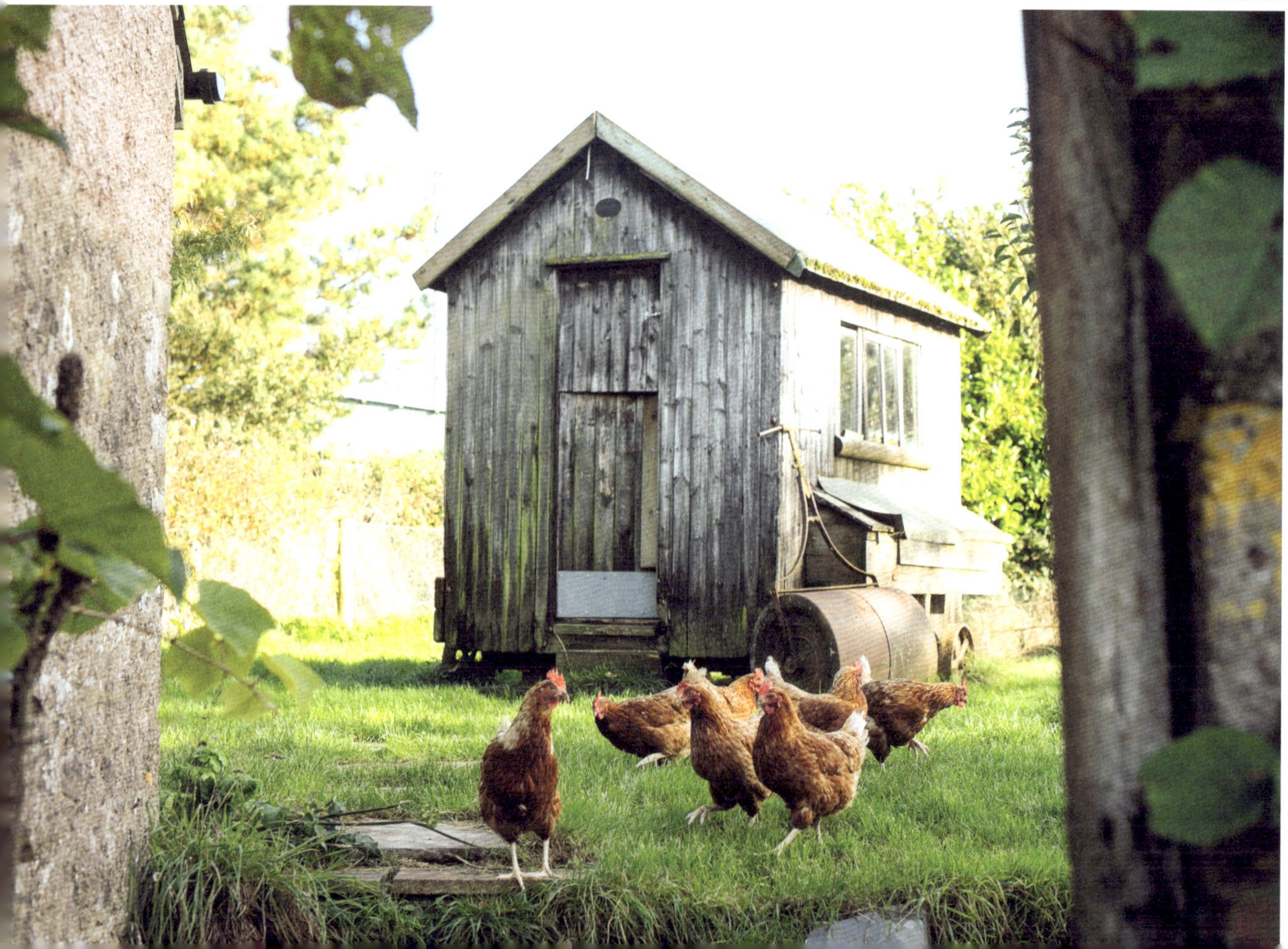

A Hint of Romany Spirit

Embracing the romance of wild living in a cluster of colourful Roma wagons

THE VINTAGE VARDOS
DEVON, ENGLAND

Big Ted, Red Rum, Little Gem, and Tippin', all nestled in a woodside meadow, make the perfect destination for family gatherings and group holidays. Lovingly restored by owners Gavin and Jemma Doyle of Fisherton Farm, the four colourful coaches offer a base from which to explore the Devonshire countryside, which brims with flora and fauna. The wagons comfortably accommodate 14 people, and occupy a secluded glade that is also home to a hand-crafted dining table and outdoor shower — with hot water. Nearby activities include the Tarka Trail cycle path, Exmoor National Park, and stunning beaches.

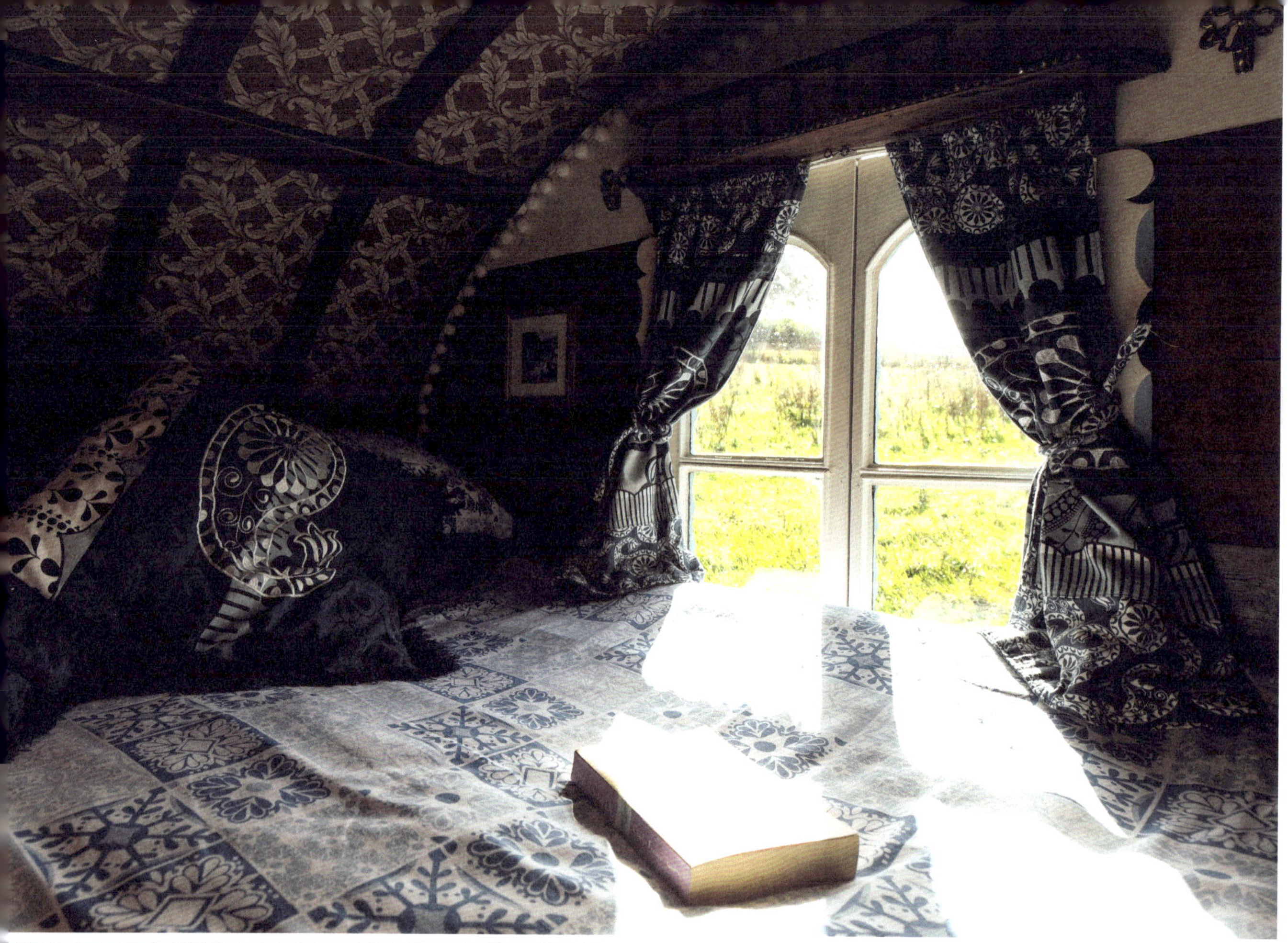
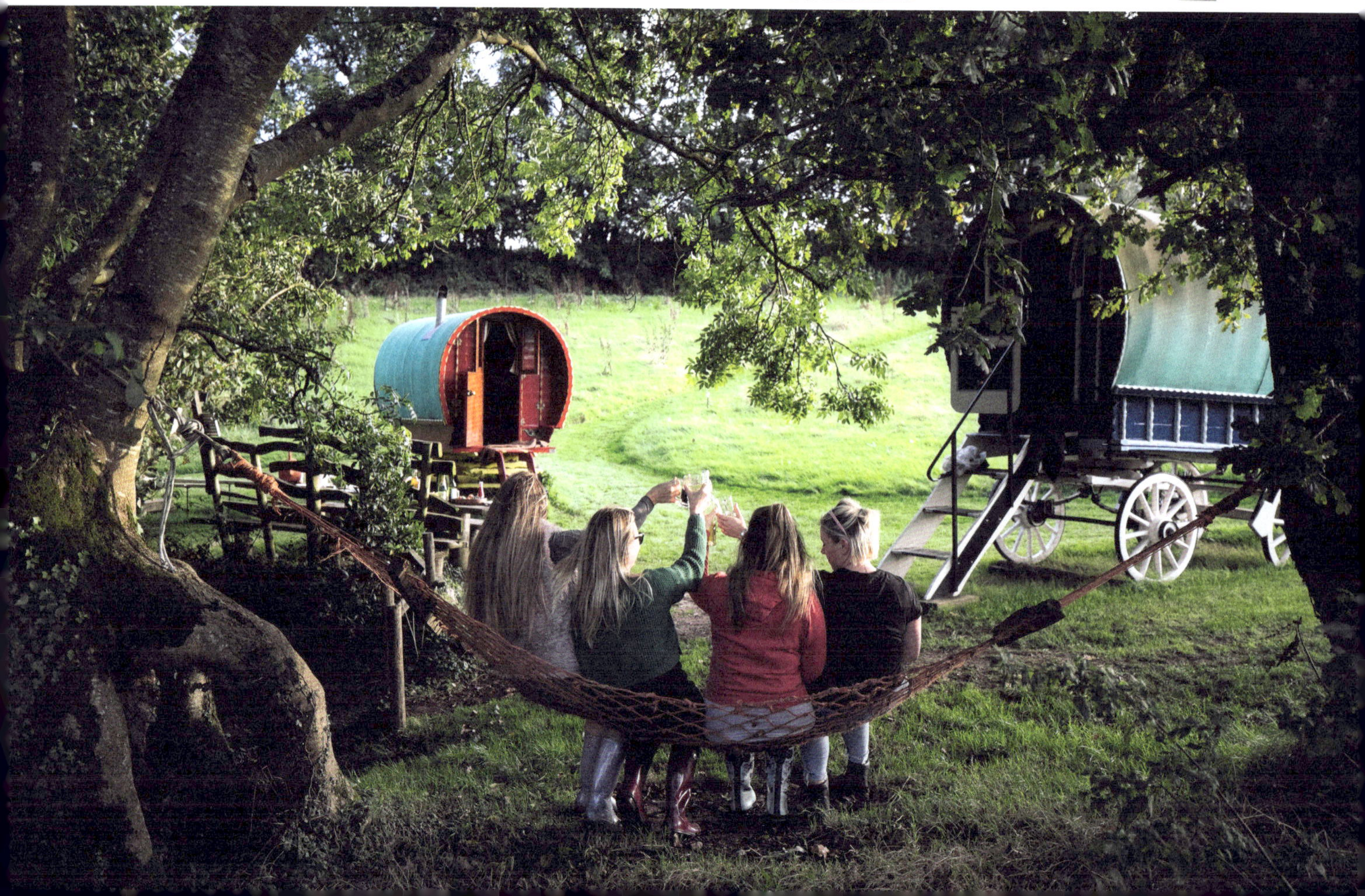

THE VINTAGE VARDOS

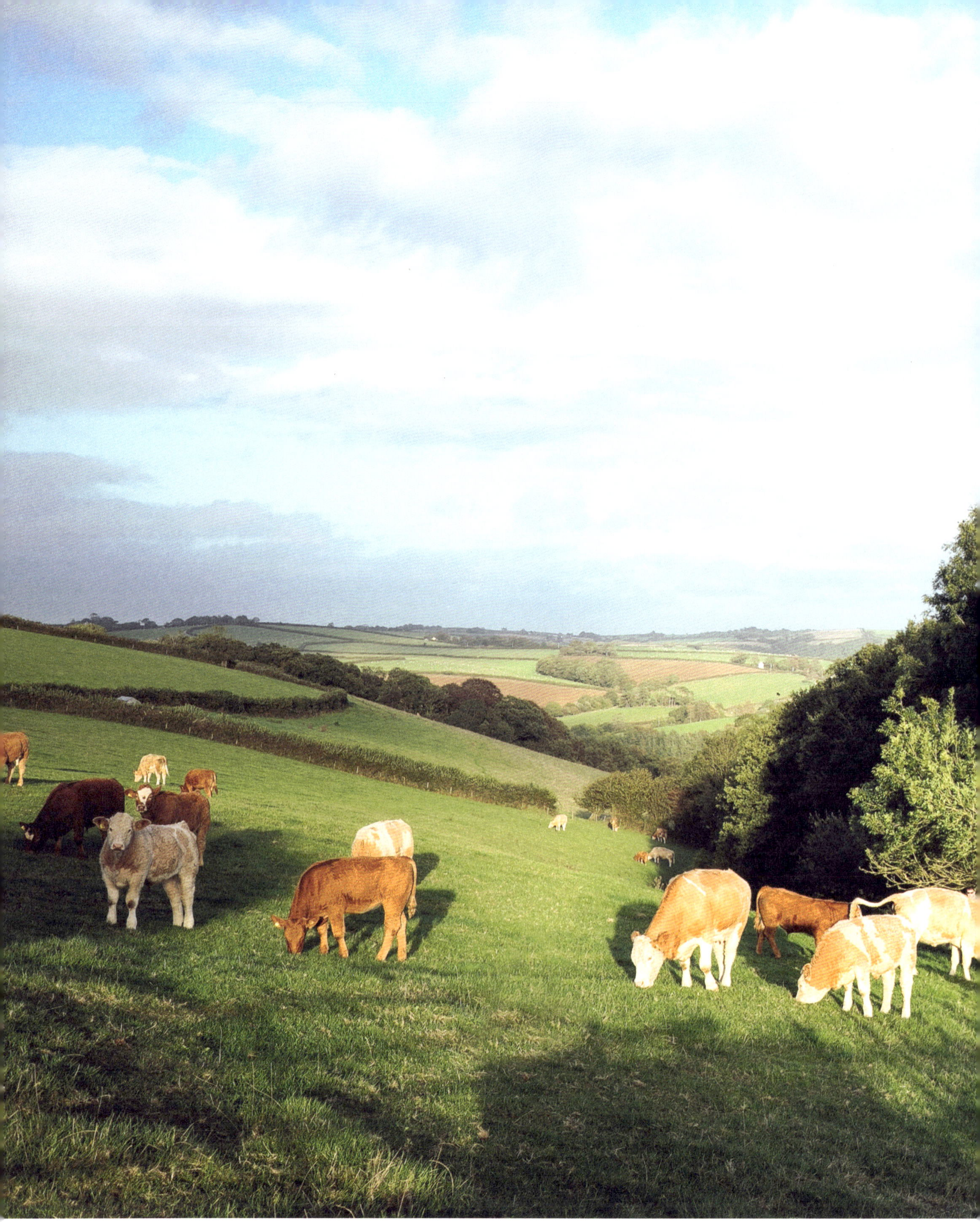

THE VINTAGE VARDOS

An Air of Exclusivity

Luxury glamping in a canvas lodge with dramatic views across Portugal's Mondego valley

MACIEIRA LODGE
BEIRA,
PORTUGAL

One of eight canvas dwellings on the 10-hectare (25-acre) Vinha da Manta estate, Macieira Lodge stands in a secluded spot that allows guests to feel totally at one with nature from sunrise to sunset. The site is planted with olive, almond, peach, cherry, and fig trees, as well as the apple trees after which this particular lodge is named, and it emphasises its natural splendour through such features as an eco-filtered swimming pool. Inside the lodge, bespoke furnishings take inspiration from the shapes and colours of the enveloping landscape. It's difficult to conjure a more peaceful and private environment in which to chill. With breakfast delivered daily, and a handy kitchen and outdoor bathroom, guests really have no reason to leave this idyllic spot, but should they want to, they can sample one of owner Menno Simon's four-course gourmet meals, all made from home-grown organic ingredients, or join his partner Jacqueline Steeman on a horseback ride. Those exploring alone will find plenty to do like hiking and wild swimming.

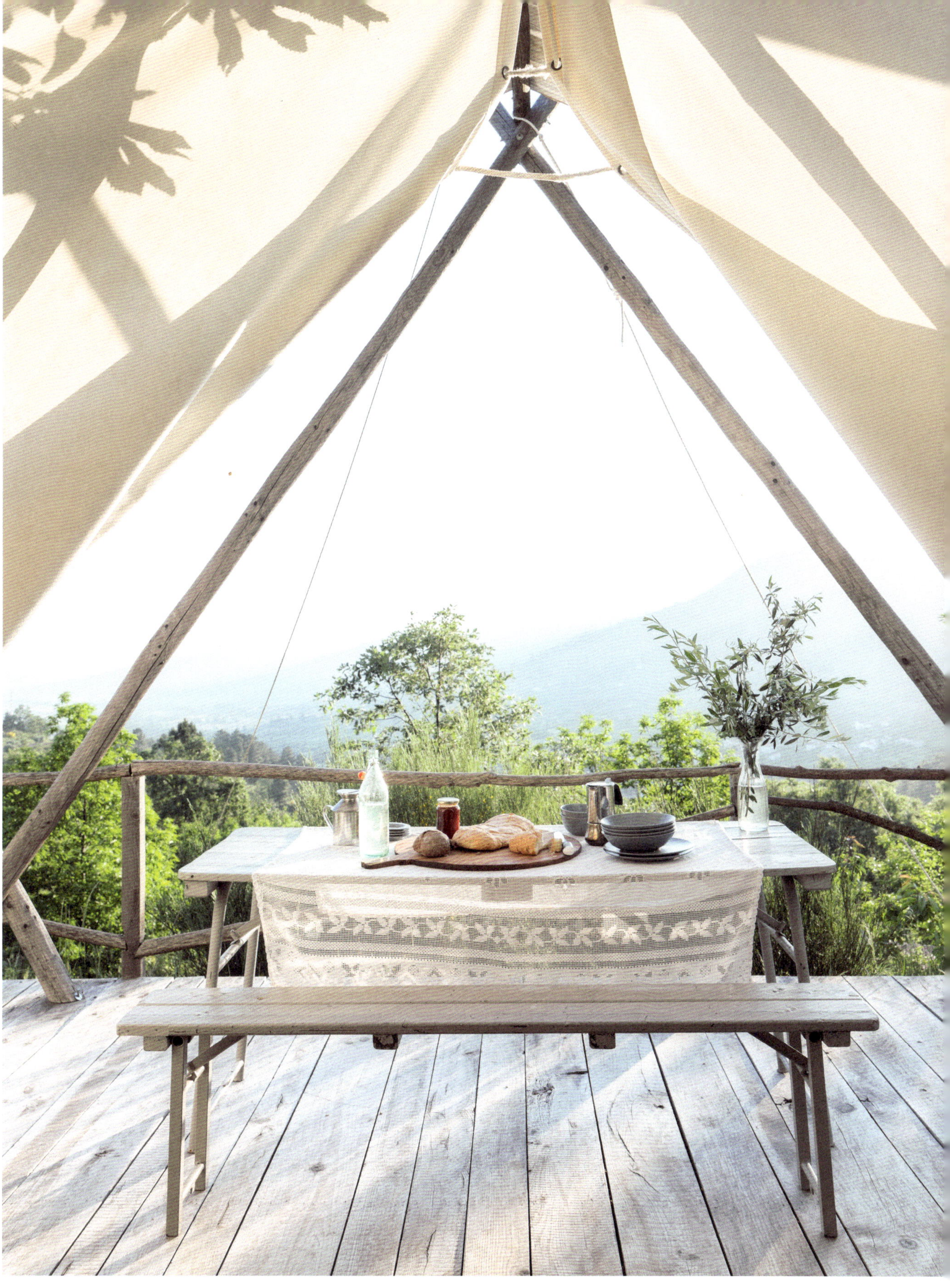

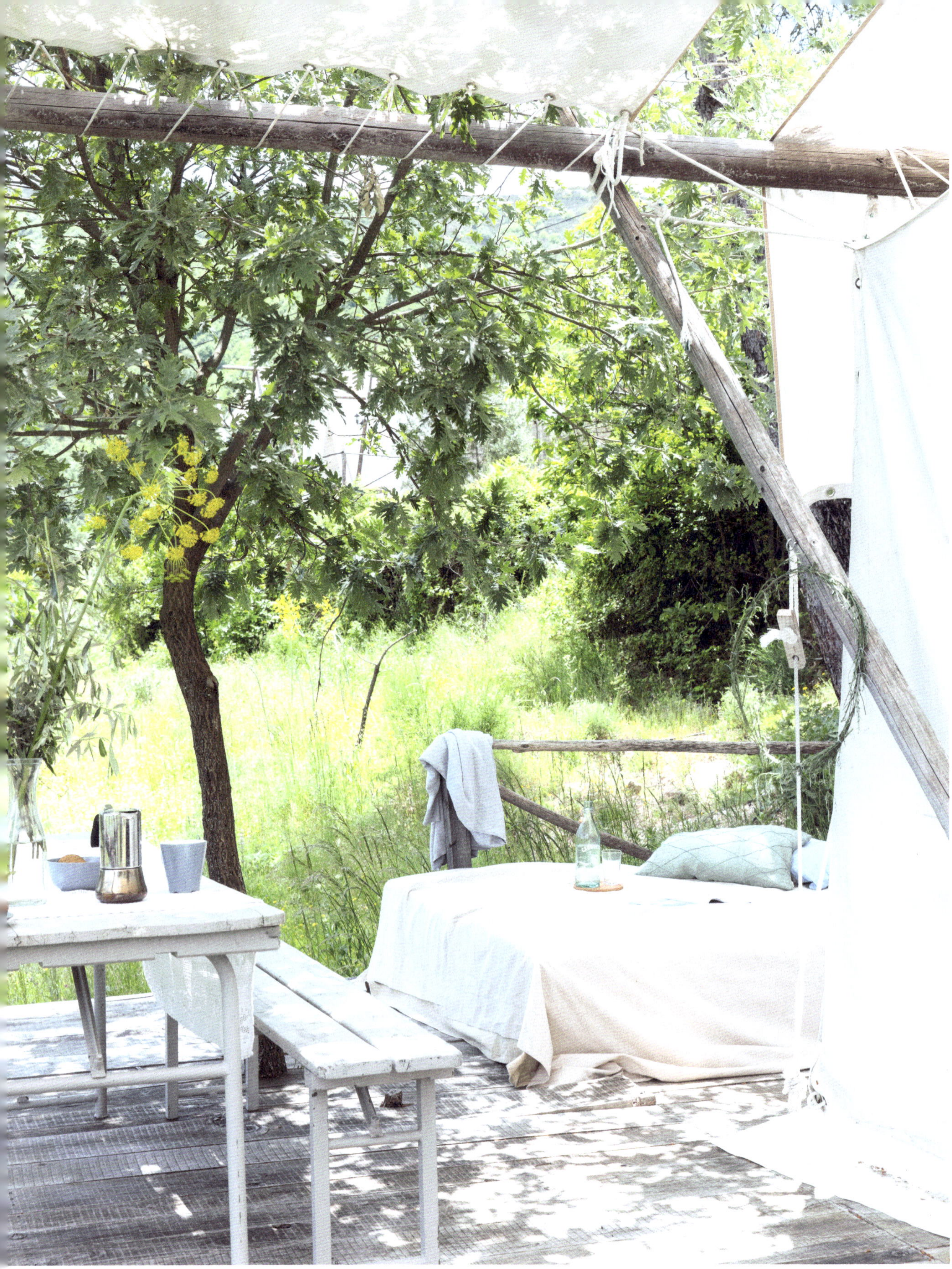

MACIEIRA LODGE

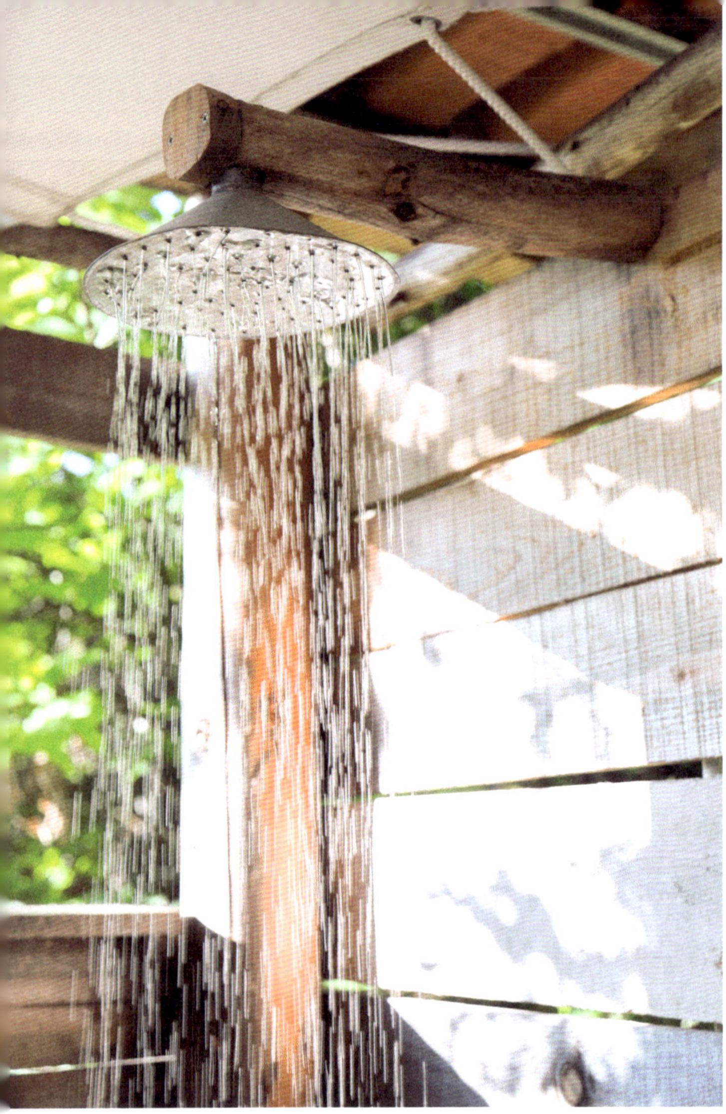

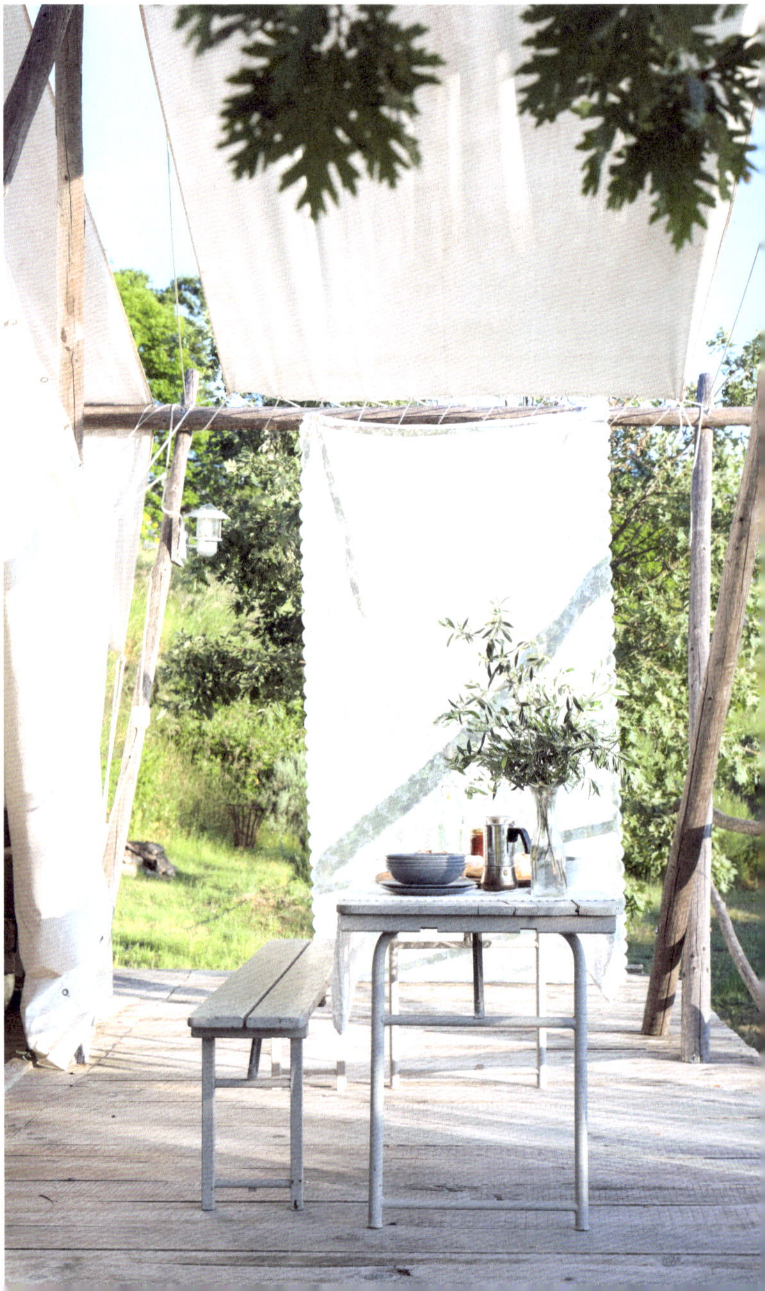

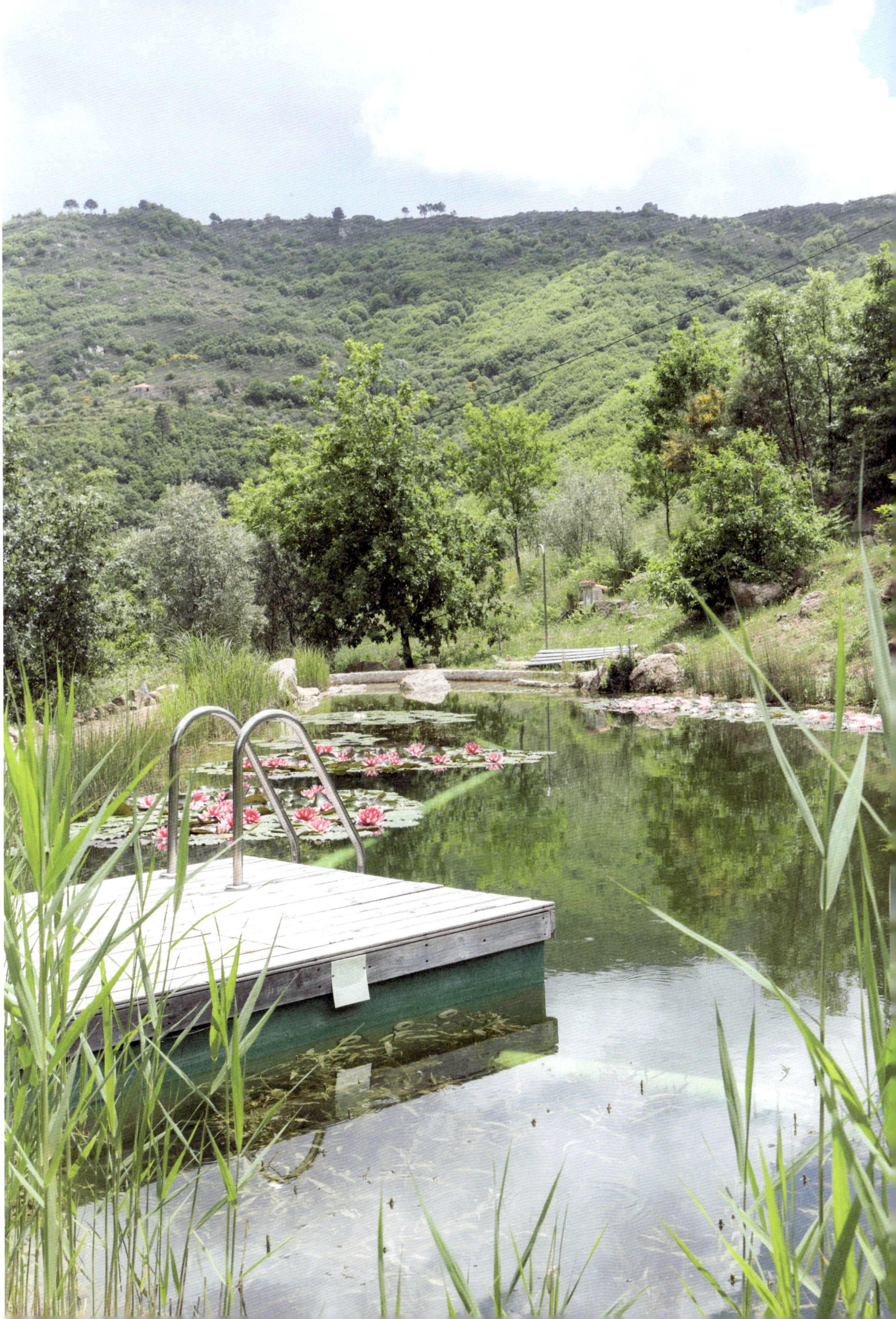

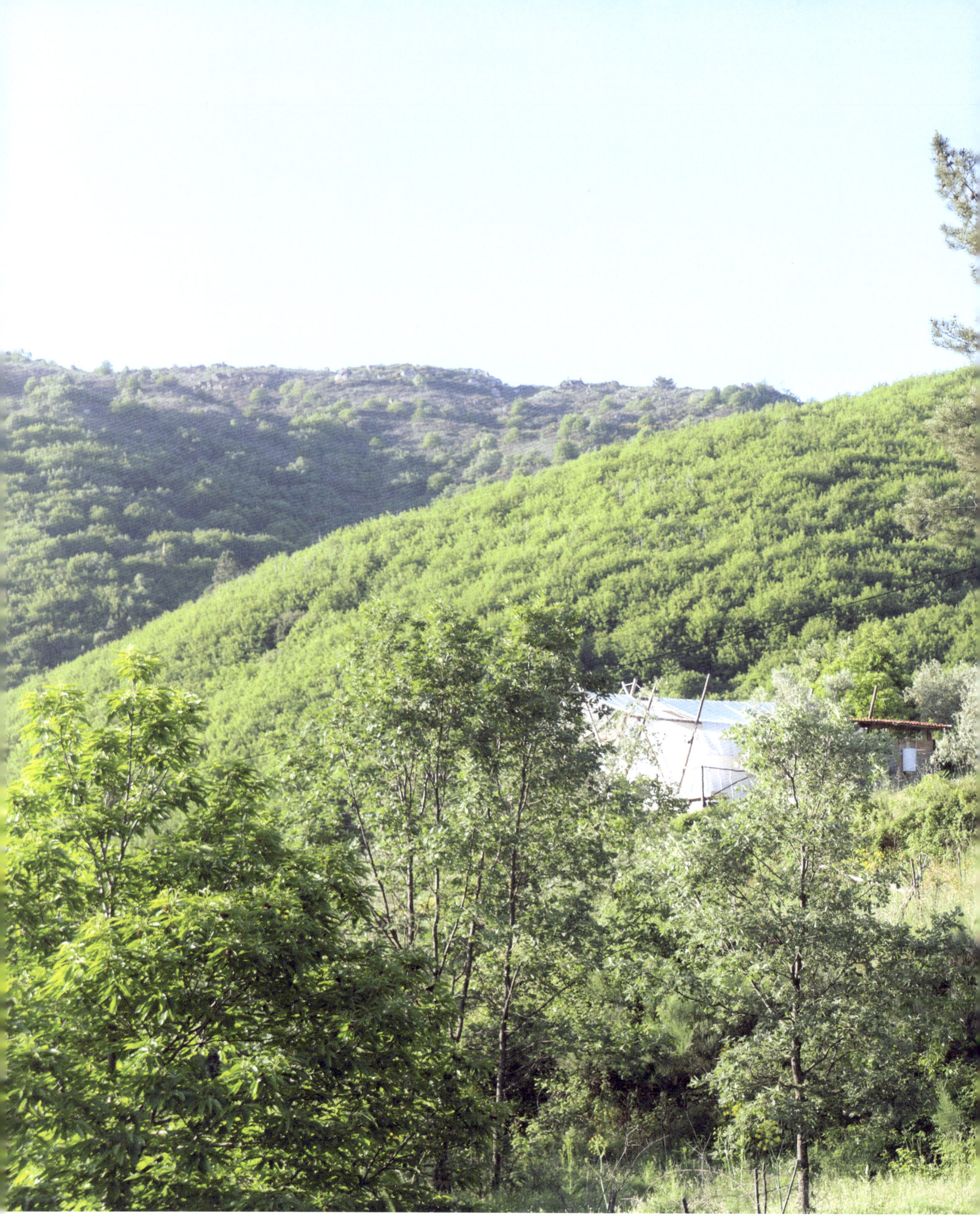

MACIEIRA LODGE

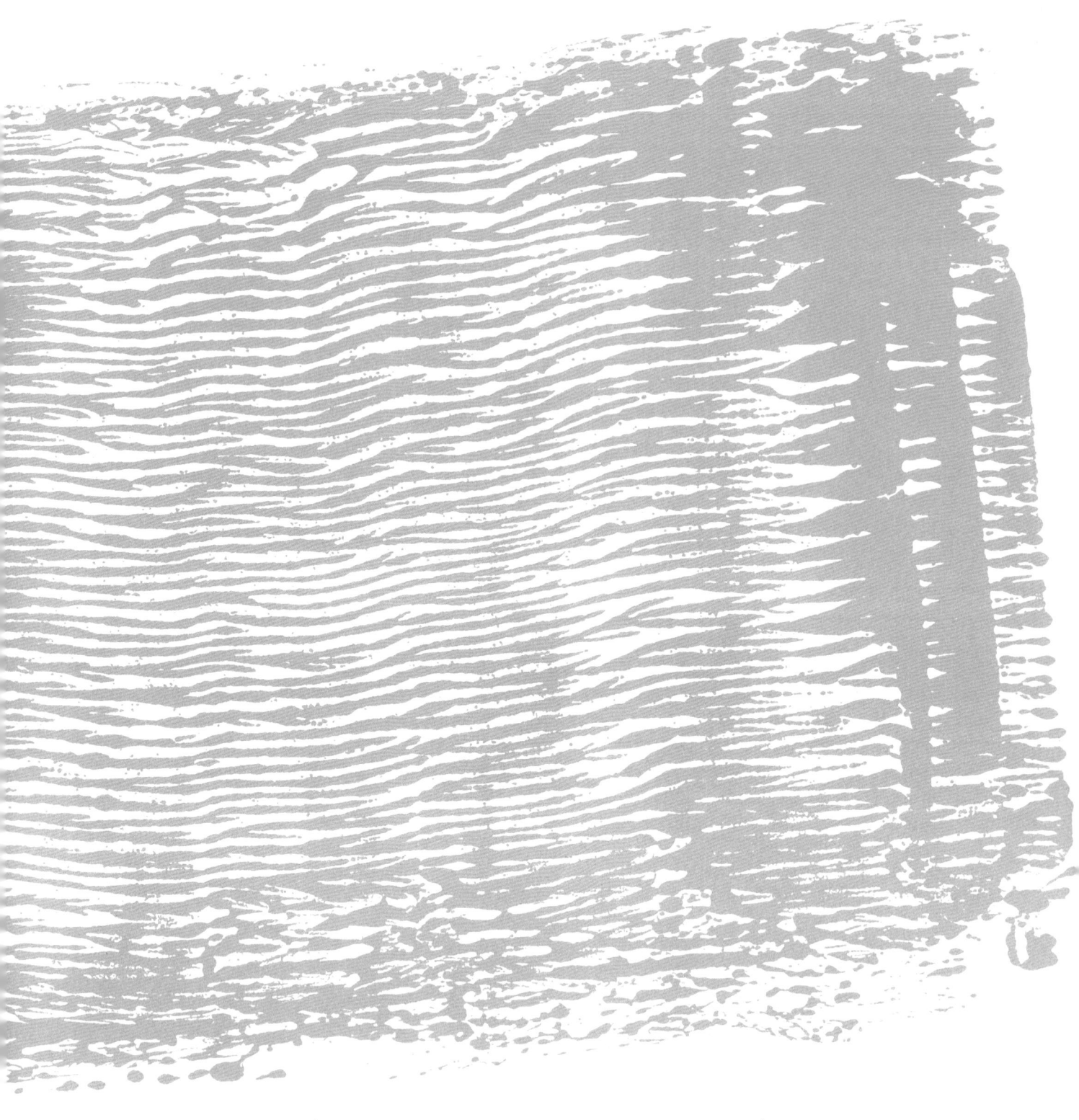

The Joy of Doing Nothing

Find out how nature is the perfect place to do nothing and feel the benefits of escaping from our over-stimulated lives

— by Canopy & Stars' David West

When was the last time you did absolutely nothing? No phones. No distractions. Nothing. Chances are you probably can't remember. We're in an age of perpetual busyness. It has been said that we are the burnout generation, one of time-poor, financially struggling, anxious, sexless workaholics with no concept of R&R. With that in mind, learning how to do nothing may be the most vital skill for surviving our frenetic, overwhelmed, over-stimulated lives.

One thing that arguably contributes to this inability to do nothing is that we increasingly occupy cities. By 2050 it's estimated that about 70 percent of the world's population will live in urban areas, up from 54 percent in 2018 and 30 percent in 1950. With this gravitation towards city life, there is an omnipresent onslaught of things demanding our attention. If it's not the billboards and flashing signs, it's the nagging feeling that with so many options, there's something out there that we could be doing. We are driven towards busyness by a fear of missing out, yet what we're really missing out on is the absence of all that. It's a fear of doing nothing.

With this in mind, you might think a holiday would provide the perfect respite from this drive to be constantly occupied, but for many of us holidays are just another block of time to fill with activities and achievements. It's for this reason — alongside many others — that a stay in the outdoors is the perfect chance to master the art of being bored. Unlike the modern city, nature asks very little of you — it only gives. It's the perfect place to practise idleness.

So, what do you need to pack for your boring holiday? Ideally as little as possible. The outdoors doesn't care what you wear — unless you're not taking a sensible coat. Add in a couple of books, a pack of cards, and a few bottles of something to drink, and you've got almost everything you need. Packing light = freedom.

> Learning how to do nothing may be the most vital skill for surviving our frenetic, overwhelmed, over-stimulated lives. A stay in the outdoors is the perfect chance to master the art of being bored.

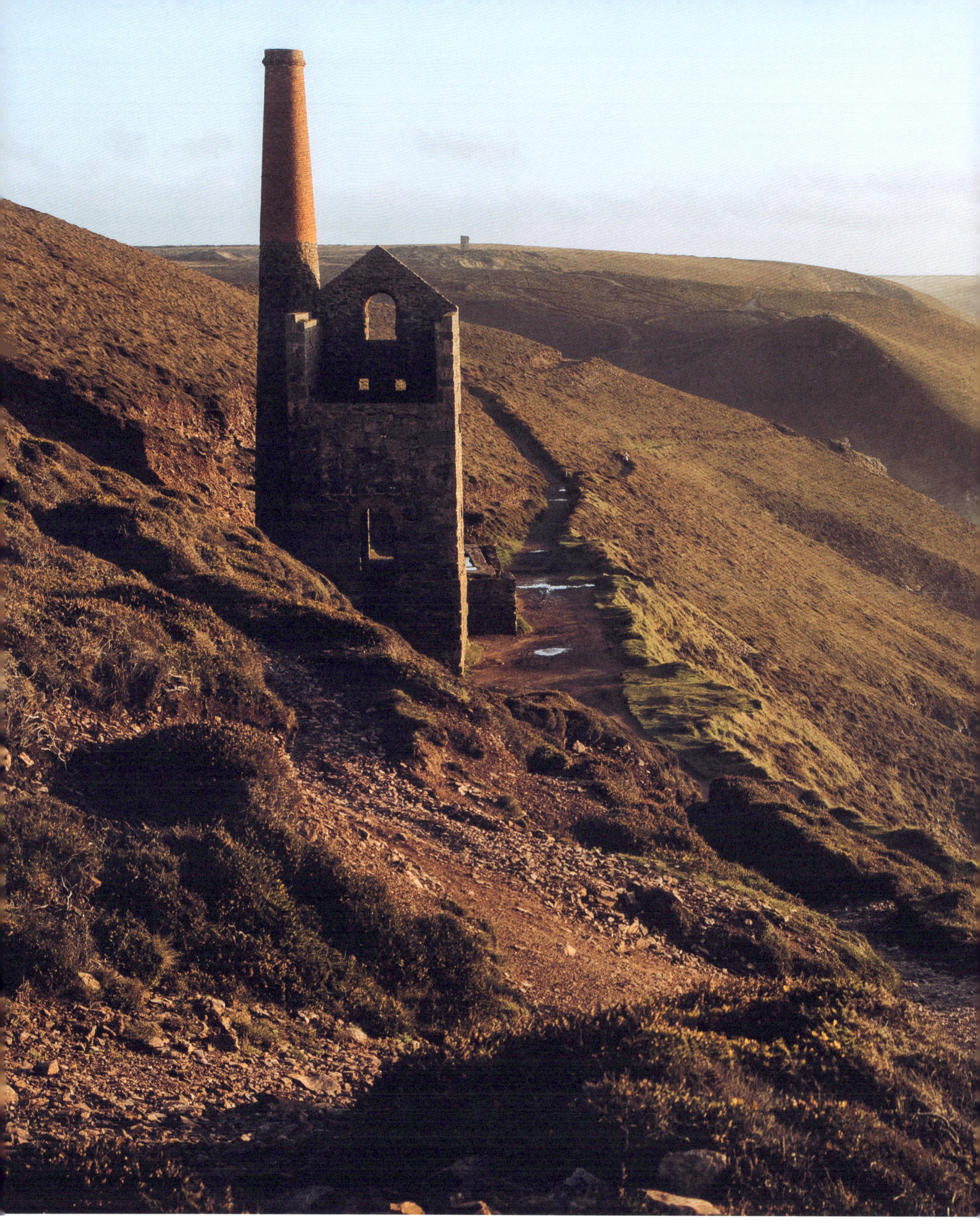

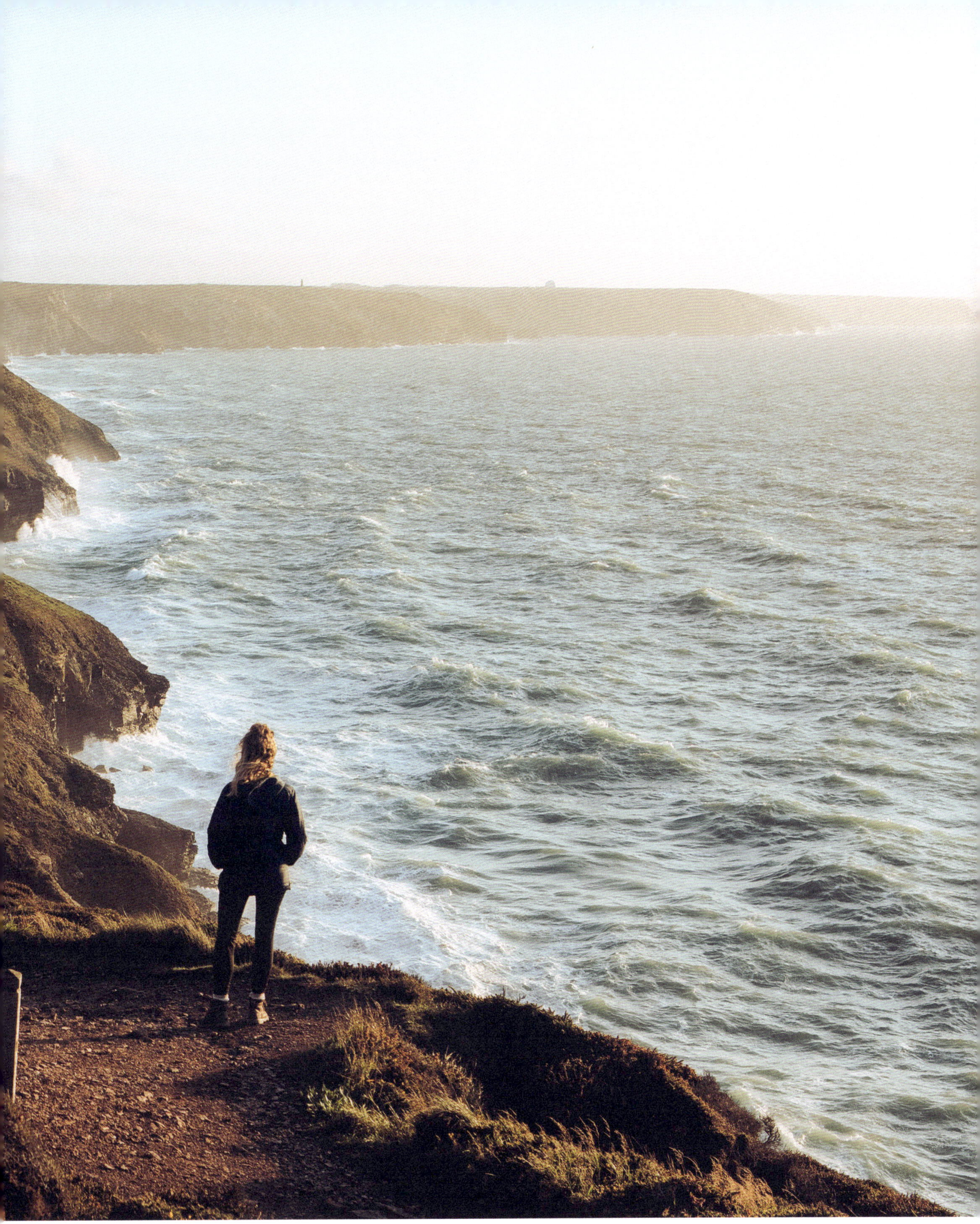

When you arrive, don't busy yourself with reading the guides and planning itineraries; press pause and immerse yourself in your surroundings. Drink in the smell of the trees, the sight of big open skies, and, ideally, your favourite tipple. It's called a break for a reason, so take this time to relax, mentally as well as physically. There is hard evidence behind this suggestion, as neuroscientists are increasingly finding that our brains depend on downtime. Moments spent being idle are vital for our mental and physical health; they let our minds make sense of what we've recently experienced, solidify memories, and can even boost creativity.

Of course, it's going to be hard at first, but doing nothing doesn't have to mean sitting still and staring into space. It can also mean remembering the joy found in tiny things, whether it's taking a long soak surrounded by nature or stoking the embers of a fire whilst a stew slowly bubbles atop. There are mental and physical benefits to be gained from seeing everyday activities not just as tasks, but as moments to be savoured — yes, even the washing up.

Even romantic relationships could benefit from a bit of boredom. As strange as it sounds, with a disconnect from your daily routine and the absence of anything to do, you'll likely find a lot more time to talk. With that comes a chance to reflect on where you are and where you want to be — deeper conversations that allow you to grow closer. If you need a bit of structure, try asking these three questions: 'What would you like to celebrate right now in your life?', 'What is a challenge for you at the moment?', 'What positive intention would you like to set going forward?'

At this point, if you find yourself itching for something more active, try going for a walk. The key to this one is to set off with no destination in mind — see where your feet take you. Instead of focusing on getting from A to B, think of it as going from A to ahh. As you walk, focus on the environment around you: the sound of the birds, the squelch of a boot in mud, the sensation of grass brushing against your legs. Take it slow and enjoy the feeling of walking without having to be somewhere.

When you return, if you haven't already banished your phone to a distant corner of the cabin, now is the time to do it. And

Even a short break can be enough to boost the immune system and reduce stress. When you return home and your friends or colleagues ask what you did on your holiday, simply respond: 'Nothing.' Be proud.

get rid of your watch, too, whilst you're at it. We've become slaves to those two tiny hands/four tiny digits. For many of us, it is our watches, not the rumble of our stomachs, that tell us when we should eat, and our phone alarms, not the rising sun or a crowing cockerel, that tell us when to wake up. The great outdoors is the perfect remedy to this. Let your natural instincts take over, and you may just find your days seem longer, and that you feel more relaxed and get a proper night's kip.

It's increasingly well documented that sleep is the best thing you can do for your health, yet our busy days don't always lend themselves to restful nights. It's a familiar story for anyone who has ever crawled into bed after a frantic day only to find that, despite all logical explanation, sleep still won't come. Studies have shown that new surroundings can do wonders for the quality of your shuteye, and one of the reasons for this is 'association'. Even if your bedroom is a sanctuary of peace and tranquillity, it still contains an association to the sleepless nights you've spent tossing and turning. There's no danger of that after a day spent doing nothing outdoors — replace counting tomorrow's jobs with counting the stars, and you'll soon nod off.

Even a short break can be enough to boost the immune system and reduce stress. When you return home and your friends or colleagues ask what you did on your holiday, simply respond: 'Nothing.' Be proud. Be unapologetic. Don't feel guilty or ashamed that you can't reel off a list of the places you visited.

Though it sounds easy, doing nothing takes a lot of time and effort, so don't get discouraged if you find it uncomfortable or difficult. Idleness is like exercise: it takes practice. At first you might get sore, but the more you do it, the easier it becomes. If you haven't got time for a holiday in the wild, then the next time you find yourself waiting for the kettle to boil, stuck in a queue, or sat on public transport, look up from your phone and out at the world. You're bound to get bored and maybe even a few strange looks, but hopefully in time we'll all become a bit more comfortable just being, rather than being busy.

> Though it sounds easy, doing nothing takes a lot of time and effort, so don't get discouraged if you find it uncomfortable or difficult. Idleness is like exercise: it takes practice. At first you might get sore, but the more you do it, the easier it becomes.

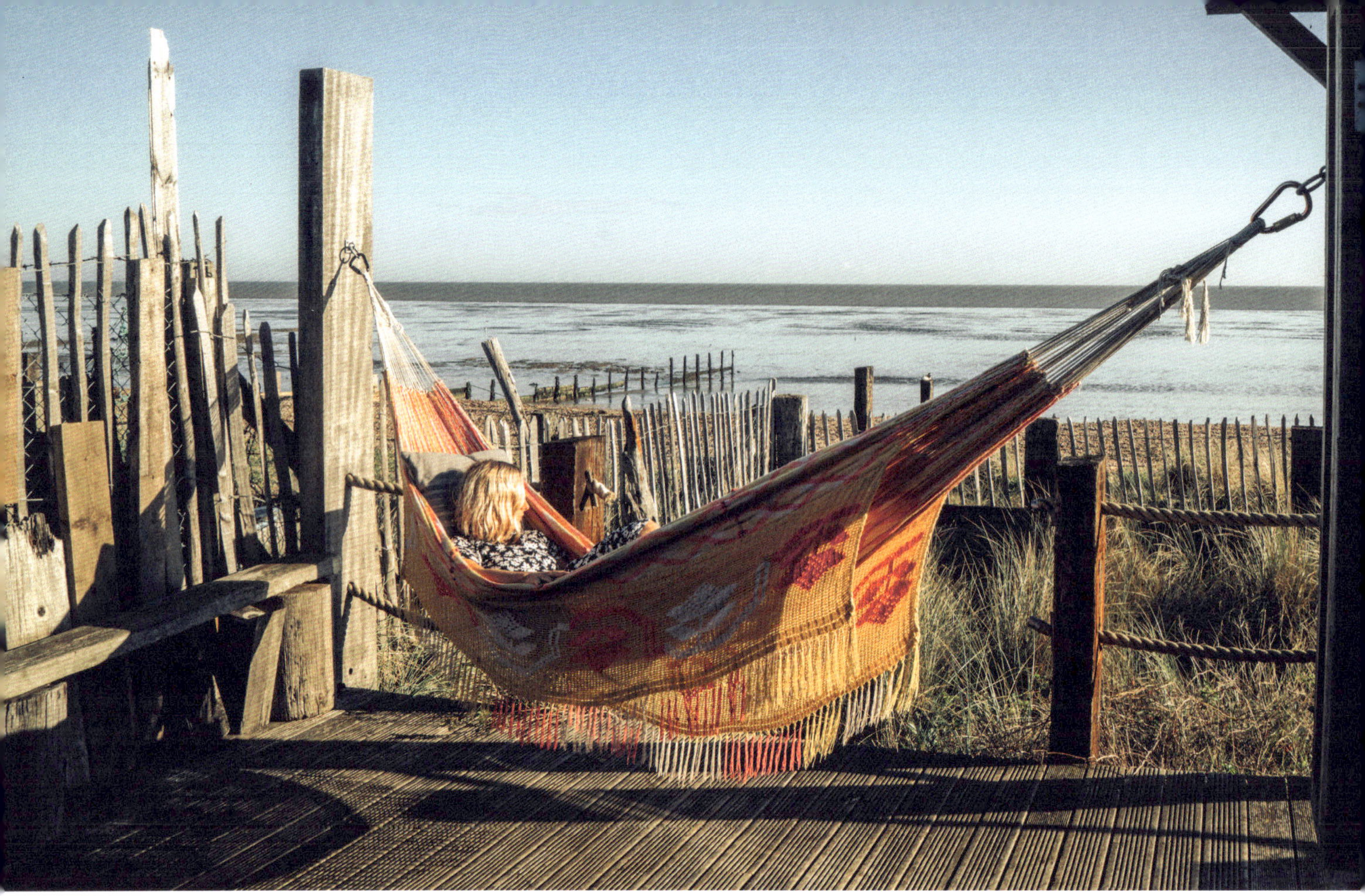

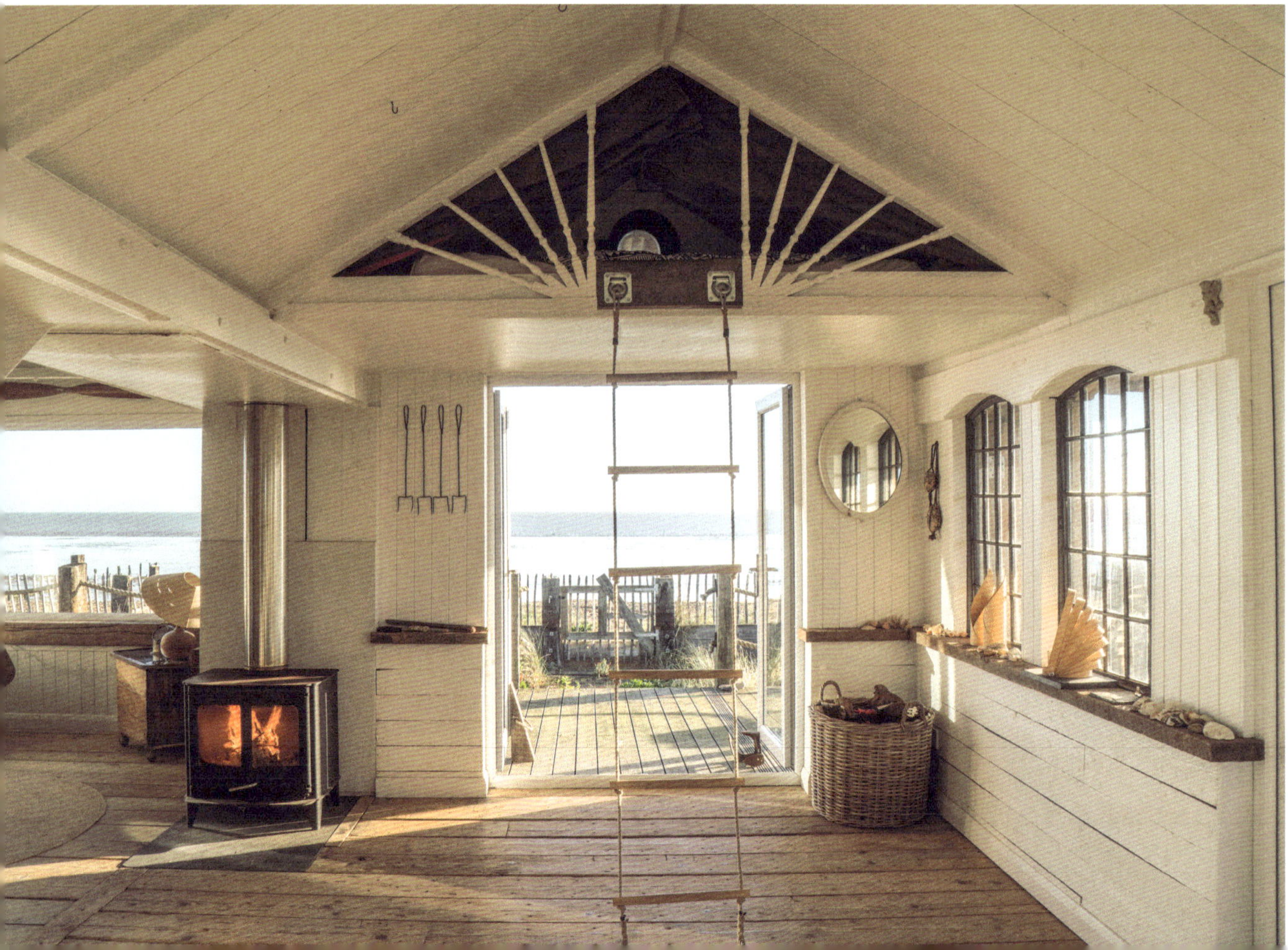

At Home Beside the Seaside

A renovated coastal cabin with a casual upcycled feel and wide-open views of the sea

THE BEACH HOUSE
KENT,
ENGLAND

Planted on grassy shingle a pebble's throw from the sea, what was once an abandoned, dilapidated home is now a two-bedroom open-plan beach house with bare-board floors, whitewashed walls, and rooms scattered with found and foraged objects. Lovingly restored by owners Simon (a designer and builder of cool, sustainable living spaces) and Anna Abbott, part of the charm of this seaside dwelling is its low impact on the environment. Completely off-grid, it uses solar power and, for cleaning purposes, harvested rainwater from the roof — you have to bring your own drinking water. Comfort comes in the form of a glowing wood burner and a gas-heated shower. With a lounge swing in the living room and a hammock on the wraparound deck, this is the ultimate place to chill and relax away from the city, and to tune in to the sound of the sea. The beach, usually deserted, lies in the middle of a bird reserve, featuring a six-mile (10-kilometre) circular hike populated with such wildlife as marsh harriers, owls, waterfowl, and butterflies.

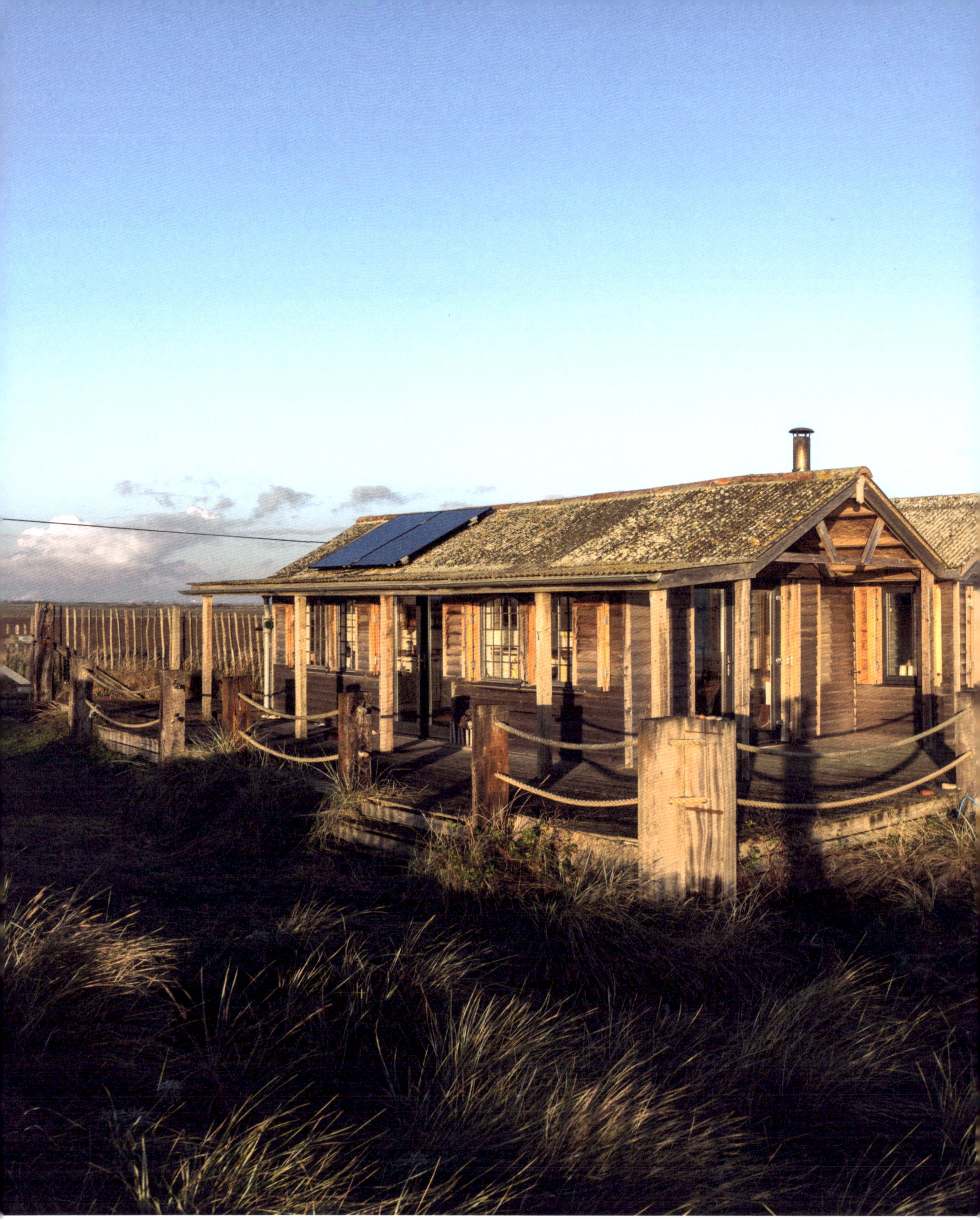

THE BEACH HOUSE

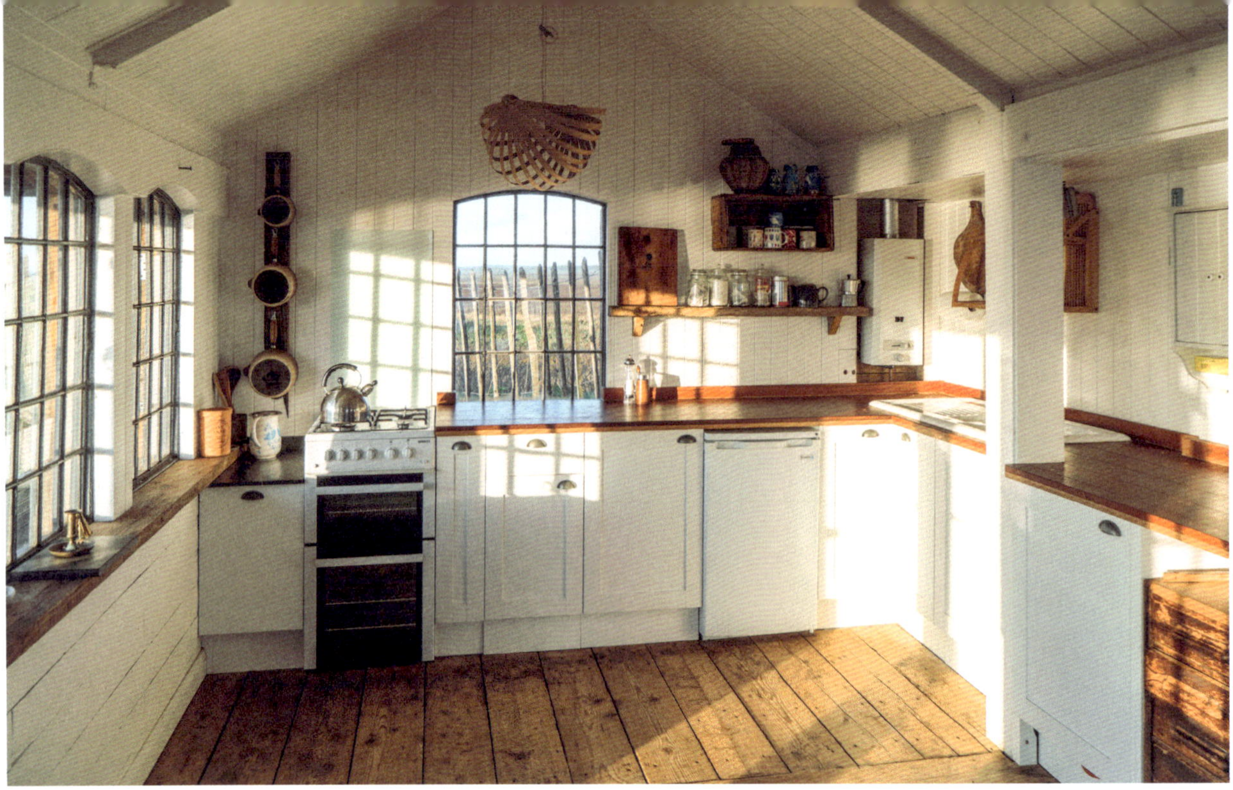

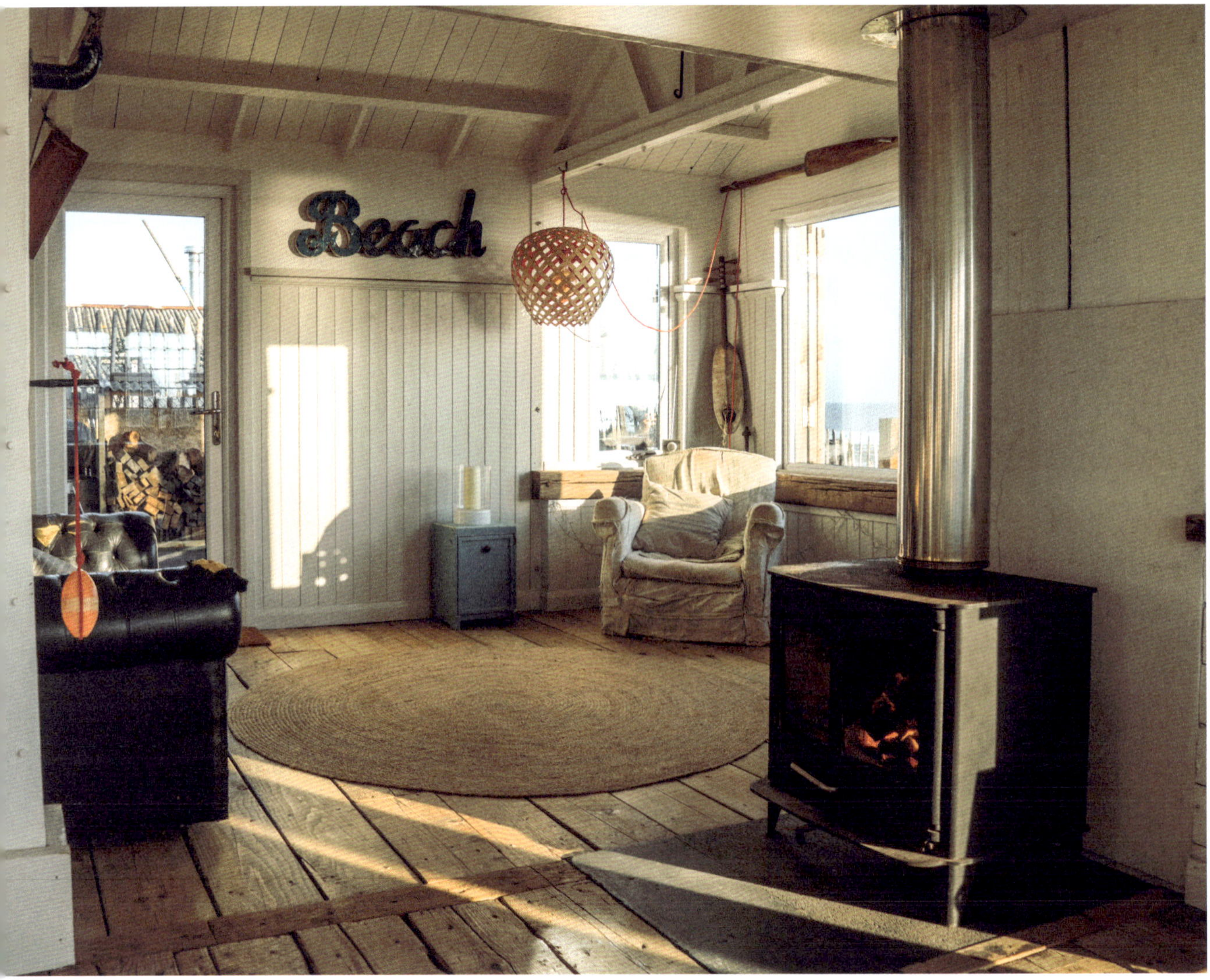
Beach

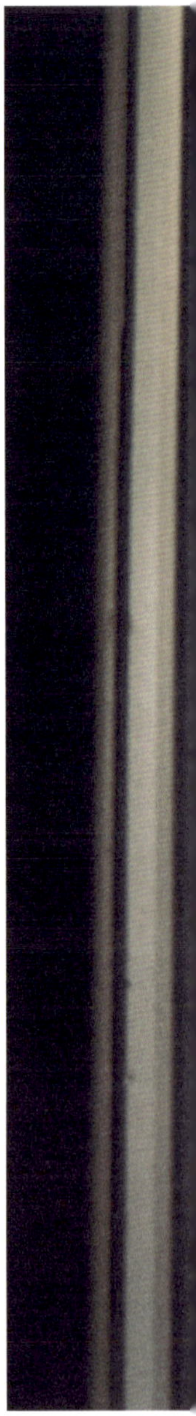

THE BEACH HOUSE

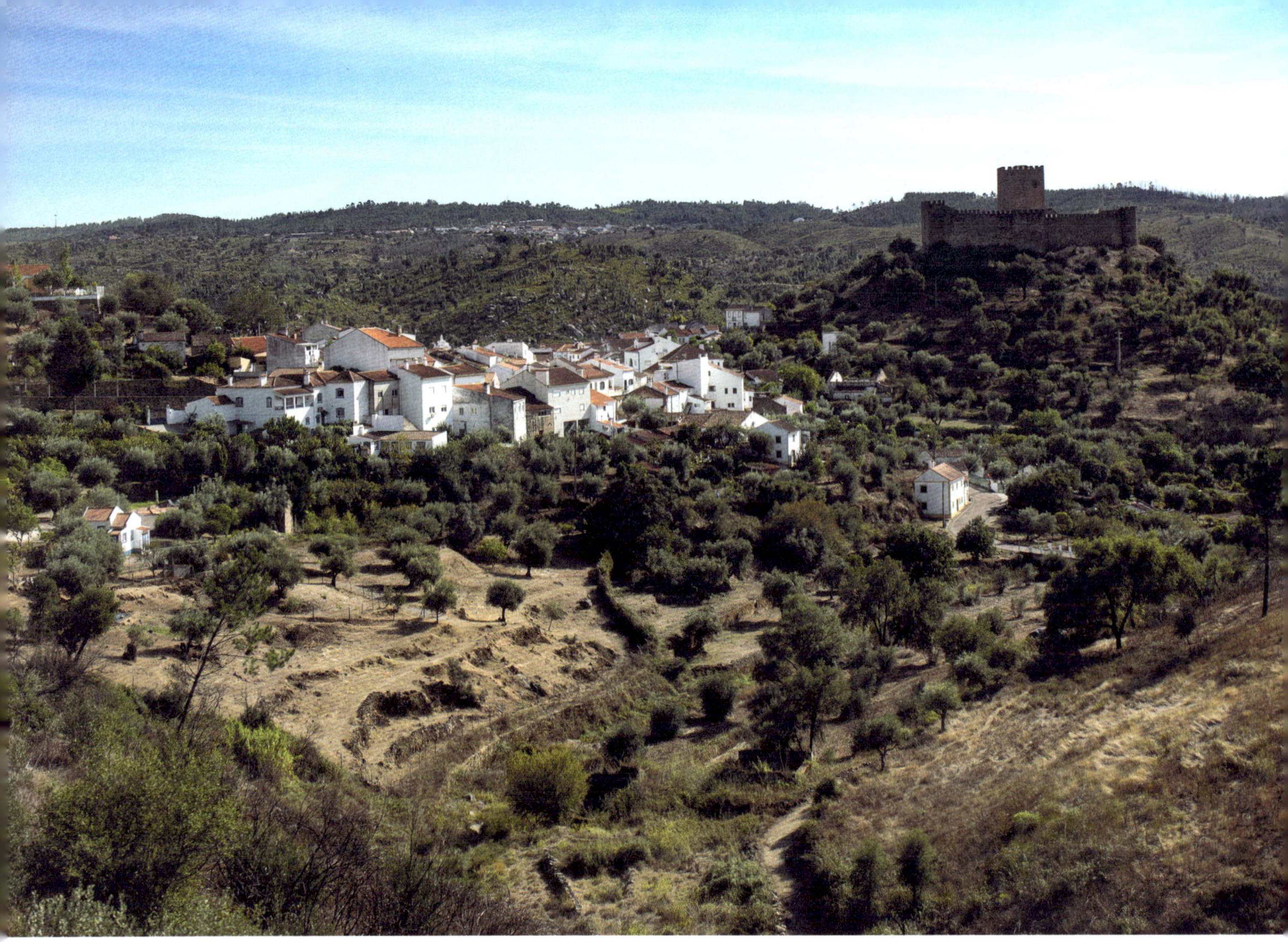
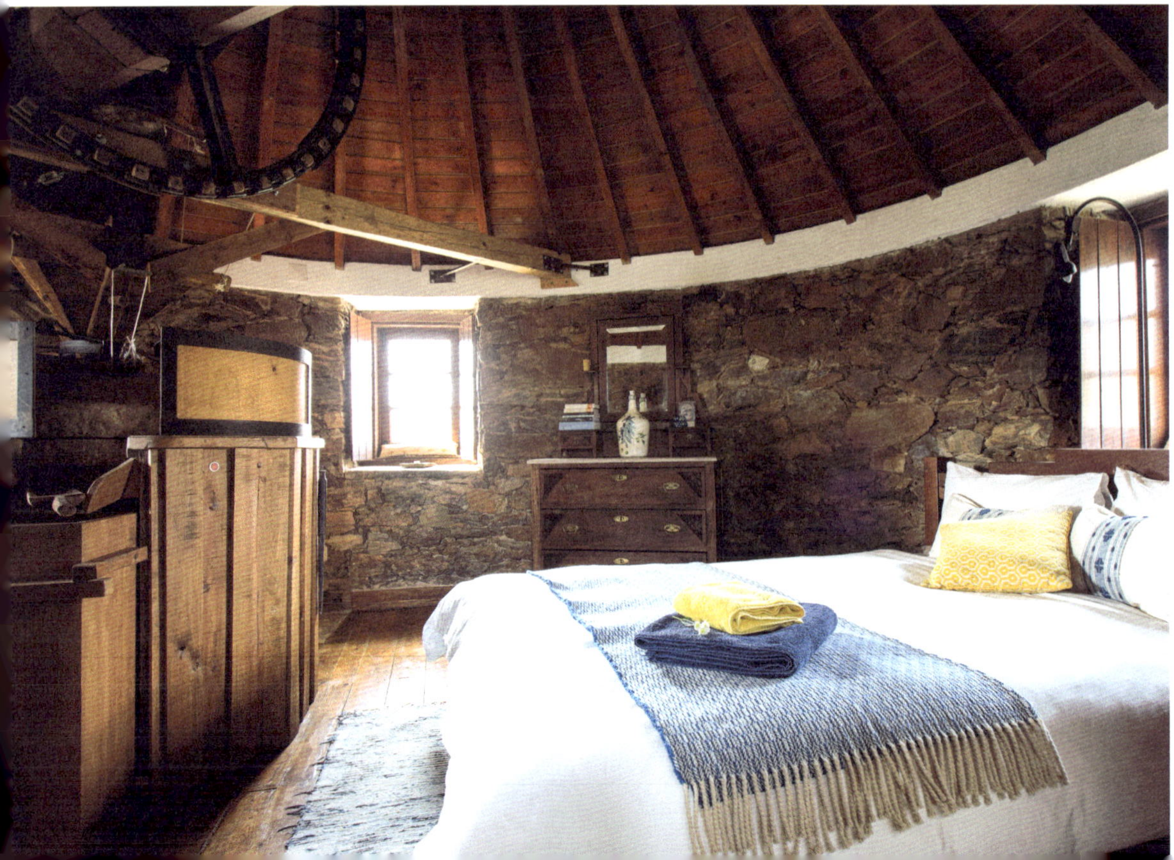

The Charm of a Century-Old Windmill

A rural getaway for two with 360-degree views of the rolling hills of central Portugal

MOINHO DA FADAGOSA
ALTO ALENTEJO,
PORTUGAL

This once-derelict stone windmill has seen a sensitive makeover at the hands of British owners Simon Broad and Fiona McCready, who have worked hard to preserve its original character. Guests will find the old mill machinery upstairs in the bedroom and, downstairs, a desk fashioned from a timeworn millstone. The sink is made from a stone chicken bath, and even the shower was once a cow trough. There's a table outside for al fresco dining with the most incredible views of the surrounding hills, and if things turn chilly, there are comfy chairs beside a big open fireplace inside. The windmill is a stone's throw from the river Tagus, a haven for wild swimmers who share the water with otters, turtles, and crayfish. For those who prefer country walks, several trails lead through the hills and into the mountains, but it is at the day's end when the charm of the place really casts its magical spell. As night falls, the sky begins to fill with stars to a backing track of tawny owl hoots and, perhaps, even the song of a lonely nightingale.

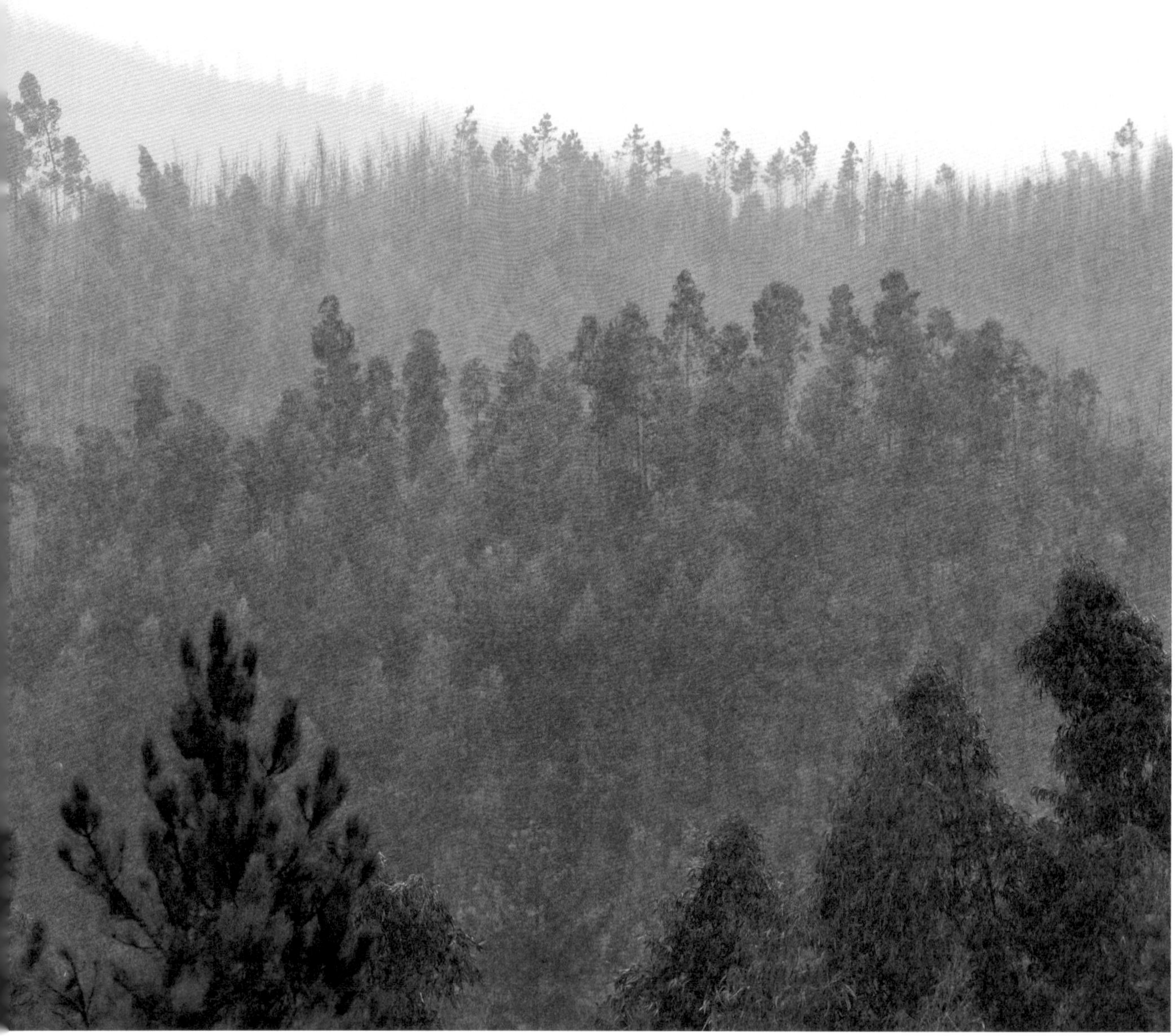

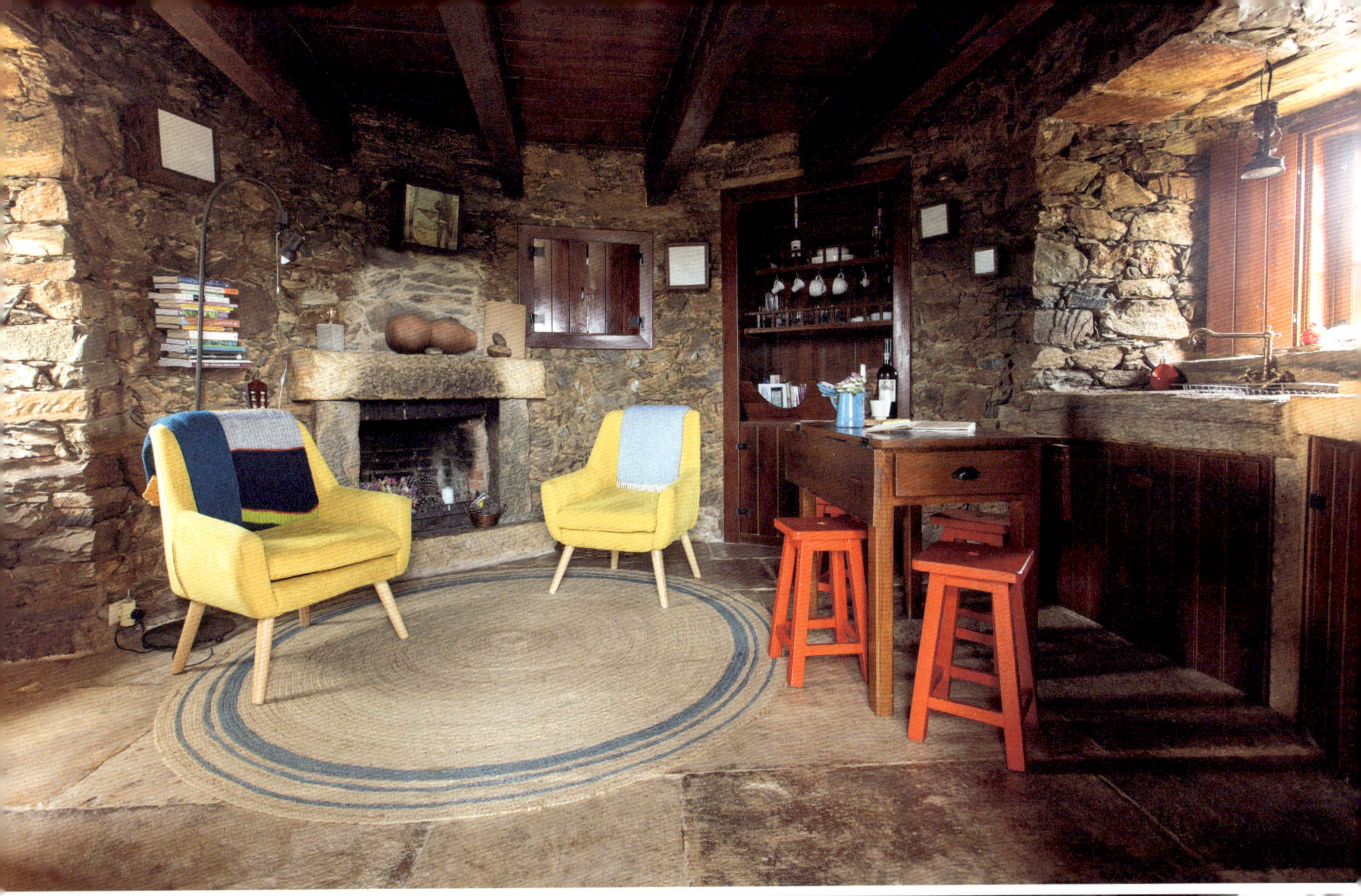

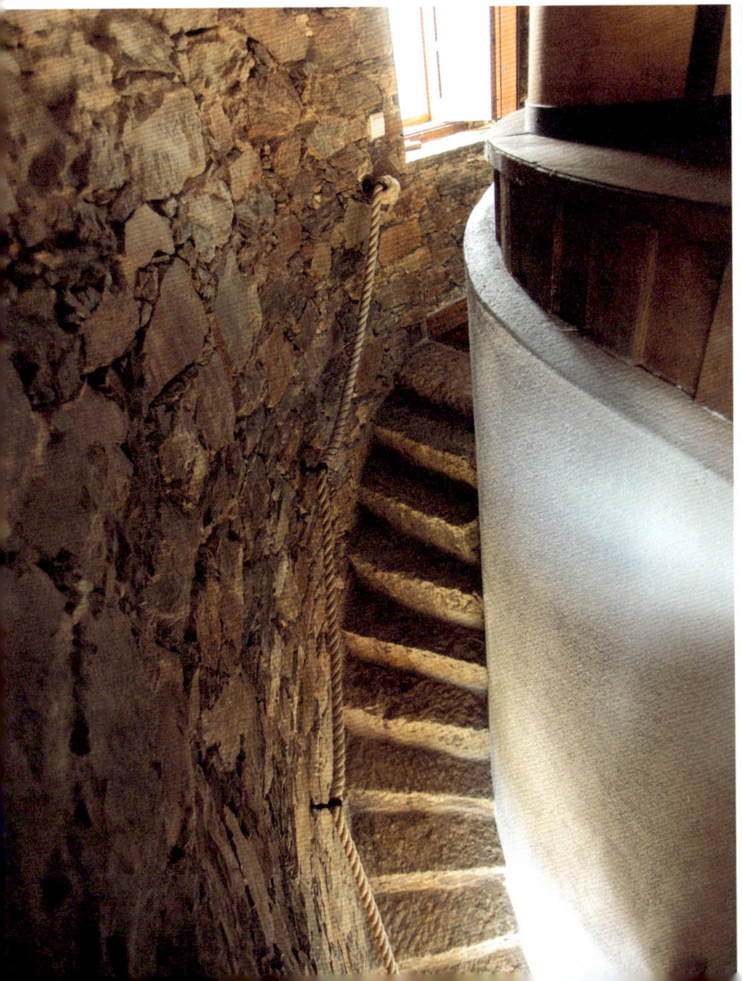

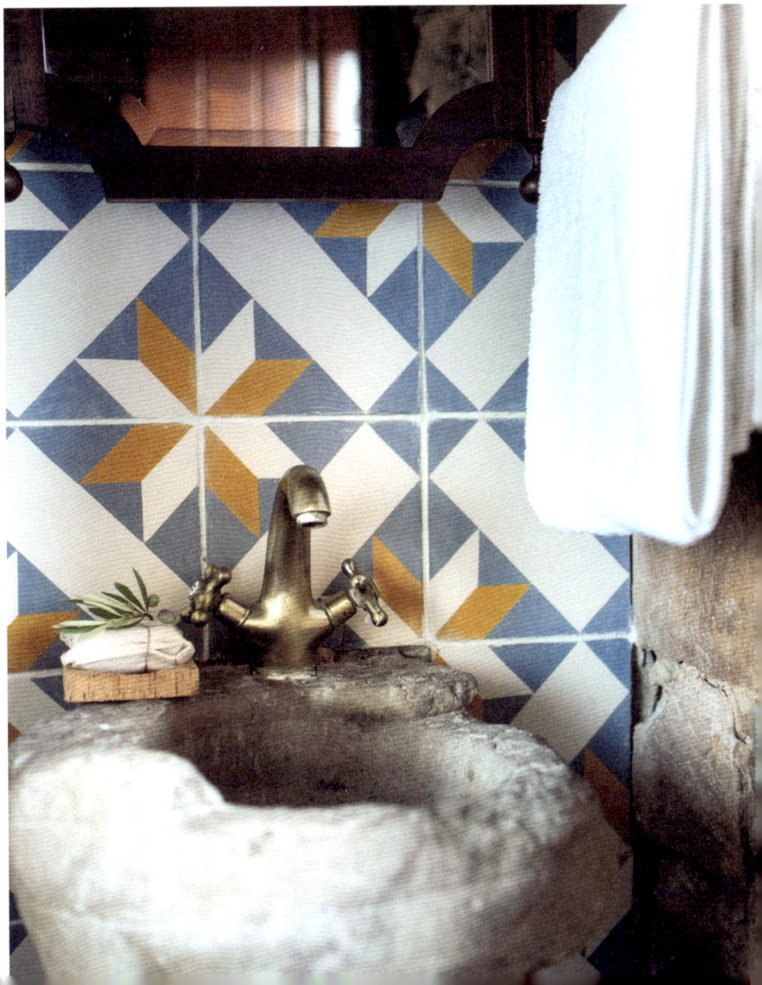

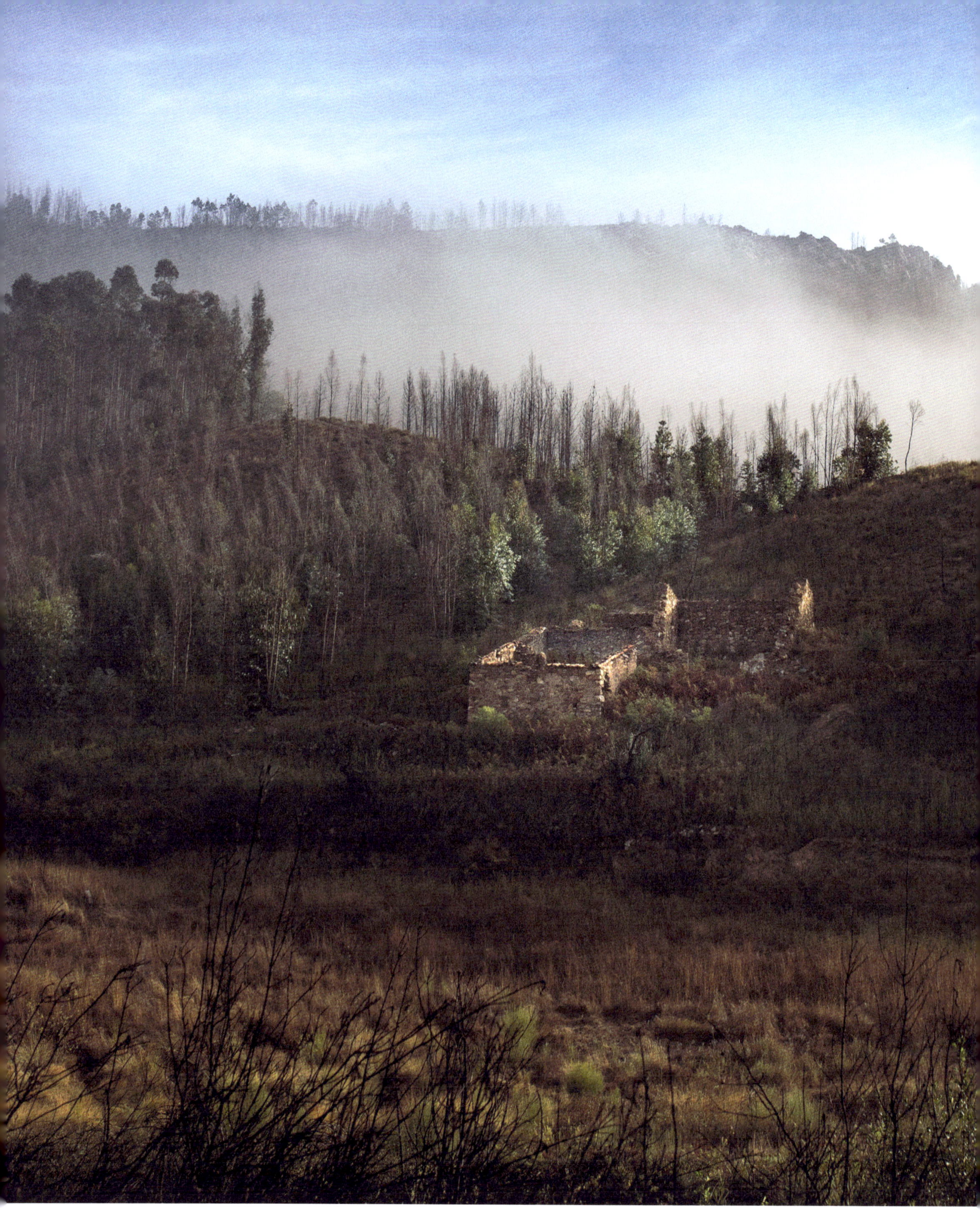

MOINHO DA FADAGOSA

Canopy & Stars

For over a decade, Canopy & Stars has been inspiring people to reconnect with nature. As curators of a unique collection of places to stay, they have connected thousands of guests to properties in Europe's great outdoors. Their inspection team visits every single location, looking for experiences that will show people the joy, benefits, and importance of living a life more wild. They believe in business being a force for good, environmentally and socially. They are majority employee-owned, 24 percent owned by a charitable trust focused on environmental causes, part of a B Corp, and they plant a tree for every booking at one of their amazing spaces.
www.canopyandstars.co.uk

Ruth Allen
The Science of Stepping Outside

Ruth Allen is a psychotherapist, trainer, and writer based in the Peak District, England, specialising in ecopsychotherapeutic/outdoor practice. Her works bring together elements of traditional talking therapy, body work, movement, and existential philosophy, and takes them outside into wild spaces. She is interested in the inner and outer journeys we make, the stories we tell about them, and the time we spend in solitude cultivating a two-way relationship with the living planet.

Jack Boothby
The Meaning of (Cabin) Life

Jack Boothby is the founder of Cabin Folk, a celebration of simple life in simple spaces. He uses his photography and his Instagram platform to bring the outdoors to time-poor people and inspire them to reconnect with nature. He is based in the north-east of England, but draws on cabins and landscapes from all over the world in his work. He is driven by the desire to tell a story or capture a moment with every picture.

Mya-Rose Craig
Our Wild Future

Mya-Rose Craig, aka Birdgirl, is an avid birdwatcher and president of an organisation she established, Black2Nature, which campaigns for equal access to nature for all, with a focus on visible minority ethnic (VME) communities who are currently excluded from the countryside. She is the youngest ever Briton to have been awarded an honorary doctorate and also the youngest person to have seen half the world's birds.

Emily Eavis
Foreword

Emily Eavis is the co-organiser of the world-famous Glastonbury Festival. She grew up on Worthy Farm in rural Somerset, where the festival takes place each year, and where she lives now with her husband and three children. From her teenage years onwards, she has played a vital role in every part of the organisation of the festival, making the magic happen for nearly 200,000 people on site, as well as millions watching live on the BBC. Passionately committed to Glastonbury's charity partners, Oxfam, Greenpeace, and WaterAid, and protecting the environment; she spearheaded the festival's much-heralded ban on the sale of single-use plastic bottles.

Chris Elmes
The Ultimate Life More Wild & Slowing the Pace

Chris Elmes is Canopy & Stars' copywriter and was the second employee at the company, joining when it was run out of a small room above a drumming and dance workshop space. He has travelled and taught all over the world, and he is never happier than when nobody knows where he is, even if it means he ends up walking in New Zealand for two days with nothing to eat but a kiwifruit.

Siân Lewis
Weekend Wanderings

Siân Lewis is an award-winning travel writer, outdoors journalist, speaker, blogger, and presenter based in Bristol in the U.K. Her work has taken her around the world, from Central American jungles to Greenland, Australia, and Thailand, where she learnt that peeing on a jellyfish sting doesn't help. Along with her global travels, she is dedicated to finding happiness outside and championing easy adventures that beginners can try.

Gill Meller
Our Outdoor Pantry

Gill Meller is a chef, food writer, and the author of several award-nominated books who developed his philosophy at River Cottage. He is passionate about simple, seasonal cookery that makes the most of a few ingredients and the natural qualities they possess. He sees cooking as a reflection of his surroundings and takes inspiration from the landscape and locality, and from the amazing farmers, growers, and fishermen that produce what he uses.

David West
The Joy of Doing Nothing

David West has been a key member of the Canopy & Stars team since 2014, masterminding the growth of its social media. Combining his work with a passion for music, he has run a record label for many years and collaborated with artists from all over the world. He also loves being outdoors, whether that means hiking through the countryside or tinkering on his allotment.

Index

7TH ROOM
Norrbotten, Sweden
pp. 116–119
Images by: Johan Jansson

AURORA DOME
Lapland, Finland
pp. 120–121
Images by:
Sarah Rodgers
p. 120
Jack Anstey
p. 121

BIG SKY LOOKOUT
Devon, England
pp. 24–31
Images by: Owen Howells

BLUE CONE
Norrbotten, Sweden
pp. 172–175
Images by: Peter Lundström

BOWCOMBE BOATHOUSE
Devon, England
pp. 200–205
Images by: Owen Howells

CABAN COPA
Powys, Wales
pp. 196–199
Images by: Iris Thorsteinsdottir

CHÂTEAU DANS LES CHÊNES
Hérault, France
pp. 214–219
Images by: Vincent Bartoli

DABINETT TREEHOUSE
Somerset, England
pp. 140–143
Images by: Owen Howells

DIGITAL DETOX CABIN
Essex, England
pp. 162–165
Images by: Gwilym C Pugh

DRAGONFLY
Norrbotten, Sweden
pp. 166–171
Images by: Peter Lundström

DRAGON CRUCK
Powys, Wales
pp. 60–63
Images by: Owen Howells

ESKO'S CABIN
Lapland, Finland
pp. 130–135
Images by:
Jack Anstey
pp. 130–131, 132 (top and bottom left), 134–135
Sarah Rodgers
pp. 132 (bottom right), 133

GWENNOL
Black Mountains, Wales
pp. 20–23
Images by: Nigel Wilson

HINTERLANDES
The Lake District, England
pp. 16–19
Images by: Stuart McGlennon

HUMBLE BEE
Devon, England
pp. 94–95
Images by: John Barwood

KINTON CLOUD-HOUSE YURT
Shropshire, England
pp. 36–41
Images by: William Bunce

KUSHTI
East Sussex, England
pp. 88–91
Images by: Iris Thorsteinsdottir

LAYÉNIE UNDER THE STARS
Lot-et-Garonne, France
pp. 46–49
Images by: Jérôme Paressant

LE CÈDRE BLANC TWO
Corrèze, France
pp. 180–183
Images by: Alain Smilo

LILLA STUGAN
Worcestershire, England
pp. 68–73
Images by:
John Jordan
pp. 68–71
Annika Rose Brown
pp. 72–73

LOG JAM CABIN
Cornwall, England
pp. 96–99
Images by: Olivia Whitbread-Roberts

MACIEIRA LODGE
Beira, Portugal
pp. 226–233
Images by: Margriet Hoekstra

MIDSUMMER MEADOW BED
Dartmoor, England
pp. 32–35
Images by: Matt Austin

MIRRORCUBE
Norrbotten, Sweden
pp. 124–129
Images by: Kent Lindvall

MOINHO DA FADAGOSA
Alto Alentejo, Portugal
pp. 246–251
Images by: Bryce Groves

ORCHARD TREEHOUSE
Worcestershire, England
pp. 10–15
Images by: Iris Thorsteinsdottir

POACHER'S CABIN
Périgord-Limousin, France
pp. 76–81
Images by: Jérôme Paressant

RUFUS'S ROOST
Yorkshire, England
pp. 100–105
Images by:
Daniel Alford
pp. 100–101, 103–105
Jack Boothby
p. 102

SKY DEN
Northumberland, England
pp. 144–147
Images by: Jack Boothby

STAR SUITE
Yorkshire, England
pp. 50–53
Images by: Iris Thorsteinsdottir

STARGAZER'S WAGON
Herefordshire, England
pp. 54–55
Images by: Iris Thorsteinsdottir

THE BEACH HOUSE
Kent, England
pp. 240–245
Images by: Ellis Anastasiades

THE BEERMOTH
The Cairngorms, Scotland
pp. 92–93
Images by: Walter Micklethwait

THE BIRD'S NEST
Norrbotten, Sweden
pp. 122–123
Images by: Peter Lundström

THE CABIN
Norrbotten, Sweden
pp. 176–179
Images by: Peter Lundström

THE CHAPEL
Shropshire, England
pp. 64–67
Images by:
  Claire Penn
  pp. 64–65
  Joanna Nicole
  p. 66
  Sabina Ruber
  p. 67

THE DANISH CABIN
Cornwall, England
pp. 206–213
Images by: George Fielding

THE FERRY WAITING ROOM
Loch Lomond and The Trossachs
National Park, Scotland
pp. 6–9
Images by: Melanie Lewis

THE ISLAND CABIN
Agder, Norway
pp. 110–115
Images by:
  Knut Eivind Birkeland
  p. 110 (top)
  Ingeborg Lindseth
  pp. 110 (bottom), 111, 113
  Kasper M. de Thurah
  pp. 112, 114–115

THE LAKE
Cornwall, England
pp. 148–151
Images by: Rupert Hanbury-Tenison

THE ROUNDHOUSE
Cornwall, England
pp. 56–59
Images by: Emma Mustill

THE VINTAGE VARDOS
Devon, England
pp. 220–225
Images by: Owen Howells

THE WOODSMAN'S TREEHOUSE
Dorset, England
pp. 188–195
Images by:
  Alexander Steele-Perkins
  pp. 188–190, 191 (right), 192, 193
  (top right, bottom left and right),
  194–195
  Haarkon
  pp. 191 (left), 193 (top left)

WOODLAND CABIN
Cornwall, England
pp. 74–75
Images by: Owen Howells

ESSAYS

OUR OUTDOOR PANTRY
pp. 136–139
Images by:
  Andrew Montgomery
  pp. 137 (top), 138
  Daniel Alford
  pp. 137 (bottom), 139

OUR WILD FUTURE
pp. 106–109
Images by:
  Harry Baker
  pp. 107 (bottom), 108
  Kate Peters
  pp. 107 (top), 109

SLOWING THE PACE
pp. 152–157
Images by:
  Harry Baker
  pp. 153 (top), 154 (bottom), 156 (top)
  Ellis Anastasiades
  pp. 153 (bottom), 156 (bottom)
  Adam Partridge
  pp. 154 (top), 157
  Chris Buxton
  p. 155

THE JOY OF DOING NOTHING
pp. 234–239
Images by:
  Daniel Alford
  pp. 236–237
  Ellis Anastasiades
  p. 235 (bottom)
  Harry Baker
  p. 238 (top)
  Chris Buxton
  pp. 235 (top), 238 (bottom), 239

THE MEANING OF (CABIN) LIFE
pp. 158–161
Images by: Jack Boothby

THE SCIENCE OF STEPPING
OUTSIDE
pp. 82–87
Images by:
  Ellis Anastasiades
  p. 83 (bottom)
  Owen Howells
  pp. 83 (top), 85 (bottom)
  Daniel Alford
  pp. 84, 87
  Knut Eivind Birkeland
  p. 85 (top)
  Chris Buxton
  p. 86

THE ULTIMATE LIFE MORE WILD
pp. 42–45
Images by:
  Natalie Reid
  p. 43 (top)
  Paul Ligas
  p. 43 (bottom)
  Harry Baker
  p. 44 (bottom)
  Owen Howells
  pp. 44 (top), 45

WEEKEND WANDERINGS
pp. 184–187
Images by: Jacob Little

STAY WILD

Cabins, Rural Getaways,
and Sublime Solitude

CANOPY & STARS

This book was conceived, edited, and designed by gestalten.

Edited by Robert Klanten and Lincoln Dexter
Co-edited by Canopy & Stars (Chris Elmes, Ruth McMenamin and David West)

Preface by Emily Eavis

Text by Anna Southgate

Essays by Chris Elmes (pp. 42–45, 152–157), Ruth Allen (pp. 82–87), Mya-Rose Craig (pp. 106–109), Gill Meller (pp. 136–139), Jack Boothby (pp. 158–161), Siân Lewis (pp. 184–187), and David West (pp. 234–239)

Editorial Management by Anna Diekmann

Head of Design: Niklas Juli

Design and layout by Johanna Posiege

Photo Editor: Madeline Dudley-Yates

Typefaces: Linotype Syntax Serif Com by Hans Eduard Meier and Bluu Next by Jean-Baptiste Morizot

Cover image by Alexander Steele-Perkins
Back cover image by Stuart McGlennon

Printed by
Grafisches Centrum Cuno GmbH & Co.KG, Calbe
Made in Germany

Published by gestalten, Berlin 2021
ISBN 978-3-89955-861-6

© Die Gestalten Verlag GmbH & Co. KG, Berlin 2021

All rights reserved. No part of this publication may be reproduced or transmitted in any form or by any means, electronic or mechanical, including photocopy or any storage and retrieval system, without permission in writing from the publisher.

Respect copyrights, encourage creativity!

For more information, and to order books, please visit www.gestalten.com

Bibliographic information published by the Deutsche Nationalbibliothek.

The Deutsche Nationalbibliothek lists this publication in the Deutsche Nationalbibliografie; detailed bibliographic data is available online at www.dnb.de

None of the content in this book was published in exchange for payment by commercial parties or designers; the inclusion of all work is based solely on its artistic merit.

This book was printed on paper certified according to the standards of the FSC®.

MIX
Paper from responsible sources
FSC® C043106